THE ARCHAEOLOGY OF THE FRONTIER IN THE MEDIEVAL NEAR EAST: EXCAVATIONS AT GRITILLE, TURKEY

Monographs
New Series, Number 3

THE ARCHAEOLOGY OF THE FRONTIER IN THE MEDIEVAL NEAR EAST: EXCAVATIONS AT GRITILLE, TURKEY

Scott Redford

with chapters by Gil J. Stein and Naomi F. Miller
and a contribution by Denise C. Hodges

Published by
UNIVERSITY MUSEUM PUBLICATIONS
University of Pennsylvania
Philadelphia 1998

for
Archaeological Institute of America, Monographs
New Series, Number 3
Boston, MA, 1998

Design and production
University Museum Publications
University of Pennsylvania Museum of Archaeology and Anthropology
Philadelphia, PA

Library of Congress Cataloging-in-Publication Data

Redford, Scott.
    The archaeology of the frontier in the medieval Near East :
excavations at Gritille, Turkey / Scott Redford ; with chapters by
Gil J. Stein and Naomi F. Miller and a contribution by Denise C.
Hodg.
    p. cm. -- (Archaeological Institute of America Monographs. New
series ; no. 3)
    Includes bibliographical references and index.
    ISBN 0-92-417165-0 (cloth)
    1. Gritille Site (Turkey) 2. Karababa Basin
(Turkey)--Antiquities. 3. Archaeology, Medieval. 4. Excavations
(Archaeology)--Turkey--Karababa Basin. [] I. Stein, Gil, 1956- II.
Miller, Naomi Frances. III. Title. IV. Series.
    DS156.G73 R43 1998
    939--dc21
                                                              98-40203
                                                                   CIP

To my parents

En büyük meselemiz budur; mazi ile nerede ve nasıl bağlanacağız . . .

Ahmet Hamdi Tanpınar, *Beş Şehir* (1946)

TABLE OF CONTENTS

LIST OF FIGURES

LIST OF TABLES

LIST OF PLATES

ACKNOWLEDGMENTS

My participation in the Gritille Project dates from 1982, when I joined the second season of excavation. Invitation came from Project Director Professor Richard Ellis of Bryn Mawr College. Over the years Prof. Ellis has applied equal measures of caution, skepticism, and intelligence in assisting and advising my work, encouraging the excavation and study of the medieval period at Gritille and enabling my work to progress. To him I owe a large debt of thanks.

I would like to thank others who carried out the medieval excavations at Gritille: Marie-Henriette Gates, Mary Voigt, Matt Adams, Julia Frane, Halsey Royden, Patty Seabolt, and Gil Stein. I wish to acknowledge a special debt to Christine Eslick and Charles Gates, whose exemplary fieldwork contributed much to the stratigraphic analysis in this study. Also working on the medieval period as part of the Gritille Project were Nikki Clark, Osman Dalgün, Branwen Denton, Tuğrul Dilek, Ria Ellis, Kathryn Gleason, Ann Gunter, Julie Perlmutter, Gianni Ponti, Bill Remsen, Connie Royden, Susan Trammel, Pat Thomas, and Andy Weiss.

I would like to thank the Director of the Adıyaman Museum, Bay Emin Yener, and his staff for their cooperation and courtesy, not least in providing cups of hot menengiç to a long-stayer in the museum's unheated basement.

I would also like to remember the kindnesses of friends and colleagues in Turkey: David French, Ann Murray, Kirsty Norman, Stuart Blaylock, Anne Dawn Sutton, Geoffrey and Françoise Summers of the British Institute of Archaeology at Ankara, Prof. Dr. Harald Hauptmann, Otto Fass and Brigitte Katzenwadel of the Lidar excavations, and Prof. Dr. Nimet Özgüç and Prof. Dr. Gönül Öney of the Samsat excavations.

Dr. Toni Cross, Director of ARIT Ankara, assisted in almost every aspect of my research. Also in Ankara, I would like to thank Chrystal and Melih Türkmen, Güler and Canan Phillips, Pat and Gary Leiser, İhsan Çetin, Canan Öztürk and Gülden Çağlı.

The following also assisted at various stages in the long gestation of this book: Robert McC. Adams, Tommaso Astarita, Michael Bates, M. James Blackman, Massumeh Farhad, Clive Foss, Bonnie Magness-Gardiner, Oleg Grabar, Antony Greenwood, Ann Gunter, Machteld Mellink, Naomi Miller, David Mitten, Gil Stein, and Patricia Wattenmaker.

Research for the dissertation that forms the basis for part of this book was supported by a Fulbright-Hays Dissertation Research Grant. The Gritille Project itself was sponsored by Bryn Mawr College, Bryn Mawr, Pennsylvania, with the cooperation of the University of North Carolina at Chapel Hill, and participation by the University Museum at the University of Pennsylvania. It was funded through generous grants from the National Endowment for the Humanities, the Metropolitan Museum of Art, the University Museum, Philadelphia, and private donors.

It is again thanks to the National Endowment for the Humanities, as well as to a Graduate School of Georgetown University Junior Faculty Research Grant, that I was able to complete my work on this manuscript. Figures and maps in Chapters 1 through 4 and 7 are the work of Julie Perlmutter, principal of the Visual Communication Studio, Washington, D.C., a patient and omnicompetent collaborator.

This book is dedicated to my parents, Lora C. and Ralph H. Redford, who first introduced me to archaeology and to the Near East at an impressionable age.

Washington, D.C.
December 1995

PREFACE

I first saw the mound of Gritille in September, 1977, and was not impressed. This was chiefly because we had reached the site just at dusk, after walking about a kilometer and a half over plowed fields in the rain, and we were in no mood to appreciate its situation and characteristics. My colleagues and I were there at the invitation of the Lower Euphrates Project and its Director, Professor Ekmel Derya, and of the Director-General of Antiquities and Museums, Mr. Nurettin Yardımcı, our purpose being to become familiar with the area and to investigate the possibilities of excavating some of the sites threatened with flooding by the reservoir of the Atatürk Dam, which was then in the planning stage. Despite this first impression, the survey data collected and published by Dr. Mehmet Özdoğan and his team from the University of Istanbul[1] showed the site to be quite interesting—so interesting, in fact, that Gritille became one of the goals of our investigation during another trip I made to the area, in January, 1980, accompanied by Professor Machteld J. Mellink of Bryn Mawr College and Dr. Marie-Henriette Gates, then Director of the Ankara branch of the American Research Center in Turkey. Although we saw the site this time in the snow, our judgment was that the size, location, and periods of occupation of Gritille made it suitable for excavation by a Bryn Mawr expedition.

The survey carried out by Dr. Özdoğan and his party was entirely professional and as thorough as it could have been in the time available. But the area in general was almost unknown ar-

chaeologically; what excavation had been undertaken had not been published in detail. My interest was originally in the Bronze and Iron ages, and from surface indications we thought that Gritille had valuable deposits of these periods. As for medieval remains, the paucity of scraps of glazed pottery seen on the surface suggested that there had been little such occupation of the site. It turned out, however, that some of the pottery that the survey had tentatively identified as Iron Age (the red-slipped and splash/drip-painted wares, particularly) was in fact medieval. The excavations at Lidar, which began in 1980, had already shown this to be the case before the work of the Gritille Project began in 1981.

During the course of the first season of the Gritille Project,[2] in the summer of 1981, it became clear that the medieval component was extensive and interesting. We realized that the project very much needed a staff member familiar with the archaeology of the medieval period if an important aspect of the site was not to be seriously slighted.

During 1981–82 Scott Redford was working at the University of Pennsylvania with Dr. Renata Holod, preparing for publication material from excavations at Rayy in Iran. Redford became aware of our need for an expert, and we of his extensive experience with excavated material of the type we had been finding. Discussions between Redford, Dr. Mary Voigt, and me resulted in his coming to Gritille for the next season and remaining in charge of the medieval

---

[1] Özdoğan, *Lower Euphrates Basin 1977 Survey*, 121–22, pls. 57, 81–82.

[2] The Gritille Project was sponsored by Bryn Mawr College, with the cooperation of the University of North Carolina at Chapel Hill, and participation by the University Museum of the University of Pennsylvania. It was funded through generous grants from the National Endowment for the Humanities (both for excavation and for postexcavation publication preparation), the Metropolitan Museum of Art, the Kevorkian Foundation, the James G. Hanes Fund/Foundation, the University Museum, and several private donors.

phase of the work for the rest of the project (1982–1984). At Gritille he was responsible for analyzing the artifactual finds of the medieval phase, and he also played an important role in the strategic planning of the course of excavation. After the final season in 1984, Redford was awarded a Fulbright fellowship to study the material in Adıyaman to prepare his dissertation on the medieval pottery of Gritille[3] and the present publication. Scott Redford's hard work, expertise, and dedication, at the site and subsequently, have resulted in the present book.

Richard S. Ellis
January 1997

---

[3] Redford, "Ceramic Sequence from Medieval Gritille, Southeast Turkey," Ph.D. diss., Harvard University, 1989.

Introduction

The Frontier in the Medieval Near East

The land frontiers between Islam and Christianity witnessed centuries of struggle. Two of the best-known medieval epics come from a tradition of recounting that struggle, which took place in an isolated, often hostile, and self-contained world of shifting boundaries and allegiances. In the Islamic world, the frontier of al-Andalus with the Christian states of northern Spain and the marchlands between Greek and Arab states in southeastern Anatolia were called by the same name, *thaghr* /(pl.) *thughūr*.[1] The epic of Digenes Akritas and *El Cantár del mio Cíd* both recount or resume the movement of raiding parties and armies across a depopulated zone between antagonistic polities.[2]

A simple look at the names of the protagonists of these epics, however, is enough to cloud the picture of an impermeable frontier between opposed polities, languages, and faiths. Digenes' name proclaims his mixed ancestry (his father was an Arab emir and his mother the daughter of a Byzantine general), and el Cíd bears an Arabic honorific, *sayyid*. The marchlands between Islamic and Christian states in both Spain and Anatolia, then, were, like all frontiers, a destination for outlaws, adventurers, and those seeking the glory of their God, a hybrid, a mix, of different languages, cultures, and creeds.

In Arabic, the term *thaghr* /(pl.) *thughūr* means "forward places" or "passes," quite specifically not a fixed border, but forward points.[3] This term is appropriate to the geography of southeastern Anatolia, where fewer than a handful of passes through the rugged Taurus and Anti-Taurus mountains gave onto the central Anatolian plateau to the north and west, or to Smooth Cilicia and the northern Syrian plain to the south and east. The remoteness of the strongholds that guarded these passes gave rise to quasi-independent strongmen in these regions.[4]

The term *thaghr/thughūr* was current during the time frame of this study, the twelfth and thirteenth centuries A.D.,[5] although the epic days of confrontation between the Byzantines and Abbasids were long past. Earlier, in the mid to late tenth century, the Byzantines had overrun the borderlands, extending their control into northern Syria for the first time since the Arab

---

[1] *Akrai* in Greek sources. In medieval Christian sources, broad, vague terms for the frontier zone are replaced in the thirteenth century by the word *frontera* when the fluid and sparsely populated frontier of the Iberian plateau is replaced by more constant and direct contact with the more thickly populated frontiers of the Kingdom of Granada. See Bazzana, Guichard, and Sénac, "La frontière," 52–53.

[2] For a comparison of the two literary traditions, see Hook, "*Digenes Akrites* and the Old Spanish Epics," 73–85.

[3] "Any gap, opening, interstice, or open intervening space, in a mountain, or in the bottom of a valley, or in a road along which people pass." Lane, *An Arabic-English Lexicon*, 1:338. In sources referring to the Spanish marchlands, the term is usually used in the singular; in sources referring to the Arab-Byzantine frontier it is usually used in the plural. The coastline was also considered to be part of the *thughūr*; see Bianquis, "Les frontières de la Syrie," 140.

[4] Many authors stress the autonomy of the frontier zone, but none stronger than André Miquel ("La perception de la frontière," 131): "Ici pas plus qu'ailleurs, on ne aurait donc parler, au propre, de frontière, mais, en l'espèce de pays littéralement, interstitiel."

conquests. Then they withdrew from this area following the defeat of the armies of Emperor Romanos IV Diogenes at Manzikert in 1071 at the hands of the Seljuk sultan Alp Arslan.

The dynamic of this frontier is understood in its general parameters from the works of historians and military strategists of the time. Contemporaneous frontier epics and romances offer indirect historical content,[6] and are often combined with the invaluable work of historical geography. The archaeological investigation of this region, then, can provide an independent base of inquiry for comparison with historical and other textually derived information.

Historical archaeology is too often used simply to match finds and strata with textual data, or simply to "flesh out" a picture only partially visible from historical sources.[7] This study, by contrast, aims to establish a dialogue between historical data—derived from chronicles, geographers, inscriptions, and coins—and the archaeological record of sites within the frontier region between the Anti-Taurus mountains and the northern Syrian plain. To that end, it presents the results of excavations in medieval (twelfth- and thirteenth-century) levels at the site of Gritille in southeastern Turkey. It also attempts to situate Gritille, its architecture, and material culture within a larger context, encompassing historical, geographical, and economic factors of the Near East at that time.

The broad questions posed by this investigation involve some of the main issues of medieval Near Eastern society. For example, how did the economic and social systems found in the Near East at the turn of the eleventh century adjust or react to the establishment of Crusader states? How did a sedentary agriculturalist populace cope with the massive influx of Türkmen pastoralists into Anatolia, Syria, and northern Mesopotamia? How did these provincial agriculturalists, often Christian, interact with or participate in the dominant Islamic culture of the Near East? How did all communities survive the almost constant warfare of the twelfth and early thirteenth centuries?

Most of all, though, Gritille can be considered as a point in the defensive web of the marchlands, tattered by centuries of thrust and parry. Disputed for centuries between Anatolian and Syrian or Jazīran (northern Mesopotamian) power, in earlier centuries this region had constituted the boundary between Roman and Parthian, Byzantine and Sasanian, and Byzantine and Arab forces. In the twelfth and thirteenth centuries, the stretch of the Euphrates River on which Gritille was located became part of the zone of confrontation between Crusaders and Turks and their allies, and finally between Muslim powers of Anatolia, Syria, and the Jazīra—the Seljuks, Ayyubids, and Artuqids.

Granted, Gritille was merely a small site lying on the right bank of the Euphrates River near the head of a small valley called the Karababa basin. How is it possible to address the macrohistorical issues of the day using data from such a small, provincial settlement? One focus of this study will be synechdocal. Gritille can stand as part for the whole of Near Eastern exurban society at a time when the vast majority of the population still dwelled outside of cities.

In this respect, the general outlines of life in a small rural settlement resonate against this larger background. Thus Gritille's archaeological remains—the buildings and building materials, the fabric of quotidian existence as expressed by the vessels and other objects and implements of work and war that Gritille's inhabitants employed, the crops they harvested, the flocks they tended, the food they ate—typify the shared material culture of the medieval Near East, as evidenced from comparative material from farther north in Anatolia and farther south in Syria.

At the same time as they shared many features of material culture and environment with others in the region, the inhabitants of Gritille also bore an exceptional burden. This was the burden of living in the marchlands, in territory disputed by the many parties attendant on the collapse of Byzantine power in Anatolia, the coming of the Turks, and the establishment of Crusader states of the Outremer. A major argument of this study will be the importance of fortified settlements in determining patterns of set-

---

[5] Yāqūt, *Mu'jam al-Buldān*, 2: 79–81.

[6] E.g., Grégoire, *Autour de l'épopée byzantin*.

[7] Russell, "Transformations," 141: "Particularly serious is the temptation to obscure the complexities or inconsistencies of stratigraphy by conflating strata . . . in the hope of constructing a more intelligible picture. Such rationalization is especially liable to occur where there is some incentive to relate the evidence to some known historical event." Also, Pesez, "Archéologie et stratification culturelle," 253: "Si l'étude du peuplement est un thème fréquent de l'archéologie, dans la mesure où celle-ci met au jour des témoins de la présence humaine, la notion de frontière est loin d'être familière aux archéologues. Comment, en effet, traduire des faits qui relèvent du politique, du juridique, de l'événementiel, à partir du matériel, de la structure, de l'objet?"

tlement and trade. The fortification of even rural settlements is a hallmark of the feudal order in the marchlands. Despite the small size of the mound, Gritille was heavily fortified in three different phases of its medieval occupation. The importance of fortified sites both as military strongpoints in a defensive system and as settlement vectors will be explored.

A river can be a border or a byway. The Euphrates River brought commerce and a measure of prosperity to this region, just as its broad flow attracted those interested in the movements of raiding parties and their larger kin, armies. The interplay between geography and history is especially important in this piedmont region of broken uplands lying between the Taurus and Anti-Taurus mountains of southeast Anatolia and the flat plains of northern Syria and Mesopotamia. Trade routes threaded along and across the river valleys that scoured the piedmont and led through the mountain passes that stitched the eastern Anatolian plateau and Syria together.

Armies climbed and descended through these same passes and traveled along these same routes. Settlement in the region may have owed much to the passage of caravans and the patronage of merchants, but in greater measure it depended on fortifications and garrisons. The ability of a peasant populace (and, to a lesser but still important extent, its flocks) to seek refuge behind walls and to guard the points of access to their lands, counted for much in the history of settlement in this region.

The border areas were linked by a system of communication and fortification. For a time and under particular circumstances, Gritille functioned as one node in a defensive system. A primary aim of this study is to locate Gritille within a hierarchy of sites and settlements with strategic value. In this respect, the survey and salvage excavation in this region of southeastern Turkey prior to its flooding permits us to compare Gritille with its neighboring settlements, fortified and unfortified, larger and smaller, in order to look at combinations of the accidents of geography and history that made for the archaeological record in the medieval period.

The word *medieval* encapsulates the complex of dynasties, religions, and languages at play in this period in the Near East. In this study it is often used also as a substitute for a more accurate if clumsy term coined several decades ago by historian Marshall Hodgson. In describing a society dominated by one religion and its culture without denying the many elements that were independent of that society in one or several ways, Hodgson coined the term *Islamicate*. By confining the adjective *Islamic* to religious matters, he used *Islamicate* to refer to "the social and cultural complex historically associated with Islam and the Muslims, both among Muslims themselves and even when found among non-Muslims."[8]

As a historian, Hodgson was concerned with many issues of medieval society not perhaps apparent to the tillers, herders, and fishermen of Gritille. Moreover, Gritilleans were not co-religionists with their Artuqid and Ayyubid overlords. Still, they were part of a complex with Islamic culture as the dominant element, and this study will examine the ways in which the material culture of Islamicate society intruded into provincial lives. Even while under Crusader hegemony, the identification of *medieval* with *Islamicate* is valid: there was no opportunity during the brief and violent life of the Crusader state (the County of Edessa [1098–1144]) for any rival to the region's established ways and means to take hold.

Like all archaeological endeavors, this book is a shared project, logistically and intellectually. It begins with four chapters on the history, archaeology, pottery, and coins and small finds of Gritille. Gil Stein contributes two chapters on the faunal remains and settlement patterns around Gritille (Chapters 5 and 7), and Naomi Miller analyzes plant remains from medieval Gritille (Chapter 6). Denise Hodges follows with an appendix on the human skeletal remains from Gritille, most of them found in the remains of the conflagration that swept the site at a point early in the medieval sequence. Chapter 8 presents an overall interpretation of the issues examined throughout the book.

This study, encompassing as it does different fields of expertise, subject matter, and authors, resolves into two different but complementary focuses. The first is a regional consideration of the Karababa basin and its important sites, from which relevant and critical contextual information is gleaned. The second is a detailed study of a broad range of data from Gritille proper, allowing reconstruction of the economic, geographical, and social factors that formed the medieval settlement there. And while the main focus remains that of the site that forms the center of its inquiry, this focus does not blur but gains in clarity from the regional considerations that form so much of the book's argument.

---

[9] Hodgson, *Venture of Islam*, 1, 59.

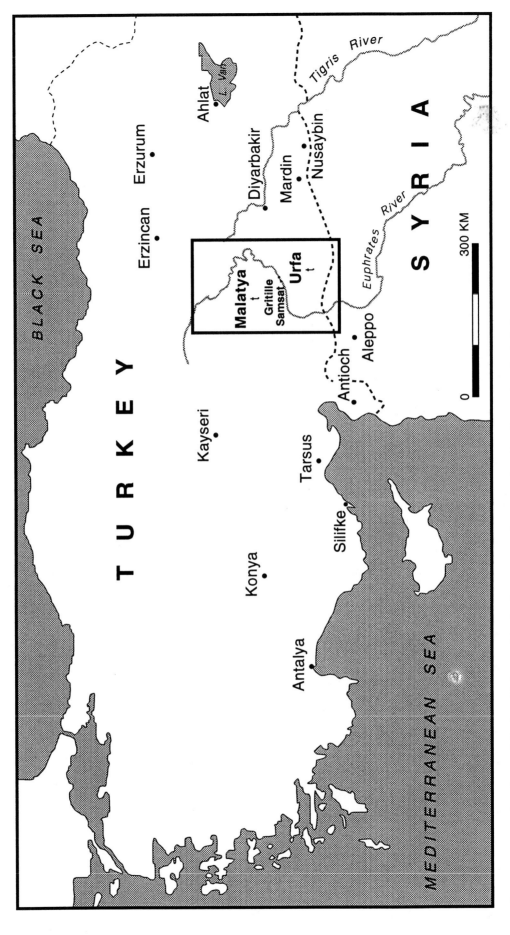

Figure 1:1. Map of Turkey and Syria with inset of Turkey's Lower Euphrates region showing archaeological sites.

I

A History of Gritille and the Karababa Basin in the Medieval and Modern Eras

A history of Gritille must of necessity begin with a regional consideration because there is no incontrovertible evidence in the medieval historical record for the site of Gritille itself. This chapter therefore presents historical material from a variety of sources—medieval chronicles, biographical dictionaries, epigraphy and numismatics, travelers' accounts from the nineteenth and twentieth centuries, and an Ottoman Turkish tax register—in order to examine the record of Gritille's largest neighbor, Samsat, and its hinterland, the Karababa basin. Evidence will be presented and examined with a view to determining the historical importance of this region. That importance will be tied to three major factors: Samsat as a major fortified river crossing on a route between north Syria and Anatolia, Samsat as the chief site in the Karababa basin, and Samsat's relation to the largest city in the region, Urfa, both militarily and economically.

The absence of Gritille in the historical record constitutes a major argument for the regional approach adopted in this book. The site of Gritille proper becomes the focus of attention in subsequent chapters. The concluding chapter will reconcile the site-specific and regional approaches to the extent possible given the nature of the evidence.

The Setting and Its Importance

Gritille is the modern name for a mound that lay on the right bank of the Euphrates River in southeast Turkey (Pl. 1:1).[1] The site was situated some 10 kilometers upstream from the main settlement in the region, Samsat (Byzantine and Crusader Samosata, Arab Sumaysāṭ), and almost directly across the Euphrates from the other major mound of this area, Lidar (Armenian Ltār) (frontispiece; Pl. 1:2). A natural topographic feature, the Karababa basin, embraced these three sites, as well as other mounds downstream from Samsat. The basin, now flooded by the Atatürk Dam, formerly comprised the expansion of the Euphrates floodplain and a surrounding valley after the river left an extended series of gorges to the northeast. Some 10 kilometers downstream from Samsat proper, the limestone hills surrounding the valley again descended to the river's edge at the Karakaya (Halfeti) Gorge, site of the present-day Atatürk Dam. The basin was long and nar-

---

[1] The site was as often as not pronounced by the Kurdish inhabitants of the valley as "Girt-tille." In colloquial Persian, the word *gerd* refers to flat-topped, steep-sided mounds. (I would like to thank Lee Horne for this information.) This characteristic profile results when the foundations of a bygone fortification wall *gird*ing the site retain the deposit on top of the mound. This was the profile of the mound of Gritille.

Whatever its etymology, the name Gritille, like Til or Tille, is a generic one. It is not a regional toponym of antiquity like Lidar or Samsat. Markwart (*Südarmenien und die Tigrisquellen*, 180–183), in the course of identifying Till Ḥamdūn with one "Tell Hüjügü," lists many sites with the name Thil, Tilia, etc. As mentioned below, the name recorded for this site by Humann and Puchstein was simply "Til," the Arabic and Syriac word for "mound."

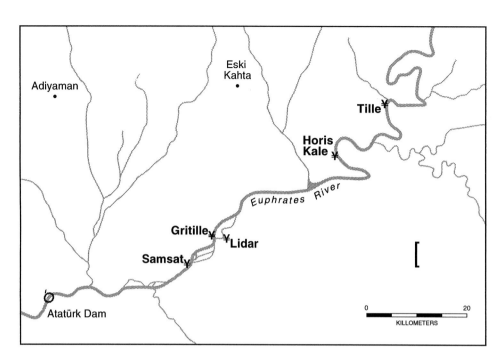

Figure 1:2. Map of the Karababa basin and sites upstream.

Figure 1:3. Map of southeastern Turkey and northern Syria with major medieval sites.

row, some 35 kilometers long and 10 wide at its greatest extent (Figs. 1:1, 1:2).

To the south, low limestone hills give way to the watershed of the Balīkh River and the north Syrian plain, while to the north these hills rise to form tableland, eventually meeting the Anti-Taurus mountains south of Malatya (Byzantine and Crusader Melitene, Arab Malaṭiya). These uplands are scored by numerous river valleys, affluents of the Euphrates like the Gök Su (Arabic Nahr al-Azraq) and the Kâhta Çayı (Classical Nymphaios) to the southwest and northeast of Samsat, respectively. Downstream from Samsat, the Euphrates continues its southwesterly course before commencing a great, lazy curve south and then east through Syria.

The location of the Karababa basin has ensured it an importance incommensurate with its size (Figs. 1:2, 1:3). In this chapter, Samsat will be examined in relation to three functions. First, Samsat served as the only river crossing on one of the major routes between Syria and Anatolia. Added to this was Samsat's position as a kind of hinge between northern Syria, Anatolia, and northern Mesopotamia (Arabic al-Jazīra). Second, Samsat was a local agricultural center, controlling a small but highly fertile valley, whose produce gained value given the relative aridity of the surrounding area. Along with other tracts to the west around Keysun (Arabic Kaysūm), Samsat produced an agricultural surplus that supplied the needs of the city of Urfa (Byzantine and Crusader Edessa, Arabic al-Ruhā) some 50 kilometers to the south. The fertility of the river floodplain in these areas was, until the completion of the Keban Dam to the north, renewed annually by spring flooding. A third function noted by medieval and modern authors alike was the navigability of the Euphrates beginning at Samsat.

Because of its propinquity to Samsat in this valley, Gritille and its history are inextricable from Samsat, its larger neighbor. Both temporally and spatially, all events that affected Samsat affected Gritille. In fact, the very existence of set-

tlement at Gritille can be seen as a function of the defense and exploitation of the hinterland of Samsat, that is to say, the Karababa basin itself.

THE SAMSAT REGION IN CLASSICAL TO MEDIEVAL SOURCES

THE REGION AS FRONTIER

The Euphrates valley was for a long time the boundary between rival powers in the area. Before the Roman Empire absorbed the Kingdom of Commagene in A.D. 72, this small state had served the Romans as a buffer against the Parthians to the south and east. As Strabo reports, "Commagene is rather a small district. It contains a strong city, Samosata, in which was the seat of the kings. At present it is a [Roman] province. A very fertile but small territory lies around it."[2] Samsat, then, served as the capital of Commagene. It was by far and away the largest and most important city of the area (even if the present-day repute of the kingdom lies at the mountaintop funerary sanctuary at Nemrut Dağı). Under Emperor Hadrian, Samsat served as headquarters for a Roman legion, the XVI Flavia Firma. Previously the frontier of the Roman Empire had moved considerably to the east, as it was to return thereafter.[3] A bridge across the Euphrates linked Samsat with Seleucia, a Hellenistic foundation across the river. The emplacement of Seleucia exemplifies the Seleucid habit of locating colonies opposite settlements at river crossings in order "to secure bridgeheads," a principle that will be examined in relation to the twinning of the sites of Lidar and Gritille on opposite shores of the Euphrates.[4]

One author notes that the Euphrates, although it lay along much of the Roman frontier in the east, did not constitute the actual border, maintaining that "except for the Euphrates gorge through the Kurdish Taurus, the Euphrates does not pose a formidable military obsta-

---

[2] Strabo, *Geography of Strabo*, 7, 240. Strabo counted Commagene to be one of the four regions of Syria.

[3] Warner, "Die Römer am Euphrat," 68–82, 75 for legions. For Roman itineraries in the trans-Euphrates region (Osrhoene), see Dussaud, *Topographie historique de la Syrie*, 479, and more recently, Crow and French, "New Research on the Euphrates," 903–912, and French, "New Research on the Euphrates Frontier," 71–101.

[4] Jones, *Cities of the Eastern Provinces*, 216. Seleucia has not been localized, although it has been identified with the mound of Lidar; Goell, "Samosata Archeological Excavations," 90. Prof. Hauptmann, the excavator of Lidar, has made no such claim for the site.

cle."[5] While this assessment may be true for large armies without substantial opposition, it does not hold for the smaller raiding parties of the medieval period. Certainly, however, the Romans, in the Karababa basin as elsewhere, must have controlled both sides of the Euphrates.

Samsat is mentioned in Byzantine sources during accounts of campaigns against the Sasanians; its walls were rebuilt by Justinian the Great.[6]

Samsat fell to the Arabs in 639. With the advent of the Umayyads and the Abbasids, the area between Urfa and Malatya once again constituted a border region, with the dominant military party extending the frontier one way or another. In general, though, this frontier area was subject to yearly raiding which sought not so much to alter the balance of power as to extract material gain through conquest and booty.

A standard definition of the Roman frontier consists of forts along a road.[7] This was the case in the Karababa basin, although work remains to be done on Roman military installations in this region.[8] A recent study has criticized a fixed, static model for defense of the eastern frontier of the Roman Empire and the concept of strictly defined boundaries to that empire.[9]

Certainly in the medieval period, as we shall see below, zones of marchland lay between opposing states. Contrary to many published assertions, these were not "no man's lands." Rather, they were areas of uncertain terrain and allegiance whose strategic importance demanded the maintenance of a series of strongholds. Until the tenth century, however, Malatya, not

Samsat, served as the great forward base of Muslim raiders;[10] Samsat must have served primarily as a key link on the road between Muslim centers of power in Aleppo, Antioch, and Manbij in north Syria and redoubts such as Malatya on the edge of the Anatolian plateau. Between Samsat and Malatya, several small fortresses were established by the Abbasids, including Ḥiṣn Manṣūr, predecessor of present-day Adıyaman. These fortresses controlled the routes to and from the edge of the *thughūr* and were probably garrisoned.[11]

It may be useful to recall that the nexus of conflict and communication between highland and lowland in this most strategic corner of the Mediterranean has always lain to the west of the Samsat region, in Smooth Cilicia. The Cilician plain and Cilician Gates afforded much easier access to the Anatolian plateau and were nearer centers of Byzantine military strength there, most notably the fortresses of Amorium and Ankyra. The thirteenth-century geographer Yāqūt devotes the lion's share of his entry on border regions, *al-thaghr*, to a synopsis of the ups and downs of Umayyad, Abbasid, and Hamdanid fortunes in fighting in and by way of Cilicia, which had replaced the eastern frontier passes more convenient for the passage of Islamic armies, after the development of Tarsus as the main Cilician base in the early ninth century.[12]

Preoccupation with the defense of this avenue can be seen as the root cause of the Byzantine determination to capture and hold Antioch, key to Cilicia. Only in times when the Cilician plain was effectively sealed off from Muslim in-

---

[5] Wheeler, "Rethinking the Upper Euphrates Frontier," 506.

[6] Humann and Puchstein, *Reisen in Kleinasien und Nordsyrien*, 1:181 ff. For Samsat in the early 7th century, see Stratos, "Les frontières de l'empire," 427–428, 431.

[7] Parker, *Romans and Saracens*, 1–2.

[8] For a critique of work in Turkey, see Lightfoot, "Tilli, A Late Roman *Equites* Fort," 509–510.

[9] Isaac, *Limits of Empire*, e.g., 394 ff. Isaac argues that what others would see as a highly organized border defense system was rather a means of controlling the movement of peoples and goods both within and without the empire.

[10] For the fortunes of Malatya in the 10th century, see Honigmann, *Ostgrenze des byzantinischen Reiches*, 57–59, 64–67, 72–73; also Canard, *Histoire de la dynastie des Hamdanides*, 262–263, 733–736.

[11] Haldon and Kennedy, "Arab-Byzantine Frontier," 109. Dalliere-Benelhadhj ("Le 'chateau' en al-Andalus," 64) writes: "Le *ḥiṣn* peut désigner une ville entière mais c'est alors pour en souligner l'aspect défensif. . . ." For the use by a central government of *ḥuṣūn* as settlement vectors in frontier zones in medieval Spain, see Azuar Ruiz, "El Sur del Pais Valenciano," 100, and as centers of state (as opposed to local) administration, 102–103. For an example of a *ḥiṣn* as the expression of local or regional power by serving as a refuge and settlement vector, but not as a frontier outpost, see Sénac, "Une fortification musulmane au nord," 123–145. C.-P. Haase, *Untersuchung zur Landschaften Nordsyriens in der Umayyadenzeit* (Kiel, 1975), was unavailable to me.

[12] Yāqūt al-Rūmī, *Mu'jam al-Buldān*, 2:79–81; Haldon and Kennedy, "Arab-Byzantine Frontier," 108.

Panorama of the Karababa basin from the top of the mound of Gritille, August 1984. Visible across the river, rising from a copse of

rees, is the mound of Lidar. Downstream, in the distance, the mound of Samsat is distinguishable across the fields.

cursions did the more easterly route via Samsat assume primary importance along the border regions.[13] This sealing off was accomplished by the rise of the Crusader principality based in Antioch following 1098, followed immediately by a small but well-defended Armenian principality in Cilicia in the twelfth century.[14]

Until the tenth century, Samsat and environs were controlled by Islamic dynasties, Umayyad, Abbasid, or Hamdanid. Muslim geographers placed Samsat in one of two regional classifications relating to the frontier zone. The first was 'awāṣim, or "strongholds," the term employed for the area immediately behind the marchlands themselves, whose principal military function was the provisioning and assembly of troops. The second was as a part of the marchlands themselves, the thughūr.[15] Samsat was never listed as part of a jund, or province, of Syria, plain and simple.

Although it lay on the right bank of the Euphrates, that is, to the north of the traditional demarcation of the Jazīra proper, some Muslim geographers considered Samsat to be on the frontiers of that region, no doubt by virtue of its location on the Euphrates after it had descended from the Anatolian plateau. Others, ignoring the traditional demarcation of the Jazīra, included Samsat in listings of the cities in the Diyār Muḍar, the westernmost of the three regions of the Jazīra. Samsat was never considered to lie in traditionally Byzantine territory, although Yāqūt wrote that Samsat lay on the banks of the Euphrates ". . . on the side of the lands of Rūm."[16] Administratively, Samsat was sometimes considered part of Syria,[17] sometimes part of the Diyār Muḍar.[18] Sometimes authors equivocated within the same text. Ibn Khurdādhbih, writing early in the ninth century, described Samsat as one of the thughūr al-Jazīra,[19] as well as one of the cities of the Diyār Muḍar.[20] The same term was taken up by the tenth-century geographer Ibn Ḥawqal,[21] as well as by al-Iṣṭakhrī,[22] both of whom place Samsat in chapters on Syria. Al-Mas'ūdī, also writing in the tenth century, mentioned Samsat only in passing, but gave it a sobriquet not reproduced elsewhere: Castle of Clay.[23] Al-Muqaddasī, another tenth-century author, continued the Syrian tradition, but did not mention Samsat as one of the cities in the Diyār Muḍar, nor did he describe it in relation to the Jazīra in any other respect.[24] Ibn Rusta described Samsat as lying in the north of Syria and considered it to be located in the thughūr

---

[13] For the premedieval period, the Samsat region has been named, perhaps hyperbolically, by F. K. Dörner as a "neuralgischen Punkt der Weltgeschichte" comparable to the Bosphorus and the Dardanelles (cited in Warner, "Die Römer am Euphrat," 68).

[14] Edwards, Armenian Fortifications of Cilicia; Hellenkemper, Burgen der Kreuzritterzeit; Ter-Grigorian Iskenderian, Die Kreuzfahrer.

[15] Yāqūt (Mu'jam al-Buldān, 4:165) defined 'awāṣim as "well-fortified settlements (ḥuṣūn [see n. 7 above] mawān'i) and the province (wilāya) surrounding them between Aleppo and Antioch." See Canard, Histoire de la dynastie des Hamdanides, 265, for the bivalence of Samsat. The same author later asserted that the two terms were often confused and ended up being used interchangeably: Canard, "al-'Awāṣim," Encyclopaedia of Islam, 761. See Honigmann, Ostgrenze des byzantinischen Reiches, 39–43, for Islamic grenzzone in this region, and Hellenkemper, "Zur mittelalterlichen Landschaftsgeschichte," 82–85. For the Syriac term tagrā, applied to the mountains between Malatya and Samsat, see Honigmann, Le couvent de Barṣaumā, 36.

[16] Yāqūt, Mu'jam al-Buldān, 3:258.

[17] al-Muqaddasī (Aḥsan al-Taqāsim fī Ma'rifa'l-Āqālīm, 54), wrote that it depended on Aleppo.

[18] Ibn al-Faqīh (Kitāb al-Buldān, 136) listed the somewhat improbable kharaj revenues from Samsat as well as other of the districts (kuwar) of the Diyār Muḍar.

[19] Kitāb al-Masālik wa'l-Mamālik, 97.

[20] Ibid., 73.

[21] Kitāb Ṣūrat al-Arḍ, 172.

[22] Kitāb Masālik w'al-Mamālik, 67.

[23] Murūj al-Dhahab wa Ma'ādin al-Jawhar, 1:118: ". . . wa qad ajtāza (al-Furāt) taḥt Qal'at Sumaysāṭ wa hiya Qal'at al-Ṭīn." This name may reflect the mudbrick walls of the citadel, which appear not to have been rebuilt in stone between Roman/Byzantine and Artuqid hegemony. See Özgüç, "Sümeysat Definesi," 444–445, for a discussion of the walls of the Samsat citadel and an Artuqid building inscription found there.

[24] See Al-Muqaddasī, Aḥsan al-Taqāsim fī Ma'rifa'l-Āqālīm, 137, for a listing of cities in the Diyār Muḍar; ibid., 154, for a listing of Samsat as one of the cities of the kura, or district, of Qinnasrīn.

zone, but elsewhere listed it as one of the districts of the Jazīra.[25] Al-Idrīsī wrote of Samsat as one of the cities of Raqqa, which was the capital of the Diyār Muḍar.[26] Ibn al-Faqīh, in delimiting geographical regions, actually defined the Jazīra as beginning in the administrative district (*ʿamal*) of Samsat.[27] And, in describing the course of the Euphrates, all geographers concurred that the river begins to turn south at Samsat. In these descriptions, no site is mentioned as lying between Malatya and Samsat along the Euphrates, and rarely is any place mentioned as being between Samsat and Jisr Manbij or even Raqqa. The ambivalence of Samsat's place in this Islamic frame of reference—in which it was part of Syria, but in the border region, a border region on the edge of the Jazīra, or part of the Jazīra itself—underlines its mediatory position between important districts of the region (Fig. 1:3).

MEDIEVAL TRADE AND COMMUNICATION ROUTES

Samsat's strategic importance was enhanced upon the reassertion of Islamic control over the whole of the Diyār Bakr, that part of upper Mesopotamia around the present-day cities of Diyarbakır and Mardin, after Byzantine withdrawal from the area following 1071. In the twelfth century, most of the military activity in the region followed an east–west axis. This was distinct from the north–south route favored in the first half of the thirteenth century, when Samsat enjoyed a certain importance as a border post on the route to and from the eastern Anatolian plateau.

Concomitant with its border location was Samsat's position as a trade post and major crossing point of the Euphrates. Throughout the medieval period, Muslim geographers placed Samsat in a chain of stops along the major route from Syria to eastern central Anatolia, as well as a stop along a secondary route from Diyarbakır (Arabic Āmid or Āmida) and parts east toward Maraş (Byzantine and Crusader Germaniceia, Arabic Marʾash), Birecik (Greek Zeugma, Arabic al-Bīra), Cilicia, and Antioch.

Ibn Khurdādhbih described an itinerary from Raqqa to Malatya that proceeded as follows:

Raqqa to ʿAyn al-Rumiya:	6 *parasangs*
from there to Tall ʿAbdā	7 *parasangs*
from there to Sārūj	7 *parasangs*
from there to Muzaniyya	6 *parasangs*
from there to Samsat	7 *parasangs*
from there to Ḥiṣn Manṣūr	6 *parasangs*
from there to Malatya	10 *parasangs*[28]

Later, the same author described the route differently. The route proceeded from al-Ḥiṣn (read Ḥiṣn Maslama[29]) through Ḥarrān, Urfa, Samsat, and Ḥiṣn Manṣūr (present-day Adıyaman), and distances are given in *sikka* (pl. *sikak*).[30]

Ḥiṣn Maslama to Ḥarrān	12 *parasangs*
from there to Urfa	8 *parasangs*
from there to Samsat	12 *parasangs*
from there to Ḥiṣn Manṣūr	8 *parasangs*

Al-Iṣṭakhrī, on the other hand, described itineraries in terms of days of travel. For this area, he outlined several routes:[31]

Manbij to Samsat	2 days
from there to Ḥiṣn Manṣūr	1 day
from there to al-Ḥadath[32]	1 day
from there to Maraş	1 day

[25] *Kitāb al-ʿAlāq al-Nafīsa*, 97, 106, 107.

[26] Al-Idrīsī, *Kitāb Rujār*, fasc. 6, 649.

[27] Ibn al-Faqīh, *Kitāb al-Buldān*, 128.

[28] Ibn Khurdādhbih, *Kitāb al-Masālik waʾl-Mamālik*, 97.

[29] The *parasang* was about 6 km; see Hinz, "Farsakh," *Encyclopaedia of Islam*, 2:812–813. For the identification of Ḥiṣn Maslama with Madīnat Fār in contemporary Syria and excavations there, see Haase, "Madinat al-Far/Hisn Maslama," 206–225.

[30] Ibid., 229. R. Dozy (*Supplément aux dictionnaires arabes*, 1:666) gives the following definition of a *sikka*: "Une *sikka* de poste, c'est -à-dire la distance d'une relais de poste à une autre est de quatre parasangs."

[31] Al-Iṣṭakhrī, *Kitāb al-Masālik waʾl-Mamālik*, 67 (for the first itinerary), 72 (for those following).

[32] Al-Ḥadath (Byzantine Adata) lay between the present-day towns of Gölbaşı and Pazarcık near the highway from Gaziantep across the mountains to Malatya. See Hartmann, "al-Ḥadath al-Ḥamrā," 40–50. Friedrich Hild (*Das byzantinische Strassensystem in Kappadokien*, 139–140) notes the importance of this fortified town: "Al-Hadaṯ' war demnach nicht nur ein Schlüssel punkt für die Antitaurusdurchquerung, sondern auch ein Straßen-knotenpunkt für straßen nach Armenien, in die Kommagene, nach Nordsyrien und Kilikien."

Samsat to Diyarbakır	3 days
Samsat to Jisr Manbij	4 days
Raqqa to Ḥarrān	3 days
from there to Urfa	1 day
from there to Samsat	1 day

Ibn Ḥawqal reproduced this last itinerary exactly, also giving the traveling time between Diyarbakır and Samsat as three days, and the same time for traveling from Samsat to Malatya. He also gave the following (somewhat conflicting) times.[33]

Manbij to Samsat	2 days
from there to Ḥiṣn Manṣūr	1 day
from there to Malatya	3 days

Al-Idrīsī, too, gave *marāḥil* (meaning units of one day's travel) as units between towns in this region, although occasionally he simply gave times in days and miles.[34]

Diyarbakır to Samsat	3 *marāḥil*
From there to Nīṣībīn	90 *amyāl*
From there to Ra's 'Ayn	3 *marāḥil*
Also: Manbij to Samsat	3 days

("It is [also] said two days," the author reports.)

Samsat to Ḥiṣn Manṣūr	"marḥala kabīra"
From there to al-Ḥadath	"yawm kabīra"
(a long day)	

As can be seen from this short excursus into medieval itineraries, the major routes upon which Samsat is mentioned as a stop are north-south ones. There were two of these. The first one originated in Raqqa, capital of the Diyār Muḍar and major stop for caravans following the Euphrates across the desert between Syria and Iraq. Proceeding north, this route hugged the Jullāb River and then the Bālīkh River, which flows almost due south until debouching in the Euphrates just west of Raqqa, and passed through or near Harran and Urfa before attaining Samsat.

The second route north came from northern Syria proper, proceeding either from Manbij (a fortified town due east of Aleppo) or Jisr Manbij (another name for the fortified river crossing at Qal'at Najm). The only other fortified river crossing between Qal'at Najm and Samsat was at Birecik, whose proximity to Antioch gave it increased prominence.

From Samsat, the route climbed onto the tableland and attained Ḥiṣn Manṣūr, a fortified mound surrounded by a town and fields.[35] Subsequent passage was more difficult, as the way wound through the mountains following the watercourse of the Cendere Çayı, an affluent of the Kâhta Çayı, after leaving the watchful eye of the fortress of Yeni Kale at Eski Kâhta (Classical Arsameia ad Nymphaios).[36] In the twelfth century, this Commagenian fortress was rebuilt by Armenians seeking to carve out small *Raüberhöhlen* in the mountains.[37] When the American traveler Vincent Yorke crossed the mountains along this route in the month of May in the early 1890s, he crossed from Kâhta to Malatya in only 18 hours and 20 minutes, although he noted that "(t)he path by which we traveled can only be used in summer, and was not fairly practicable for beasts at the date when we crossed the mountains."[38]

In addition to providing refuge for renegade Armenians and Crusader garrisons in cas-

---

[33] Ibn Ḥawqal, *Kitāb Ṣūrat al-Arḍ*, 190.

[34] Al-Idrīsī, *Kitāb Rujār*, 652.

[35] Abu'l Fidā' (*Kitāb Taqwīm al-Buldān*, 269) describes it as being in ruins, even though the surroundings were still cultivated. This passage, however, does not seem to date to the 14th century, when this work was composed. Ibn Ḥawqal (*Kitāb Ṣūrat al-Arḍ*, 166), writing in the 10th century, described much the same situation, the result of Byzantine-Hamdanid warfare.

[36] The bridge, built by Septimius Severus, still spans the Cendere Çayı. It seems often to have been confused or conflated by Muslim geographers in their accounts of this region with another, far less spectacular Roman bridge over the Nahr Sanja (classical Singas) near Besni (Arabic Bahasnā). It was this latter bridge that was considered by medieval Muslim geographers as one of the wonders of the world, the other one in this region being the church of the Haghia Sophia in Urfa: al-Mas'ūdī, *Kitāb al-Tanbīh wa'l-Ashraf*, 64; Ibn Ḥawqal, *Kitāb Ṣūrat al-Arḍ*, 166; Canard, "al-'Awāṣim," 1:266. However, it seems likely that a conflation of the two occurred in accounts of this region, since the bridge by Besni is the less "wonderful" of the two by far.

[37] Dörner and Goell, *Arsameia am Nymphaios*, passim.

[38] Yorke, "Journey in the Valley," 325.

tles like Eski Kâhta and Gerger (Classical Ar-sameia-on-the-Euphrates, Byzantine Karkaron, Arabic Karkar)[39] to the east, these mountains were home to a host of Syriac monasteries, including the seat of the Syriac patriarchate, the large and prosperous monastery of Barṣaumā.[40] This monastery, too, lay to the east of the main route through the mountains to Malatya.

The main east–west route across this section of the Near East passed to the south of Samsat. It followed a lowland path across the northern Syrian plain from Nīṣībīn (Classical Nisibis) to Urfa or Harran and thence Birecik. This is the path followed by the Spanish traveler Ibn Jubayr in 1184.[41] The other east–west route left Diyarbakır and must have passed through Siverek (Arabic Al-Suwayda[42]) and crossed the Euphrates at Babūlā.[43] From there it followed the old Roman road to Eski Kâhta and Ḥiṣn Manṣūr (3 km from Classical Perrhe) before descending to Samsat.

From Samsat, the way west proceeded to al-Ḥadath, where the road proceeded across the Anti-Taurus to Maraṣ. By traversing the many river valleys that furrowed these uplands, the way was no doubt more difficult than the more popular and southerly route traversed by Ibn Jubayr. In addition, the traveler on the northerly route bypassed major towns such as Nīṣībīn and Urfa or Harran.

MEDIEVAL AGRICULTURE IN THE REGION

Samsat itself never acceded to the upper ranks of Syrian or Jazīran cities. The town's most notable features were always its agriculture and its citadel, never its size. Urfa was clearly the most important city of the region, surpassed in northern Syria only by Antioch and Aleppo. In several geographers' accounts, Samsat is paired with Jisr Manbij, and they are described as *madīnatāni ṣaghīratāni ḥaṣīnatāni*, two small fortified cities.[44]

Al-Idrīsī provided interesting information about the Samsat region.[45]

> The city of Samsat is on the Euphrates and possesses a well-protected citadel. Samsat lies to the east of al-Lukām Malaṭa (the Anti-Taurus) on the Euphrates. Big mountains ring it and in them grow walnuts and grapes and other fruits, summer and winter fruits alike; these grow wild and have no owner.

Ibn Shaddād, too, noted the variety of fruits that grew in the mountains around Samsat.[46] Ibn Ḥawqal called attention to the presence at Samsat of dry farming as well as irrigation, *saqī* as well as *mabākhis*.[47] Al-Iṣṭakhrī's description does not actually mention irrigated fields by name,

---

[39] Hellenkemper, *Burgen der Kreuzritterzeit in der Grafschaft Edessa*, 79–83; Dédéyan, "Razzias 'turcomanes' et contre-razzias arméniennes," 49–58, provides a detailed history of the vicissitudes of Armenian and Crusader control over Gerger and its surroundings.

[40] Honigmann, *Le couvent de Barṣaumā*, passim. Michael the Syrian (*Chronique de Michel le Syrien*, 3, fasc. ii, 198–199) noted the often hostile coexistence of Syriac Christians and Armenians in these mountains.

[41] Ibn Jubayr, *Riḥla*, 214–223.

[42] Honigmann, *Ostgrenze des byzantinischen Reiche*, 136.

[43] This toponym is spelled (and transliterated) a number of ways, including Bābalū. Cahen, "Le Diyār Bakr au temps des premiers Urtukides," 254. The proximity of this crossing to Gerger may have been its main attraction. What relation it had to Tille, its downstream neighbor, remains to be explored.

[44] Abu'l Fidā', *Kitāb Taqwīm al-Buldān*, 267, quoting Ibn Ḥawqal. Likewise al-Iṣṭakhrī, *Kitāb al-Masālik wa'l-Mamālik*, 76, who, however, changed the adjective to nazīhatāni, "decent," or "upright."

[45] Al-Idrīsī, *Kitāb Rujār*, 166.

[46] Ibn Shaddād, *Al-'Alaq*, 114.

[47] Ibn Ḥawqal, *Kitāb Ṣūrat al-Arḍ*, 166. Dozy (*Supplément aux dictionnaires arabes*, 1:55) defines the later term as follows: "Terres qui ne sont pas arrosées d'une manière artificielle, mais seulement par l'eau de la pluie." Ibn Ḥawqal actually uses the term *zurū' mabkhūs*, but al-Iṣṭakhrī uses the form defined by Dozy. For the importance in Islamic law of the distinction between irrigated and non-irrigated lands, see Cahen, "Le service de l'irrigation en Iraq," 131.

but his enumeration of fields (*zurū'*), gardens (*basātīn*), and nonirrigated fields (*mabākhis*) seems to imply the same thing.[48]

Travel on the River

Navigability of the Euphrates from Samsat serves as the third function that raised the importance of Samsat in the medieval period. The use of inflated skins to travel the rivers of upper Mesopotamia is attested as far back as the ninth century B.C.[49] Ibn Khurdādhbih noted that boats (*sufun*) and rafts of inflated skins (*aṭwāf*) were loaded for travel downstream; his information was copied by Ibn al-Faqīh and al-Idrīsī, who added that this traffic proceeded all the way to Baghdad.[50] Al-Iṣṭakhrī adds travel times to his description of the Euphrates; from the border (*ḥadd*) of Malatya to Samsat is given as two days' travel, and from Samsat to Jisr Manbij as four days.[51]

Until the introduction of inner tubes to the region, rafts made of inflated goatskins (Turkish *kelek*) continued to be used, as were rafts made of reeds and hollow gourds.[52] And until the completion of the dam, large rafts would float down the Euphrates with cargoes of wood allegedly destined for Syria; they traveled through populated areas at night to avoid detection.

Nevertheless, aside from the brief instances cited by medieval geographers, historical testimony for the long-distance transport of significant amounts of goods by river is slight. Many geographers transmitted more than they described, as witnessed by the verbatim repetition of Ibn Khurdādhbih's phrase.[53] No doubt river traffic did occur, primarily on shallow draft *aṭwāf*, but its importance in long-distance commerce, and hence to the importance of Samsat specifically, must be called into question. The detail geographers devote to the delineation of land itineraries points to the traditional caravan as the major means of transport employed. Samsat's importance consisted in assuring the safe crossing of the Euphrates more than its utilization as a port of embarkation.

A Source for the Samsat Region in the Sixteenth Century

Only a study utilizing the tax registers and other archival material in the Turkish archives allows the history of this region to be traced through the Ottoman period. Evidence of the richness of documentation available there is presented in a transliterated tax register for the province of Malatya in the year 1560.[54] At this time, Samsat was the seat of a township (*nahiye*) bound to the Kâhta district (*kaza*) of Malatya subprovince (*liva*). (For most of its later history, until Adıyaman became a separate province of the Republic of Turkey in 1954, this area was tied to an administrative center in Malatya.)

In the section of the 1560 tax register devoted to the administrative district of Samsat, the number of houses, the ownership, and sometimes the agricultural produce of individual villages are listed.

Three ferries (*sefine*) are listed for *nahiye* of Samsat. One was at Samsat itself. Another, called the ferry of Cemceme, was located in the fields of Uzamış near Bekircek (= Birecik).[55]

---

[48] Al-Iṣṭakhrī, *Kitāb al-Masālik wa'l-Mamālik*, 76.

[49] Neo-Assyrian reliefs from the palace of Ashurnasirpal (reg. 885-860) at Nineveh show soldiers floating across a river on inflated skins: Budge, *Assyrian Sculptures*, Pls. 21, 22. In addition, Xenophon (*Persian Expedition*, 172) mentions the crossing of the Tigris on inflated skins in his *Anabasis:* "I shall need two thousand bags made of hide, and I can see that there are numbers of sheep and goats and oxen about. When we have skinned them and inflated their hides they will give us an easy means of getting across."

[50] Ibn Khurdādhbih, *Kitāb al-Masālik wa'l-Mamālik*, 174; Ibn al-Faqīh, *Kitāb al-Buldān*, 175; and al-Idrīsī, *Kitāb Rujār*, 650.

[51] Al-Iṣṭakhrī, *Kitāb al-Masālik wa'l-Mamālik*, 68.

[52] Humann and Puchstein, *Reisen in Kleinasien und Nordsyrien*, 1:174. An Iranian bureaucrat writing in the late 19th century noted travel on the Tigris River from Diyarbakır to Samarra by this means took seven days: Farmayan and Daniel, *Shi'ite Pilgrimage to Mecca 1885–1886*, 106, where the rafts are called *qoffeh kalak*, using the Iraqi Arabic word for river boat in addition to *kelek*.

[53] For the issue of the replication of information in the works of medieval Islamic geographers, see Miquel, *La géographie humaine du monde musulman*, e.g., 1:354 ff.

[54] Yınanç and Elibüyük, *Kanunî Devri Malatya Tahrir Defteri*.

[55] Ibid., 431.

Using modern toponyms, we can propose an identification with a crossing of the Euphrates near the village of Birecik to the village of Cümcüme, both downstream from Samsat.[56] The third ferry mentioned in this tax register was near Herduyan (= Hardiyan) at the northern end of the Karababa basin.[57]

The tax register does not mention the sources of revenue for most villages. When they are noted, millet, barley, wheat, and cotton are included. Wheat and barley are listed for the small (two-household) village of Til (karye-i Til), which depended on Samsat. Til was part of the *timar* (fief) of Ali and Ahmed the porter and Mustafa, members of the guardians (*müstahfizân*) of Samsat citadel.[58]

No Christians are listed in this register. Instead, tribes (*taife*) of Kurdish and Arab (Bargi, read Bakri)[59] origin are listed when any information is given.

THE SAMSAT REGION IN MODERN TRAVELERS' ACCOUNTS

THE NINETEENTH CENTURY

The first traveler's account pertaining to this region is that of Baptistin Poujoulat, who traveled with an Ottoman army through southeastern Anatolia and northern Syria in 1837. The trip inspired him to note that "[l]es trois grands fléaux de l'Orient sont la peste, l'incendie et les drogmans."[60] A few pages after this observation Poujoulat's narrative brought him to Samsat, where he noted that

> Les terres qui environnent la cité sont fécondées par les eaux du grand fleuve, et produisent des grains, des raisins excellents et du tabac.[61]

In the town of Samsat he found two thousand families of Kurds. After crossing the Eu-

phrates at Samsat, his party reached Urfa after a march of 12 hours.[62]

The Prussian count Helmut von Moltke floated past Samsat the following year and was impressed with the Euphrates after it left the gorges above Samsat around Horis Kalesi.

> . . . von hier breitet sich der Euphrat aus und fliesst in weiten Windungen am Castell Choris vorüber, der berühmten Stadt Samosata zu; dort ist das Thal weit, unter Fluss gleicht der Oder nahe oberhalb Frankfurt. . . . Der Strom fliesst nun in einem 800 Schritt breiten Bett, das er jedoch nur selten ausfüllt (und zwar ganz anders, als die Karten angeben) westwärts.[63]

Other travelers passed by Samsat in the nineteenth century, but none stopped to take its measure until the Austrians Humann and Puchstein, famed for their rediscovery of the Commagenian sanctuary at Nemrut Dağı, visited Samsat on June 29, 1883. They, too, were impressed with the breadth of the Euphrates in the Karababa basin.

> Der Euphrat fliesst hier von Nordosten nach Südwesten, ist sehr breit, seicht und mit mehreren Sandinseln durchsetzt. Ein Teil des Ufers ist so flach, dass es regelmässig überschwemmt wird, gehört auch vielleicht von Zeit zu Zeit einmal zum Flusse der hier sein Bett bis zu einer gewissen Grenze hin verändern mag, da er nicht von Felsen eingeschlos-sen ist.[64]

It is as "Til," or "mound," plain and simple, that Gritille makes its debut in western scholarship, on the map accompanying the text of Humann and Puchstein's travels.[65]

The American Vincent Yorke traveled in this region in the early 1890s, following the river val-

---

[56] Wilkinson, *Town and Country in Southeastern Anatolia*, 1:127, Fig. 5.7, for this area.

[57] See Özdoğan, *Lower Euphrates Basin*, Pl. 41, for the location of this village.

[58] Yınanç and Elibüyük, *Kanunî Devri Malatya Tahrir Defteri*, 436.

[59] I owe this suggestion to Wheeler M. Thackston, Jr.

[60] Poujoulat, *Voyage à Constantinople*, 1:203.

[61] Ibid., 207.

[62] Ibid., 208.

[63] von Moltke, *Briefe über Zustände*, 236.

[64] Humann and Puchstein, *Reisen in Kleinasien und Nordsyrien*, 1:182.

[65] Ibid., 2, Map 2.

ley of the Euphrates up to Samsat, whence he followed the traditional route across the mountains to Malatya. He observed that

> [t]he country through which we travelled on the left bank is flat, treeless, and mostly dreary in character. . . . The villages, however, are thickly distributed wherever the rocky soil admits of cultivation.[66]

THE TWENTIETH CENTURY

Ewald Banser floated down the Euphrates in the early years of the twentieth century, and before he entered the rapids of the Karakaya gorge, he passed through the Karababa basin, ". . . wo der ärmliche Kurdenflecken Samsat ein nicht unwichtiger Färpunkt ist."[67]

The most informative account of the crops and conditions in the Karababa basin comes from another German, the geologist Arnold Nöldeke, who floated down the Euphrates on a raft in 1917–1918, stopping every so often to reconnoiter. Aside from a rather involved discussion of the geology of the region, Nöldeke animates his article with a remarkable number of precise observations concerning (in addition to geology) crops and game.

> Auf der lehmigen Boden der höheren Uferbänke finden sich verhältnismässig zahlreiche Dorfsiedelungen. Vor allem wird Mais und Tabak gebaut. Einige Dörfer liegen in Gärten von Feigen-, Nuss-, Pistazien- oder Maulbeerbaümen ganz eingebettet. Die Hochfläche trägt Gerste und Mais; die Hänge sind vielfach mit Weinkulturen bestellt.[68]

The picture he paints is one of very fertile land, with many of the same varieties of fruit that al-Idrīsī had mentioned as growing wild in the eleventh century now being cultivated. The author continues with his description of the Karababa basin as seen from his raft (and here the reader must remember that his raft had a draft of only 55 cm):

> Die hohen Uferränder pflegen in kurzen, fast regelmässigen Zwischenrämen von Ravinen durchrissen zu sein, die aber nur selten wasserführend sind; oft hat sich darin, namentlich, wenn sie der Südsonne abekehrt sind, eine reiche Vegetation von Strauch- und Baumwerk, Feigen, Platanen, Brombeeren, verwildertem Wein aufgetan. In diesem letzen breiten Schlauch strömt der heutige Euphrat, sich ungeregelt zu Armen vielfach verzweigend; nur Niedrigwasserzeit für die Schiffahrt ein ungünstiges Fahrwasser! Der landschaftliche Charakter dieser flussstrecke erhellt aus dem Gesagten ohne weiteres: flache uferbänke erscheinen beiderseits, Kiesbänke und lehmige, mit Tamarisken bestandene Inseln. Die Wasserarme zwischen den flachen Inseln sind der Aufenthalt für zahlreiche Wasservögel: Reiher, Gänse, Enten; auch ein bis zwei familien von Pelikanen pfleft man hier anzutreffen. Auf den Tamarisken Inseln treiben in mondhellen Nächten Wildschweine gern ihr Wesen. Eine ganze Anzahl von Dörfen liegen beiderseits auf den niedrigen Ebenen; einige auch auf der Kante des Nagelfluhabbruches.[69]

Two Germans, epigrapher Friedrich Karl Dörner and architect Rudolf Naumann, followed in the footsteps of Humann and Puchstein in the late 1930s, conducting a survey of the remains in the ancient Kingdom of Commagene. Gritille was marked on a map resulting from this survey but was not investigated because of its lack of standing ruins.[70]

THE EXCAVATORS

Theresa Goell's two seasons of excavation at Samsat in 1964 and 1967 were a coda to her pioneering work with F. K. Dörner in the previous decade. These excavations were undertaken in response to an oft-heard threat, that of a massive dam to be built on Turkey's lower Euphrates.

---

[66] Yorke, "Journey in the Valley," 321.
[67] Banser, *Die Türkei,* 265.
[68] Nöldeke, "Der Euphrat von Gerger," 16.
[69] Ibid., 17–18.
[70] Dörner and Naumann, *Forschungen in Kommagene.*

The dam project finally began to be realized in the late 1970s.

In response, Turkish scholars initiated a national and international salvage effort. The first step in this effort was the publication of two surveys of the reservoir area by the prehistorian Mehmet Özdoğan and the classical archaeologist Ümit Serdaroğlu. The mound of Gritille is featured in both surveys and is named both Tille and Gritille.[71]

INFERENCES FROM THE HISTORICAL RECORD

AGRICULTURAL POTENTIAL OF THE REGION

No one who has visited the Near East should be surprised by Nöldeke's images of flora and fauna concentrated in a well-watered area. An oasis the Karababa basin is not: as al-Idrīsī noted, the Anti-Taurus to the north contained vines (no doubt a factor in locating monasteries in this region) and other fruit- and nut-producing flora. Writing on Ḥiṣn Manṣūr, located in the middle of the uplands to the north of Samsat, Abu'l Fidā stressed the fertility of the land.[72] In addition, winter rains in north Syria provide for a crop of winter wheat, and dry farming is feasible over large parts of the area. Ellsworth Huntington, who spent four years in eastern Turkey in the late nineteenth century, has left a vivid description of the climatic and agricultural conditions on those plains:

> No dweller in a green land like the eastern part of America can fully realize the beauty of the brief snatch of spring verdure which in this semi-arid land is gone from the lower mountains almost as soon as it comes, and stays on the plains but two or three short months. During the time of the spring showers, from the middle of March to the middle of June, the plains resemble our prairies, except for the universal background of mountains. . . . Before the end of June the last showers have fallen, the bright flowers have given place to this-

> tles and a few other hardy inconspicuous compositae, the wheat and barley are turning yellow, and soon the plains assume the same dull grayish or yellowish-brown which the mountains always wear. After the long cloudless summer a few autumn rains in October bring out such flowers as the yellow crocus, and the winter wheat gives some verdure to the plain, but in general the brown remains until it is covered with snow in late December or January.[73]

Still, only irrigated areas would have remained green and productive for the half of every year that the land is barren, and the rich soil of the river valley would have produced higher yields than surrounding areas. If we envisage the mix of dry and irrigated agriculture mentioned by medieval geographers as occurring in the Karababa basin, then we can assume that the area of lowest-lying land next to the river must have been irrigated. Nöldeke, in the citation above, describes the relative high clay banks of much of the valley, but he, Humann and Puchstein, and von Moltke all mention the breadth of the riverbed. The shifting course of the river between these relatively high banks would have left substantial tracts of irrigable land. Some, it is true, would have been wild with tamarisk and game, but if recent practice is any guide, even river islands not used for crops would have served as pasturage for livestock in the dry summer months. Here, then, would have been located the gardens mentioned by Ibn Ḥawqal, while the major portion of the valley would have grown the crops appropriate to dry farming (modern cultivation concentrates on wheat, barley, and lentils). The fact that three travelers mention the cultivation of tobacco shows that irrigation was widely practiced before the diesel pump was introduced into the region, as tobacco is a crop requiring both abundant water and rich soil. Until recently, the use of diesel pumps allowed large portions of the valley which could not have been irrigated in the past to be exploited in this manner.

---

[71] Özdoğan, *Lower Euphrates Basin*, 4, Pl. 1; Serdaroğlu, *1975 Surveys in the Lower Euphrates Basin*, 59, Pl. 64, Fig. 19.

[72] Abu'l Fidā, *Kitāb Taqwīm al-Buldān*, 269.

[73] Huntington, "Valley of the Upper Euphrates River," 307.

The agricultural potential of the Karababa basin has been examined here in some depth in order to situate Gritille and other sites properly. Gritille and Lidar constituted the two major medieval settlements in the hinterland of Samsat. As such, they must be identified with the exploitation of the region in the eleventh through thirteenth centuries. Gritille was not occupied earlier in the medieval era, while Lidar, compared with its rehabilitation in the eleventh to thirteenth centuries, comprised a small earlier medieval settlement, believed by its excavators to have been a caravansaray.[74]

SAMSAT'S ROLE AS A POINT ON THE RIVER

The river crossing at Samsat has been established as a major one by a review of the medieval geographers' itineraries, and we shall see in the historical summary that in this time period it held a military importance equal to, if not exceeding, its commercial one. At the same time, the importance of the river as a means of transport has been discounted beyond local trade. Since both Gritille and Lidar were fortified for much of their medieval incarnations, it stands to reason that the protection of the flanks of Samsat was a major reason for their existence.

Recent scholarship has focused on settlement at Gritille and Lidar as a function of the protection of a river crossing near Samsat.

> [T]he economic and strategic importance of specific crossing points must also have been affected by historical factors, particularly the location of political boundaries that would restrict the use of the most convenient crossings and encourage the use of less favorable ones. *It is particularly in periods of political fragmentation and upheaval, with conditions of decreased security in some areas, that the importance of minor river crossings would be enhanced.*[75]

Another view posits communication along the Euphrates as a prime determinant of settlement in the Karababa basin. According to this hypothesis, a pattern of larger settlements located upstream from smaller settlements "may suggest that the latter formed the receiving settlements for goods or people disbursed from the larger upstream settlement."[76] Gritille, according to this model, was the smaller settlement linked to Lidar, and Şaşkan Büyüktepe the downstream "receiver settlement" of Samsat.

I shall argue that the importance of these sites was due to their presence as fortifiable and defendable eminences on the river rather than to any particular characteristics of the river at that point. While riverine communication and trade may have been crucial for the settlement of the Karababa basin in earlier eras, as we have seen, the primary mode of communication and transport was by land in the medieval period.

Between Lidar and Gritille, it is true, the Euphrates channel was particularly broad, but it was so at other points much closer and much farther from Samsat. The ford became important because the presence of forts on both sides of the Euphrates allowed an army or a caravan to cross the river (a dangerous and time-consuming operation in the most peaceable of circumstances) in relative security. The fortifications were built there, and also probably at Şaşkan Büyüktepe,[77] because there already existed tells, or habitation mounds, whose human development may have been due to the river-traffic theory outlined above as well as other factors such as the presence of springs (found at the base of the mound at both Lidar and Gritille). The most important fortified river crossing was always that of Samsat; the existence of other sites on the Euphrates in the Karababa basin depended on the degree of Samsat's importance.

Because a river passage left forders exposed to attack, the Euphrates constituted a natural barrier, protecting the local peasantry against

---

[74] Hauptmann, "Lidar Höyük 1981," 94. Prof. Hauptmann dates this building to the 4th to 7th centuries; he has subsequently mentioned in conversation with the author that the building may date to the Abbasid period. The other major 11th to 13th century medieval settlement in the Karababa basin has been identified at Şaşkan Büyüktepe by survey: see Wilkinson, *Town and Country in Southeastern Anatolia*, 1:157–159, Fig. A.5. This site is located across the river and downstream from Samsat.

[75] Ellis and Voigt, "1981 Excavations at Gritille, Turkey," 321. Emphasis added.

[76] Wilkinson, *Town and Country in Southeastern Anatolia*, 1:101.

[77] Wilkinson (ibid., 129) notes that the medieval occupation of the summit of this mound probably points to its use as a small fortified stronghold.

swift cavalry raids. The importance of the Euphrates in this respect is recorded by an extraordinary circumstance, when a harsh winter in 1121 caused the river to freeze. As Michael the Syrian noted, "In the year 1432 there was a severe winter, for forty days, the Euphrates froze as did the other rivers; they provided a passage like the solid ground."[78] This particular cold snap allowed Artuqid forces to cross the Euphrates and attack Gerger castle.

As established by the preceding review of modern and medieval travelers' and geographers' accounts, the agricultural potential of the Karababa basin was great. As shall be shown in the historical section that follows, this potential was exploited to the utmost at some point in the period spanning the lifetime of the County of Edessa (1098–1144) and the brief interregnum that preceded the capture of Samsat by Muslim forces in 1150.

Therefore, it is as protectors of the rich agricultural hinterland of Samsat that I prefer to view these medieval settlements in the Karababa basin. To use medieval Arabic terminology, these settlements would have been *rustāqs* of Samsat. This term is often translated as "village," but if we translate it as "rural canton," together with the idea of a rural settlement goes the idea of a collection center.

The existence of fortified rural cantons dependent on a larger town is attested by Matthew of Edessa for the region of Ḥiṣn Manṣūr. In 1113, he writes, Tancred defeated Kogh Vasil, the Armenian lord of Keysun, and exchanged the castle of Ra'bān for

> the district of Ḥiṣn Manṣūr also T'orêsh and Uremn; for Vasil had captured this district of Ḥiṣn Manṣūr, together with the fortified P'ersin, Raghtip, Ḥart'an, T'orêsh and Uremn, and now returned them to the Franks.[79]

These toponyms have not been identified, but the configuration conforms to that which the archaeological record gives for the Karababa basin, with the fortified outposts of Gritille and Lidar dependent on Samsat. In addition, survey data for the uplands around the area mentioned by Matthew seem to confirm a pattern of numbers of fortified settlement in the medieval period.[80]

The History of the Karababa Basin (11th to 13th Centuries)

The Shifting Balance of Power

The Crusades hold such sway over the historical imagination of the West that it is easy to view any and all events in the medieval Near East as issuing from that historical phenomenon. And yet, for the history of the peoples of the area, the Turkic invasions of the eleventh century onward had a greater and more permanent impact than any other single event.

For the first time since the seventh century, the balance of power between Byzantines and the Islamic world was irrevocably altered. Certainly the pendulum had oscillated during that time period; from the eighth-century Arab sieges of Constantinople, Byzantines gained the ascendant under the Macedonian dynasty in the tenth century, regaining Malatya in 934 and Antioch in 969, and increasing their power well into the second half of the eleventh century.

On the Islamic side, starting in the mid-tenth century, a series of frontier dynasties of nomadic Arab tribes established power bases in and around Aleppo. The most famous of these was the Hamdanid dynasty, but it was succeeded by other dynasties of north Syrian/Jazīran origin, the Mirdasids and the 'Uqaylids, the latter still holding onto minor principalities in the face of the Turkic invasions when the Crusaders arrived on the scene in 1097.

The battle of Manzikert in 1071 is cited by historians as a marker for the arrival of Turks in eastern Anatolia, but actually they had begun to arrive seven years earlier.[81] That year, however, does mark the definitive collapse of the system of frontier defenses in eastern Anatolia, as well as the withdrawal of Byzantine military forces from the *'awāṣim*.[82]

---

[78] Michael the Syrian, *Chronique de Michel le Syrien*, 2, fasc. ii, 209.

[79] Matthew of Edessa, *Armenia and the Crusades*, 211.

[80] Blaylock, French, and Summers, "The Adıyaman Survey," 125.

[81] Cahen, "La première pénétration turque," 5–67.

[82] For more on this topic, see Oikonomidès, "L'organisation de la frontière orientale," 285–302.

Ironically, when the Crusaders arrived at the gates of Antioch, and for many years thereafter, their incursions were viewed by Muslim chroniclers as a resurgence of the power of the Byzantines.[83] Still, the confusion is comprehensible when one surveys the tumult that reigned with the Turkic influx and the collapse of the dominant military and economic force in the region.

THE BYZANTINES AND ARMENIANS IN SAMSAT

Samsat and surroundings had been captured by the Byzantines in 958 but seem not to have played a significant role in Byzantine plans, which concentrated on the region around Antioch as well as on parts of Syria farther south. The situation changed with expanding Byzantine presence in the area. As part of the strategy that led the Byzantines to overreach their military capabilities by swallowing smaller tributary states along their borders, Urfa was besieged and captured by the Byzantine *protospatharios* Maniakes from a vassal of the Marwanid ruler of Mayyāfarīqīn.[84]

Maniakes took up residence in Samsat in 1031 as *strategos* of the new theme of "the cities of the Euphrates." The Byzantine military presence in these far-flung regions proved a strain, one that was remedied in two ways. First, treaties of friendship and tribute money from the emir of Aleppo induced the Byzantines to withdraw the cavalry as well as the 20,000 soldiers they had garrisoned along the southeastern frontier northward to Gerger[85] in the face of a Pecheneg invasion of the Balkans.

Second and more substantively, the Byzantines relied more and more on Armenians to man the ʿawāṣim zone. The Armenians, previously a minor presence in the area, began to increase in numbers in the face of continuous Türkmen depredation of their ancestral lands to the north and east. In addition, when the Byzantines took over Armenia, Armenian princes had

been given lands in southern Cappadocia and had relocated there and established estates. This slow but steady migration increased to a torrent by mid-century. It is generally thought of in connection with the establishment of the Kingdom of Armenian Cilicia, but Urfa, Maraş, and other cities and regions of the area also gained large Armenian populations.[86]

The Byzantine *sebastos*, or governor, of Maraş in the 1060s was an Armenian, one Philaretos Brachamios (Arabic Filardūs al-Rūmī). After Manzikert, Philaretos seized Cilicia and eventually controlled territory stretching all the way to Antioch in his own name.[87] In 1077, Urfa fell to the armies of Philaretos, only to be captured by a Turk named Buzan a decade later in 1087. Much conflict developed between the Armenians and the incoming Muslim armies and Türkmen nomads in this period. One of these hostilities, described by Matthew of Edessa as occurring in either 1081 or 1082, took place in the Karababa basin and very likely involved Gritille, which was probably fortified at that time.

> In this period a certain emir by the name of Khusraw came with many troops from Persia and reached the territory of Edessa, devastating many places [as he advanced]. At this time a battle was fought near the Euphrates River, at a place called Mknik, which is close to the fortress of Ltar; for all the garrisons of the neighboring fortresses had gathered together to give battle to this emir. However, on that day the Turks were victorious and slaughtered many of the Christians.[88]

Thoros, another Armenian who had been in Byzantine service, managed to regain Urfa from the Turks in 1094. In 1097, the first Frankish armies arrived in Cilicia, and one of them, under the leadership of Baldwin of Boulogne, set out east, lured by the promises of Armenian advisors. Thoros and the other petty Armenian rul-

---

[83] Gibb, "Notes on the Arabic Materials," 744.

[84] Honigmann, *Ostgrenze des byzantinischen Reiche*, 134–135; Felix, *Byzanz und die islamische Welt*, 146–148.

[85] Honigmann, *Ostgrenze des byzantinischen Reiche*, 116.

[86] Georges Tate ("Frontière et peuplement en Syrie," 155), maintains that Armenians began moving into this region earlier, in the 10th century, as military adventurers.

[87] Laurent, "Byzance et Antioche," 61–72, 148–159; idem, "Des grecs aux croisés"; and Segal, *Edessa. The Blessed City*, 215 ff.

[88] Matthew of Edessa, *Armenia and the Crusades*, 146.

ers of the region were eager to use the Franks as mercenaries to protect their principalities from the forces of the Seljuks of Rum and the Danish-mendids, Turkic states to the north and west.

Baldwin, however, had more ambitious plans. Leaving the main Crusader army at Mar-aş, he set out to capture the castles of Till Bashīr (Crusader Turbessel) and Ruwandān (Crusader Ravendal) to the west of the Euphrates and south of Maraş. The possession of these two fortresses kept lines of communication open with the main Crusader forces advancing on Antioch.

In 1097, the main powers in this region were the Armenian principalities of Thoros at Urfa, Kogh (meaning "Robber") Vasil ruling Keysun and Besni, Kogh Vasil's father-in-law, Gabriel, at Malatya, and Constantine at Gerger.[89] Needless to say, power, even at a time of political fragmentation, still resided with the sovereigns of the major cities of the region, Duqāq at Damascus, Ruḍwān at Aleppo, and Yaghī Siyān at Antioch.[90]

Samsat, which had been taken over by Philaretos, was conquered from the Armenians by an emir of Harran, Sharaf al-Dawla.[91] When Baldwin and his troops arrived in the area, rule of Samsat had passed to a Türkmen chief named Balduk.[92] Balduk had joined forces with Sukmān, emir of Diyarbakır, in 1095, sending cavalry against Urfa at harvest time.[93]

Baldwin and a small force of knights were invited to Urfa by Thoros in February 1098.[94] The difficulties encountered by this Crusader force in making its way to Urfa help illuminate the problems faced by the local Armenian po-

tentates in their eagerness to embrace the Crusaders as new allies. Baldwin made to cross the Euphrates near Birecik on his way from Maraş to Urfa:

Meanwhile, the Turks who lived on the farther side of the river had learned that he was coming and had prepared ambushes for him. There was, however, a fortified town on his route ruled by a certain Armenian, and thither he withdrew to avoid the pitfalls prepared for him. He was kindly received by the lord of the place with gracious hospitality, and there he rested for two days, not daring to proceed. Then the Turks who had lurked in ambush during that time grew weary of waiting longer. With standards raised, they suddenly appeared with a strong force before the place and began to drive off cattle from the pastures near by. As the Christians were unequal to their adversaries both in strength and numbers, they did not venture to go out against them but remained in the fortress, and on the third day the Turks departed.[95]

When Baldwin and his troops finally reached Urfa, Baldwin was adopted and made co-regent of the city. Almost immediately thereupon, Baldwin, his knights, and a force of Armenians set out against Balduk but were unable to take Samsat. As Albert of Aachen put it:

---

[89] Hellenkemper, *Burgen der Kreuzritterzeit in der Grafschaft Edessa*, 68 for Kogh Vasil, 85 for Gerger: "[I]n den 'nördlichen Landschaften von Gargar' sitzt um das Jahr 1100 die armenische Familie des Sanbīl, die die Oberhoheit des Kogh Vasil anerkennt. Die Söhne des Sanbīl, Konstantin, Tābtūg und Christophoros, teilen sich das Land; Konstantin had die Herrschaft in Gargar, auf Tābtūg und Christophoros entfallen vermutlich Gaktaj und Bēt Bōlā (Bābūla, heute Bibol).

[90] For an introduction to the Levant at the time of the First Crusade, see Gibb, *Damascus Chronicle of the Crusades*, 14–40.

[91] Bar Hebraeus, *Chronography of Gregory Abu'l Faraj*, 229.

[92] Osman Turan (*Doğu Anadolu Devletleri Tarihi*, 140, n. 21), identifies Sulaymān bin Īl-Ghāzī with the Balduk mentioned in Christian sources. This identification is based on two references by Ibn al-'Adīm. The first of these is in his biographical dictionary *Bughyat al-Ṭalab fī Tārīkh Ḥalab* (p. 89). The second is in his *Zubdat al-Ḥalab min Tārīkh Ḥalab* (p. 126). Both mention that in 490 A.H./A.D. 1096–1097 Ruḍwān bin Tutush asked for assistance from Sulaymān bin Īl-Ghāzī, lord (*ṣāhib*) of Samsat, who sent many troops to Aleppo.

[93] Matthew of Edessa, *Armenia and the Crusades*, 162, where Balduk is called emir of Samsat and son of Amir Ghazi.

[94] Matthew of Edessa (ibid., 168) reported sixty knights; William of Tyre (*History of Deeds Done Beyond the Sea*, 1:190), reported eighty.

[95] William of Tyre, ibid.

Baudouin, voyant qu'il lui serait impossible de s'emparer de la citadelle de Samosate, occupée par des Turcs vaillans dans les combats et infatigables, laissa ses hommes, revêtus de leurs cuirasses et de leurs casques et munis de leur chevaux, dans le bâtiment de Saint-Jean, situé non-loin de la citadelle, afin qu'ils pussent opposer une résistance continuelle aux Turcs et les harceler sans relâche.[96]

Since Albert reports that Baldwin was accompanied by two hundred knights, that he lost six in the fray, and that he left Samsat with twelve, a substantial force, approximately one hundred and eighty knights, must have been left behind to continue guerrilla actions against the Muslim forces. The "bâtiment de Saint-Jean" referred to in the text must surely, then, have been larger than a mere building; more likely it was a fortified settlement like those referred to by Matthew as occurring in the hinterland of Samsat.[97] However, because Baldwin had arrived at Urfa with so few Crusader knights, we must envisage the garrison as consisting mainly of non-Crusaders.

THE COUNTY OF EDESSA

Only a month after entering Urfa, Baldwin managed to rid himself of Thoros and establish himself as sole ruler, count, of a new state, the first in the Outremer, the County of Edessa. This state, which was to last only forty-six troubled years, stands as an anomaly. Historians of the Crusades, not knowing how to categorize its existence, have tended to slight it owing both to its distance from the Holy Land and its brevity of duration.[98] Perhaps Edessa's anomalous character was reinforced as well by the swiftness with which the tiny population of Frankish knights resident in the county intermarried with and took up the intrigues of the local Armenian aristocracy. Baldwin himself married the daughter of a wealthy Armenian noble who was related to Constantine of Gerger. Many of his nobles, too, followed suit, taking brides, dowries, and fiefs in the area, although we will see that when the lot of the county worsened, the Franks did not hesitate to break with their Armenian allies. The position of the County in an exposed, inland location also stood in contrast to the other, coastal, Crusader states, and this relative difficulty of access may have discouraged a more numerous transfer of Frankish families from Antioch.

It is not known how long the knights camped out against the citadel at Samsat, but Balduk saw fit to relinquish his isolated stronghold after the murder of Thoros when it became clear that Baldwin had consolidated his power. Balduk sold Samsat to Baldwin for 10,000 bezants, and the safety of Urfa was insured. Samsat, which had long been the seat of a Syriac bishop, now gained an Armenian bishop, who stayed in residence until the fall of the County.[99]

The County of Edessa, newly established, expanded its borders. Birecik was soon conquered, thus completing the Frankish hold over the westward sweep of the Euphrates, and forts were established in the Shabakhtān, a group of mountains to the southeast of Urfa which served as important advance posts for raids to (and from) the east. Nominal suzerainty was also extended far across the Euphrates to the north and east to include the mountain baronies such as that of Constantine of Gerger. Ibn al-Athīr offered his description of the territory under the control of the County at its height only after recounting the capture of Urfa by the forces of Zangī many years later. Once they had been vanquished, the Crusaders' ability to penetrate to the heartland of the northern Mesopotamia could be mentioned:

---

[96] Albert of Aachen (Albert d'Aix), *Histoire des croisades*, 20:129–130; Matthew of Edessa, *Armenia and the Crusades*, 168–169, portrays the initial siege in a darker light.

[97] This impression is reinforced by a reading of William of Tyre (*History of Deeds Done Beyond the Sea*, 1:192), who recounts the event in the following manner: "He left behind, however, knights in an adequately fortified place near by who were ordered to keep up a continual warfare which would leave the people of Samosata no respite."

[98] Runciman, *History of the Crusades* 1:209: "It was not to set up Baldwin and his like in semi-oriental monarchies that Urban had appealed to the faithful at Clermont." The County of Edessa's neglect has been partially redressed in monographic fashion by a Crusader historian using non-Western language sources in translation: see Amouroux-Mourad, *Le comté d'Edesse*.

[99] Hellenkemper, "Zur mittelalterlichen Landschaftsgeschichte," 76.

Their (the Franks') kingdom in these regions (*Diyār*) was from near Mardin to the Euphrates (with towns) like al-Ruhā (Urfa), Sarūj (Suruç), al-Bīra (Birecik), Sinn ibn 'Uṭayr, Jamlīn, al-Mawzar, al-Qirādī, and others.[100]

When Jerusalem fell to the Crusaders, Baldwin of Boulogne was chosen as King of Jerusalem, and rulership of the County fell into the hands of Baldwin's cousin, Baldwin of LeBourg, known as Baldwin II. He, too, found it politic to forge alliances with local Armenian rulers and soon married Morphia, daughter of Gabriel, the ruler of Malatya.

In 1101, Baldwin's cousin, Joscelin of Courtney, arrived in Urfa and was enfeoffed with all of the regions of the county lying to the west of the Euphrates and to the south of the lands of Kogh Vasil, with the residence of this fiefdom at Till Bashīr (Crusader Turbessel).[101]

William of Tyre recounts this even more fully:

> As Joscelin had neither lands nor other wealth, Baldwin conferred upon him extensive possessions so that he might not be compelled to turn to a stranger to earn a livelihood. This grant included all that part of Baldwin's own land lying adjacent to the great river Euphrates. It contained the cities Coritium and Tulupa, the exterior and well-fortified castles Turbessel, Hamtab, Ravendal, and others. The count reserved for himself the region beyond the Euphrates, as being nearer to the enemy's domain, and retained only one city of the interior, namely Samsat.[102]

It appears as if Baldwin wished to devote his full attentions to the aggrandizement of his realms to the north and east.

In 1104, these hopes were cut short when the combined armies of Antioch and Edessa were decimated while attempting to take Harran. The remaining history of the County of Edessa is very involved, with scarcely a month passing between raids and a year between alliances. The most elemental of solidarities, those of blood and faith, seem to have evaporated in the face of the quest after personal gain. To quote one eminent scholar,

> The real mainspring of Syrian politics, it can hardly be doubted, is to be found in the principle of "beggar-thy-neighbour" which had long governed the relations of the amirs of Syria and Mesopotamia ever since the disintegration of the Caliphate.[103]

Across the Euphrates to the north and west, the Crusaders garrisoned forts belonging to allied Armenian lords such as Kogh Vasil or Constantine or Michael of Gerger, but to the east and south they were fully exposed to the brunt of Artuqid and Zangid attacks across the plain. Because of chronic manpower shortages as well as difficulties in combating the more mobile Turkic archers and cavalry, the County adopted a strategy that was to prove to be the mainstay of the Crusader states of the Outremer in general. This lay in garrisoning key fortresses and not allowing troops to stray too far from these. As Ibn al-Athīr wrote, these included the castles along or to the west of the Euphrates, as well as the forts of the Shabakhtān. Artuqid and Zangid incursions invariably began with the spring but became heavier as the summer progressed, concentrating on ravaging the countryside outside the walled cities and fortresses of the County. Fields were burned and orchards and vineyards chopped down. As examples, I would cite two contemporary sources. The first is a brief description of the investment of the countryside

---

[100] Yāqūt (*Mu'jam al-Buldān*, 3:269, under "al-Sinn") locates this fortress "in the Jazira near Samsat." Honigmann (*Le couvent*, 151), identifies al-Mawzar with the present-day town of Viranşehir; Ibn al-Athīr, *al-Kāmil fī al-Tārīkh*, 11, 98. For a similar passage, see the same author's *al-Tārīkh al-Bāhir fī al-Dawlat al-Atābakiyya*, 67. The enumeration of castles in Frankish hands in the Shabakhtān and farther east is more detailed in these accounts than Frankish possessions across the Euphrates because Zangī failed to dislodge completely Frankish forces from across the Euphrates. Also, most of the forts mentioned in this list lying in the land (*balad*) of Mardin had been taken by Zangī in the previous year (idem, *al-Kāmil fī al-Tārīkh*, 11, 94).

[101] Cahen, *La Syrie du nord*, 236.

[102] William of Tyre, *History of Deeds Done Beyond the Sea*, 1:450–451.

[103] Gibb, *Damascus Chronicle of the Crusade*, 743.

around Urfa by the armies of Mawdūd, Emir of Mosul, in 1112:

> At the turn of the year at harvest Mawdud with a great army marched straight on Edessa, camped against the town, devoured the land and crops, and cut down the gardens and trees that remained. . . . Distress in the town grew with the scarcity and their spirits failed them, for year after year they planted and laboured but did not reap.[104]

The second quote is from Matthew and describes a campaign undertaken by the armies of the Artuqid Īl-Ghāzī in the spring of 1119:

> With this army the emir arrived at the gates of the city of Edessa. He remained there for four days without being able to do any harm to the city. Then, he crossed over the Euphrates River and, marching forth like a galloping horse out of breath, ravaged many places because all the areas occupied by the Franks were left unfortified. The emir seized fortresses, farming villages, monasteries, and also slaughtered everyone including old people and children.[105]

THE ROLE OF SAMSAT IN URFA'S SURVIVAL

The scorched earth policy evident from these quotations is confirmed in a variety of chronicles from the afflicted local Christian populace: the anonymous Syriac author and Matthew of Edessa quoted above, as well as Bar Hebraeus and Michael the Syrian. One wonders, then, just how the populace, especially that of the larger towns like Urfa, did survive. It is here that the role played by Samsat in the survival of Urfa becomes clear.

Two examples serve to underline the importance of Samsat to Urfa; they came into the historical record only because they were accompanied by disaster, but we may assume that they were a normal part of the economic order of the area.[106] First, in 1123, Baldwin II was captured while setting out to restock his capital with ". . . corn from Kaisun and Sumaisat."[107] Second, in October 1137,

> . . . a great multitude assembled in Sumaisat to go to Edessa, for only a great company could travel by reason of the enemies who always beset and ambushed the roads. There were carriers of fodder, wine, and all the necessaries of life, men and beasts without number, accompanied by Frankish horsemen and footmen.[108]

This caravan was ambushed by the armies of the Artuqid emir of Mardin, Timurtaş, before it reached its destination. From the enumeration of the booty, we learn that these beasts included horses, ponies, mules, and donkeys.

Although the regions to the south and east of Urfa seem to have borne the brunt of these attacks as they were more exposed, the land around Samsat itself was ravaged too, most notably in 1114, after another unsuccessful siege of the capital by Aqsunqur.[109] After an earlier siege of Mawdūd's in 1110 was lifted, Baldwin II surveyed the devastated countryside and made the decision to abandon all lands on the left bank of the Euphrates except Urfa and a few castles; the peasantry was left with no choice but to move to lands to the west and north.[110] Matthew of Edessa reported the retreat as follows:

> At this point Tancred learned of a plot hatched against him by the other leaders, and so taking his troops, reached Samosata and descended to the banks of the Euphrates. Soon all the Frankish

---

[104] Anonymous, "First and Second Crusades," 83.

[105] Matthew of Edessa, *Armenia and the Crusades*, 223.

[106] Matthew of Edessa (ibid., 54) notes a similar provisioning from Samsat of Urfa under duress during the initial Byzantine occupation of that city almost a century earlier.

[107] Anonymous, "First and Second Crusades," 91.

[108] Ibid., 278. Bar Hebraeus (*Chronography of Gregory Abu'l Faraj*, 265) put the number of Frankish knights at 300, accompanied by 4,000 foot soldiers. This underscores the importance of the caravan and suggests that its aim might have been the victualing of Urfa for the entire winter.

[109] Bar Hebraeus, *Chronography of Gregory Abu'l Faraj*, 246.

[110] Ibn al-Qalānisī, *Dhayl Tārīkh Dimashq*, 103–104.

forces followed him. Now, when the inhabitants of Edessa and those of the surrounding countryside who had taken refuge in the city heard of this withdrawal, they all left, even the women and children, and followed after the Frankish forces.

In this account, Matthew emphasizes the Euphrates as a boundary, difficult to cross. When Mawdūd learned of this retreat, he invaded. Again Matthew:

> Reaching the banks of the Euphrates, Maudud slaughtered a countless number of the inhabitants of the area and carried off the remaining together with their possessions. The Franks had already crossed over to the other side of the river. . . . Many drowned in the river. Those who tried to swim across were unable to reach the other side. Many tried to cross over on boats, but five or six of them sank full of people because too many persons got in them. So on this day the entire territory of Edessa was devastated and depopulated.[111]

The Collapse of the County of Edessa

Copper coins, which had been minted in Edessa since 1098, ceased to be issued sometime before 1118, signaling the economic collapse of the County. These coins were often palimpsests, often overstruck, with the crudely drawn figure of a knight in chain metal and helmet standing with his sword raised, superimposed on a barely effaced eleventh-century Byzantine *folles*. A bust of Christ on the obverse, a bellicose knight on the reverse, a legend in Greek proclaiming the figure of the knight to be the count himself: no more boastful gauntlet could have been thrown down at the edge of the Mediterranean

Christian world.[112] The challenged were the Turks, interlopers from the Seljuk realms to the east, and they responded as they had responded to the Byzantines. The power base of the Artuqids and Zangids may have lain with the great tribal confederations farther east in the Diyār Rabī'a and the Diyār Bakr. The Türkmen who served as the backbone of their armies may have been fickle and greedy for booty. Nevertheless, tribes and flocks moved ever westward, taking up the lands emptied by the devastation of economic collapse and war.

The increased importance of lands north and west of the Euphrates and intimations of Armenian plots against the Franks brought an inevitable move starting in 1116–1117. One by one, the Armenian principalities of the right bank were subdued and their rulers replaced by Franks, from Birecik all the way to Gerger.[113] However, despite the enfeoffing of lands to the south and west, Samsat always remained directly under the rule of the count.[114]

With the growing power of 'Imād al-Dīn Zangī, Emir of Mosul, the Crusader state became even more beleaguered. Artuqid forces, especially those of Timurtaş, son of Īl-Ghāzī, also joined in the attacks. Finally, in 1144, Zangī's forces stormed the walls of Urfa, and Joscelin II, then count, fled with a few survivors to Samsat. Nūr al-Dīn, son of and successor to Zangī, crushed a last attempt by Joscelin to retake the city in 1146.[115] In doing so, he completed the depopulation of that mainly Christian city.

News of the fall of Urfa reverberated throughout medieval Christendom; as far away as Ethiopia, a town was named Roha after the lost city.[116] The Second Crusade was organized in response to the fall, but the city was never retaken. There was, it seems, little to retake. Bar Hebraeus estimated that thirty thousand people were killed and sixteen thousand carried off into captivity:

---

[111] Matthew of Edessa, *Armenia and the Crusades*, 205–206.

[112] Porteous, "Early Coinage," 171. Also, Metcalf, *Coinage of the Crusades*, 8–9. The title of count, or *komes* in Greek, is largely a military one by this time in Byzantine history.

[113] Matthew of Edessa, *Armenia and the Crusades*, 211 ff. First Prince Vasil, son of Kogh Vasil, lost all of his lands to Baldwin, and then the Armenian Abu'l-Gharīb, governor of Birecik, had his town seized and handed over to the Frank Galeran of Le Puiset.

[114] See note 95 for quote from William of Tyre. This impression is reinforced by Joscelin's escape to Samsat in 1144, and his wife Beatrice's brief reign there.

[115] Michael the Syrian, *Chronique de Michel le Syrien*, vol. 3, fasc. ii, 271, "L'inique Josselin se sauva à Samosate."

[116] Roha was the original name for the site of Lalibela, which was renamed after its most famous ruler, who lived in the 13th century.

And Edessa remained a waste place, and saturated with blood, and filled with the limbs of her sons and her daughters; and the sirens used to go into it during the nights to feed upon the flesh of the slain. And it became a habitation for jackals.[117]

Michael the Syrian also couched his account of the fall in Biblical language: "The Assyrian boar prevailed and devoured the delicious grapes."[118] Baldwin, Count of Maraş and master of Keysun, foreseeing the final assault on Crusader lands to the north and west of Urfa, undertook the refortification of Keysun, tearing down its mudbrick wall and erecting one of stone and lime (mortar).[119] In 1149, Reinald, who succeeded Baldwin after his death in 1146, lost Maraş to Mas'ūd the Rum Seljuk sultan, and in 1150 Joscelin himself was captured and imprisoned in Aleppo by Sultan Nūr al-Dīn. The Crusaders were at bay, and Countess Beatrice, Joscelin's wife, decided to sell the remaining fortresses on the right bank of the Euphrates to the Byzantines.[120]

THE TURKIC TAKEOVER

A rapprochement between Nūr al-Dīn and Mas'ūd allowed the armies of those two sovereigns to take the lands to the west and southwest of Samsat.[121] The Artuqid armies of Mardin, Hasan Keyf, and Harput, advancing from the east, took Bābūla in 1149 and Gerger, Kâhta, Kores (Horis Kalesi), Ḥiṣn Manṣūr, and Samsat in 1150.[122]

The fate of Gritille, however, may have been sealed in the previous year, 1148, during the course of another Turkic raid. According to the anonymous Syriac chronicler writing in 1234,

At that time the Turks took the fort named Tell Adana or Agangatal above Sumaisat, killed the men, enslaved a great number of women and children, and destroyed the fort by fire.[123]

As mentioned at the beginning of this chapter, Gritille is a modern name, and all nineteenth- and twentieth-century travelers' accounts referred to it, if at all, as Til, or Tille: "mound" plain and simple. Nevertheless, the location of this fort upstream from Samsat, the Christianity of its inhabitants, as well as the fact that Gritille was burned at about this time make the coincidence striking.

THE SOCIAL STRUCTURE DURING THE CRUSADES

We may conclude that the whole area gained immeasurably in strategic importance with the establishment of an independent Franco-Armenian state here. Increased mayhem and bloodshed aside, when we examine the written sources, it is difficult to assess any change in the lot of the common man or woman in this period. In a seminal article, Claude Cahen pointed out that for the peasantry of Crusader lands, the coming of the Crusaders meant little more than the replacing of one overlord by another. For the Muslims the case was often different, but in the County of Edessa, with the notable exception of Suruç, most of the population was Christian. Cahen indicates that, by and large, each rural settlement, or *casal*, had one overlord, who himself owed allegiance to higher authorities.[124] This arrangement, of course, was not unique to Cru-

---

[117] Bar Hebraeus, *Chronography of Gregory Abu'l Faraj*, 273.

[118] Michael the Syrian, *Chronique de Michel le Syrien*, vol. 3, fasc. ii, 261.

[119] Ibid., 269.

[120] Lilie, *Byzanz und die Kreuzfahrerstaaten*, 157–158. Byzantine intentions in this region remain obscure. Of course the Byzantine Empire still held claim to the region, but how, in fact, it could have hoped to assume and maintain control over such a far-flung region is obscure.

[121] Matthew of Edessa, *Armenia and the Crusades*, 257 ff. Mas'ūd took Keysun and Besni, and turned them over to his son and successor, Qilij Arslān II, but he was unable to take Till Bashīr, which surrendered to Nūr al-Dīn in 1151.

[122] Cahen, "Le Diyār Bakr au temps des premiers Urtukides," 254; Ibn al-Azraq al-Fāriqī, *Tārīkh Mayyāfāriqīn wa Āmid*, 133; Gerhard Väth (*Geschichte der artuqidischen Fürstentümer in Syrien*, 108–109) argues that it was good relations between Fakhr al-Dīn Qara Arslān and Nūr al-Dīn that permitted the Artuqid armies to occupy territories that could have been conquered easily by the more powerful Zangids.

[123] Anonymous, "First and Second Crusades," 299.

[124] Cahen, "Le régime rural syrien," 228–229, 297.

sader lands, corresponding to the traditional system of the village headman, or *mukhtār*, prevalent in the Near East.

Thoros had ruled Urfa as an *iqṭā'*, or feudal appanage, from the Iranian Seljuk Sultan Malik-shāh; the major difference between *iqṭā'* and western-style feudalism seems to have been the nonhereditary nature of the post at this point in the development of this institution.[125] At the beginning of the County of Edessa, when Armenians were enfeoffed, or later, when only Franks were granted territories, the western hereditary feudal system seems to have applied. In it, the lord extracted a certain percentage of the harvest of lands under his protection and reserved the right to use able-bodied men as soldiers. However, as noted above, Samsat, vital for the survival of Urfa, seems never to have lapsed from the direct control of the Count of Edessa. What difference, if any, this had on taxes and corvée labor cannot be determined from the sources.

The only indication that seems at any variance with William of Tyre's statement concerning direct control of Samsat by the Crusader Count of Edessa comes from a reference to a "queen" of Samsat, with whom Aqsunqur intrigued before laying waste to her lands in 1114.[126] It is attractive but unfounded to suppose that this "queen" was Morphia, Baldwin's Armenian bride.

There is no reference to a Crusader governor of Samsat, but it stands to reason that there existed some sort of garrison with a commander. And although not confirmed, it seems likely that the freestanding structure that rose on the southeastern corner of the citadel mound at Samsat was the Crusader keep.[127]

Of all ethnicities, Armenians seem to have predominated in the County of Edessa; Syriac Christians were by and large excluded from positions of influence. In fact, there is ample evidence that Syriac Christians, wearying of continuous strife with Armenians, preferred Islamic rule, just as they had preferred it to Byzantine. As noted above, both Jacobite and Armenian Monophysite bishops were resident in Samsat during the life of the County, and both groups must have been present in the Karababa basin in substantial numbers. Yāqūt, writing during the reign of the Ayyubid prince al-Afḍal at Samsat, reported that the citadel there contained an Armenian section.[128] There were, in addition, Armenians resident in Samsat who still followed pre-Christian Armenian Zoroastrian rites, among them reverence for the sun and the poplar tree.[129] Both Armenian and Syriac Christians had moved into this region from areas to the north and east in large numbers at Byzantine invitation after its conquest in the tenth century.[130]

Under the Bedouin dynasties that had preceded the Byzantine advance, Arab tribal lead-

---

[125] There are hereditary *iqṭā'*s found after the middle of the 12th century. For a discussion of the rights of an *iqṭā'* holder, see Humphreys, *From Saladin to the Mongols*, 371–380.

[126] Bar Hebraeus, *Chronography of Gregory Abu'l Faraj*, 246.

[127] I owe this suggestion to Richard Brotherton. This judgment awaits final publication of the Ankara University excavations at Samsat. For an earlier opinion on this structure, see Goell, "Samosata Archeological Excavations," 93; also 91, Fig. 4, whose caption calls this structure "the medieval keep, or entrance gate."

[128] Yāqūt (*Mu'jam al-Buldān*, 3:258): "wa lahā qal'a fī shiqq minhā yaskunuhā al-Armin."

[129] Their presence is attested by a pastoral letter written sometime in the 12th century from St. Nerses the Graceful to T'oros, bishop of Samsat, concerning these people, called *arewordik'* in Armenian. See Russell, *Zoroastrianism in Armenia*, 517, 534–537, for a complete translation of this letter.

[130] Tate, "Frontière et peuplement en Syrie," 155. In earlier centuries, the population of this region had often been altered by imperial resettlement programs; see, e.g., Haldon and Kennedy, "Arab-Byzantine Frontier," 109–110, for Abbasid efforts at settling Muslims and garrisoning the frontier regions. J. M. Fiey ("Syriac Population of the Thughur al-Shamiya and the 'Awasim," 46 ff.) details the forcible resettlement of the Christian populations of the *thughūr* by both Byzantine and Muslim polities during the same time period, including Samsat and Keysun; this is also noted by C. E. Bosworth ("Byzantium and the Syrian Frontier," 58). Only part of these uprootings seem to have been due to a "scorched earth" policy. Nevertheless, depopulation seems definitely to have been a net effect, as the number of identifiably Abbasid (vs. later medieval) sites found by Blaylock, French, and Summers indicates. Haldon and Kennedy ("Arab-Byzantine Frontier," 100) suggested on self-admittedly meager evidence that one side effect of the depopulation of the border regions would have been an increase in pastoral nomadism and other forms of herding. Herding (and rustling) were certainly a large, if not the largest, component of the upper frontier around the valley of the Ebro in Spain, although that territory was more naturally suited to a herding-based economy than the border regions of northern Syria and southeastern Anatolia.

ers, too, had acquired territory and built castles along the Euphrates, structures large enough to shelter their flocks and families when they left to wage war.[131] In particular, members of the Banu Numayr, the Bedouin dynasts of Harran, owned land in the vicinity of Samsat, which the Franks seized in 1118.[132] This may have been Sinn ibn ʿUṭayr, a castle near Samsat founded by one of the Banu Numayr.[133]

The presence of transhumants in this region before the arrival of the Turks in the late eleventh century complicates the sedentary/nomadic dynamic. As is well known, most sedentary agriculturalists keep flocks; this was certainly the case at Gritille. However, traditionally, fields in cultivated regions are used as winter pasturage by nomads, and no doubt Bedouins used the Karababa basin and other areas along the Euphrates in a similar fashion, and a complex, overlapping dynamic between herder and tiller evolved.

The arrival of Türkmen tribes and their flocks added a surplus of pastoralists to the equation, but at the same time the Byzantine collapse in Anatolia and the disorder of late eleventh-century Syria opened Asia Minor and much of Syria and the Jazīra to their exploitation.[134] It is possible that at this time the pattern of Türkmen migration from summer pasture on the Anatolian plateau to winter pasture on the plains of northern Mesopotamia was established; certainly it is attested by the time of the Aqqoyunlu in the fourteenth and fifteenth centuries.[135] Ibn al-Qalānisī, in reporting a raid by Count Joscelin on nomads and their flocks in the

valley of the Euphrates farther south in Syria in 514 A.H./A.D. 1120–1121, mentions both Arab and Türkmen tribes grazing their flocks in the valley:

> And it is reported that Joscelin raided the Arabs and the Türkmen living in Ṣiffīn and carried away some of them and some of their herds (which were) on the bank of the Euphrates and on his return he destroyed Ḥiṣn Buzāʿa. . . .[136]

Until their recent submersion, the fields of the Karababa basin were grazed in winter by the flocks of Türkmen nomads from Malatya.[137] Poujoulat, traveling in 1837, may have seen the ancestors of these nomads in the mountains between Malatya and Adıyaman where he observed "des tentes noires des Turcomans, des chevaux superbes et de grands chameaux."[138] This pattern must have been well established farther east by Kurdish tribes, who are not mentioned this far west in the medieval era. One nineteenth-century traveler observed that

> Vielen Kurdentribus leben im Winter in Mesopotamien und suchen dann in Sommer mit ihren Heerden die Weideplätze im Hochgebirge auf.[139]

Thus, the fluidity of social structure common to most frontier regions was compounded in the Karababa basin during the medieval period by the coming of the Crusaders and the failure of any one power to establish firmly its hegemony over the area for any length of time.

[131] Bianquis, "Les frontières," 146.

[132] Rice, "Studies in Medieval Harran," 77.

[133] Yāqūt, *Muʿjam al-Buldān*, 2:269, entry for "al-Sinn"; see also note 100 above. Thierry Bianquis ("Les frontières," 142) writes: "Un parallèle peut être fait entre ces édifices relevant de populations de montagnards sédentaires et ceux que les grands chefs bédouins kilabites construisirent sur les plateaux calcaires de Syrie du Nord, au coeur de leur *iqtâ'*, comme refuges pour leurs familles et pour leur bétail. Chaque chef de grande famille, en édifiant une place forte pour les siens, participait ainsi à la mise en place d'une ceinture collective de forteresses et à la défense de la région frontière, allégeant d'autant l'effort financier et militaire des autorités byzantines d'Antioche ou kilabites d'Alep."

[134] See Cahen, "Les tribus turques," 178–187; and Bianquis, "L'ânier de village," 103, for Türkmen/Bedouin rivalry in Syria.

[135] Woods, *Aqquyunlu. Clan, Confederation, Nomadism*, 41, Map 2 (opp. 43), shows the Samsat region in the winter pasture (*kishlaq*) area of eastern Anatolia/northern Mesopotamia.

[136] Ibn al-Qalānisī, *Dhayl Tārīkh Dimashq*, 203.

[137] Personal observation, Biriman village, November 1985.

[138] Poujoulat, *Voyage à Constantinople*, 206.

[139] Wünsch, "Meine Reise in Armenien und Kurdistan," 518.

Samsat Under Islamic Rule

Historians have been puzzled as to why Nūr al-Dīn, by far the strongest monarch in the area, allowed Timurtaṣ, the bested rival of his father, to take possession of any territories in this region. Cahen went so far as to posit that the Artuqids were acting in concert with Nūr al-Dīn, and that a corps of Artuqids was serving in his army.[140] Timurtaṣ had submitted to Nūr al-Dīn's father Zangī in 1130, although he used the occasion of Zangī's death to seize territories once ceded to the Zangid state, but it is possible that Timurtaṣ had once again made peace with Nūr al-Dīn.[141] Whatever the case, Timurtaṣ died two years subsequent to the capture of Samsat, and the reins of power passed to his son Najm al-Dīn Alpī.[142]

For the next twenty-five years or so, Samsat was passed from emir to emir as an *iqṭāʿ* of the Mardin branch of the Artuqids. Usually it was ruled in concert with the Shabakhtān, giving rise to the impression that this particular *iqṭāʿ*, encompassing as it did the westernmost parts of the Artuqid realm, was a border fiefdom.

Alpī gave Samsat to the *ḥājib* (chamberlain) Saʿd al-Dawla Altuntāsh. With the death of Altuntāsh two years later, an Artuqid prince, Shams al-Dīn Sawīnj bin Sīyāwush bin Artuq, acceded to the post. He was imprisoned by Alpī in 559 A.H./A.D. 1164–1165 and was replaced by another *ḥājib*, al-Dikrī, and then by a homonym of the first governor under Alpī.[143] This Altuntāsh was put to death by Alpī's successor, Qutb al-Dīn, in 570 A.H. /A.D. 1174–1175 after having revolted. Qutb al-Dīn himself died in 580 A.H./A.D. 1184–1185 and was succeeded by his ten-year-old son, Yuluk Arslān.

The region experienced a severe earthquake in 1170. Afterward, it seems as if the walls of Samsat citadel were rebuilt in stone by the Artuqids. The Ankara University team excavating Samsat in the late 1970s and 1980s discovered an Artuqid building inscription of Fakhr al-Dīn Qarā Arslān, Artuqid ruler of Hasan Keyf (reg. 1144–1174),[144] who had participated in the invasion of the former Crusader realms, seizing Gerger and Ḥiṣn Manṣūr.[145] This inscription indicates that close cooperation between the Mardin and Hasan Keyf branches of the Artuqids continued for decades after the conquest.

Two conflicting accounts of the end of Artuqid rule in the Samsat region arise. The first claims that Muẓaffar al-Dīn Kūjak (Küçük), who had been given the governorship of Harran by Saladin, took Samsat, and then assumed it as an *iqṭāʿ* from Saladin, founder of the Ayyubid dynasty, in 1182–1183.[146] The other account has Saladin himself taking Samsat and giving it to Muẓaffar al-Dīn as an *iqṭāʿ*.[147]

Whichever account is more accurate, it may be stated that Samsat passed under Ayyubid control circa 1182–83. Muẓaffar al-Dīn Kūjak kept Samsat along with Harran and Urfa until the death of his brother in 586 A.H./A.D. 1190–1191,[148] whereupon he left for his brother's *iqṭāʿ* in Irbīl. Saladin's nephew, al-Malik al-Muẓaffar, prince of Hamā, then ruled Samsat until his death in 587 A.H./A.D. 1191–1192.[149] Then Samsat passed to his son, Nāṣir al-Dīn Muḥammad (d. 617 A.H./A.D. 1220–1221).[150]

In 588 A.H./A.D. 1192, Saladin granted his eldest son al-Malik al-Afḍal Samsat as an *iqṭāʿ*, along with other cities of the region. However, in the course of the power struggle attendant on the death of Saladin, al-Afḍal lost out to his

---

[140] Cahen, "Le Diyār Bakr au temps des premiers Urtukides," 254, n. 1.

[141] Cahen (ibid., 249) makes the following comment concerning Crusader relations with the Artuqids: "Leurs rapports avec les Urtukides semblent n'avoir été pendant plusieurs années que d'une hostilité adoucie; les uns comme les autres étaient trop occupées ailleurs par Zangi ou les Danišmendites."

[142] Ibid., 254; Ibn Shaddād, *Al-ʿAlaq*, 115.

[143] Cahen, "Le Diyār Bakr au temps des premiers Urtukides," 262.

[144] The end of Fakhr al-Dīn Qarā Arslān's reign has been extended from 562 to 570 A.H. on the basis of numismatic evidence; see Spengler and Sayles, *Turkoman Figural Bronze Coins*, 23. For the building inscription, see Özgüç, "Sümeysat Definesi," 444–445.

[145] Ibn al-Azraq al-Fāriqī, *Tārīkh Mayyāfāriqīn wa āmid*, 133.

[146] Ibn Shaddād, *Al-ʿAlaq*, 115.

[147] Ibn al-Athīr, *Al-Kāmil*, 12:83; Ibn Waṣīl, *Mufarrij al-Kurūb fī Akhbār Banī Ayyūb*, 5:53.

[148] Ibn al-Athīr, *Al-Kāmil*, 12:163.

[149] Ibid., 56, 62.

[150] Ibn Shaddād, *Al-ʿAlaq*, 116.

uncle al-'Ādil and in 597 A.H./A.D. 1200–1201 was relegated to the territories of Shabakhtān and Sinn ibn 'Uṭayr, and Samsat.[151] In 598 A.H./A.D. 1201–1202, al-Afḍal revolted against his uncle, but he was defeated, and all of his *iqṭā'* except Samsat was taken away from him.[152]

Not content with his lot within the Ayyubid realm, and possessed of ambitions larger than the territory of Samsat, al-Afḍal traveled to Kayseri, where he met with the Rum Seljuk sultan Ghiyāth al-Dīn.[153] Acknowledging his suzerainty in 601 A.H./A.D. 1204–1205, al-Afḍal struck silver coins in the name of the Seljuk sultan.[154] This risky alliance finally began to bear fruit for the lord of Samsat when 'Izz al-Dīn Kaykāwus became Rum Seljuk sultan; in 615 A.H./A.D. 1218 he invaded northern Syria accompanied by al-Afḍal and took Till Bashīr before being called back to Anatolia.[155]

Al-Afḍal died suddenly at about age fifty-seven in 622 A.H./A.D. 1225,[156] and it is unclear whether or not Samsat remained in Seljuk hands. This is unlikely, for it was very far from the Seljuk realm. Be that as it may, the Seljuks, ever intent on returning to the Islamic heartland, again descended on northern Syria via Samsat in 1238.[157] Ibn Shaddād maintained that the Seljuks continued to control Samsat until 1260, when the area was taken over by Mongol forces.[158]

The Benedictine monk Simon de Saint Quentin traveled through Anatolia in 1246 on his way to Tabriz, meeting along the way Frankish mercenaries who had helped put down the revolt of Baba Resūl. Baba Resūl was a Türkmen from Kafarsūd, a town near Samsat. His millenarian preaching and Türkmen constituency allowed Baba Resūl to seize most of the region. Sweeping north to Amasya, he and his forces were finally defeated by the Seljuks in 1240.[159] Simon included Samsat (as well as Urfa!) in a list of cities of the Seljuks.[160]

The revolt of Baba Resūl exemplifies the cultural flux that this region witnessed in the medieval period and will be included in the discussion of the final chapter. It is an episode prefatory to another movement of peoples from east to west, namely, the coming of Mongol-led armies into the Near East. In the eastern half of Anatolia and in this region, the Mongols took over the position of highland power from the Rum Seljuks, who themselves had dispossessed the Byzantines, and the Ayyubids had inherited the lands in northern Syria formerly held by the Hamdanids, but the ensuing power struggle was played out along similar routes and confined to similar border regions. With the coming of the Mongol armies into the region in the early 1260s, the border was momentarily pushed very far south into Syria. Following the victory of the Mamluks and internal Mongol disruptions, the Mamluks expanded their control northward into eastern Anatolia, with Malatya and Kemah (Arabic Kamakh) once again forming the advance posts of the lowland power.

Samsat must have been held by the Mamluks as part of their *arrière pays*, but the focus of Mamluk interests in the region lay farther north, and so at this time Gerger and Kâhta received new fortifications, as did Besni. Habitation and

---

[151] Bar Hebraeus (*Chronography of Gregory Abu'l Faraj*, 350) reported that al-Afḍal was given Samsat, Suruç, Rā's al-'Ayn, and Jumlīn (a fort in the Shabakhtān; see n. 100 above); Ibn al-Athīr, *Al-Kāmil*, 12:163.

[152] Ibn al-Athīr, *Al-Kāmil*, 12:182; Bar Hebraeus, *Chronography of Gregory Abu'l Faraj*, 351.

[153] Ibn al-Athīr, *Al-Kāmil*, 12:201.

[154] Bar Hebraeus, *Chronography of Gregory Abu'l Faraj,* 351.

[155] Ibn al-Athīr, *Al-Kāmil*, 12:248.

[156] Not 1125 as reproduced in Eddé-Terasse's translation of Ibn Shaddād (*Al-'Alaq al-Khaṭīra fī Dhikr Umarā' al-Shām wa'l-Jazīra*, 117). See also Ibn al-Athīr, *Al-Kāmil*, 12:428, and Ibn Khallikān, *Wafayāt al-A'yān*, 3:419–421, for a biographical notice on al-Afḍal, including his love of poetry. Perhaps out of sympathy with the lowly exile that was the fate of Saladin's son, the author emphasized the isolation of Samsat by stating definitely that it was located outside of Syria in a district of Rum.

[157] Bar Hebraeus, *Chronography of Gregory Abu'l Faraj*, 403; Ibn Bībī, *Das Seltschukengeschichte des Ibn Bibi*, 206.

[158] Ibn Shaddād, *Al-'Alaq*, 117–118.

[159] Yāqūt (*Mu'jam al-Buldān*, 4:469), under "Kafarsūt" called it close to Besni. Mustafa Sucu (*Adıyaman İli ve İlçeleri*, 16), identified it with the modern village of Keferdiş in Kâhta subprovince but does not locate the village on his map. For the religious context of this uprising, see Ocak, *La révolte de Baba Resul.*

[160] Simon de Saint-Quentin, *Histoire des Tartares*, 67: "Samsat, where it is said there was one of the crosses of the two thieves."

fortification at Tille, too, continued through the end of the thirteenth century and possibly into the early fourteenth.[161]

The Rupenid Armenian allies of the Mongols allowed them complete access to Smooth Cilicia, and the main Mongol lines of advance were to the west at Birecik. Subsequent to the Mongol defeat at the hands of the Mamluks, the independent Armenian Kingdom of Cilicia (as well as the Crusader states, including the Principality of Antioch) were conquered by the Mamluks, and Cilicia once again became the major avenue for traffic between Anatolia and Syria.

Despite the continual replacement of governors of Samsat between 1150 and 1225, no doubt the constancy of the *iqṭā'* system permitted a degree of prosperity in the Karababa basin. No doubt, too, the populace increased, although a larger Turkic nomadic population arriving with the Artuqids may have proven deleterious to the exploitation of areas previously under cultivation. Nevertheless, the city of Urfa was decrepit, and with it went the principal market for the agricultural surplus of the fertile valleys along the Euphrates and its tributaries. No amount of strategic importance could revive the economy of the area or the potent lines of demand that drew produce from *rustāq* to *madīna* to *qaṣaba*, that is to say, from rural settlements such as Lidar and Gritille to Samsat to Urfa.

By the middle of the thirteenth century, Samsat's strategic value had dwindled, too, a situation that was to continue until the building of railroads in the region in the mid-nineteenth century (one of the causes of the flurry of European travelers then). The final phase of occupation at Gritille can be dated on numismatic and stratigraphic evidence to the mid-thirteenth century, just before this region started to enjoy the status it officially received upon the completion of the Atatürk Dam—that of a backwater.[162]

THE ROLE OF HISTORIC ARCHAEOLOGY IN THE REGION

The writings of nineteenth- and twentieth-century European and American travelers allow us to compare modern conditions (crops, climatic conditions, habitation patterns, building materials, etc.) to those of the recent past, lending more certitude to ethnographic observations. Medieval geographers provide more information on climate and crops, as well as on routes of trade and communication. Medieval Muslim chroniclers such as Ibn al-Athīr, Ibn al-Qalānisī , and Ibn al-'Adīm furnish a wealth of detail about political and military activity as well as urban issues.

And, extraordinary for the medieval Near East, the presence of large numbers of monasteries in this region gave rise to Christian chroniclers with intimate knowledge of non-urban areas. Bar Hebraeus, Michael the Syrian, Matthew of Edessa, and the anonymous thirteenth-century Syriac chronicler provide much information about this region in the twelfth and early thirteenth centuries, information of a quantity unrivaled in the medieval Near East. Still, even their descriptions of the lives and living conditions of the populace are incidental.

The benefits of an archaeological investigation of this time period are both obvious and real. Instead of merely confirming the written word, archaeology permits the intensive investigation of the military and domestic architecture of the time, to reconstruct the goods that flowed along the travel routes frequented by medieval geographers, and in general to recover information about levels of society living and regions lying beyond the normal compass of urban literate society. In the chapters that follow, the archaeological investigation of medieval Gritille will be presented, adding dimensions to the historical and topographical information presented above.

---

[161] For Mamluk inscriptions at Eski Kâhta, see Dörner and Goell, *Arsameia am Nymphaios*, 305–316. For Mamluk Gerger, see Hellenkemper, "Zur mittelalterlichen Landschaftsgeschichte," 83; for the dating of Tille, see Moore, *Tille Höyük* 1, 197–198. For a Mamluk building inscription from the Ulu Cami and the Çarşı Camii in Besni, see *Türkiye'de Vakıf Abideler ve Eski Eserler*, 1:80–81. There are also unpublished Mamluk era inscriptions on the fortifications of Besni.

[162] Cahen ("Contribution à la histoire du Diyâr Bakr," 94) blamed the decline of this adjacent region on the depredations of the Mongols as well as "moins brutales mais à la longue plus graves, les dégâts résultant pour l'agriculture de l'expansion des pasteurs nomades. . . ."

II

EXCAVATIONS IN MEDIEVAL LEVELS AT GRITILLE

THE MOUND OF GRITILLE

The mound of Gritille, ovoid in shape, with a flat top measuring some 80 by 40 meters, lay on the right bank of the Euphrates River. It was oriented in a northeast–southwest direction and was located at a bend in the river in the upper reaches of the Karababa basin (Fig. 2:1). At the base of the mound, next to the river, was a spring. This eastern slope of the mound was considerably more abrupt than other sides, a feature indicating fluvial erosion. The distance from the river's edge to the top of the mound was approximately 20 meters, while the mound rose only about 10 meters from the fields to the west (Fig. 2:2).

The fields lying on three sides of the mound at Gritille were used for the cultivation of tobacco, lentils, and wheat, as well as for the grazing of sheep, goats, and occasionally cattle. Thus, Gritille was ideally situated for the exploitation of the Euphrates valley at this point. Even though the mound itself was uninhabited when excavation began (it was planted with grapevines), the presence of the small village of Halilan less than 2 kilometers south of Gritille as well as the foundations of an Ottoman or early Republican village directly to the north of Gritille reinforce the suitability of this location for a farming village.

The riverbed between Lidar on the left bank of the Euphrates River and Gritille and Samsat on the right bank was dotted by large, flat islands used as sources of brushwood and as summer pasturage for cattle from neighboring villages (Fig. 2:1). It is on one of these islands that Nöldeke camped in 1918 and from which he drew such a rich picture of the region's fauna.[1] The presence of mounds on opposite banks of the Euphrates and the relative shallowness and division of the river here into several channels have given rise to speculation about a second function for a settlement at Gritille, that of a river crossing. Villagers seldom traversed the river at this point, although many possessed the innertubes used to cross the river or to reach the islands (Pl. 2:1).

INTRODUCTION TO THE ARCHAEOLOGY

In the mid-1970s Gritille was recorded as part of survey activity along stretches of the Euphrates River valley slated to be flooded by dam building.[2] In response to an invitation from the Directorate General of Antiquities of the Republic of Turkey, Professor Richard Ellis of Bryn Mawr College, Bryn Mawr, Pennsylvania, organized excavations at Gritille under the auspices of the Lower Euphrates Salvage Project.[3] Pro-

---

[1] See Nöldeke, "Der Euphrat von Gerger," 16.
[2] Özdoğan, *Lower Euphrates Basin*, 121–122, Pls. 51, 81, 82.
[3] Ellis and Voigt, "1981 Excavations at Gritille," 319.

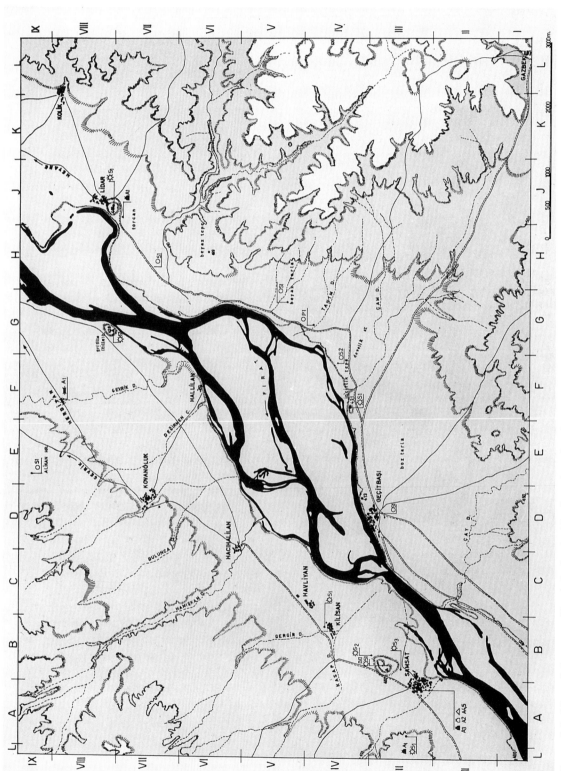

Figure 2:1. Map of the upper Karababa basin (Serdaroğlu, Pl. 64).

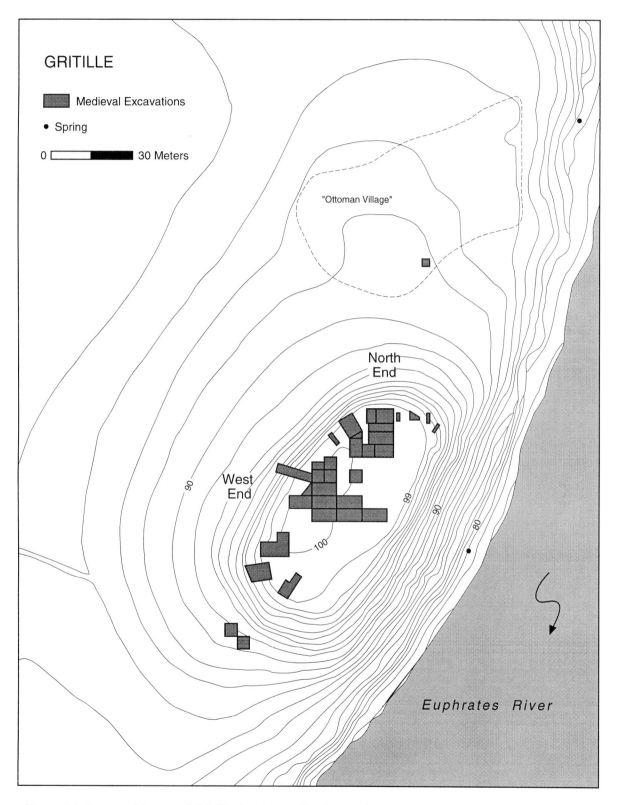

Figure 2:2. Topographic map of Gritille showing medieval operations.

fessor Ellis and his team undertook four campaigns at Gritille in the summers of 1981 to 1984.

In order to understand better the presentation and discussion of medieval levels at Gritille, it is important to understand two items
concerning excavations at Gritille in general.
First, archaeologically speaking, this region of
southeastern Turkey was practically terra incog-
nita when the Lower Euphrates Salvage Project
began its survey activities. Excavations at Eski
Kâhta (Arsameia-on-the-Nymphaios) and Samsat had recovered little of the pre-Roman period.
And the ceramics and small finds from Theresa
Goell's excavations at Samsat remained unpublished.[4] Within a very short period in the mid-
1970s, over 200 sites were recorded and surveyed by Turkish archaeologists working in this
area.

Second were the pressures and demands of
salvage archaeology. According to reports of the
General Directorate of State Hydraulic Works
(DSİ) of Turkey, the Karababa basin, with Samsat in its center, was scheduled to be flooded in
1985. While this target date looked increasingly
unlikely as time progressed (the region was not
flooded until the early 1990s), the commitment
of personnel and resources to the Gritille Project
were made according to those early projections.
Within a short period of time, the archaeology of
this border zone between historic Syria, Anatolia, and upper Mesopotamia had to be explored. The largely unknown character of the
region and the limited timeframe of operations
were two constraints of this salvage project. The
best aspect of the Lower Euphrates Salvage Project was that it was a group endeavor. Communication between the Turkish, German, British,
and American teams working in the area contributed substantially to easing intractable problems.

THE MEDIEVAL OCCUPATION

According to the published survey reports
available to Professor Ellis and his team at the
beginning of excavations, Gritille comprised a
rich deposit of pre- and early historic material,
with little evidence of medieval occupation.[5] In
almost all respects, surveys of the area were ad-
mirable in their accuracy and thoroughness in
the face of limited resources and time. But because so little was known of this area before the
surveys began, the extent of the medieval occupation at Gritille, Lidar, and other sites of the region was underestimated. On the basis of survey information, Gritille was chosen for excavation by Professor Ellis, and a team of prehistoric
and Bronze Age archaeologists was assembled.
Excavations in 1981 at Gritille, however, revealed an extensive medieval component to the
occupation sequence. Medieval remains were
found on the southwest flanks of the mound, in
a step trench along the eastern edge of the
mound, and atop the mound in its northwestern
area.[6]

The gradual understanding of the extent of
medieval deposits at Gritille continued during
the 1982 season. The step trench down the eastern slope of the mound in 1981 had been the only one to encompass the medieval deposit on
top of the mound. At the eastern edge of the
mound, the medieval deposit was only 1.5 meters deep.[7] As 1982 excavations on the top of the
mound revealed no end to the medieval deposits, a test trench was sunk toward the end of the
season and only breached the medieval deposit
after 4.5 meters.[8] The 3 meter discrepancy in the
thickness of the deposit between the eastern and
western edges of the mound was largely due to
the preservation of a fortification wall along the
western edge of the mound, while the steep,

---

[4] Dörner and Goell, *Arsameia am Nymphaios*, passim. Based on excavation records found in the Theresa Goell
archive at Harvard University's Semitic Museum, I have subsequently studied and published medieval glass
and ceramics from Goell's Samsat excavations: see Redford, "Ayyubid Glass from Samsat, Turkey," and idem,
"Medieval Ceramics from Samsat, Turkey."

[5] Özdoğan, *Lower Euphrates Basin*, 122: "The surface finds show that the site was occupied continuously from
the Late Chalcolithic to Classical times, and for a certain length of time during the Middle Ages. The surface
material indicates the most important levels as belonging to the Late Chalcolithic and the Iron Age." See also
Serdaroğlu, *1975 Surveys in the Lower Euphrates Basin*, 117.

[6] Ellis and Voigt, "1981 Excavations at Gritille," 3:2.

[7] Ibid., 326.

[8] Redford, "Excavations at Medieval Gritille," 106.

eastern edge of the mound had been eroded by the Euphrates River. Plate 2:2 shows the excavations in Operation 12, just to the south of the initial step trench, with upper-level domestic walls extending until they were broken by the steep slope of the riverine edge of the mound.

The difference in thickness of deposit from riverside to inland side of the mound was paralleled at the site of Lidar, directly across the Euphrates from Gritille. At that larger site, the medieval fortification wall, too, was missing from the riverine edge of the mound, and the medieval habitation was terraced down the slope of the mound toward the river.[9] At Gritille, suffice it to say that further efforts to excavate the medieval levels concentrated on the better-preserved western portions of the mound.

EXCAVATION STRATEGY

The discovery of the depositional discrepancy and the fortification wall led to a three-pronged excavation strategy. The large area along the landward edge of the site (the West End), excavated for all four campaigns, was the only section in which the entire medieval sequence was recovered. As a control for this area, an adjacent 10 by 10 meter area (Operation 26/27) in the center of the mound was also excavated (Fig. 2:3).

Because the fortification wall was the most significant architectural feature of the medieval levels at Gritille, efforts continued during all seasons to understand it, its massive presence on the west side of the mound, and its absence on the east. In 1982 the wall and its construction, as well as its relationship to the western slope of the mound, were explored through excavations down the western edge of the mound (Operation 8). In 1983, the wall and its relationship to the stratigraphy of the intramural settlement were explored. Finally, in 1984, careful stratigraphic excavation was abandoned in favor of slit trenches cut in order to track the fortification wall along the northern, southern, and southwestern edges of the mound and possibly to recover its gate.

The first two elements of excavation at medieval Gritille entailed intensive analysis of the central-western part of the mound. In 1984, the final season, settlement variation was explored,

adding extensive exposure to the intensive exposure of the first three campaigns. In addition to the expanded exploration of the fortification wall, excavations in the northern half of the mound uncovered an enclosure separated from the rest of the site by another defensive wall. While excavation continued to be stratigraphic, the pace of excavation was speeded by the selective elimination of sieving and the more extensive use of larger excavation units and larger digging tools.

These differing excavation techniques, necessitated by the salvage nature of the excavation, led to differing emphasis in the presentation of material in this report. While all areas were excavated stratigraphically, the complete medieval sequence was uncovered only in the West End. Analysis of the ceramics from the West End of Gritille formed the basis of the author's dissertation. As a result of these factors, this area furnishes the largest and most carefully excavated and studied medieval exposure of the site. It is also in this area that the defensive wall was best preserved and excavated. As a result, the general outlines of the occupational sequence at Gritille will be first exposed by reference to this area, extending to the adjacent Operation 26/27 in the middle of the mound. From there it will continue to a discussion of the fortification wall and the North End and other excavation areas.

THE MEDIEVAL STRATIGRAPHIC SEQUENCE

The medieval stratigraphic sequence at Gritille can be divided into eight phases. These phases are a combination of architectural and stratigraphic data, some of them small and precisely delineated (Phases 1–4), some of them larger and composed of a greater variety from operation to operation (Phases 5 and 6). In the pages that follow these phases will be discussed in greater detail, but at the beginning a brief outline of the occupational sequence at medieval Gritille may help the reader.

Phase 1 was nonarchitectural. It consisted of an isolated burial recovered in Operation 12 along the eastern edge of the mound.

Phase 2 consisted of the first medieval occupation of the site. The first fortification was built, and from it, walls radiated inward toward

---

[9] Hauptmann, "Lidar Höyük 1981," 259.

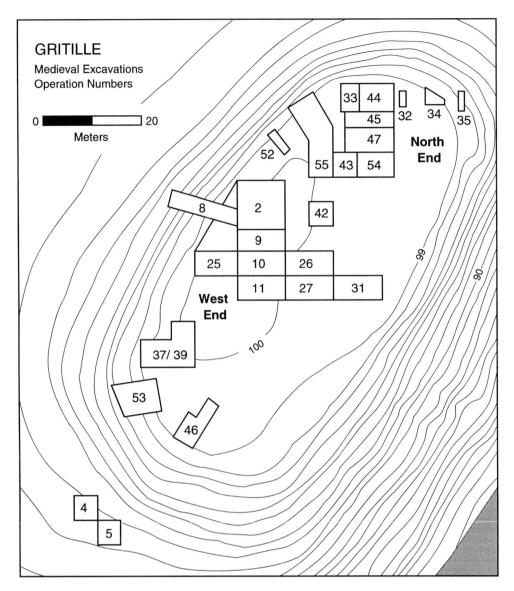

Figure 2:3. Key to medieval operations showing location of section drawings.

the middle of the mound. These walls were in turn subdivided to form smaller units. Occupation seems to have been brief.

Phase 3 was marked by the massive reinvestment of the site, a rebuilding of the fortification wall and the reuse of the Phase 2 "spoke walls" around the site. It was marked by domestic habitations in the West End and elsewhere on the site. However, in the North End, an area was separated from the rest of the settlement by the building of a large towered defensive wall across the site, behind which was a large courtyard area.

Phase 3 was also called the Burnt Phase because it ended in a conflagration that engulfed the site. In the ruins of this level the remains of

eight skeletons were recovered, as was a hoard of Crusader silver.

The site seems to have been reinhabited immediately and repaired in Phase 4. A pebbled street was laid up the middle of the mound, and walls were reused and rebuilt. This phase is also notable for the recovery of several distinctive two-chambered ovens fronted by panels with geometric decoration.

Phase 4 was of short duration despite the obvious efforts made to repair and reinhabit the site. It was succeeded by Phase 5, during which the mound was only intermittently inhabited, while settlement continued along the terrace to the north of the mound. This phase is marked by the decay and collapse of the mudbrick struc-

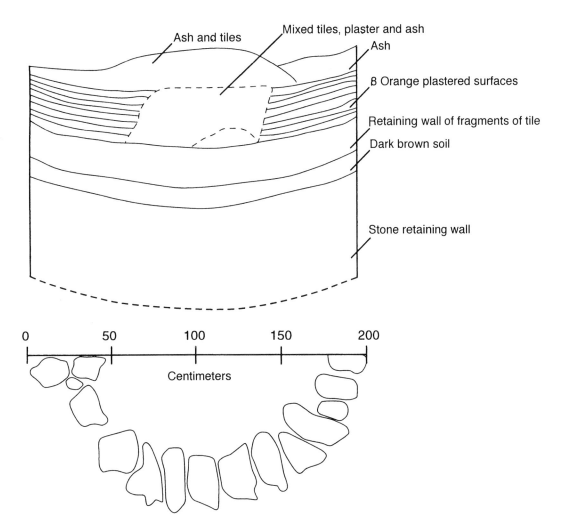

Figure 2:4. Sketch section and plan of pyrotechnic feature, West Balk, Operation 11.

tures of Gritille, including the fortification wall, and the construction of a large pyrotechnic feature (Fig. 2:4) which may have been a lime kiln and generated immense amounts of ash.

During Phase 6 the lime kiln fell out of use, and the mound was used intermittently, with construction activity limited to hearths, ovens, bins, and a few scrappy walls and floors.

Phases 7 and 8 mark the return of habitation to the mound of Gritille. A pebbled street was laid and flanked by domestic structures. The sole defensive structure seems to have been a freestanding tower erected near the northwestern edge of the mound. The ovens, curb walls, and other domestic features of the last phases of habitation continued to the very top of the deposit.

THE WEST END EXCAVATIONS

The West End of Gritille consisted of excavations in an area over 25 by 10 meters in extent, bordered by the fortification wall that ran along the western edge of the mound. This was first excavated in 1981 (Operations 2, 3, 6, and 7) in four adjacent 5 by 5 meter squares.[10] In 1982, the area immediately to the south was excavated in three contiguous 5 by 10 meter units (Operations 9, 10, and 11). The larger excavation units

[10] Ellis and Voigt, "1981 Excavations at Gritille," 326–328. When excavation continued in this area in 1984, the whole 10 by 10 m area was called Operation 2.

better suited the large number of walls and other architectural features encountered in the medieval deposit. In 1983, excavation continued in Operation 11 and in Operation 10, which was extended to the west to encounter the fortification wall (Operation 10/25). In 1984, the final season of excavation, with the exception of Operation 11, the entire area was excavated.

The Beginning of the Medieval Sequence (Phases 1 and 2)

The beginning of the medieval sequence was reached in four places: at the eastern, north-ern, and western edges of the mound and in the center, in Operation 26/27. In Operation 1 (the step trench that was extended down the steep eastern slope of the mound in 1981), a series of hearths, floors, and rubble walls marked the medieval period. That some of these walls were cut off at the eastern riverine edge of the mound indicated that a portion of this deposit had been cut into by the Euphrates River, which flowed at the base of the site (Pl. 2:2).

To the north of the mound, 1984 excavations uncovered the remains of several walls that extended from the center of the mound out toward the edge (Fig. 2:5). That these broke off at the

Figure 2:5. North End. Stone plan; Phase 3.

edge of the mound indicated that there, too, erosion and/or robbing by the villagers of the Ottoman period settlement to the north of the mound had deprived these walls of their continuation.

In Operation 26/27, a sounding in the southwestern corner of the area revealed a hearth, walls, and two pits. Here as elsewhere, there was a layer of fairly artifact-free soil separating the beginning of the medieval deposit from the preceding late Iron Age habitation levels.

In the West End excavations, too, the first period of medieval occupation was uncovered in a small sounding in 1984, adjacent to the 1982 deep sounding in Operation 9 and against the fortification wall, and again in Operation 25 against the fortification wall. In these small soundings, the remains of walls, beaten earth floors, and one hearth were uncovered. These deposits were covered by a layer of brown, particulate soil.

As was the case elsewhere at Gritille, the walls in this first architectural phase consisted of mudbrick laid on a stone footing. This footing, which could rise as many as ten to fifteen courses, was generally laid on the ground level, or in only a shallow trough. There were very few walls with bona fide foundation trenches. The stone footings consisted of rubble: unhewn or roughly hewn pieces of the local limestone, with occasional pieces of water-worn stone. As just mentioned, these rocks were placed in rough courses, usually with the stones of one course laid lengthwise in the opposite direction from those of the previous course, forming a rough sort of herringbone pattern (Pl. 2:2). The chinks between these larger rocks were often stopped by smaller stones or sherds of thick varieties of pottery, often base and rim fragments of storage jars, or handles. Likewise, the middle of one of these courses would be filled with smaller stones and occasional larger pieces of pottery. Care was taken to place larger stones at the corners or ends of walls.

This level was considered the first architectural phase of the medieval period for two reasons. The first was the test trench in Operation 9, which had reached a premedieval deposit just below this level. The second was the bottom of the first fortification wall, whose stone foundation courses were uncovered by the test trench in Operation 25. There were four stone foundation courses to the fortification wall at this point; all in all they reached a total of 70 centimeters in height. The lowest course of the first phase of the fortification wall was some 15 centimeters below the first course of the interior walls belonging to this first medieval occupation level.

Conclusions concerning the nature of this occupation on the basis of this small exposure are of limited value. From this probe, as well as others in Operation 26/27 and in the North End, one can say that the occupation seems to have been brief.

A layer of decayed mudbrick almost devoid of potsherds, bone, or other artifacts lay between this phase of occupation and the one following it. In several spots throughout the West End excavations, however, the second architectural phase of occupation was penetrated, and the continued descent of a series of walls into Phase 2 was noted. As a result, it became possible to propose with a fair degree of certainty a set of walls originating in this first phase, even if it was not possible to excavate fully this area down to the first medieval occupation. These walls are colored gray on Figure 2:6. The most important of these walls is a series of long spoke walls radiating toward the center of the mound from the fortification wall. This phenomenon, also present in the North End, seems to have furnished the principle by which the original medieval settlement was organized.

PHASE 3, "THE BURNT PHASE"

Despite the layer of clean fill that covered Phase 2, some of the walls must have been still visible when the mound was reoccupied, for several of these walls were reused, either wholly or in part. This reuse of walls was not simply a matter of convenience. As became evident in the first seasons of excavation in medieval levels at Gritille, the settling of walls was a constant problem. The inconsistent nature of the ground on which these medieval walls were built led to frequent buckling, tilting, and consequent repair. Walls built over ancient pits fell into them, and walls near the edge of the mound slid off. Therefore, throughout the medieval period, constant reincorporation of earlier walls or wall footings occurred. In addition, as we shall see, in Phase 7 lime plaster floors were also laid to provide a more solid footing above particularly soft and shifting deposits laden with ash and

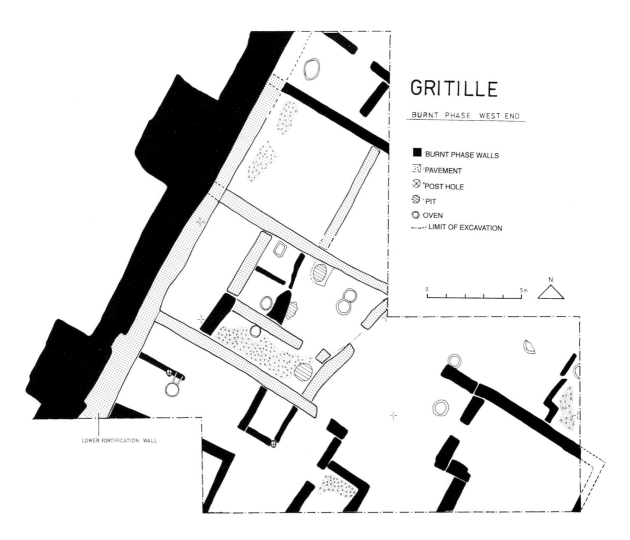

Figure 2:6. The West End: Plan of the Third ("Burnt") Phase.

other organic matter. Plate 2:3 shows a Phase 2 spoke wall that tipped and was rebuilt in Phase 3.

During Phase 3, the fortification wall was also rebuilt on top of the earlier one. For reasons that are not entirely clear, but may have to do with the same desire for stable foundations, the Burnt Phase fortification wall was built at a re-move of approximately 20 centimeters from the edge of the earlier fortification wall, leaving a small ledge of mudbrick jutting out into the in-tramural settlement (Pl. 2:4). Against this ledge were built most of the walls of this second phase, obviating almost all attempts to connect stratigraphically the Burnt Phase occupation with the second fortification wall. Nevertheless, it is possible to argue that the second fortifica-tion wall belongs to this phase when we exam-ine the subsequent history of the mound, which

involved a substantial period of intermittent use and little habitation during Phase 5, at which time the fortification wall fell into disuse. This point of view was supported by the presence of one wall, the long wall running east–west across the mound in Operations 25 and 9, which was actually found to be leaning against the second phase fortification wall.

The reuse of the second phase "spoke walls" in the Burnt Phase gave a regularity to the disposition of the structures built at that time. These consisted of a series of interconnect-ed structures with courtyards and enclosed areas that sheltered behind the fortification wall (Pl. 2:5). In between the long walls, a series of di-vider walls stretched (e.g., in Fig. 2:7, between D and E/F/H, between B and C, and so on), parti-tioning the space into a series of open and closed spaces. Within these spaces there oc-

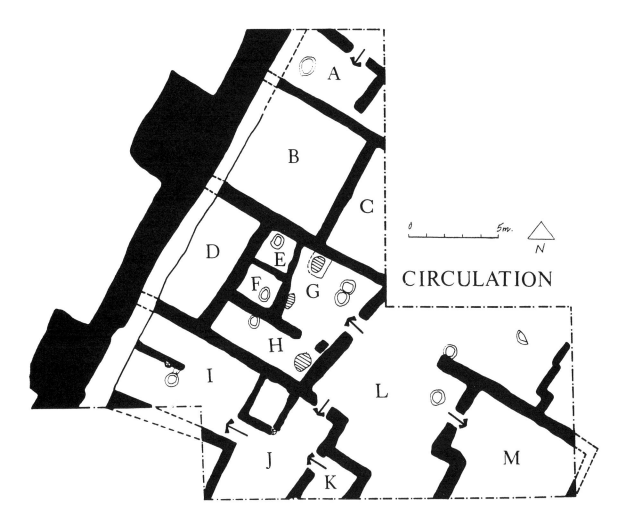

Figure 2:7. The West End: Circulation and area identification of Phase 3 structures.

curred a further enclosure in the subdivision of space by insubstantial walls. Some of these walls were only one brick thick; often they meandered quite extravagantly (e.g., the wall between areas E and F and G). It is impossible to ascertain how high these walls rose, but most certainly they were used as screens for discrete activity areas, since often they enclosed a small space containing only one feature (Pl. 2:6).[11] This kind of wall was called a *curb wall*. Curb walls were another constant of the medieval architecture at Gritille. In this phase, they were found in areas I, J, E, F, and in the area to the north of M.

Toward the center of the mound, the structures found along the inside of the fortification wall came to a halt, giving way to an open space of irregular dimensions (Fig. 2:7L). This, in turn, gave way to another structure, seemingly freestanding (Fig. 2:7M; Pl. 2:7). There were three entrances into the structures along the western edge from the open area in the middle of the mound, and one entrance into structure M.[12] Although some areas did not have obvious means of ingress (Fig. 2:7B, D), in general circulation seems to have occurred within five general areas in the West End. The first of these was

---

[11] The term *feature* denotes any construction that is not a load-bearing wall, that is to say, hearths, ovens, bins, pits, drains, curb walls, etc.

[12] The entrance into J from K was screened by two small walls to the east and south; these must have functioned as a sort of vestibule into the area from the main circulation space L.

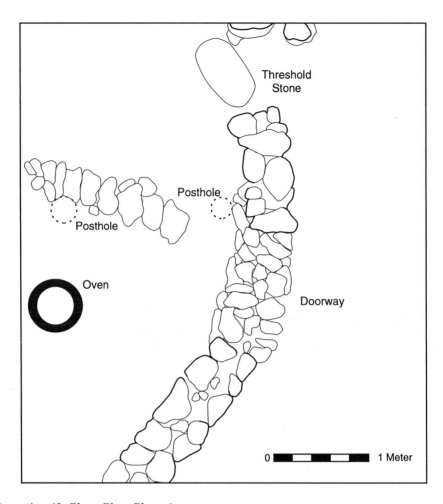

Figure 2:8. Operation 42, Phase Plan, Phase 4.

M. The inside of this structure was barren of features in this phase, but the areas outside M to the north and west contained ovens, a rough pavement, and low curb walls indicating domestic activity.

The wall dividing areas D and H from I and J functioned as a major architectural divider. The area I/J/K and the area D/E/F/G/H can be considered as separate. The space divided by curb walls into E, F, G, and H seems to have been a major focus of activity, with bins or cuvettes, ovens or pits in each of the subdivided spaces. By contrast, the floor of D was covered with lime, but did not have any features at all.

Another long wall separated D and E/F/G/H from B and C, as well as from A to the north. C constituted a separate unit unrelated to the rest of this area, while it is possible, although not certain, that B communicated with A. C, we can assume from Operation 42 to the east (see Fig. 2:8), was entered from that direction and was used separately from A and B. The wall be-

tween B and C was high, and the doorway between them had been blocked sometime during Phase 2 or at the beginning of Phase 3.

If we take Phase 4 as a model, then we can assume that the wall between A and B somehow allowed circulation between these two areas. The mound sloped gently from north to south, and in Phase 4 a couple of steps led down from A to B through a doorway punched through the wall, but it is possible that part of this wall may have been low enough to allow access to B earlier. In Phase 3, B possessed a rough stone paving in the area near the fortification wall, but that is all. Area A lay at the north edge of the West End. In the middle of this area was a large oven that was rebuilt several times. This space was entered from the north and the east from other parts of other structures that lay in those directions.

At the south edge of the West End lay the fifth area, comprising spaces I and J. J was entered from the main circulation area L, as well as from

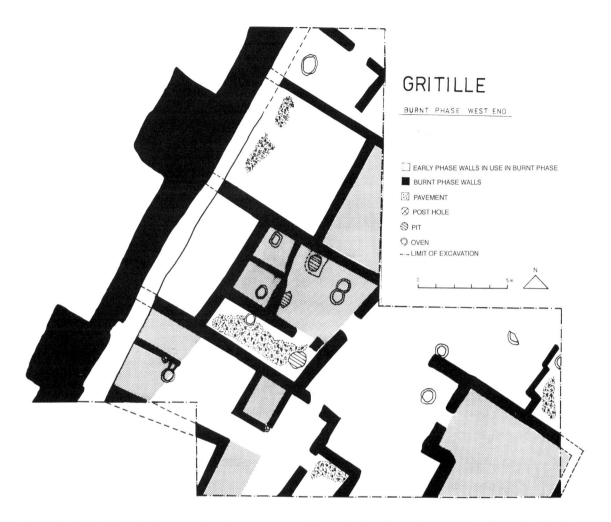

GRITILLE

BURNT PHASE WEST END

☐ EARLY PHASE WALLS IN USE IN BURNT PHASE
■ BURNT PHASE WALLS
⊡ PAVEMENT
⊗ POST HOLE
⊖ PIT
○ OVEN
–··– LIMIT OF EXCAVATION

0 ____ 5 m

N △

Figure 2:9. The West End: Covered and open spaces of Phase 3 plan. Covered areas are indicated by shading.

the east via K. A small rectangular area to the north of the main area, J was partitioned by two small curb walls, but otherwise this space was empty of features at the end of this phase. J was unusual by virtue of the number of its entrances and exits, the third of which led to I, a long narrow space partitioned at the back by a small curb wall. To the left of this curb wall was a shallow basin made of mudbrick with a drainhole atop a channel leading underneath the curb wall.

INDOOR AND OUTDOOR SPACES

The fire that terminated Phase 3 preserved evidence of roofing systems not present at any other level. Despite its relative abundance in this phase, as compared with other levels, this evidence is inadequate for proposing anything but a hypothetical reconstruction of roofed areas in this phase.

There were four major indicators of enclosed spaces. The first two are distinct archaeological features: postholes and door sockets. Post-holes, indicated on Figures 2:6 and 2:9 by small circles with crosses inside them, were, as their name implies, holes sunk in an earthen floor or curb wall for the accommodation of a wooden pole or post that would have supported some sort of a roof. Oftentimes these holes were lined with small stones, and some even had a stone at the bottom of the hole. Door sockets at Gritille, found by the score reused in walls, consisted of smaller rocks with holes partially gouged, partially worn by the rotation of a doorpost. The presence of a door implied a space closed from the outdoors.

The two other telltale factors were the size of the space presumed to have been roofed and the thickness of the walls. There is no index for the latter, although curb walls were obviously inadequate to the task. Based on the accumulation of material inside walls constructed identically to those of Gritille, the excavators of Taşkun Kale estimated the height of the walls of intramural structures there at 4 meters.[13]

Before proceeding with an analysis of the covered and open spaces of Phase 3 (Fig. 2:9), a word about roofs and ethnography. Although the ethnographic analogy is at best only that, under certain conditions it can be revealing. Insofar as construction methods are concerned, the similarities between the medieval architectural remains at Gritille and the houses of the twentieth-century village of Biriman, some 3 kilometers distant from Gritille and home to the Gritille Project, were cause for examining the roofs of Biriman (Pl. 2:8) with some attention.

The most striking coincidence of evidence was that of roof rollers (Turkish *loğ taşı*), cylinders of limestone 1 to 2 meters long used in Biriman and other villages to roll the flat, mud-plastered village roofs free of water after a rain. Such stone cylinders were also found in abundance in lower and upper levels at Gritille, giving rise to the probability that the structures of medieval Gritille, too, were flat-roofed.

Ethnographic analogy is based on an assumption that environmental factors such as climate and topography determine the parameters of human activity to such an extent that that activity and its products remain recognizably similar over time. Given the likelihood that both medieval Gritille and late twentieth-century villages such as Biriman shared the feature of flat-roofed structures, one can then postulate certain similarities in the use of said shared feature. In Biriman, roofs are reached by staircases, upper stories, and changes in terrain; and they serve as a major living and sleeping area during more than half of the year when the weather is hot or temperate (Pl. 2:8). Although four seasons of excavation at Gritille failed to turn up archaeological evidence of staircases, ladders, and the like, in discussing the function of medieval structures at Gritille, it is important to bear in mind this possibility.

Because of the scarcity of wood, the straight poplar trunks used to roof a village mudbrick house constituted by far and away the most expensive part of the house. They were laid atop

the walls and covered with layers of matting, brush, mud plaster, and mudbrick. No other wood was used structurally in the construction of village houses built in this traditional style. This stands in contrast to the evidence from medieval Gritille, especially during Phase 3. Postholes imply the use of wood as a means of roofing support. We can propose the deforestation of the Karababa basin as the reason for this change. (In Chapter 5, Naomi Miller proposes deforestation even during the course of the medieval settlement at Gritille.) The houses of the village of Tille incorporated wood as structural elements in the form of posts, and Tille lies near sources of wood in the surrounding hills.

The most direct evidence for a covered space at Gritille was furnished by an area of approximately 1.5 meters by 75 centimeters at the western edge of J (Pl. 2:9). There a series of burned pieces of wood were found. Seven in all, these pieces were flat and, in their ruinous and no doubt incomplete state, measured 50 to 75 centimeters in length and 2 to 4 centimeters in breadth. In size and shape, they resembled sawn or hewn planks.

Three of these boards lay roughly at right angles to the wall at the west of this space. There was a 50 to 75 centimeter gap between these pieces of wood. At the edge of these three planks ran a row of three planks laid end to end and parallel to the back wall of J. The seventh board lay outside this fairly regular disposition to the east.

Although no evidence of a posthole was uncovered in this area, the boards indicate that there existed some sort of roofing over this otherwise open area. This covering did not extend to the north and east across the entrance to area I, but a posthole found at the junction of two small curb walls to the north of this entrance indicated that this small division of courtyard J was also probably covered.

Similarly, the posthole found near the end of the curb wall horizontally dividing the end of area I can be cited to support the idea that at least the end of the space was covered (Pl. 2:10). In this case, burnt planks, twigs, and clay were also found scattered about the area to the south of the divider wall at the western end of the space. Although the planks fell in a more haphazard fashion than those in area J, better pre-

---

[13] McNicoll, *Taşkun Kale*, 8.

servation of another kind allows us to propose a roofing system similar to the village one discussed above. Naomi Miller has analyzed a botanical sample from this area, identifying the chunks of charcoal present in the sample as poplar/willow, which is consistent with the ethnographic model proposed for Taşkun Kale.[14]

Evidence suggests that areas E/F/G were roofed (Fig. 2:9). No charred beams were found here, but the size of the space and the range and number of features found within it strongly suggest that it was enclosed. H seems to have been an open space, only because it had a rough stone paving, a feature that we can observe in this phase only in the manifestly open areas of B and the area outside and to the north of M and along the east balk.

A door socket was found next to the northern entrance wall of the E/F/G/H area from L. This increases the likelihood that this space was covered in Phase 3. As for spaces C and M, both had distinct entrances (that to C being found in Operation 44 to the east) off large open spaces. Both, too, had thick walls preserved to a substantial height.

All in all, then, one finds a series of fairly fluid spaces: divided open courtyards and indoor rooms. Indices of activity—ovens, bins, troughs, and the like—are to be found in both open and closed areas. For example, M was roofed but empty, while the area outside this structure was littered with ovens and curb walls. E/F/G, by contrast, seems to have been enclosed but was full of the same features.

As for the actual roofing systems themselves, the best-preserved evidence, that of space J, seems to indicate that a sort of impermanent lean-to-like structure, possibly a simple sun-shade, existed in essentially open areas, further enriching the gradation between closure and exposure.

In addition to the myriad domestic activities associated largely with exterior or partially covered spaces, one must think of the stabling of animals as another function of these spaces. Miller's analysis of samples of burnt organic matter from Burnt Phase area I found dung ash and "essentially pure wheat deposits," consistent with the floor of an animal pen and fodder.

Roofing over this area also seems to have been poplar/willow, with twiglets and small branches of poplar, tamarisk, and ash probably representing firewood. Samples of vetchling seeds and fava beans mixed in with the roofing material were also probably stored in this area.[15]

THE BURNT PHASE OCCUPATION

It is hard to estimate the duration of this phase of occupation. Certainly, as we have seen, a great deal of building took place. Although the materials and methods of construction were simple, there was a substantial outlay of time and resources in the reoccupation of the site. Not the least of this consisted in a continued military aspect to the mound of Gritille, expressed by the rebuilding and maintenance of the defensive perimeter wall.

The second phase was penetrated only in three areas in the West End. Two of these, the 1982 test trench into area D and the 1984 test trenches in D and I, did not reveal anything below the floor level which marked the burning at the end of this phase. The lack of substantial accumulation of occupational debris in these areas makes it seem as if, despite the extensive building activity in this phase, it was short-lived.

Nevertheless, the test trench sunk between the burnt "planks" at the western end of J revealed ovens, pits, and other features indicative of prolonged habitation before the termination of this phase by burning. This test trench, visible in the south section of Operation 11 (Fig. 2:10) descended only 50 centimeters below the burnt floor. Consequently, the layer of artifact-free mudbrick debris intervening between occupation phases in those other test trenches was not reached.

We may conclude that, in this level as in others at Gritille, occupation patterns and the accumulation of occupational debris were uneven, reflecting partial or differential use of the area comprising the intramural settlement.

PHASE 4

The Phase 3 occupation ended in haste. In addition to the burned debris found in D, I, and J, the surfaces of E, F, G, H, and J were found strewn with abandoned pottery, including sev-

[14] Miller, "Crusader Period Fortress" (MASCA Ethnobotanical Report 3), 4. I am grateful to Dr. Miller for permission to cite her work.

[15] Miller, "Crusader Period Fortress," *Anatolica* 18 (1992), 90–91.

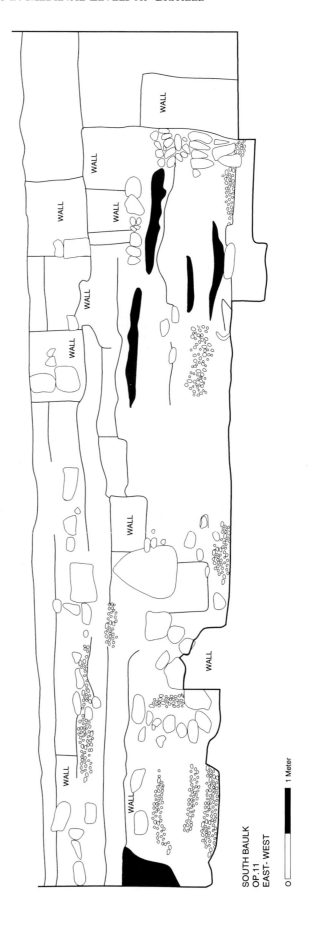

Figure 2:10. Section: South Balk, Operation 11.

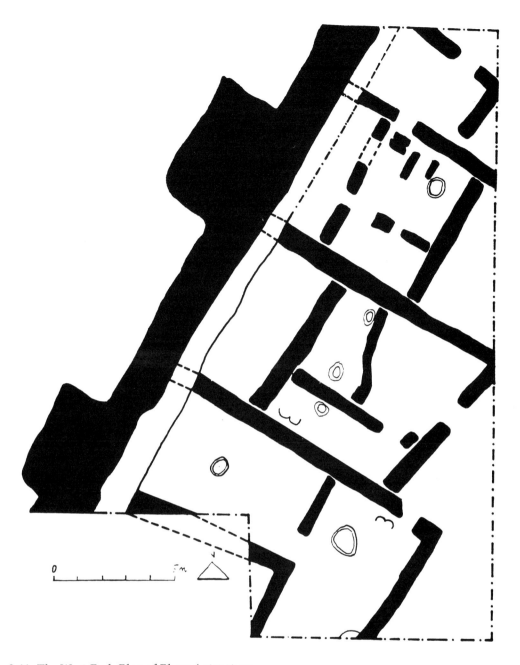

Figure 2:11. The West End: Plan of Phase 4 structure.

eral nearly complete vessels. Damage must have been sustained by the structures of the West End, for we find the substantial rebuilding of at least one major wall, that long wall delimiting the northern edge of area I. This wall must have collapsed entirely, for its stone footing was rebuilt and a buttressing second skin of stones and mud plaster was added to its north face.

All in all, though, the buildings of Phase 3 were reinhabited. Courtyard J, barren of features in Phase 3, received several ovens, pits, and bins in this phase. So did E/F/G/H. In this

phase, too, the curb wall between E and F was eliminated, and the meandering curb wall between E/F and G became even more so. To the north of this area, courtyard B, which had been devoid of features except for patches of stone paving in the previous phase, now received a new entrance from area A, complete with two steps down. On either side of this entrance, as well as elsewhere in B, the remains of small curb walls, sometimes no more than a line of stones, were encountered.

The major constructional activity of Phase 4

(Fig. 2:11) consisted in the laying of a paved street along L. This street ran north–northeast up the center of the mound, skirting structure M. The small area K, found in Phase 3, was eliminated, and courtyard J was entered directly from this street, which ran right by its entrance. This street was laid with some care. First, a substrate of large stones was placed in the area, then covered with smaller stones and pebbles which served as the actual surface. Whether by design or through use, the dismantling of this layer yielded the heaviest concentration of bone found in the medieval levels.[16] A piece of this feature can be observed in the east and south sections of Operation 11 (Figs. 2:10, 2:12) and in the west section of Operation 26/27. The heavier stone underpinning is visible in Figure 2:10.

Another characteristic of this phase of occupation at Gritille was a novel type of pyrotechnic feature, one not found in any other phase. It consisted of several double-chambered ovens, most of them preserving traces of elaborately molded and incised flanking front panels with geometric designs. The entire structure of these ovens was composed of mudbrick. The geometric designs had, in turn, small chips of glazed ceramics inserted at intersections in the design. The most complete of these ovens was found at the rear wall of M (Fig. 2:13). Ovens bearing this distinctive shape and designs were found in H, J, and M (Pls. 2:11–2:16). In all cases they were placed against the back wall of the space. The inside of most of the chambers revealed slight but not heavy indications of burning. In a stratigraphic sequence that showed a continuous re-use and repetition of objects, features, and building techniques, this oven type (whatever its actual function, it does not seem suited for daily cooking) was unique at Gritille.

Many similar ovens were found at Lidar. Excavators there suggested assigning them some cultic significance because of the objects found associated with them. For example, one of the Lidar ovens, found behind a colonnade as the only feature in a pebbled court, contained deer bones, a luster bowl, and four holes that contained the remains of fire brands 30 to 35 centimeters high. Also at Lidar, another double oven in area F/43 was found with bronze crosses in it.[17]

Similar ovens were found at sites to the north. At Pirot, excavators found only one of these ovens; it was in a level dated to the twelfth century.[18] At Tille, a portion of a decorated side panel was found.[19]

The continuity of regional traditions over the course of a millennium is emphasized by late Roman/early Byzantine levels at Eski Malatya, which yielded ovens of similar shape and not dissimilar geometric designs.[20]

Phase 5

Phase 5 constituted the major stratigraphic divider of the medieval sequence in the West End, as elsewhere at Gritille. As noted above, the phases outlined in this chapter have been defined as those in which changes in architecture as well as stratigraphy occurred. Speaking strictly from a stratigraphic standpoint, Phase 5 consisted of a series of phases: floors, differing features, and uses of different areas of the West End. However, because Phase 5, which comprises the largest middle belt of the Gritille sequence visible in Figures 2:10, 2:12, 2:14, and 2:15, was largely devoid of building or other signs of permanent habitation in this area, it has been considered here as one unit.

A considerable expenditure of effort in the reoccupation of the site after the Burnt Phase is evident, including the repair of existing walls, the modification of certain smaller walls, and the laying of an extensive pebble pavement street. However, in almost every area of the West End this level, and the architecture associated with it, was engulfed in layer after layer of

---

[16] The construction of a paved street at Korucutepe was strikingly similar, with bones and sherds mixed in with the pebble pavement; see van Loon, *Korucutepe*, 2:43.

[17] Akkermans, "Lidar Excavation Notebook F/G/H 42, 1980–81," 85. I am grateful to Prof. Harald Hauptmann, Director of the Lidar Excavations, for permission to consult the Lidar archive, housed in the Institute for Prehistoric Archaeology of the University of Heidelberg. See also Hauptmann, "Die Grabungen auf dem Lidar Höyük, 1979," 260–261, Pls. 156:1 and 157:1, showing a Maltese cross in the middle of one of the decorated panels, comparable to the fragment found at Tille.

[18] Karaca, "Pirot Höyük 1980 Çalışmaları," 110.

[19] Moore, *Tille Höyük* 1, Fig. 74:142.

[20] Equini Schneider, *Malatya*-II, 19, Pls. 18, 19, for these features, called "focolare a ferro de cavallo."

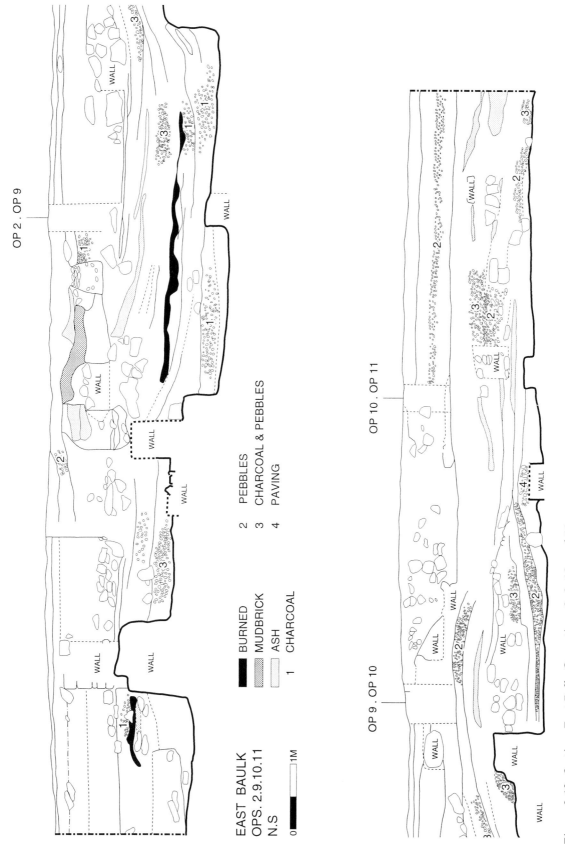

Figure 2:12. Section: East Balk, Operations 2, 9, 10, and 11.

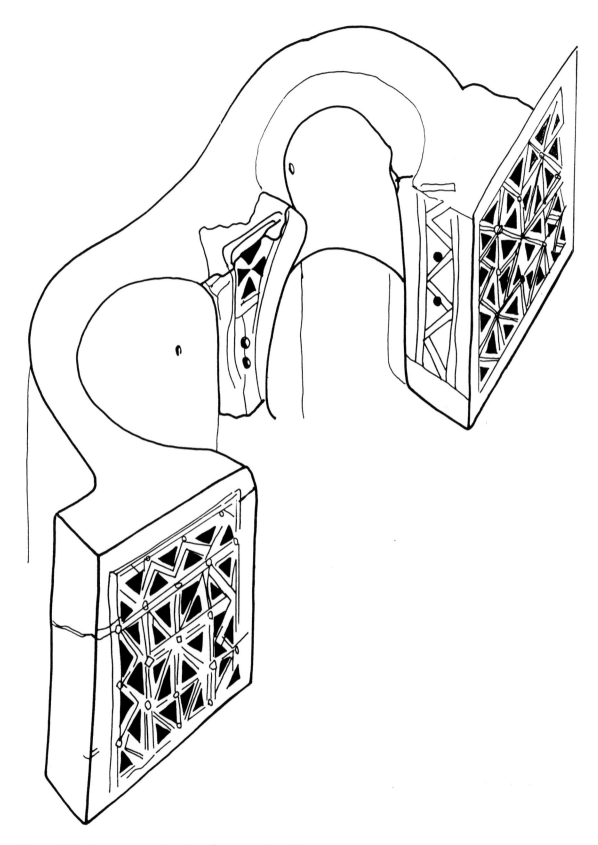

Figure 2:13. Axonometric drawing of oven in Area M.

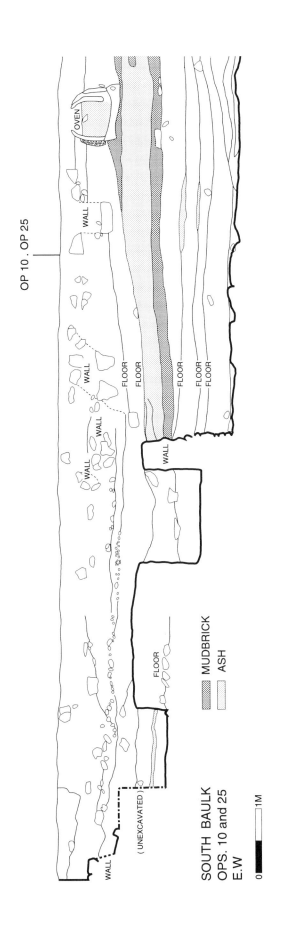

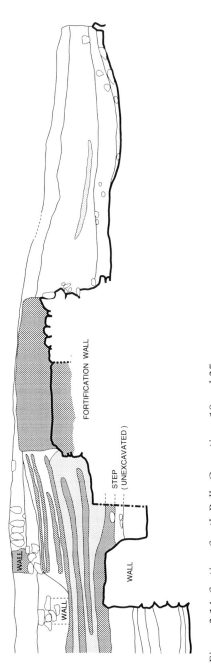

Figure 2:14. Section: South Balk, Operations 10 and 25.

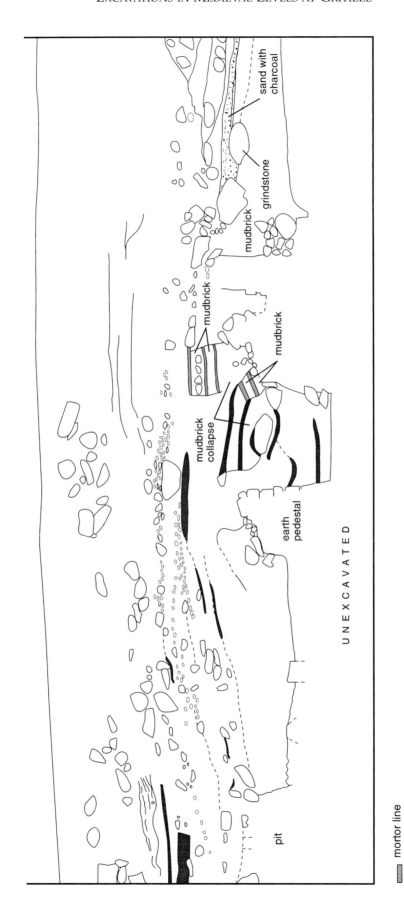

Figure 2:15. Section: West Balk, Operation 26/27.

mudbrick collapse, ash, and decayed organic debris of mottled hues of brown and green. In all of the section drawings, the walls of Phases 2, 3, and 4 can be seen covered with these layers, which in part must have consisted of the collapsed mudbrick superstructures of these same walls. The decay of the fortification wall, too, can be noted at the end of this sequence. In Figure 2:14, layers of mudbrick wash can be seen clearly in the section to the east of the wall.

This is not to say that the site was abandoned in this phase. The area comprising Operations 10/25 and 11 especially witnessed a certain amount of activity, although it did not involve the construction of buildings. Instead, it may be useful to think of the West End in this period as a kind of industrial zone, with habitation largely moving off the mound. The north end of Operation 2 did not reveal the same accumulation of ash as did the south, although the space between walls was filled with stone tumble and decayed mudbrick wash with some ash lenses. Continued wall building in this area, and the extensive rebuilding of Oven 21 in area A, however, indicate that this area was still in use for some time after Operations 9, 10, and 11 had ceased to be used domestically.[21]

Activity in this southern sector of the West End can best be seen in Figure 2:14. Here, excavation had descended to the Burnt Phase, which is shown as the bottommost level in the western 2 meters of Operation 10 and inside the fortification wall in Operation 25 (Fig. 2:7I).

A series of packed mudbrick floors of a slight pinkish tint succeeded each other in this area, the earliest associated with a small retaining wall built up against the inside of the fortification wall. These floors had patches of charcoal and ash on and between them. This area was still sheltered by the remains of walls, which presumably furnished the rationale for activity in this area in this phase. The slow accumulation of debris and floors was capped at the top of these walls by a thick layer of mudbrick, in which distinct and regular lines could be observed.

A similar situation applied to the southeast in Operation 11, in the former area of courtyard J. Although distinct floors were not observed here, there were patches of ash and charcoal indicative of occasional use, as well as large amounts of stone tumble. This area, too, was filled with a thick mudbrick cap, but in the midst of the area a few unattached curb walls were extant.

To the north of area I, the uneven accumulation of debris against walls observed in the east section (Fig. 2:12) applied throughout the area of D/E/F/G/H (mostly contained in Operation 9). This debris contained many stones as well as the patches of ash and charcoal mentioned earlier. Since some of the mudbrick superstructure of all of the walls remained, the source of the entire quantity of stone cannot be readily explained.

Although area C underwent the same accumulation of layers of debris, the history of the rest of Operation 2 is different. The Phase 3 occupation here did not endure as briefly as it did farther south in the West End. The modifications to areas A and B were not overlaid with the same deposits indicative of architectural collapse and organic decay. Indeed, the area did not suffer the burning at the end of Phase 3 that made the differentiation of phases farther south so apparent. Instead, a gradual abandonment seems to have taken place in which these areas were covered with fine layers of mudbrick wash and silt.

This period of general disrepair, with only a few areas used intermittently, constituted the first part of Phase 5. The second part of this phase is also by and large nonarchitectural. It is, however, marked by the introduction of two conspicuous features into this area, namely, two pyrotechnic areas that produced large amounts of ash. The function of both of these "ovens" is not clear. The ash produced was fine and contained nothing more than small pieces of charcoal and lime. Archaeobotanical analysis of a sample of this thick ash layer revealed an "assemblage (that) is consistent with somewhat scattered hearth/oven debris."[22] The few artifacts found—occasional pieces of pottery or bone—were burned but were so infrequent as to

---

[21] An analysis of the ceramics from Operation 30, the one area off the mound that yielded domestic architecture, showed that most of the sequence there pertained to the time period corresponding to Phase 5 and its successors. This, in turn, led to the idea that, in the main, occupation at Gritille shifted off the mound in Levels 5 and 6, only to return in Level 7.

[22] Miller, "Crusader Period Fortress," *Anatolica* 18 (1992), 90. "The deposit seems to have a low density of charred remains, consisting primarily of wood charcoal."

be justly considered accidental inclusions. No conclusions could be drawn about the nature of the industrial process undertaken in these two areas, but almost all of Operations 10, 25, and 9 was blanketed with ash.

The first and more impressive of the "ovens" was only partially excavated, as it lay partially in the west balk of Operation 11 (Fig. 2:4; Pls. 2:17–2:18). As observed above, the remains of mudbrick walls from earlier phases provided shelter for the activity areas of this phase, and such is the case with this oven. It was nestled in the crook formed by the walls at the end of Operation 11. It consisted of several layers of Roman roof tiles (a common insulation material for ovens up until the flooding of this region; they were probably brought from Samsat, as they were until recently to the village of Biriman) packed around a baked mud ring.

Inside this area, the heart of the feature, were seven floors of lime plaster with clay or other soil baked orange by heat layered between them like a cake. Whether or not these plaster floors were the result of successive use of the feature, or were the byproduct of the lime used in whatever manufacturing process was employed here, they do indicate multiple, perhaps prolonged, use. Multiple depositions of lime could be seen within the feature itself during the process of dismantling (Pl. 2:19).

There is a possibility that this feature was a lime kiln. Although small compared even with traditional lime kilns, it could have performed the task of converting the local limestone into lime. All the necessary ingredients were at hand: limestone (from the footings of abandoned buildings in the vicinity), water, and fuel (charcoal or wood). Furthermore, since the process is odoriferous, a location at a distance from inhabited areas is usually preferred.[23] A fully excavated "oven" at Tille furnishes the closest parallel; there the floor of the pyrotechnic feature was "made from a coarse, gravelly, white/gray substance similar to mortar."[24]

In addition to its use on floors, lime was also found on portions of the lower walls in Operation 11. Lime appears to have been widely used in the region. It was used for floors at Gritille and Tille and on walls at Gritille, Tille, and Pirot.[25] At Horis, the excavators found lime used as mortar for limestone ashlar blocks as well as for floors and wall plaster; lime mortar was also used at Korucutepe.[26]

Phase 5 also produced a second enigmatic pyrotechnic feature: an oval depression lined with stones (visible in the right center of Pl. 2:19). This depression, measuring 75 centimeters in length, was sunk into the mudbrick top of the remains of a long wall which had marked the northern limit of area I in Phase 2. The result of burning had turned a zone of several meters around this oval a bright orange, the color made even more vivid by the thick layer of ash (visible in Fig. 2:14) atop it. This burnt surface is uneven; it plunges precipitously to the north where not supported by the remains of the earlier wall. It is visible in the east section of Operation 10 (Fig. 2:14), where it is marked as a floor. The accumulation of ash was limited by the wall marking the southern boundary of B and C. By the time of this phase, the fortification wall was definitely out of use, as witnessed by the lenses of mudbrick debris found in the ash layer next to the fortification wall.

PHASE 6

The last three phases of the medieval deposit at Gritille proved to be more difficult than earlier phases to excavate and interpret, principally because of a marked decrease in preservation. Walls were preserved only as stone footings; almost all lacked traces of mudbrick superstructure. Floors or other habitation surfaces were fugitive, difficult to find in the desiccated soil of the upper levels. Vine roots intruded into the deposit. Last but not least, the differential settling of walls (especially atop the thick ash layer of Phase 5) added to the scarcity of floor levels, which made it difficult to link walls into contemporaneous structures.

This phase marked a rehabitation of the West End. In Operation 11, three walls were laid out on top of the mudbrick debris at the top of Phase 5. In the middle of this room was a large flat stone, the basis for a roof support. In Opera-

---

[23] Ortega, "Basic Technology," 77–81.
[24] Moore, *Tille Höyük* 1, 32.
[25] Karaca, "Pirot Höyük 1980 Çalışmaları," 110; Moore, *Tille Höyük* 1, 33.
[26] Doruk, "Horis Kale Kazıları," 168; Işık, "Horis Kale Kazıları 1981," 317; van Loon, *Korucutepe*, 2:44.

tion 25, a small rectangular structure with an internal divider wall was erected on top of the fortification wall, finally proving that it was out of service. This small structure (Fig. 2:16, Pl. 2:20), far too small for human habitation, must have served as a storage bin.

To the north in Operation 2, two long walls were found running in the same orientation as the lower phase "spoke walls," but the intrusion of Phase 7 fortifications destroyed whatever association between them that may have existed.

One of these walls, too, extended over part of the fortification wall.

PHASE 7

Phase 7 (Fig. 2:17) was marked by three major architectural elements. The first of these was a large square structure that ran out over the top of the fortification wall in Operation 2 (Pl. 2:21). Its depth of foundation, size, and lack of apparent entrance all suggest the structure's

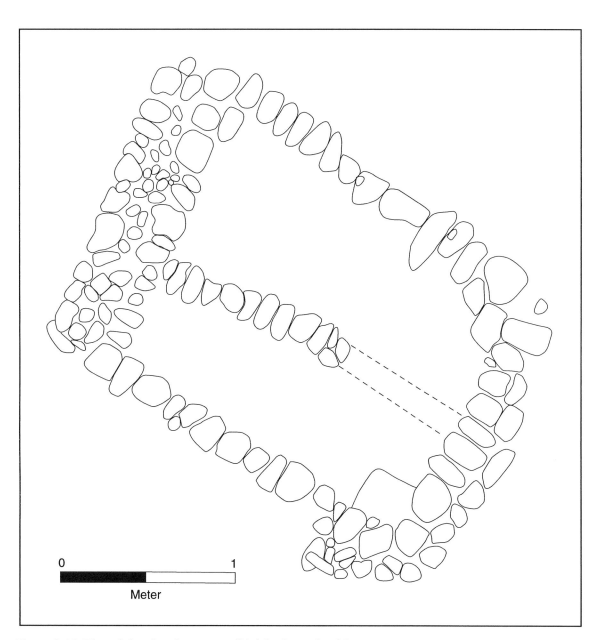

0   1

Meter

Figure 2:16. Plan of chambered structure (bin) in Operation 25.

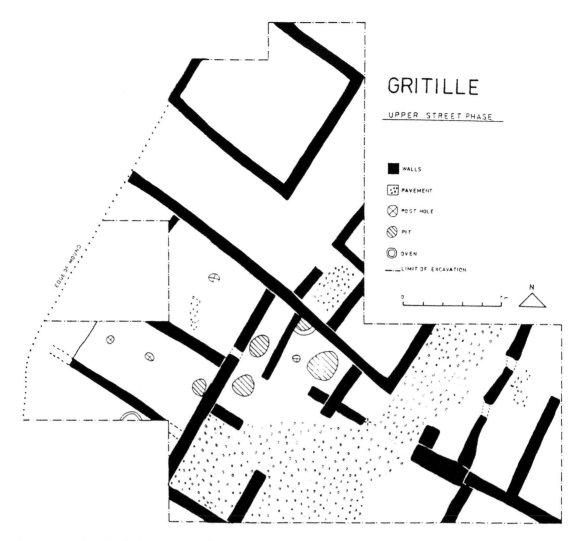

Figure 2:17. West End plan in Phase 7.

use as a tower, perhaps a watchtower.[27]

A space of approximately 2 meters separated this building from the other Phase 7 structures to the south and east. These constructions, consisting of partially enclosed areas often with roughly laid pebble pavements, and enclosed rooms with postholes for roofing, were organized around two long walls, one of them running parallel to the edge of the mound, the other perpendicular. Domestic structures stretched across the mound to its eastern edge.

Because this level was erected to a great extent on top of the ash layer at the top of Phase 5, it was necessary for its inhabitants to provide solid living surfaces. This was accomplished in the area to the southwest of the West End in Operation 25, where a thick lime plaster floor was laid (Fig. 2:14). Similarly, a plaster floor was also laid in the rectangular room to the north of this area.

In addition to the domestic areas and tower, the third major characteristic of this phase was another pebble-paved street. In alignment it duplicated the pebble pavement of Phase 4. It was laid in a similar fashion, with a large stone substructure topped by smaller stones and pebbles. This street is visible in all four balk sections (Figs. 2:10, 2:12, 2:14, 2:15). In Operation 11,

---

[27] For a stone plan of this structure, see Ellis and Voigt, "1981 Excavations at Gritille," ill. 3.

where the pavement entered a cul-de-sac (Pl. 2:22), its alignment is novel.

As it had in Phase 4, the street separated a series of structures along the western edge of the mound from structures lying toward its center. However, despite these similarities, there were basic differences of organization between the layout of Phase 7 and that of Phases 3 and 4. In Phase 7 the layout of structures seems to have been much more haphazard. Instead of open and enclosed areas entered from a street or central circulation space, some areas were completely closed off from the street (the two plaster-floored rooms in Operations 25 and 9), whereas some discrete units were immediately accessible from the street (the cul-de-sac and the area with the two pits and posthole in Operation 10).

As a result, despite the presence of two long divider walls and of the street itself, the development of this phase, as well as the subsequent modifications of Phase 8, assumes a less regular aspect. The street, tower, and long walls point to some kind of planning, but the subsequent development of the site seems to have been more like a series of responses to individual functions or needs than maintenance of an ordered scheme. These conclusions are based on a comparison with the original organization of the intramural settlement, wherein divider walls at regularly spaced intervals provided the second, third, and fourth phases of medieval Gritille with their underlying order.

PHASE 8

Found at the uppermost limit of the medieval sequence, scant and poorly preserved remains of two subphases, here lumped together as Phase 8, proved primarily domestic in nature. In the arid topsoil, stratigraphy well-nigh disappeared (Pl. 2:23). In the remains from this phase, minor alterations to the structures of Phase 7 could be determined, as could the addition of features such as pits and ovens. The uppermost medieval remains consisted of nothing save the sheared-off bottoms of ovens, some of them visible beneath the brush cleared prior to the commencement of excavation. This level, too, was found across the entire top of the mound.

THE FORTIFICATION WALL

Excavations of the medieval fortification wall at Gritille allowed us to reconstruct the wall's circuit over a stretch of the landward section of the mound between West End operations and Operations 53 and 46 at the southwestern edge of the mound (Fig. 2:18). However, at no time during the excavation of medieval Gritille was an entrance to the intramural settlement found.

Excavations along the northern and eastern edges of the mound failed to recover a fortification wall. It is probable that the fortification wall in these areas fell prey to erosion, other natural catastrophes, and/or stone-robbing. The fortification walls at Tille and Lidar were also incompletely preserved, and at Tille there were significant rebuildings of portions of the wall in order to shore them up.[28]

While the fragmentary preservation of the Gritille perimeter wall presented one problem, a second problem was raised by the nature of the materials used to construct the wall. As is well known, mudbrick architecture demands almost constant upkeep. The portions of the fortification wall excavated—especially in Operation 8, where the construction of the wall was investigated in the greatest detail—showed significant repair and modification. Although these modifications can be presented convincingly in sequence, the relation of that sequence to the main stratigraphic sequence of the mound is an argument neither proved nor disproved by the stratigraphic sequence.

In broad outline, there were two main phases to the construction of the fortification wall at Gritille. The first coincided with the initial investment of the site in Phase 2. In the West End, this wall was represented by a narrow mudbrick ledge capping eighteen courses of stone that descended below the intramural settlement. Investigation of the earlier fortification wall was hindered by the presence of another one atop it and slightly to the outside in Phase 3. This wall was modified, reinforced, and thickened but did not prevent the sack of the site at the end of Phase 3, nor the abandonment of the site after Phase 4. By the end of Phase 5 (but probably earlier), the fortification wall had definitively been abandoned.

---

[28] Moore (*Tille Höyük 1*, 37) notes the slippage of the limestone footings of the Tille fortification wall.

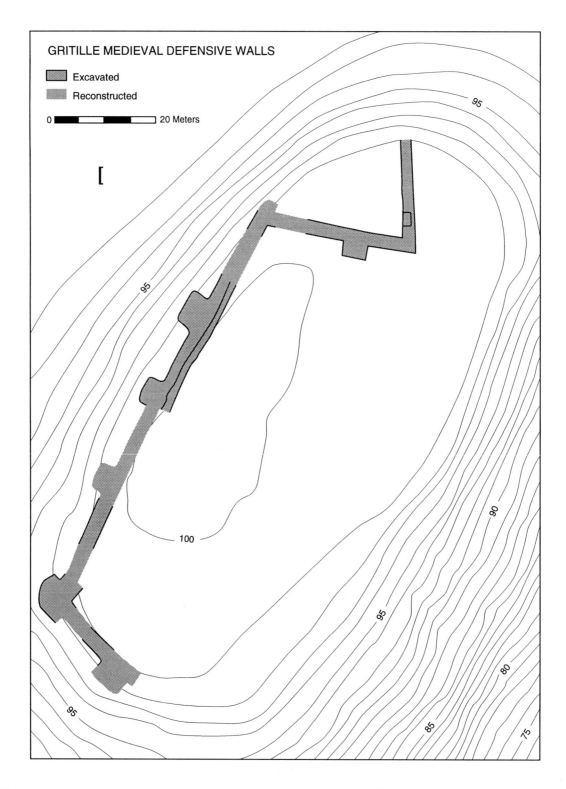

Figure 2:18. Topographic site map showing the medieval fortification wall.

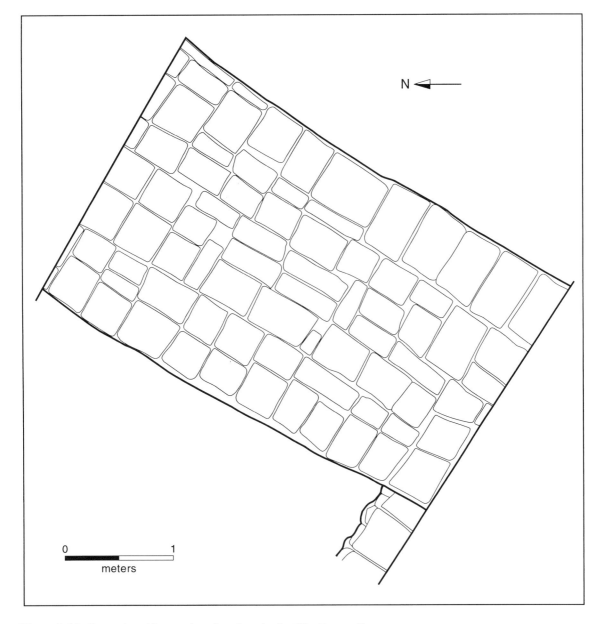

Figure 2:19. Operation 46, top plan showing the fortification wall.

The first phase of the fortification wall was best preserved at the southern end of the site, in Operations 46 and 53 (Figs. 2:19, 2:20). Operation 53 uncovered a bastion at the southwest corner of the mound (Pls. 2:24, 2:25). The mudbrick superstructure was eroded in three levels down the edge of the mound (represented by the thicker lines in the drawing), with the stone footings constituting the exterior base of the corner exposed at the bottom. The bastion thus formed was massively built, with lines of mudbricks intersecting in the middle of the bastion,

and the interstices at the southernmost corner filled in at an angle. Figure 2:20 shows a stretch of the curtain wall, approximately 2 meters thick, with the edge of a tower protruding from the corner. Here as elsewhere, the size of the mudbricks varied considerably within one phase. Also, it was impossible to detect the relatively minor changes in mudbrick size between phases that excavators detected at Lidar.[29]

If there had been a second fortification wall atop this stretch of the first fortification wall, it had eroded. Erosion is a possibility, since the

---

[29] Hauptmann, "Die Grabungen auf dem Lidar Höyük, 1979," 261.

N ←

0 ▬▬▬▬▬ 100
meters

Figure 2:20. Operation 53, top plan showing the fortification wall.

first fortification wall was recovered close to the surface. This was not the case with Operations 37 and 39, closer to the West End (Pl. 2:26). Here a stretch of the upper fortification wall was uncovered, lying atop the same shelf of mudbrick from the earlier fortification wall projecting into the intramural settlement.

Operation 8, a step trench along the western edge of the mound, yielded the most information about all phases of the fortification wall. Figure 2:21 is a drawing of the south section of

Operation 8, with a section through the reinforcement of the wall that occurred in Phase 4. Figure 2:22 is a plan of the tower of the second fortification wall in Operation 8 showing mudbricks over a rubble socle surrounded by a slightly raised border of stones. This tower is also evident in Plate 2:27.

From Figure 2:21, two things are evident. First, as was the case at Tille,[30] reinforcements were not bonded into the fortification wall; indeed, here a slight but distinct separation is

[30] Moore, *Tille Höyük 1*, 37.

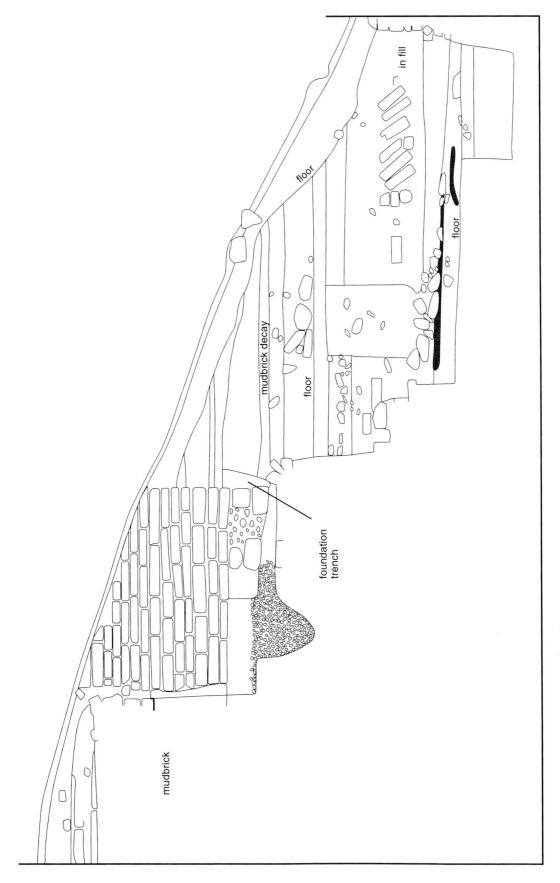

Figure 2:21. Section: Operation 8, South Balk.

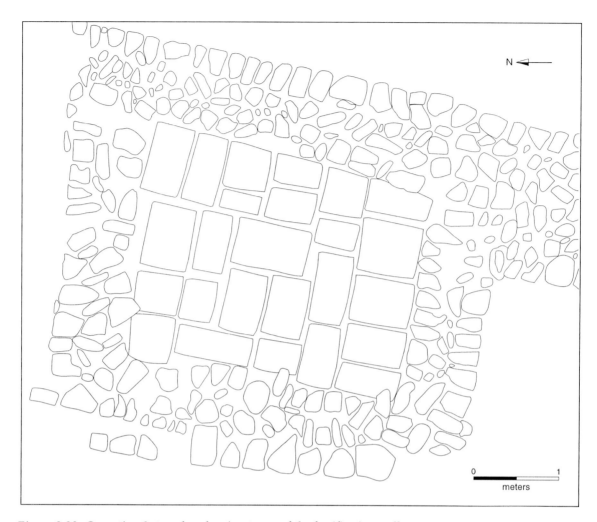

Figure 2:22. Operation 8, top plan showing tower of the fortification wall.

visible. Second, the method of construction consisted of a footing of larger stones filled in with river pebbles. This was also the construction technique used for the perimeter walls at Tille and Lidar.[31] Although the fortification wall at Gritille was not dismantled any further than this section, it may be assumed that this method of construction was used for the entire wall.

Excavation in Operation 8 revealed the following construction sequence to the fortification wall. First, a fortification wall with towers was constructed. Second, another fortification wall was built atop the first. It had irregularly built stone foundations and a pinkish mudbrick superstructure. It was approximately 2 meters wide. One tower had stone surrounding a mud-

brick infill (Fig. 2:22) and was topped with a mudbrick superstructure.

The third stage in the wall's construction consisted of a repair to a corner of the tower in Operation 8 and a massive infilling between the towers. This was accomplished by means of a foundation trench at the bottom of which a stone foundation wall was built, and behind which large numbers of river stones and pebbles were placed. This trench was then filled with mudbrick. After this last enlargement, the wall was 4 to 4.5 meters thick. It was subsequently abandoned.

The south section of Operation 10/25 uncovered a different, if incomplete, sequence of repairs (Fig. 2:14). Visible in the section are re-

---

[31] Ibid., 29; Hauptmann, "Die Grabungen auf dem Lidar Höyük, 1979," 251.

pairs to the outside of the wall, with mudbrick atop a two-course stone wall added to the top of a larger, lower mudbrick wall, but with no evidence of the massive infilling farther north. Plates 2:28 and 2:29 show the tower in Operation 10/25, first with its surviving mudbrick articulated, and then stripped to the stone socle.

If the first wall pertains to Phase 2, then the second fortification wall must belong to Phase 3, although, as stated above, its placement slightly to the west of the first fortification wall eliminated most stratigraphic connection between it and Phase 3 intramural structures (Pl. 2:27). As the fortification wall was definitely abandoned sometime in Phase 5—as evidenced by the mudbrick decay, abandonment of the domestic structures atop the mound and, finally, the building of structures atop the mound—the infilling observed in Operation 8 must belong to Phase 4. Although Phase 4 consisted of a brief reoccupation of the site, it was typified by a massive cleanup of the debris from the burning at the end of Phase 3 and an equally large intramural project, the laying of the lower street.

At Lidar, across the Euphrates from Gritille, there were also two major fortification walls built in the medieval period. The first wall had a thickness of 1.5 meters, and the second varied in thickness from 1 to 1.8 meters.[32] Poor preservation of these perimeter walls prevented recovery of towers at Lidar.

THE NORTH END EXCAVATIONS

The major feature of the northern part of the mound was an area separated from the rest of the mound (Fig. 2:5). Separation was effected by a towered wall that faced inward toward the rest of the site. To the west, this wall joined the fortification wall (Fig. 2:23, Operation 52). To the east of the tower, the wall narrowed and turned abruptly northward, extending toward the edge of the mound where formerly there had been a fortification wall. The area thus cordoned off from the rest of the site constituted the northwestern corner of the mound.

Because the fortification wall was missing, ingress and egress were impossible to calculate. There was only one (blocked) doorway preserved among the remaining walls; it was in the north–south wall at the east of the enclosure.

(The lower right-hand side of Plate 2:30 shows this doorway unblocked by excavators.) The interior of the enclosure was different from the rest of the site not in building materials but in scale. It consisted of a large courtyard which was at least partly covered. Five large stone post supports were found (four forming a square), as were an oven or hearth, a drain, and pits (Pl. 2:31). North–south walls trailed off at the end of the mound. In addition, there were remains of a wall running roughly parallel to the edge of the mound near its modern edge. This raised the possibility that there were smaller rooms or casemates between the main courtyard and the fortification wall at the north of the mound, as was evidently the case in Phase 2.

The plan of this part of the mound in Phase 2 was at least partially recovered by assuming that the walls protruding into the floor of the Phase 3 enclosure were remains of Phase 2 walls. They are indicated in the plan (see Fig. 2:5) by dotted lines, as well as by stones when those were evident. In a few places at the edge of the mound where this phase was excavated, it proved similar to Phase 2 in the West End. That is to say, the walls rested on a mainly sherd- and artifact-free fill of brown dirt that overlay the Hellenistic deposit underneath. Here there were no hearths or other indications of occupation; in the few areas in which Phase 2 levels were investigated, the matrix consisted largely of bricky fill from the collapsed walls. A parallel set of walls near the eastern edge of the Phase 3 enclosure appears to define a passageway.

The North End enclosure, also burnt at the end of Phase 3, yielded a Crusader coin hoard and the majority of the human skeletal remains recovered from the Burnt Phase (e.g., Pl. 2:32). These finds suggest that the North End enclosure constituted a sort of keep, home to a small garrison meant to defend the site. Given the manpower shortages of the Franks everywhere in the Outremer, it seems unlikely that the defenders of this rude keep were members of the Frankish component of the County of Edessa. However, the coin hoard may indicate a close link with the Franco-Armenian military elite of the remnants of the County.

Certainly the North End did not resume its previous function in Phase 4. Several small di-

---

[32] Hauptmann, "Die Grabungen auf dem Lidar Höyük, 1979," 251.

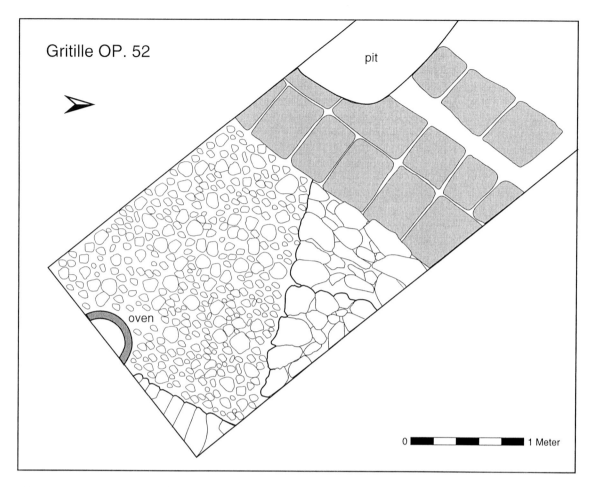

Figure 2:23. Operation 52, plan.

vider or curb walls were built, including two incorporating elements of a press (Pls. 2:33, 2:34; Figs. 2:24, 4:6) probably used as post supports. The doorway in the eastern enclosure wall may also have been walled up in this phase. Subsequent to Phase 4 the area seems to have been sporadically used. Several pits were sunk into the collapse from surrounding walls. The area was reoccupied and rebuilt with domestic structures in Phases 7 and 8.

OTHER OPERATIONS

INVESTIGATING THE PAVED STREET (OPERATIONS 42 AND 43)

One major organizing element of the site, the street that ran up the spine of the mound in two different phases, was investigated in the final excavation season by Operations 42 and 43. Both were 5 by 5 meter squares, placed to the north of Operation 26/27. Operation 43 uncovered not the street, but largely the tower of the North End enclosure wall, which extended about halfway into the square (Pl. 2:35). The stratigraphic sequence for this operation (Fig. 2:25) is the same as that outside the North End enclosure wall in neighboring Operation 54 to the east.

Phase 2 was not reached in Operation 43, although it was represented by walls protruding into the floor of the Phase 3 occupation. Likewise, the base of the tower in Operation 43 was not reached, but it was probably not much below the level reached at the end of excavation, some seven stone courses deep. The occupation in this area in Phases 3 and 4 consisted of floors and walls that directly abutted the North End enclosure wall and tower. Ovens and pits com-

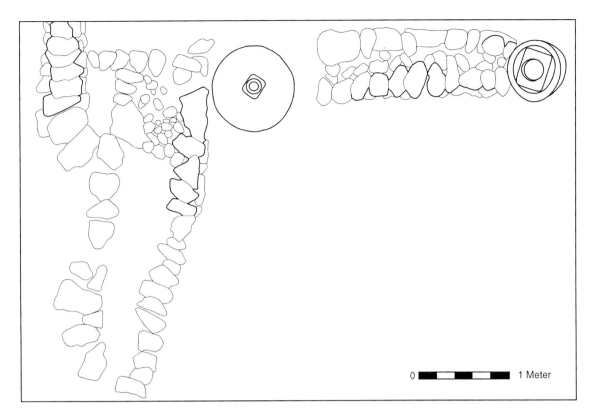

Figure 2:24. North End. Operation 47. Phase 4 walls with millstones.

pleted the picture of domestic occupation little different from that in other parts of the mound outside of the North End.

Phases 5 and 6 were represented by fugitive surfaces in a bricky deposit pocked by ash, probably denoting collapse from the mudbrick superstructure of the North End tower and fortification wall mixed with debris and occasional occupational surfaces. Here, too, the site was reoccupied by domestic structures in Phase 7, represented by a stone wall at the southern edge of the section.

Operation 42 (Figs. 2:8, 2:26; Pl. 2:36) was divided in Phases 3 and 4 between a domestic structure and an outside circulation area, which was paved in Phase 4. The central architectural feature was the divider wall which curved approximately north–south through the square. At first, a doorway was present in the wall; this was blocked and another doorway was opened to the north. This doorway was unusually marked by a large threshold stone. At this time, an oven and posthole were added to the west of the wall. When the site burned at the end of

Phase 3, ash and large chunks of charcoal were deposited on the floor. In Phase 4, the area was reoccupied, with a curb wall added to the interior. In Phase 4, too, the lower street was laid before the area was abandoned. Both phases of the pebbled street are visible in Figure 2:26, as are the ashy wash lenses that underlay the first street, debris from collapse of structures in Phase 3.

Phases 5 and 6 were marked by the collapse of the structure, with large amounts of brick wash mixed with burnt material accumulating inside and wash and mixed debris building up on top of the street. During Phase 7 the upper street was laid, and a wall following the alignment of the earlier wall was built.

In later phases the street seems to have fallen out of use. A pit was dug in the middle of it, and debris was built up on top of it. More poorly preserved domestic structures mark the final stages of occupation, with the western half of the square covered with a rough stone pavement, presumably an exterior surface covering the soft ash laden deposit below.

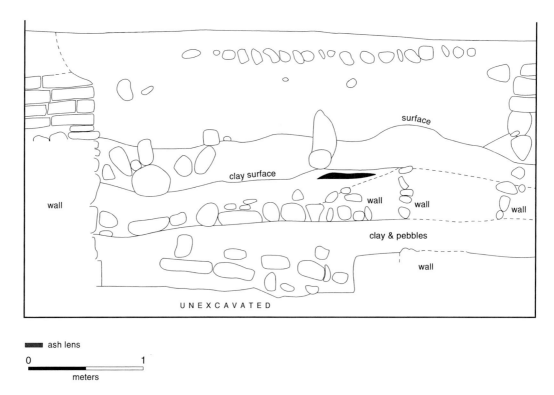

Figure 2:25. Section: Operation 43, East Section.

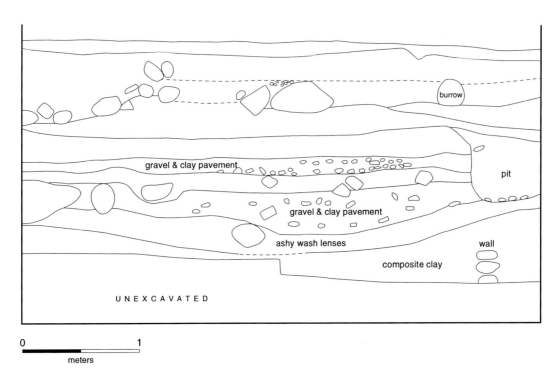

Figure 2:26. Section: Operation 42, East Balk.

Exploring the Extent of the Fortification Wall
(Operations 37 and 39)

Operations 37 and 39 were opened in 1984 to trace the fortification wall. After the discovery of the enclosure area of the North End, the first major sign of settlement differentiation in medieval levels at Gritille, it was decided to expand and combine these operations in order to probe the nature of the medieval settlement in the southern half of the site.

Figure 2:27 is a phase plan of Level 7 in this area (also visible in Pl. 2:37). Part of the wall at the top of the plan extended over the top of the abandoned fortification wall. The configuration of domestic architecture found here was familiar from the West End just to the north: longer walls running roughly at right angles to the edge of the mound were bisected by smaller divider walls to form open and closed spaces; and here a series of mudbrick bins was similar in shape and size to those found in Operation 25.

Although the Burnt Phase was not reached in this area, the excavator noted that the long walls continued to descend below the level of the cross-walls, again conforming to the pattern of long divider walls found in the area just to the

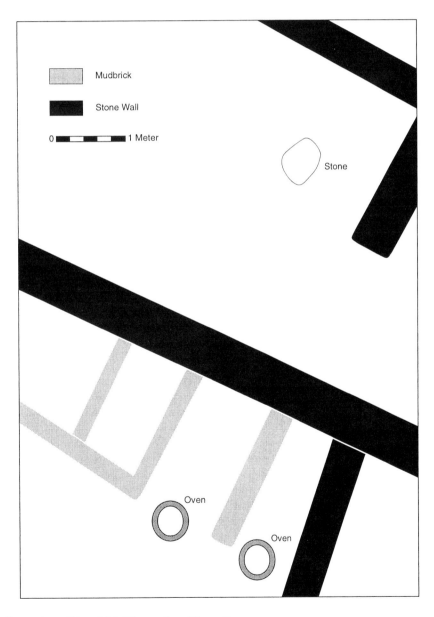

Figure 2:27. Operations 37 and 39, Phase plan, Phase 7.

north. Also similar to the West End, a ledge constituting the inner edge of the lower fortification wall was found, with the upper fortification wall built on top of it and slightly to the outside.

THE STORAGE PITS (OPERATIONS 4 AND 5)

Operations 4 and 5 were located on a terrace below the southwest edge of the mound.[33] These two operations did not yield evidence of domestic occupation as did the test trench to the north of the mound (Operation 30) and Operation 8 for the western edge of the mound. Rather, eight large storage pits, six in Operation 4 and two in Operation 5, were recovered. The mouths of these storage pits were rectangular and formed of stone (Pl. 2:38). Below, they belled out to form cavities up to 3 meters in depth. The walls of the pits were unlined, and they were filled with wash and occasional artifacts from the mound. Figure 2:28 is a section of one of these pits in Operation 4.

It is likely that these pits were used for grain storage and possibly to hide harvest from either besiegers or tax collectors. Certainly, the tradition of underground storage is well-established in the region. To the north, in Cappadocia, the soft tufa was carved into so many depots and refuges from the Arab raiders that Cappadocia became known in Arab sources as *al-maṭmūra*,[34] literally, the "underground grain storehouses," but by extension probably the whole complex of underground refuges found there. The pits found in Operations 4 and 5 at Gritille were excavated from the soil and were convenient to the settlement, but do not seem to have been associated with any dwellings. Therefore, it is distinctly possible that they were used for the purpose discussed here.

ARCHITECTURAL PARALLELS

TAŞKUN KALE

The best parallels for the spatial organization of Gritille in the first phase of its medieval occupation are furnished by Taşkun Kale and Lidar. Taşkun Kale was a small (approximately 40 by 30 meter) early fourteenth-century fort

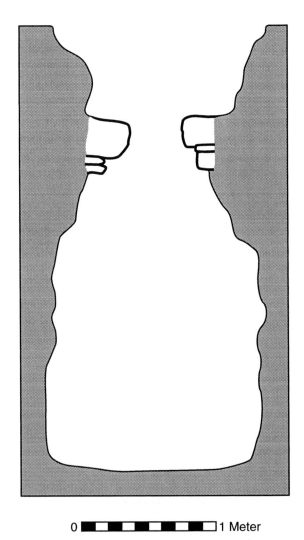

0 ▮▯▮▯▮▯▮▯▯ 1 Meter

Figure 2:28. Operation 4, section of storage pit.

guarding the approaches to a major river crossing of the Murad Su, principal affluent of the upper Euphrates River northeast of Malatya (see Fig. 1:1). Like Gritille, Taşkun Kale was organized on a roughly oval plan, with rectangular towers studding the fortification wall at approximately 10-meter intervals (Fig. 2:29). Inside the walls, a central massing and circulation space was ringed with a row of structures entered from this central space. Here, too, the primary organizing unit consisted of a series of long walls roughly perpendicular to the fortification wall itself. When the need arose, the space between these walls was filled with court-

---

[33] Ellis and Voigt, "1981 Excavations at Gritille," 330, ills. 6, 7.

[34] See Haldon and Kennedy, "Arab-Byzantine Frontier," 97, for this term.

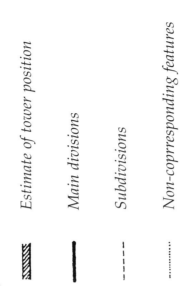

Estimate of tower position

Main divisions

Subdivisions

Non-coprresponding features

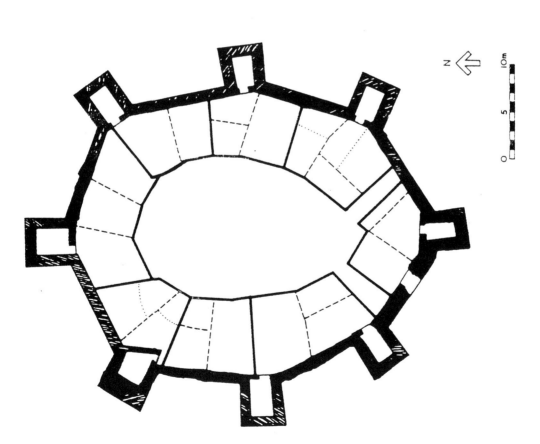

N

0   5   10m

Figure 2:29. Plan of Taşkun Kale (McNicoll, Fig. 100).

yards or enclosed areas. As time passed, these structures completely ringed the interior of the fortification wall, encroaching more and more on the central space.[35] Similarities between Phase 2 Gritille and Taşkun Kale extend to construction materials and techniques. The walls of Taşkun Kale were built using the same herringbone technique found at Gritille, and they consisted of the same rubble footings underpinning a mudbrick superstructure.

The excavators of Taşkun Kale believed that its regular layout and distance from a local Christian village lent credence to its functioning as a garrison fort. This garrison would probably have been a company of soldiers in the employ of the Ilkhanid Mongol dynasty which controlled this part of Anatolia in the early fourteenth century.[36]

It is easy to note similarities between Taşkun Kale and Gritille. We know that the site of Lidar was fortified by the Byzantines as part of the campaign to protect their supply lines when trying to capture Urfa in 1031. We also know from Matthew of Edessa that there were other forts in the vicinity.[37] A military treatise dated to the 960s and attributed to the Byzantine Emperor Nikephoros Phokas discusses elements of campaigning on the Byzantine oriental frontier which bear on the likelihood of selecting a site like Gritille for fortification.[38] Two elements singled out as important in such a choice are the keeping of an expeditionary force in a circle, and the siting of a camp next to a river, preferably near a ford. While the camps mentioned in this treatise are unfortified, temporary ones, the resources necessary to transform a hilltop guarding a ford into a secure fort using the prevalent mudbrick construction technique of the area would have been minimal compared with stone construction.

In a recent study of the medieval Armenian fortifications of Smooth Cilicia, R. Edwards has noted that medieval Byzantine military architecture displays an inconsistency of masonry types. Characteristics of Byzantine fortifications in Cilicia are crude masonry and a readiness to reemploy building stones lying at hand.[39] While stonemasonry may have been the building norm in Cilicia and areas on all sides of the Samsat region, it must be assumed that mudbrick was used for fortifications of less than primary importance throughout eastern Anatolia, northern Syria, and northern Mesopotamia.[40] Consequently, even though Gritille's construction does not resemble that of other fortifications of the middle Byzantine period, it is not anomalous to propose that the first, mudbrick fortification of Gritille was undertaken during the Byzantine rule of this area.

LIDAR

This conclusion is reinforced by an examination of the medieval remains from Lidar, Gritille's twin mound across the Euphrates. Although Lidar was much larger than Gritille, distinct similarities of layout can be noted. In all medieval phases of occupation at Lidar, the same organizational principle was observed, namely, the presence of a street paralleling the fortification wall at the edge of the mound, called by its excavators a *Ringstraße* (Fig. 2:30).[41] Between the street and the fortification at roughly 10-meter intervals ran long spoke walls. The spaces between these walls were irregularly divided into courtyards, covered areas, pitted areas, and so forth (Fig. 2:31). Unfortunately, the fortification wall at Lidar was recovered in highly fragmentary form only in the area depicted in Figure 2:31, so comparisons between fortifica-

---

[35] McNicoll, *Taşkun Kale*, 7.

[36] Ibid., 12.

[37] See Chapter 1, this volume.

[38] "Skirmishing" in Dennis, *Three Byzantine Military Treatises*, 181.

[39] Edwards, *Armenian Fortifications of Cilicia*, 19.

[40] See Chapter 1, n. 119, for a reference to Michael the Syrian's account of the rebuilding in stone of the mudbrick fortification wall of Keysun by the Crusaders under threat of attack.

[41] The following two plans are inked reproductions of sketch plans made by members of the Lidar excavation team and are reproduced here by permission of Prof. Harald Hauptmann, Lidar Excavation Director. They are to be found in the Lidar excavation archive at the Institute for Prehistoric Archaeology, The University of Heidelberg. For a view of one part of this feature, see Hauptmann, "Die Grabungen auf dem Lidar Höyük, 1979," Pl. 157:3.

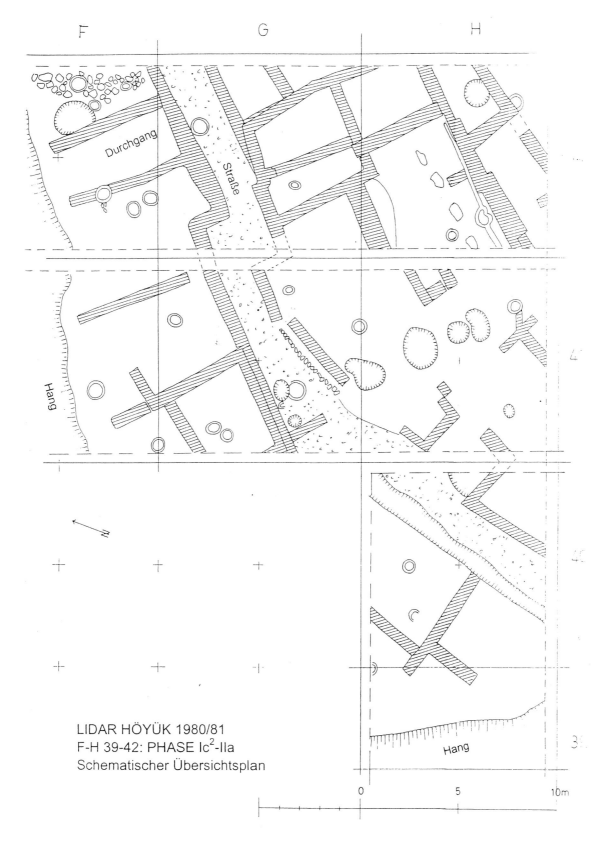

LIDAR HÖYÜK 1980/81
F-H 39-42: PHASE Ic²-IIa
Schematischer Übersichtsplan

Figure 2:30. Plan of Lidar 1980–81 excavations F–G 41/42. (Courtesy of Prof. H. Hauptmann, Institute of Prehistory, Heidelberg University.)

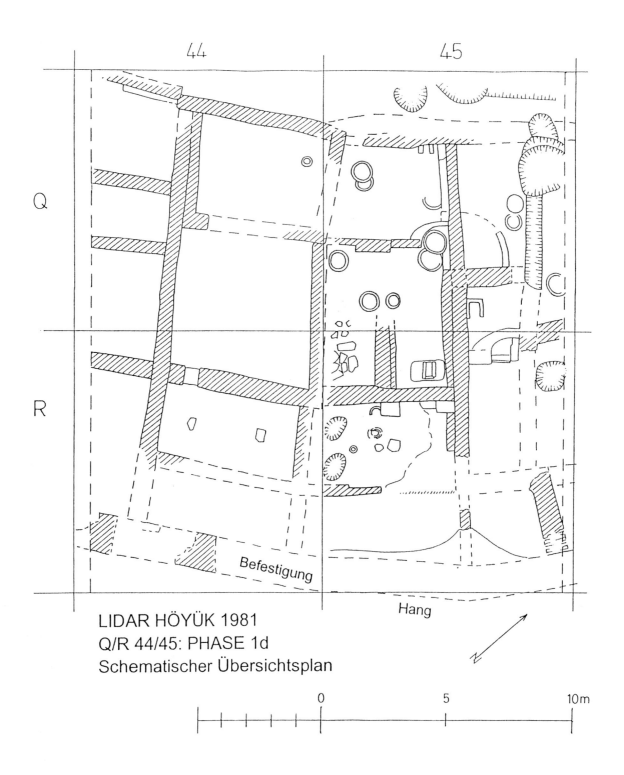

LIDAR HÖYÜK 1981
Q/R 44/45: PHASE 1d
Schematischer Übersichtsplan

Figure 2:31. Plan of Lidar 1981 Excavations Q–R 44/45. (Courtesy of Prof. H. Hauptmann, Institute of Prehistory, Heidelberg University.)

tion walls of the two sites are of limited value. Nevertheless, it can be ascertained that the defensive wall at Lidar, like the one at Gritille, consisted of a mudbrick superstructure erected on a rubble socle.

The regularity of layout found at Taşkun Kale, Lidar, and Gritille can be attributed to the intervention of state or military authority. Military concerns for ease of communication and assembly require a certain amount of regularity. Perhaps more important, however, is the simple fact that it is inherently more expedient, and easier, for a state to construct a settlement with a regularized system. In the Greco-Roman world, the layout of army camps and colonies alike was accomplished per strigas.[42] While notions of grid-plans are absent from all three of these settlements, it is clear that medieval states, both Islamic and Christian, employed simple but effective systems for the laying out of fortified settlements, be they garrisons or not. The top of an eminence was surrounded by a fortification wall, and a street or open area parallel to the contours of the enclosed space provided for circulation. Dwellings and other structures ran along the interior of the fortification wall, delimited by long divider walls set at regular intervals. The space between these walls was subdivided and used as needed.

TILLE

A habitation model of a different kind is furnished by Tille, a site overlooking a crossing of the Euphrates downstream from the castle of Gerger. Here excavators recovered the entire plan for the top of the mound, save for peripheral areas where the mound had been eroded or structures such as the fortification wall had been robbed for their stones. In the early phase, a pebbled road led up to the middle of the site from a lost gateway, debouching into a large cobbled courtyard (Fig. 2:32).[43] A series of fragmentary outbuildings (some of them surmised by excavators to be stables) lay to the south. To the north, abutting the fortification, lay a more regularly disposed structure containing a pebbled hall, in the middle of which were two stone column bases.

The model chosen by the excavators to explain this arrangement was that of a local *derebey* or strongman who lived with his retinue and minions behind the walls of the fortified hilltop settlement, with a settlement of his subjects spread around the base of the mound.[44] The columned building would have served as the residence of this minor potentate, whose major concern would have been to secure the nearby river crossing and approaches to Gerger.

A later medieval phase at Tille shows an expansion and aggrandizement of the structures in the intramural settlement, including the construction of a bath house and the laying of limestone pavement, but the basic organization of space does not differ much.[45]

At Tille, then, we can observe a different type of spatial and social organization, in which a high place was fortified and inhabited, but whose plan evolved gradually. As such, it did not possess the regularity of a settlement planned and laid out by a larger, bureaucratic entity of nonlocal origin. The situation of its buildings was dictated by functional criteria, but the underlying order of an initial, overall plan for the space was not present.

An analogy for the ruler's residence at Tille can be found in Matthew of Edessa, who mentions a raid by a small band of Turks against Keysun, the seat of the Armenian lord Kogh Vasil in the late 1130s. This detachment surprised the town, which was substantially larger than Tille, sacked it, and set it on fire.

---

[42] See, e.g., Castagnoli, *Orthogonal Town Planning in Antiquity*, 115 ff.

[43] French, Moore, and Russell, "Excavations at Tille 1979–1982," Fig. 2.

[44] Ibid., 168: "The type of site at Tille during the 12th–13th centuries on the top of the höyük [mound] appears to be a *beylik*—a defended stronghold of a minor chieftain. . . . The unit would appear initially to be a small single family with their servants. As the family grew, the need for more housing increased so that during the second level the site expanded until the whole höyük was intensively used." See also Moore, *Tille Höyük 1,* 23, 36–37, 47, for summaries of the main residence building in the first three major levels of medieval occupation at Tille.

[45] Ibid., Fig. 3.

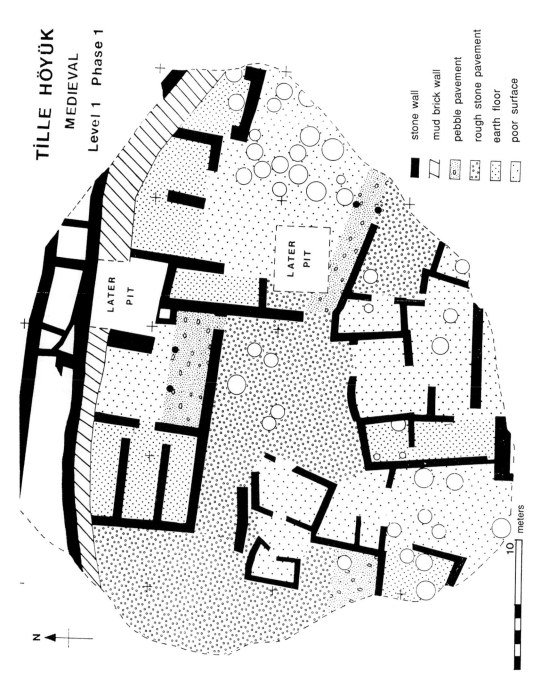

TİLLE HÖYÜK

MEDIEVAL
Level 1 Phase 1

LATER
PIT

LATER
PIT

stone wall
mud brick wall
pebble pavement
rough stone pavement
earth floor
poor surface

N

10 meters

Figure 2:32. Plan of Tille, Level 1, Phase 1 (French, Moore, and Russell, "Excavations at Tille," Fig. 2).

After marvelling at the magnificent palace built by the great Armenian prince Kogh Vasil and also the other splendid buildings (of the town), they departed. . . .[46]

Dédéyan, in a detailed study of Armenian Türkmen relations in the chaotic twelfth century, contrasts the brigandage of the loose feudal order of the Armenian lords of Gerger and their dependents with the *razzias* of Türkmen and apostate Armenian lords across the Euphrates between Gerger and Siverek.

Gogh (sic) Vasil, émule, initialement, des Turcomans pillards, avait terminé sa carrière en seigneur arménien traditionnel, ami du faste et de la culture, modèle de justice, protecteur de l'Église. Les seigneurs de Karkar, quant à eux, ne surent jamais se départir d'une ardeur primitive qui, certes, intimidait les Turcs, mais ne pouvait assurer à leur possessions le minimum d'organisation qui en aurait assuré la pérennité.[47]

The feudal order, here deprecated by Dédéyan for the twelfth century, survived the Turkish conquest of this region in the mid-twelfth century, with the major residential complex rebuilt and reoccupied after two fires well into the thirteenth century.

Horis Kale and Pirot

The site of Horis Kale, located near the confluence of the Euphrates and the Kâhta Çayı upstream from the Karababa basin, contained a large structure within the castle enclosure. This structure was dated by its excavators to the thirteenth century and was thought to have been the residence of a local strongman or military commander.[48] Unfortunately, it is difficult to comment on the spatial organization of Horis Kale, owing to both the lack of published plans as well as the extensive reuse of the Commagenian walls in the medieval period.

Likewise, a paucity of plans makes it difficult to comment on the twelfth-century occupation of the mound of Pirot, located at a river crossing on the right bank of the Euphrates east of Malatya. However, Pirot did share with Gritille, Lidar, Samsat, Tille, and other sites certain basic features: a fortification wall and the use of internal walls of mudbrick on stone footings.[49]

Samsat

At Samsat, we encounter a site of a different order. True, the site of Lidar was much larger than any of the other sites mentioned above, but Samsat was a regional military and administrative center outstripping any of these. The one published plan from medieval levels was the result of a trench cut across the middle of the mound at Samsat by American archaeologists in the 1960s.[50] In it, one can observe a regular disposition of structures laid out off long walls running northwest–southeast and perpendicular to the edges of the citadel mound. The only complex readily distinguishable from this plan was one consisting of a series of rooms centered around a court at the eastern edge of the mound. Although the construction materials were similar to those of Lidar, Gritille, Tille, and other sites, the size of this complex dwarfed all of the buildings found on other sites.

Goell and subsequent Ankara University excavators of Samsat assumed this structure to be the residence of the governor of Samsat, dated to the Artuqid and Ayyubid periods on the basis of the finds recovered within its confines.[51] Turkish archaeologists state that this structure was last repaired in the thirteenth century.[52]

---

[46] Matthew of Edessa, *Armenia and the Crusades*, 242.

[47] Dédéyan, "Razzias 'turcomanes' et contre-razzias arméniennes," 53.

[48] Işık, "Horis Kale Kazıları 1981," 315.

[49] Karaca, "Pirot Höyük 1980 Çalışmaları," 110–111.

[50] Goell, "Samosata Archeological Excavations," Fig. 5.

[51] Redford, "Ayyubid Glass from Samsat, Turkey," 83.

[52] Özgüç, "Sümeysat Definesi," 445. These later excavations also recovered a bathhouse associated with this complex.

CONCLUSION

The medieval levels at Gritille betray a layout consistent with the regional explanation advanced in Chapter 1. The military component of the first phases of this site's medieval history relate it to the defense of the hinterland of Samsat by virtue of its proximity to Lidar and the Euphrates River. Other than these two factors, there was likely little to distinguish it from the other agricultural settlements found by Stein's regional survey. This mixture of state intervention into the lower rungs of the agricultural order and that order itself is expressed in differences in site layout and defensive architecture, but not in building materials and the overall disposition of domestic/residential structures.

III

THE CORPUS OF GRITILLE MEDIEVAL CERAMICS

THE CERAMIC SAMPLE

Ceramics from medieval levels at Gritille were analyzed based on a sample from the West End excavations. The West End was chosen because it represented the largest exposure, the greatest depth and, in places, the complete sequence of medieval occupation levels. Over 3,200 sherds—all glazed sherds and all un-glazed indicator sherds from all West End operations excavated in 1982–1984—were coded. After a review of the West End stratigraphy, over two hundred items were deleted because the potsherds came from unreliable contexts. The final coded sample consisted of 2,984 potsherds.

The ceramic sample is quantified by phase in Table 3:1. "Count" represents the number of sherds in Phases 2 through 8, while "Value"

TABLE 3:1. SHERD COUNT PER PHASE

Phase

Value label	Value	Frequency	Percent	Valid Percent	CUM Percent
	2	86	2.9	2.9	2.9
	3	155	5.2	5.2	8.1
	4	231	7.7	7.7	15.8
	5	1112	37.3	37.3	53.1
	6	650	21.8	21.8	74.9
	7	579	19.4	19.4	94.3
	8	171	5.7	5.7	100.0
	Total	2984	100.0	100.0	

Count	Value	One symbol equals approximately 24.00 occurrences
86	2.00	* * * *
155	3.00	* * * * * *
231	4.00	* * * * * * * * * *
1112	5.00	* *
650	6.00	* *
579	7.00	* *
171	8.00	* * * * * * *

```
I.........I.........I.........I.........I.........I
0        240       480       720       960      1200
```
Histogram Frequency

Valid cases: 2984
Missing cases: 0

TABLE 3:2 GLAZED SHERDS PER PHASE

Phase

Value label	Value	Frequency	Percent	Valid Percent	CUM Percent
	2	9	1.1	1.1	1.1
	3	13	1.6	1.6	2.8
	4	21	2.7	2.7	5.4
	5	296	37.5	37.5	43.0
	6	188	23.8	23.8	66.8
	7	210	26.6	26.6	93.4
	8	52	6.6	6.6	100.0
Total		789	100.0	100.0	

Count	Value	One symbol equals approximately 8.00 occurrences
9	2.00	*
13	3.00	* *
21	4.00	* * *
296	5.00	* *
188	6.00	* *
210	7.00	* *
52	8.00	* * * * * * *

```
    I.........I.........I.........I.........I.........I
    0         80        160       240       320       400
```
Histogram Frequency

Valid cases: 789
Missing cases: 0

names the phases. Given the small exposure of the first occupation phase, it is not surprising that it had the smallest sample: 2.9 percent of the total. Largest by far was Phase 5, with over one-third of the sample (37.3%).

Glazed Ceramics

As stated above, all glazed sherds—body sherds included—were coded and quantified by phase (Table 3:2). The total number of glazed sherds came to 789. Glazed pottery at medieval Gritille consisted of either earthenware or artificial paste bodied ware (*fritware*). At the time of the analysis, it was suspected that some of the coarser frits were not fritware at all; subsequent neutron activation analysis bore this out, finding that some sherds had calcareous clay fabrics. Nevertheless, at the initial stage, all glazed sherds with a body color of tan/buff to white were coded as frit.[1] Noncalcareous clay earthenwares were covered with a range of opacified green, brown, and/or yellow glazes. They were also found with slip-incised designs, a technique known as *sgraffiato*.[2]

Fritwares were covered with clear, turquoise, manganese (a deep purple sometimes verging on brown), and cobalt (dark blue) glazes. In addition, sherds of green and brown luster were found at Gritille. Other techniques of fritware decoration included molding, incision, and applied decoration.

In addition to the glazes listed above, lighter versions of all glazes were used (usually on the inner surface) on vessels of all fabric types. The presence of these lighter glazes may be attributed to their dilution, or to differences in firing temperatures between the inside and the outside of a vessel. All further discussion of glazed ceramics will be undertaken later in this chapter. Representative examples of glazed sherds are illustrated in Figures 3:15 through 3:20.

---

[1] Blackman and Redford, "Calcareous Clay Glazed Ceramics," 32–35.

[2] For a description of the technique of manufacture of sgraffiato, see Mitchell, *Aşvan Kale*, 74–75.

UNGLAZED WARES

Unglazed wares were categorized by shape types, which were also tabulated by phase (Table 3:3). First, a type collection was used to draw up categories of vessel shapes. These categories were based on shared attributes of shape and rim diameter, as well as on frequency of occurrence.

During the course of the excavation, there was a continual intrusion of potsherds from earlier levels into the medieval strata. The presence of, say, Bronze Age pithos rims and Hellenistic fish-plate fragments in medieval levels can be attributed to the digging habits of the medieval inhabitants of Gritille. Those inhabitants had dug many pits into earlier strata, including pits used for storage or refuse disposal, as well as larger pits created by the practice of extracting earth for the manufacture of mudbrick. As a result, excavators of Bronze and Iron Age levels at Gritille provided invaluable advice in distinguishing medieval pottery shapes from those of the premedieval levels. Unglazed sherds that were of uncommon shape or fabric and were also not known to belong to earlier levels were noted and drawn. However, these sherds were not included in the corpus of medieval ceramics unless they were encountered on more than one subsequent occasion.

TABLE 3:3. MORPHOLOGICAL TYPES BY PHASE

Morph	Phase							Morph Total
	2	3	4	5	6	7	8	
Cooking pot	15	18	22	105	70	45	18	293
	1%	1%	1%	5%	3%	2%	1%	13%
Lid	12	15	17	73	29	18	2	166
	1%	1%	1%	3%	1%	1%	0%	8%
Basin	1	8	9	31	22	12		83
	0%	0%	0%	1%	1%	1%		4%
Pithos	3	2	9	14	13	8	1	50
	0%	0%	0%	1%	1%	0%	0%	2%
Jug	6	19	25	128	70	58	23	329
	0%	1%	1%	6%	3%	3%	1%	15%
Bowl		2	2	9	9	14	6	42
		0%	0%	0%	0%	1%	0%	2%
Lamp		1		2	2			5
		0%		0%	0%			0%
Ring base		2	2	36	19	25	1	85
		0%	0%	2%	1%	1%	0%	4%
Other base	20	19	25	89	70	62	29	314
	1%	1%	1%	4%	3%	3%	1%	14%
Handle	22	49	86	335	165	135	35	827
	1%	2%	4%	15%	8%	6%	2%	38%
Phase total	79	135	197	822	469	377	115	2194
	4%	6%	9%	37%	21%	17%	5%	100%

TABLE 3:4. MORPHOLOGICAL TYPES BY AMALGAMATED TEMPER CATEGORIES

	Morph								Total
Temper	Cooking Pot	Lid	Basin	Pithos	Jug	Bowl	Lamp	Handle	
All vegetal	99	105	52	5	10	3	5	69	348
	34%	64%	61%	13%	3%	7%	63%	8%	20%
All nonvegetal	191	58	33	34	317	37	3	747	1420
	66%	36%	39%	87%	97%	92%	38%	92%	80%
Total	290	163	85	39	327	40	8	816	1768
	100%	100%	100%	100%	100%	100%	100%	100%	100%

Shape categories fell into the following order: closed-form, necked vessels; everted-rimmed closed-form vessels squat of profile; large, thickly potted, square-rimmed closed-form vessels; open-form vessels with flat rims; and shallow, open-form vessels. These were considered to be jugs, cooking pots, pithoi or storage jars, basins, and bowls, respectively. In addition, there was a separate category for lids. For purposes of this study, we will use the functional names for these shapes, even though they convey associations that cannot in certain cases be proved definitively.

The categories of the unglazed ceramic corpus are presented in Figures 3:1 through 3:14. Because some sherds were drawn before the coding system was devised, these pieces did not have their temper and other fabric inclusions recorded.

The distribution of shape types by phase (Table 3:3) shows that handles formed the largest type category (38%) across all phases. This statistic led to an attempt to link handles to the morphological categories described below. Of the major shape categories, cooking pot (13%) and jug (15%) were the largest. The bowl category (2%) did not include glazed examples. The other major type categories, pithos (2%) and basin (4%), formed small percentages of the total, as did lid (8%).

DEFINITION OF WARES

In the section that follows, the morphological types set up here will be examined to establish the presence or absence of wares in those types. R. Adams has defined *ware* as "shared paste and preparation criteria,"[3] but the term *ware* will be used here to describe pottery with a coincidence of fabric color, temper, and decoration.

During the processes of excavation, assembling a type collection, and coding, it became clear that certain decorative techniques (such as splash/drip painting) and certain fabric types (orange colored and grit- and sand-tempered bodies, for instance) were common to several type categories, while certain other types had specific characteristics not shared with other morphological categories. For this reason it was decided to investigate temper, fabric color, and decoration in relation to morphological types.

TEMPER

The major morphological types were cross-tabulated by temper (Table 3:4). The thirty-two temper categories in the initial coding were reduced to two: those with vegetal inclusions, and those without. Overall, there was a 4 to 1 preponderance (80% to 20%) of nonvegetal, that is

---

[3] Adams, "Tell Abū Sarīfa," 90. By preparation criteria, we may assume that the method of firing, as well as the technique of manufacturing, is implied. Since all but a handful of the Gritille medieval ceramics were wheel-made, this leaves fabric color as the major "preparation criterion" in Adams's terminology, although decoration will be used as another in this study.

to say, grit- and sand-based tempers over tempers containing vegetal (chaff) inclusions. This ratio was inconsistent within the various morphological types. Three type categories showed a higher than average percentage of nonvegetal to vegetal tempers. Cooking pots, for instance, showed a 2 to 1 ratio of nonvegetal to vegetal tempers (66% to 34%), lids a ratio close to 1 to 2 (36% to 64%), and basins a 2 to 3 ratio (39% to 61%).

The three other major type categories, pithos, jug, and bowl, all showed a lower than average percentage of vegetal tempers: 3 percent for jugs, 7 percent for bowls, and 13 percent for pithoi.

FABRIC COLOR

Munsell soil color charts were not used to determine fabric color for two reasons. First, color accuracy could not be assured under the differing lighting conditions available during coding. Second, we felt it was inaccurate to assign an exact color to a fabric that often ranged in color from core to edge. Because of over- or underfiring, the color of cooking pots, basins, and pithoi often varied considerably from their core

to the area closer to the surface of the vessel. Hence the large percentage in categories such as red-to-brown.

Absolute counts by fabric color were not made because of two limiting factors. Most significant was the extensive leaching of all earthenwares that took place in Phase 5. Of the 213 leached sherds, 142 came from Phase 5 contexts. When a sherd's fabric color could not be determined because of leaching, fabric color was not coded. This leaching can be attributed in part to the high ash content of much of the deposit, both of Phase 5 and of Phases 3 and 4. The other limiting factor was that many sherds in the cooking pot category had been burned, again making color determination uncertain.

The largest fabric color category overall was orange (Table 3:5), representing just over half of the sample. Next was dark brown, with nearly a quarter of the total, followed by red-to-brown with 12 percent and gray-to-black with 10 percent.

Cooking pot sherds had a high percentage at the darker end of the spectrum: two-thirds of this category was dark brown, and one-quarter was gray-to-black. Likewise, lid sherds did not

TABLE 3:5. FABRIC COLOR BY MORPHOLOGICAL TYPE

| Color | Morph | | | | | | | | Total |
	Cooking Pot	Lid	Basin	Pithos	Jug	Bowl	Lamp	Handle	
Cream to tan	1	2	2		4	1		10	20
	0%	1%	2%		1%	2%		1%	1%
Orange	11	26	67	20	269	32	5	452	882
	4%	17%	79%	53%	85%	80%	50%	56%	51%
Red to brown	8	16	10	12	29	6	1	120	202
	3%	11%	12%	32%	9%	15%	10%	15%	12%
Brown	2	78	4	1		1	3	10	99
	1%	52%	5%	3%		2%	30%	1%	6%
Dark brown	197	6	1	3	7			149	363
	67%	4%	1%	8%	2%			19%	21%
Gray to black	74	23	1	2	7		1	59	167
	25%	15%	1%	5%	2%		10%	7%	10%
Total	293	151	85	38	316	40	10	800	1733
	100%	100%	100%	100%	100%	100%	100%	100%	100%

follow the pattern of overall percentages: just over half of all lids were brown, with the rest fairly evenly distributed between gray-to-black (15%), red-to-brown (11%), and orange (17%).

The rest of the profile categories—pithos (85%), basin (91%), jug (94%), and bowl (95%)—fell preponderantly in the orange and red-to-brown range.

SURFACE TREATMENT

Seven techniques were used in various combinations to decorate the surfaces of the unglazed wares at Gritille. These were as follows: (slip)-painted, incised, comb incised, modeled/crimped, stamped, applied, and molded (Table 3:6).

TABLE 3:6. SURFACE TREATMENT BY TYPE

Surface	Cooking Pot	Lid	Basin	Pithos	Jug	Bowl	Handle	Total
Incised	38 24%	9 7%	17 39%	2 6%	4 2%		26 6%	96 9%
Splash/drip-painted	77 48%	17 13%	4 9%	6 18%	50 30%	4 13%	157 35%	315 31%
Red-painted		1 1%	5 11%	12 35%	103 61%	23 74%	244 55%	388 38%
Modeled/crimped	18 11%	87 64%	12 27%	5 15%	7 4%	2 6%		131 13%
Applied	1 1%	1 1%					5 1%	7 1%
Crimped & painted	1 1%	5 4%		2 6%	1 1%			9 1%
Incised & painted	20 13%	3 2%	2 5%	2 6%	1 1%	1 3%	8 2%	37 4%
Incised & applied	2 1%		3 7%		2 1%		6 1%	13 1%
Stamped & painted	1 1%			4 12%				5 0%
Applied & painted					1 1%	1 3%	1 0%	3 0%
Crimped & incised		7 5%						7 1%
Stamped	1 1%	1 2%	1 3%					3 0%
Crimped, incised, crimped & inc., painted	1 1%							1 0%
Crimped & painted		4 3%						4 0%
Total	159 100%	135 100%	44 100%	34 100%	169 100%	31 100%	447 100%	1019 100%

When major type categories were cross-tabulated by broad categories of intentional surface modification, it became clear that (slip) paint was the predominant decorative medium used on the Gritille medieval pottery. Almost three-quarters (69%) of the unglazed diagnostic sherds were slip-painted. The next largest category was modeled/crimped with 13 percent, although 64 percent of that category came from one type category, lids. When the painted category was broken down further into its two major constituent techniques, splash/drip-painted and full-field red-painted, further refinement became evident.

Nearly half of all cooking pots (48%) were splash/drip-painted. The other major categories of surface treatment for cooking pots were incised (24%), incised and painted (13%), and modeled/crimped (11%).

Almost two-thirds of all lids (64%) were modeled/crimped, a term that means simply that the lid edge was pinched to form a band not unlike the edge of a piecrust.

Basin decoration, when present, was varied: a plurality (39%) was incised, and not many examples were either splash/drip-painted (4%) or red-painted (11%).

The sample of pithos indicator sherds, too, was small. Just over one-third of the sample was red-painted (35%), and 15 percent was modeled/crimped, a category that, as was the case with lids, involved modification of the rim. Jugs were 61 percent red-painted, and 30 percent splash/drip-painted. Similarly, bowls were overwhelmingly painted: 74 percent red-painted and 13 percent splash/drip-painted.

From the three cross-tabulations just reviewed, it is possible to recognize distinct ware types. The two most evident were jug and cooking pot. Both had different fabric colors and tempers. On one hand, cooking pot fabric was predominantly dark brown, and over one-third of this type had temper with vegetal inclusions. Jug fabric, on the other hand, was almost exclusively orange in color and mineral in temper. Moreover, despite a common decoration of splash/drip, very few jugs were incised in any fashion, while many cooking pots were; and of the entire sample, only two sherds of the cooking pot category were red-painted (and only in combination with other techniques), by far and away the most common surface treatment of the jug category.

The bowl category shared with the jug category similar percentages of fabric color, temper, and surface treatment, allowing associations of jug and bowl categories in the same ware type.

Pithos sherds are also associated with this same ware category. Like jugs and bowls, pithos sherds had a low percentage of vegetal temper and fabric color almost exclusively in the orange to red/brown range. The surface treatment of this category, too, fit with bowls and jugs: there was a high percentage of red-painted and splash/drip-painted examples, although crimped rims on pithos sherds accounted for a larger percentage of that category than was found with bowls and jugs.

Lids, like cooking pots, formed a ware category distinct from the predominant orange found in the pithos, jug, and bowl types. In the lid category, vegetal temper predominated, as did the brown category of fabric color; by contrast, brown was not represented above 5 percent in any other type category except lamp, which had only three examples. Likewise, its surface treatment was distinct from other types of the ceramic corpus, with red-painted and splash/drip-painted decoration minor compared with plastic treatments such as modeled/crimped (76% in combination with other techniques).

The basin category seems akin to the lid category in certain respects. Like the lid category, it had a high ratio of vegetal to nonvegetal temper—3 to 2. However, unlike the lid category, its fabric color was almost exclusively in the orange and red/brown range. Most basin indicator sherds were undecorated. Only small percentages were splash/drip- or red-painted; the largest category was incised, usually a meander on top of the flat rim of the vessel. As was the case with lids, crimping was employed on edges/rims.

The main obstacle to associating the lid and basin categories is fabric color. It may be that the much smaller, thinner lids were more thoroughly fired than were the larger, thicker basins, thus creating a difference in body color, and we may associate the two in one ware category.

In this manner, three major wares can be isolated from the Gritille medieval ceramic corpus. The first is cooking pot ware, the second is orange ware, associated with the jug, pithos, and bowl types, and the third is a chaff ware associated with lids and basins.

HANDLES AND BASES

Until now, the categories of handle and base have been ignored. It is important to associate these two categories with vessel types because of their representation in the ceramic sample. From Table 3:3 we can see that ring bases numbered 85, or 4 percent of the unglazed sample, while non-ring bases numbered 314, or 14 percent. With 827 examples, detached handles constituted 38 percent of the total.

Two methods were utilized to reunite bases and handles with their type categories. The first, and simplest, consisted in examining pieces retrieved either whole or with handles attached to the rim section of the vessel. These pieces, illustrated in the typology given in this chapter, allowed direct association of handle types with vessel types.

The second method used the wares outlined above to associate handles and bases with types. This task, which will be described below, was aided considerably by the absence of handles from whole type classes of vessels. Bowls were found without handles, as were pithoi. Basins were found only with lugs as handles, easily distinguishable from the more common varieties, which attached near the rim and on the shoulder of the vessel. In sum, we were left with three types—jug, cooking pot, and lid—with which to effect analysis. Almost all jugs and cooking pots had two handles (while lids had one), although the two-handled configuration did not survive very often. Lid handles were very easily distinguishable from vessel handles by virtue of their semicircular shape, so the major issue to be addressed was the difference between cooking pot handles and jug handles.

HANDLE TYPOLOGY

First, a word about handle typology. Because it was recognized early on in our analysis that handles would form a major part of the Gritille ceramic corpus, care was taken to consider such variables as the position of the handle in relation to the rim, and the presence or absence of a thumbstop. If variables such as these were ignored, then it became possible to collapse the forty-four handle categories that evolved during coding into eight major types: round/ovoid (Fig. 3:8E–H), strap (Fig. 3:9E, G), lug (Fig. 3:1A,

G, H), unribbed strap (Fig. 3:12B, E–G), wingtip (Fig. 3:12F), rectangular (Fig. 3:8B, C), and lid (Fig. 3:13).[4] Some of these names derived from the shape of a cross-section of the handle: hence round/ovoid, rectangular, and strap, whose cross-section was long and thin.

HANDLE AND RIM CONFIGURATIONS

From surviving examples that preserved rims and handles together, it was possible to associate the ribbed strap category exclusively with cooking pots and the round/ovoid and rectangular handle categories with jugs. The wingtip handle shape, so named for its flaring edges and elevation above the edge of the vessel rim, was also found exclusively on one type class, cooking pot.

EXAMINATION OF HANDLES USING WARE CRITERIA

These incidental observations were borne out in an examination of the temper, fabric color, and decoration of handles (Table 3:7). The cross-tabulation of temper by handle category shows that round/ovoid and rectangular handle classes had a ratio of mineral to vegetal tempers almost identical to that of the jug category shown in Table 3:4: 96 to 4 percent and 94 to 6 percent compared with 97 to 3 percent. Similarly, though not as closely, lid handles and lug handles recapitulated the ratios of lids and basins. The wingtip handle sample showed a higher percentage of vegetal temper than that of the cooking pot category in Table 3:4, but the sample was restricted. The ribbed strap handle category showed a ratio of vegetal to mineral tempers between that of cooking pots and jugs.

Looking at the same handle categories cross-tabulated by fabric color (Table 3:8), lid and lug handles approximated the percentages of lids and basins. Wingtip and ribbed strap categories were overwhelmingly in the dark brown or gray-to-black range, linking them to cooking pots. Likewise, the round/ovoid type was 94 percent orange or red-to-brown, and the rectangular category was 85 percent or so, linking them to the jug type category. As was the case with temper, the fabric color of the unribbed strap handle lay between that of the jug and cooking pot types, with substantial percentages in both orange and dark brown.

---

[4] As mentioned above, it is the shape of the lid handle that is more distinctive than its cross-section.

TABLE 3:7. AMALGAMATED HANDLE CATEGORIES BY TEMPER

Handle	Temper All Vegetal	All Nonvegetal	Total
Round to ovoid	19 4%	486 96%	505 100%
Ribbed strap	49 28%	128 72%	177 100%
Unribbed strap	24 18%	107 82%	131 100%
Lug	11 65%	6 35%	17 100%
Wingtip	5 50%	5 50%	10 100%
Rectangular	5 6%	82 94%	87 100%
Lid	12 57%	9 43%	21 100%
Total	125 13%	823 87%	948 100%

Table 3:9 is a cross-tabulation of handle categories by surface treatment. The handle types associated above with the jug type—rectangular and round/ovoid—both had overwhelming percentages of either red-painted surfaces or splash/drip painting, 95 percent for round/ovoid, and 88 percent for rectangular. Likewise, unribbed strap was 64 percent red-painted or splash/drip-painted. And, in the ribbed strap handle category, which seemed to be divided between cooking pot and jug in temper and fabric color, so, too, in surface treatment were the results ambivalent. The majority of the sample seemed to belong to cooking pot ware; here only 2 percent of this category is red-painted, for instance. Since the other handle types so clearly belong to the ware types defined earlier in this chapter, we may conclude that this particular category of handle shape was quite simply found in both jug and cooking pot type classes.

BASES

Base sherds proved to be more difficult to classify than the handle type. The difference between the two was striking. First of all, only bowls were found with ring bases. All of the other bases for the other morphological type categories can be described succinctly as "flat."

TABLE 3:8. AMALGAMATED HANDLE CATEGORIES BY FABRIC COLOR

Handle	Color Cream to tan	Orange	Red to brown	Brown	Dark brown	Gray to black	Total
Round to ovoid	9 2%	372 75%	96 19%	9 2%	8 2%	3 1%	497 100%
Ribbed strap		15 9%	4 2%		105 60%	52 30%	176 100%
Unribbed strap	1 1%	38 31%	10 8%	4 3%	60 48%	11 9%	124 100%
Lug		12 71%	4 24%		1 6%		17 100%
Wingtip		1 10%			7 70%	2 20%	10 100%
Rectangular	3 4%	50 60%	21 25%	1 1%	4 5%	4 5%	83 100%
Lid		4 21%	2 11%	9 47%		4 21%	19 100%
Total	13 1%	492 53%	137 15%	23 2%	185 20%	76 8%	926 100%

Variations were slight, consisting of a rounding of the base (the coding category "rounded flat") or a raising of the center of the base (categories "flat raised" and "rounded raised").

Second, decoration often did not reach the base of the vessel, particularly splash/drip painting. Other techniques, such as crimping, incision, and applied decoration, were likewise concentrated on the upper half of the vessel, especially on the shoulder and rim. As a result, many bases belonging to characteristically decorated vessel forms were themselves undecorat-

TABLE 3:9. SURFACE TREATMENT BY HANDLE TYPE

Surface	Round to Ovoid	Ribbed strap	Unribbed strap	Lug	Wingtip	Rectangular	Lid	Total
Incised	11 / 4%	12 / 12%	14 / 21%	2 / 67%	3 / 50%	2 / 4%		44 / 8%
Splash/drip-painted	65 / 22%	62 / 63%	25 / 38%			20 / 40%	2 / 15%	174 / 33%
Red painted	214 / 73%	2 / 2%	17 / 26%			24 / 48%		257 / 48%
Modeled & crimped	1 / 0%			1 / 33%			2 / 15%	4 / 1%
Applied		5 / 5%	1 / 2%				1 / 8%	7 / 1%
Crimped & painted		1 / 1%					1 / 8%	2 / 0%
Incised & painted	1 / 0%	13 / 13%	5 / 8%			1 / 2%		20 / 4%
Incised & applied	2 / 1%	1 / 1%	3 / 5%		3 / 50%	1 / 2%	5 / 38%	15 / 3%
Stamped & painted		1 / 1%						1 / 0%
Applied & painted.						2 / 4%		2 / 0%
Crimped & incised			1 / 2%				1 / 8%	2 / 0%
Stamped							1 / 8%	1 / 0%
Crimped, incised, crimped & inc., painted		1 / 1%						1 / 0%
Total	294 / 100%	98 / 100%	66 / 100%	3 / 100%	6 / 100%	50 / 100%	13 / 100%	530 / 100%

ed. This claim is easily demonstrated by comparing the sample sizes of base sherds tabulated by temper (326 sherds; Tables 3:10) and by fabric color (345 sherds; Table 3:11) with the sample size for base sherds tabulated by surface treatment (116 sherds; Table 3:12).

TEMPER OF BASES

Base type classes (Table 3:10) adhered to ware categories to the same degree as handles. As noted above, ring bases were found only on bowls. This can also be said of flat ring bases, with the exception of one lamp base, whose vegetal temper raised the percentage of this small sample. Otherwise, the two largest categories, rounded flat and flat base types, both had low percentages of vegetal temper, 8 percent and 7 percent respectively, leading to the assumption that they belong to orange ware as defined above.

BASE COLOR

If we check the same base categories in relation to fabric color (Table 3:11), we find higher percentages of dark brown and gray-to-black (28% and 21%), but they are not exceptionally high. By contrast, orange comprised over half,

TABLE 3:10. TEMPER BY BASE

| Base | Temper | | Total |
	All Vegetal	All Nonvegetal	
All ring base	2 9%	20 91%	22 100%
Flat ring base	2 50%	2 50%	4 100%
Rounded flat	14 8%	157 92%	171 100%
Flat	8 7%	107 93%	115 100%
Rounded raised	3 38%	5 63%	8 100%
Flat raised	1 17%	5 83%	6 100%
Total	30 9%	296 91%	326 100%

TABLE 3:11. FABRIC COLOR BY BASE

| Base | Color | | | | | | Total |
	Cream to tan	Orange	Red to brown	Brown	Dark brown	Gray to black	
All ring base	7 16%	30 68%	3 7%	1 2%		3 7%	44 100%
Flat ring base	2 33%	1 17%	1 17%		1 17%	1 17%	6 100%
Rounded flat	4 2%	89 53%	42 25%	6 4%	12 7%	16 9%	169 100%
Flat	1 1%	61 54%	28 25%	1 1%	13 12%	8 7%	112 100%
Rounded raised		3 38%	2 25%	1 13%		2 25%	8 100%
Flat raised		2 33%	2 33%		1 17%	1 17%	6 100%
Total	14 4%	186 54%	78 23%	9 3%	27 8%	31 9%	345 100%

and red-to-brown one-quarter of both categories.

What can be concluded from these results? Because the rounded raised and flat raised base categories were so small (8 and 6 instances), it was not possible to compare their temper or fabric color percentages with those of the larger flat and rounded flat categories. It may be concluded that cooking pot bases (those with higher percentages of vegetal temper and a dark brown or gray-to-black fabric color) were not included in the coded sample to any extent comparable with jug bases. Cooking pot bases were more rounded than jug bases (Fig. 3:11F–H). What cannot be observed is the thinness and friability of the cooking pot ware fabric when compared with that of orange ware. Cooking pot ware tended to fragment into smaller pieces when broken, and the rounded bases, by virtue of their gently curved surfaces, were not preserved in large, recognizable pieces.

SURFACE TREATMENT OF BASES

The sample of bases preserving evidence of decoration was approximately one-third the size of that for the other two categories (Table 3:12). Of this number, 66 percent was red-painted, 28 percent splash/drip-painted. Of the two major base types, rounded flat was 69 percent red-painted, 26 percent splash/drip-painted, while flat was 61 percent red-painted and 36 percent splash/drip-painted. These percentages, too, indicate the survival of jug bases over those of any other type category.

FINAL TALLY OF MORPHOLOGY

When all of the base and handle types corresponding to morphological classes were reassigned, the overall counts of cooking pot and especially jug were enhanced (Tables 3:13, 3:14). Jug sherds weighed in at 55 percent of the total instead of 15 percent before bases and handles

TABLE 3:12. SURFACE TREATMENT BY BASE TYPE

Surface	All ring base	Flat ring base	Rounded flat	Flat	Rounded raised	Flat raised	Total
Incised		1 50%	1 2%				2 2%
Splash/drip-painted			16 26%	16 36%			32 28%
Red-painted	3 75%		43 69%	27 61%	2 67%	1 100%	76 66%
Modeled/crimped		1 50%					1 1%
Crimped & painted			1 2%				1 1%
Incised & painted					1 33%		1 1%
Incised & applied	1 25%						1 1%
Stamped & incised				1 2%			1 1%
Crimped & incised			1 2%				1 1%
Total	4 100%	2 100%	62 100%	44 100%	3 100%	1 100%	116 100%

TABLE 3:13. AMALGAMATED TYPE CATEGORIES PER PHASE

Morphology

Value label	Value	Frequency	Percent	Valid Percent	CUM Percent
Cooking pot	1	505	23.7	23.7	23.7
Lid	2	176	8.3	8.3	32.0
Basin	3	91	4.3	4.3	36.2
Pithos	4	51	2.4	2.4	38.6
Jug	5	1171	55.0	55.0	93.6
Bowl	6	132	6.2	6.2	99.8
Lamp	7	5	.2	.2	100.0
	Total	2131	100.0	100.0	

Count	Value	One symbol equals approximately 24.00 occurrences
505	1.00	* *
176	2.00	* * * * * * *
91	3.00	* * * *
51	4.00	* *
1171	5.00	* *
132	6.00	* * * * * *
5	7.00	

```
I.........I.........I.........I.........I.........I
0        240       480       720       960      1200
              Histogram Frequency
```

Valid cases: 2131
Missing cases: 0

TABLE 3:14. MORPHOLOGICAL TYPES BY PHASE REDUX

Morph	Phase 2	3	4	5	6	7	8	Morph Total
Cooking pot	27	35	48	194	105	74	22	505
	1%	2%	2%	9%	5%	3%	1%	24%
Lid	13	15	19	75	32	20	2	176
	1%	1%	1%	4%	2%	1%	0%	8%
Basin	1	10	9	32	26	13		91
	0%	0%	0%	2%	1%	1%		4%
Pithos	3	2	9	14	13	8	2	51
	0%	0%	0%	1%	1%	0%	0%	2%
Jug	29	67	100	427	248	220	80	1171
	1%	3%	5%	20%	12%	10%	4%	55%
Bowl		4	5	46	28	42	7	132
		0%	0%	2%	1%	2%	0%	6%
Lamp		1		2	2			5
		0%		0%	0%			0%
Phase total	73	134	190	790	454	377	113	2131
	3%	6%	9%	37%	21%	18%	5%	100%

were added, and cooking pot sherds saw an increase in examples from 293 to 505 and a percentage rise from 13 percent to just over 23 percent. Other type categories such as lid, pithos, and basin remained at constant percentages, but bowl, owing to the addition of ring bases, climbed from 2 percent to 6 percent of the total.

THE CERAMIC ASSEMBLAGE AT MEDIEVAL GRITILLE

Standardized ware types at medieval Gritille imply centralized production. For a site the size of Gritille, this production must have occurred outside the settlement, doubtless at the local administrative center of Samsat. Orange ware was used to make jugs, the single largest morphological type, as well as bowls and pithoi. Typical of this ware was orange body fabric, sand and grit temper, and a limited decorative vocabulary of splash/drip and red painting, and some incision.

Cooking pot ware—more thinly potted and made of a dark brown fabric with a higher percentage of temper, including chaff temper—was also splash/drip-painted to a great extent. However, this technique was also combined with incision, modeling, and other techniques more often than in the case of orange ware.

Cooking pot ware defined a discrete morphological type, a trait shared by two smaller ware categories, basin and lid. Basins were further separated from other wares by temper; lids by both temper and fabric color.

The predominance of the closed jug form in the Gritille ceramic assemblage implies a preeminent concern for the transport and storage of liquids. Pithoi, large storage vessels for grain and other stuffs, appear to have been supplemented by the use of mudbrick bins and lined pits for storage.

Cooking pots were used for food preparation and cooking. Most likely they were also used for eating out of, as only a small number of bowls were recovered. Moreover, an analogy for this use of the cooking pot is supplied by the modern Turkish *güveç*, an earthenware pot in which food is baked and from which the food is eaten without recourse to a bowl.

Lids would have been used on all classes of closed forms, but many correspond in size to the rim diameter of cooking pots. As for basins, their size and relative scarcity imply a use only with specialized food or other varieties of preparation not requiring transport. The function of basins would have also been filled by the mudbrick cuvettes and other shallow receptacles built into the floors of various rooms. In this way, the range of activities associated with the most ubiquitous of artifacts, the pot, cannot totally be encompassed; a range of activities can be associated with a vessel type, but certain quasi-architectural features extend the continuum beyond the range of ceramic vessels.[5]

DIACHRONIC ANALYSIS OF THE UNGLAZED WARES

Thus far, in defining ware and morphology types, we have concentrated on attributes shared over time. Let us also look at diachronic variations in the same sample.

BASINS

Tables 3:15 and 3:16 present the distribution of fabric color and temper by phase for the morphological category of basins. As with the simplified version of these charts found above, a constancy of fabric color and temper can be observed for this category. It is possible that the lightness that chaff provided to the body of these large basins was a reason for the high percentage of basins with vegetal inclusions.

Table 3:17, a cross-tabulation of decoration by phase, shows the modeling of a band on the outside of the vessel (20%; Fig. 3:1B, C, J, I) and the incision of a meander on top of the rim (Fig. 3:1D–F, J, I; 32%, together with other techniques) to be the two most prevalent decorative types. The high incidence of this incised meander on both wheel- and handmade vessels, as well as its location on one part of the vessel, the top of the rim and nowhere else, seems to imply a function for this incision beyond the decorative. Such a function can only be hypothesized, but it likely had to do with either grasping or covering these large, shallow vessels, which must have

---

[5] McNicoll, *Taşkun Kale*, 57–60, isolated the activities of storage, food preparation, portage, cooking, eating and drinking, and ablution as primary and matched them with vessel types.

TABLE 3:15. BASIN FABRIC COLOR BY PHASE

Color	Phase						Total
	2	3	4	5	6	7	
Cream to tan		1 10%		1 3%			2 2%
Orange	1 100%	5 50%	11 100%	24 75%	19 73%	10 77%	70 75%
Red to brown		4 40%		5 16%	3 12%	2 15%	14 15%
Brown				1 3%	3 12%		4 4%
Dark brown				1 3%	1 4%		2 2%
Gray to black						1 8%	1 1%

been unwieldy when full. Lugs alone must not have sufficed to hold these vessels. The indentations of the so-called piecrust edge would have served a similar dual function.

Even in handmade examples, the basin shapes did not present a variation. The angle of the vessel wall varied, as did the degree to which the rim was squared. The eccentric example shown in Figure 3:2M has a slightly inverted profile, but conformed in fabric color and temper.

There were more handmade basins than any other vessel type. Of the ten handmade sherds coded from West End contexts, six were basins, three were lamps, and one was a lid. Two of these handmade basin sherds were in Phase 3, one was in Phase 5, and three were in Phase 6. This high concentration (6 of 10) of handmade vessels in one category bears examining. The small percentage of basin sherds that were burnt (12 out of 237 or only 5% of all indicator sherds with signs of burning) demonstrates that, whatever their use, burning or heating had little to do with their normal function. Basins were both large and simple in form and therefore more

subject to breakage and easier to make. Size and simplicity of shape may have motivated in situ manufacture of this vessel type.

Basins (also called *casseroles*) were found in medieval levels at Aşvan Kale and Taşkun Kale in the Keban region north of Gritille, as well as at Tille and Lidar.[6]

PITHOI

Tables 3:18 and 3:19 examine pithos fabric color and temper over time. Again, most notable is the consistency, both of fabric color, in the orange and red-to-brown range, and of temper, with lime, sand, grit, and also mica found in a majority of examples.

When we turn to pithos decoration (Table 3:20), however, a clear-cut chronological indicator presents itself. This indicator is the incidence of rows of stamped decoration on pithos shoulders (Fig. 3:4A–E), represented in Table 3:20 by "Stamped & red-painted" and "Stamped design in rows."

The use of stamps on both glazed and unglazed Islamic ceramics is not unusual, especial-

[6] Mitchell, *Aşvan Kale*, Fig. 95, Nos. 1084–1087; McNicoll, *Taşkun Kale*, Figs. 67–69, 78; Moore, *Tille Höyük 1*, Fig. 43; Hauptmann, "Die Grabungen auf dem Lidar Höyük, 1979," Pl. 162:13. Lale Bulut ("Samsat İslami Devir Sırsız") did not include basins in her study of unglazed ceramics from medieval Samsat, but it is hard to believe that they were not recovered there.

TABLE 3:16. BASIN TEMPER BY PHASE

Temper	Phase 2	3	4	5	6	7	Total
Grit						1 8%	1 1%
Vegetal, mineral				1 3%			1 1%
Vegetal, lime, mineral		3 30%	3 27%	12 38%	13 50%	6 46%	37 40%
Lime, mineral	1 100%	3 30%	3 27%	4 13%	1 4%		12 13%
Vegetal, lime, mica, mineral			2 18%	1 3%			3 3%
Lime, mica, mineral			1 9%	8 25%	6 23%	6 46%	21 23%
Vegetal, lime		3 30%	1 9%	3 9%	3 12%		10 11%
Vegetal, mica, mineral					1 4%		1 1%
Vegetal, mica, lime					1 4%		1 1%
Vegetal, lime, grit			1 9%	1 3%			2 2%
Mica, lime sand				1 3%			1 1%
Grit, sand		1 10%					1 1%
Mica, lime, grit				1 3%			1 1%
Grit, lime, mica, mineral					1 4%		1 1%

ly farther south and east in the Jazīra and Iraq.[7] In the Gritille ceramic corpus, however, stamped decoration was present almost exclusively on pithos shoulders. Exceptions to this generalization were several lids (e.g., Fig. 3:13B) and an unusual type of cooking pot (Figs. 3:10L, 3:12A, all probably belonging to the same vessel). On pithos shoulders, a triangular stamp, resembling either a stylized radiant light or a pawprint, was used most often, but a rosette or

---

[7] See, for example, Sarre and Herzfeld, *Archäologische Reise*, 1:225–226. At Taşkun Kale one stamped pithos was recovered, although the stamp was not similar to those used at Gritille: McNicoll, *Taşkun Kale*, Fig. 49:30. A clay stamp with a design similar to that used on the pithos neck was also recovered: Ibid., Fig. 91:43. See also Moore, *Tille Höyük 1*, Fig. 42:147, 150, for examples from Tille similar to the triangular stamp recovered at Gritille.

TABLE 3:17. BASIN DECORATION BY PHASE

Decorex	Phase 2	3	4	5	6	7	Total
Splash/drip-painted			1 13%	1 7%			2 4%
Incised meander		1 20%	4 50%	6 40%	1 13%		12 27%
Incised reg. spaced lines	1 100%				1 13%		2 4%
Reg. puntations		1 20%			1 13%		2 4%
Red-painted allover				1 7%		4 50%	5 11%
Crimped piecrust band		1 20%	3 38%	1 7%	3 38%	1 13%	9 20%
Splash/drip w/ incised banded meander					1 13%	1 13%	2 4%
Painted line at rim						2 25%	2 4%
Reg. punctations on raised band		2 40%		3 20%	1 13%		6 13%
Crimped piecrust band & incised meander				1 7%			1 2%
Reg. incision, linear pattern				2 13%			2 4%

disc was also found. This distinctive decorative technique begins in Gritille in Phase 5 and continues through Phase 7. It was usually found in conjunction with red-painting of the body, the most common decorative technique (47%, including other techniques) for this vessel type.

The second most common technique was splash/drip painting (e.g., Figs 3:3H; 3:4F), found on 22 percent of the sample. The splash/drip technique was only found on pithos sherds in the latter part of the sequence, from Phases 5 through 7. This observation may be unreliable,

however, for the following reason. Pithos rims were massive relative to body thickness and thus tended to break from the body of the pot fairly close to the rim. As a result, splash/drip slip-painting, unlike full-field red-slip painting which covered the rim, may simply not have been evident in the small sample (5 examples) of pithos sherds from Phases 2, 3, and 4. In addition to splash/drip painting, another common kind of decoration was some sort of surface modification to the exterior of the squared rim of these vessels, such as an incised meander

TABLE 3:18. PITHOS FABRIC COLOR BY PHASE

Color	Phase 2	3	4	5	6	7	8	Total
Orange	2 67%	1 50%	3 38%	9 64%	9 69%	5 63%	2 100%	31 62%
Red to brown	1 33%	1 50%	3 38%	2 14%	2 15%	3 38%		12 24%
Brown					1 8%			1 2%
Dark brown			1 13%	2 14%	1 8%			4 8%
Gray to black			1 13%	1 7%				2 4%

TABLE 3:19. PITHOS TEMPER BY PHASE

Temper	Phase 2	3	4	5	6	7	8	Total
Grit					1 8%	2 25%		3 6%
Vegetal, mineral					1 8%			1 2%
Vegetal, lime, mineral				3 21%	1 8%			4 8%
Lime, mineral	2 67%	1 50%	1 11%	3 21%		2 25%		9 18%
Vegetal, lime, mica, mineral				1 7%		1 13%		2 4%
Lime, mica, mineral	1 33%		7 78%	7 50%	9 69%	3 38%	2 100%	29 57%
Pebble, lime		1 50%	1 11%					2 4%
Lime, grit					1 8%			1 2%

TABLE 3:20. PITHOS DECORATION BY PHASE

Decorex	Phase 2	3	4	5	6	7	8	Total
Splash/drip-painted				2 29%	3 23%	2 22%		7 19%
Banded meanders					1 8%			1 3%
Red-painted all over			1 33%	1 14%	5 38%	4 44%	1 50%	12 33%
Crimped piecrust band			1 33%					1 3%
Splash/drip & reg. punctations				1 14%				1 3%
Painted line at rim						1 11%	1 50%	2 6%
Reg. punctations on raised band		1 100%	1 33%	1 14%	2 15%			5 14%
Stamped design in rows					1 8%			1 3%
Red paint & modeled band				1 14%				1 3%
Reg. incision, linear pattern	1 100%							1 3%
Stamped & red-painted				1 14%	1 8%	2 22%		4 11%

(Fig. 3:3H), regular punctation in a linear pattern (Fig. 3:3A, C), or a scalloped or piecrust band (Fig. 3:3B).

Two unusual vessel shapes were found (Fig. 3:3F, G). As mentioned earlier, pithos sherds constituted a favorite packing material used in the construction of walls, and as such numerous large rim sherds from Bronze and Iron Age contexts were found in medieval levels at Gritille. However, although the shapes of these two vessels were unique, still they conformed to the general fabric color and type of inclusion found in medieval pithos indicator sherds at Gritille. The pithos rim depicted in Figure 3:3F bore a mark incised in three strokes on the inside rim. It was deliberately incised in the wet clay and

may have been either a potter's mark or an indication of the contents of the vessel (although in the latter case, one would expect this mark on the exterior of the vessel).

Three factors account for the small number of pithos sherds recovered from Gritille. The first is simply the size of these vessels. The one pithos that was reconstructed stood well over 60 centimeters high and measured over 40 centimeters at its widest. These were the largest vessels at medieval Gritille.

The second and third factors both concern secondary reuse. Just as medieval period walls were robbed to provide stones for buildings of later eras, and just as pithos sherds were used to pack medieval walls, so too medieval pithos rim

TABLE 3:21. JUG FABRIC COLOR BY PHASE

Color	Phase 2	3	4	5	6	7	8	Total
Cream to tan	2	1	1	8	1	3	4	20
	7%	1%	1%	2%	0%	1%	5%	2%
Orange	13	50	65	265	192	167	61	813
	43%	75%	67%	67%	78%	76%	76%	72%
Red to brown	6	9	26	96	30	28	11	206
	20%	13%	27%	24%	12%	13%	14%	18%
Brown			1	5	9	2		17
			1%	1%	4%	1%		1%
Dark brown	8	5	2	9	6	12	3	45
	27%	7%	2%	2%	2%	5%	4%	4%
Gray to black	1	2	2	14	7	9	1	36
	3%	3%	2%	4%	3%	4%	1%	3%

sherds must have been reused as filler material in later structures, such as those of the "Ottoman Village" to the north of the mound. Moreover, there was some secondary reuse strictly within the medieval period. Often, ovens at Gritille were fashioned of clay into conical shapes. Many of these ovens were rebuilt, so that surviving shells were double- and triple-ringed. Sometimes, however, a pithos would be placed in service as an oven. The base and rim were sheared off, and the pot was planted upside down in the earth. It seems unlikely that a pithos would have been acquired for primary use as an oven, although the possibility cannot be ruled out, since many ovens at Gritille consisted of handmade clay shells. More likely, only after the vessel was somehow damaged would it have been pressed into service as an oven.

Parallels to the storage vessels found at Gritille can be found in the medieval ceramics from Aşvan Kale and Taşkun Kale to the north, as well as from Tille, Lidar, and Samsat.[8]

JUGS

As with the previous expanded tables of fabric color and temper, those for the jug category (Tables 3:21, 3:22) expand upon the homogeneity noted above. As for decoration (Table 3:23), splash/drip painting (24%; Fig. 3:7) and full-field red painting (64%; Fig. 3:8G) predominated. It is possible that many of those indicator sherds preserved only at the painted rim ("painted line at rim" 5%, Fig. 3:5E, F) were splash/drip-painted further down the body of the vessel.

Both of these techniques were found throughout the sequence at Gritille. Although the origins of splash/drip painting cannot be traced, surely the technique does not date, as is often maintained for glazed "splashwares," from the introduction of Tang dynasty Chinese splashwares into the Abbasid empire. Full-field painting of vessels in a heavy, dull, dark red paint, which is sometimes subsequently bur-

---

[8] Mitchell, *Aşvan Kale*, Figs. 95: 1089–93, 105:1289–90, 1293; McNicoll, *Taşkun Kale*, Figs. 45, 80:267–268; Bulut, "Samsat İslami Devir Sırsız," Figs. 89–93. For complete examples, see Redford, "Medieval Ceramics from Samsat," Nos. II, JJ; and Moore, *Tille Höyük 1*, Fig. 47:199. Examples of the stamped decoration found at Gritille were found as well at Lidar (Hauptmann, "Die Grabungen auf dem Lidar Höyük, 1979," Pl. 162:12) and at Tille (ibid., Fig. 42:147, 150), although the latter is not a pithos. The former appears to be, although it is listed as a bowl. A pithos rim was also found at a small medieval settlement (Site 35) downstream and across the river from Samsat: see Wilkinson, *Town and Country in Southeastern Anatolia*, Fig. B.18:17.

TABLE 3:22. TEMPER OF JUG BY PHASE

Temper	Phase 2	3	4	5	6	7	8	Total
Grit					6 2%	1 0%	1 1%	8 1%
3				1 0%	2 1%		1 1%	4 0%
Mica, mineral				2 0%	3 1%	1 0%	1 1%	7 1%
Vegetal, lime, mineral		1 1%	2 2%	10 2%	7 3%	5 2%	2 2%	27 2%
Lime, mineral	15 56%	43 64%	49 50%	125 30%	42 17%	33 15%	11 14%	318 27%
12			1 1%	4 1%	6 2%	3 1%	1 1%	15 1%
Lime, mica, mineral	12 44%	21 31%	42 43%	274 65%	178 72%	164 74%	60 75%	751 65%
16						1 0%		1 0%
17		1 1%	1 1%	2 0%				4 0%
19				1 0%				1 0%
20					1 0%			1 0%
23			1 1%	1 0%				2 0%
24			1 1%					1 0%
Lime, mica			1 1%					1 0%
Grit, lime, mica, mineral		1 1%		3 1%	2 1%	13 6%	3 4%	22 2%

TABLE 3:23. JUG DECORATION BY PHASE

Decorex	Phase 2	3	4	5	6	7	8	Total
Splash/drip-painted	1 25%	2 8%	8 22%	29 16%	31 26%	34 32%	15 44%	120 24%
Incised meander	1 25%		1 3%			1 1%		3 1%
Banded meander(s)		1 4%		1 1%				2 %0
Reg. punctations			1 3%					1 0%
Applied button(s)		1 4%			1 1%			2 0%
Red-painted all over	1 25%	14 54%	23 62%	136 73%	78 67%	62 59%	13 38%	327 64%
Crimped band				1 1%				1 0%
Reg. punctations & splash/drip					1 1%			1 0%
Incised lines & applied buttons			1 3%		1 1%			2 0%
Painted line at rim		1 4%	2 5%	7 4%	4 3%	8 8%	4 12%	26 5%
Reg. punctations on raised band		3 12%	1 3%	6 3%	1 1%			11 2%
Black painted				2 1%			2 6%	4 1%
Red-painted & modeled band				1 1%				1 0%
Incised geometric design	1 25%	4 15%		3 2%				8 2%
Reg. incision, linear pattern				1 1%				1 0%

nished, is easier to assign a pedigree. This technique, along with the carinated shape, is so similar to bowls of the late Hellenistic period that one can propose this technique as a debased local survival of bowl decoration from this era.[9]

There were two basic types of jugs at medieval Gritille, those with rolled rims (Fig. 3:5B, C, E, F) and those with slightly everted rims, usually wedge-shaped, below which was a raised band (Fig. 3:5O–Q, S). Over 60 percent of all full-field red-painted jugs was of the rolled-rim variety, while examples of splash/drip painting were found on every jug type. None of the major jug types was distributed in correspondence to the stratigraphic divisions of the medieval deposit.

Rim diameters of 235 jugs were collected, and no pattern of change over time was discernible. The mean diameter of individual jug types ranged from 9.2 centimeters (45 examples, standard deviation of 2.260) to 10.7 centimeters (11 examples, standard deviation of 1.737). Rolled-rim jugs had diameters between 9 and 10 centimeters, while the everted-rim jugs had slightly larger mean diameters, ranging between 10 and 11 centimeters. The mean jug rim diameters of each phase ranged from just over 9 centimeters (Phase 4; 17 examples, standard deviation of 2.174) to 10.6 centimeters (Phase 3; 12 examples, standard deviation of 1.443).

In addition to these two major types of jug, there were also several small categories of exceptional shapes. Five examples of wavy-rimmed jugs, sometimes modeled into trefoil shapes, were found in the West End pottery (Fig. 3:8B, D). The examples were distributed almost evenly across the stratigraphic sequence: one in Phase 3, one in Phase 5, two in Phase 6, and one in Phase 8. These rim shapes were also found at Samsat and Tille.[10]

Unique jug forms can be seen in Figures 3:5R and 3:6D, while unusual, more squat shapes with rolled rims and short necks are shown in Figure 3:5K, L. The latter were akin to another squat profile vessel type (Figs. 3:5F, G; 3:7B) with the simple everted rim of cooking pots, but without the size, temper, or fabric color.

Gritille jugs were paralleled both in form as well as fabric and decoration by jugs found at other sites in the Karababa basin, Tille, Aşvan Kale, and Taşkun Kale.[11]

COOKING POTS

Confusion of unusual jug sherds with a small, handleless rim sherd of cooking pot ware is possible, because some cooking pots (5%) had orange fabric, and some jugs (4%) dark brown fabric.

More cooking pot sherds were burnt than sherds of any other vessel category, comprising 137 of 237 or 58 percent of all sherds bearing signs of burning. This helps explain the 25 percent of all cooking pot examples (Table 3:24) with a fabric color of gray-to-black.

Otherwise, as discussed above, cooking pots form a separate and distinct ware category from the orange ware (bowls, pithoi, and jugs) that predominated at Gritille. Dark brown was the most common fabric color (67%), a percentage that would no doubt have been higher save for the large number of burnt sherds. The fabric was grittier than that of orange ware, with more inclusions, including a higher percentage of vegetal matter (Table 3:25).

It is when we examine a ware type such as this and find high levels of lime and mica inclusions, levels shared by orange ware, that we are led to question the independent manufacture of these wares. The use of lime as a temper was not

---

[9] Burnishing of these red wares is called "varnishing" by some classical archaeologists. See Waagé, "Hellenistic and Roman Tableware of North Syria," in idem, *Antioch on-the-Orontes*, Vol. 4, Pt. 1:4–6, 25. See also McNicoll, *Taşkun Kale*, 165, Fig. 86:7, 9, 10; Rogers, "Mediaeval Pottery at Apamaea," 264.

Full-field red/brown painting of vessels is found in this region prior to the Hellenistic era in first millennium Iron Age pottery; see Özdoğan, *Lower Euphrates Basin*, Pl. 81:13, 15, for medieval sherds mistaken for this ware.

[10] Moore, *Tille Höyük 1*, Fig. 31:27–29; Bulut, "Samsat İslami Devir Sırsız," Figs. 19–24, 39, 73–77.

[11] Mitchell, *Aşvan Kale*, Figs. 99:1167, 1171, 1175, 1179, 1181; 103:1261, 1263; McNicoll, *Taşkun Kale*, Figs. 51:40–43; 53:58–59; 80:271–276; Hauptmann, "Die Grabungen auf dem Lidar Höyük, 1979," Pl. 159:1, 2; Moore, *Tille Höyük 1*, Figs. 28–32; Bulut, "Samsat İslami Devir Sırsız," Figs. 4–79; Redford, "Medieval Ceramics from Samsat," Nos. F–W; Öney, "Pottery from the Samosata Excavations," Pl. 284; Wilkinson, *Town and Country in Southeastern Anatolia*, Figs. B.25:39–40, B.18:1–3, B.18:21, for Şaşkan Büyüktepe, Site 23, and Site 35, respectively.

TABLE 3:24. COOKING POT FABRIC COLOR BY PHASE

Color	2	3	4	Phase 5	6	7	8	Total
Cream to tan				1 1%				1 0%
Orange	3 11%	1 3%	2 4%	8 4%	7 7%	4 5%		25 5%
Red to brown	1 4%		2 4%	3 2%	4 4%	1 1%		11 2%
Brown				2 1%				2 0%
Dark brown	20 74%	23 66%	33 69%	113 59%	75 71%	54 73%	20 91%	338 67%
Gray to black	3 11%	11 31%	11 23%	66 34%	19 18%	15 20%	2 9%	127 25%

TABLE 3:25. COOKING POT TEMPER BY PHASE

Temper	2	3	4	Phase 5	6	7	8	Total
Grit				1 1%		1 1%		2 0%
Vegetal, mineral				2 1%				2 0%
Mica, mineral					4 4%			4 1%
Vegetal, lime, mineral				4 2%	1 1%	2 3%		7 1%
Lime, mineral	3 11%		1 2%	10 5%	12 12%	4 5%		30 6%
Vegetal, lime, mica, mineral		6 17%	10 21%	69 36%	32 31%	24 32%	6 27%	147 29%
Lime, mica, mineral, sherd					1 1%	2 3%		3 1%
Lime, mica, mineral	24 89%	26 74%	26 54%	76 40%	21 20%	10 14%	9 41%	192 38%
Lime, mineral sherd				2 1%				2 0%
Grit, lime, mica, mineral		3 9%	11 23%	28 15%	32 31%	31 42%	7 32%	112 22%

widespread when compared with sand or grit, and mica certainly must be viewed as an accidental inclusion, in that it possesses no tempering qualities.[12]

In addition to the shared presence of lime and mica in orange and cooking pot ware alike, both wares used splash/drip slip painting as a major form of decoration. Splash/drip alone or together with other decorative techniques accounted for 59 percent of cooking pot decoration (Table 3:26). For these reasons, we can assume a shared production center for both orange ware and cooking pot ware, even though their temper and fabric color ratios were different.

The angle of cooking pot rims varied substantially, as did the degree of wedging and beveling at the rim. Despite the wide range of decorative techniques used on cooking pots, much wider than on any other vessel type, no one technique could be found to predominate at an earlier or later phase. In addition to splash/drip painting, punctation occurred in bands (Fig. 3:10D, M) as well as in more irregular applications to the body of the pot (Fig. 3:9F, G).

Punctation and incision were also commonly found at the top of the handle (Figs. 3:9C, E; 3:12B, E, G), although occasional applied buttons and "snakes" (Figs. 3:9A, F; 3:11B; 3:12C) were also found in the same location. Since the raised thumbstop was uncommon at Gritille, yet the same location at the top of the handle was consistently scored, punctated, or otherwise marked, we can conclude that this texturing of the handle top served a purpose other than decoration. This overlap of decoration and function has also been proposed for the incised meanders found on top of basin rims.

The use of incision on handle tops seems to be a clear case of "functional decoration," the basin rim less clearly so. A different kind of coincidence of utility and decoration, namely, the utility of decoration to the potter rather than to the user of the pot, can be postulated for the predominance of decoration on zones of juncture between separately thrown pieces of the same pot. This is seen most clearly on the shoulder of cooking pots, which were joined to the separately thrown neck and rim. Smoothing marks were easier to conceal when covered not only with a brush dripping with reddish brown paint, but also with a tool or comb quickly incising a pattern on the same area.

Two vessel profiles were found exclusively on one side of the burning and abandonment of the mound that constituted the great stratigraphic divide of the medieval sequence at Gritille. The first and more distinctive was a flat-topped, wedge-shaped, inverted rim type (Fig. 3:12D). This distinctive shape also had a distinctive handle type, the flaring "wingtip" handle. Wingtip handles occurred exclusively on this type of cooking pot. Instances of this profile were found in Phases 6 through 8: five in Phase 6, twelve in Phase 7, and five in Phase 8.

The second type of cooking pot found only subsequent to Phase 4 was one with a wedge-shaped, beveled, everted rim (Fig. 3:12E, G). Thirty of these were found: eight in Phase 5, twelve in Phase 6, seven in Phase 7, and three in Phase 8.

As measured by their rim diameters, the size of cooking pots did not change dramatically over the medieval sequence. The mean diameter ranged from 19.5 centimeters for Phase 2 (14 examples, standard deviation of 3.032 centimeters) to 20.8 centimeters for Phase 7 (40 examples, standard deviation of 3.059).

We did find some unusual rim types (Fig. 3:10 B, F) as well as a unique vessel (Figs. 3:10L, 3:11H, 3:12A, likely all from the same pot). This vessel was unique not only for its stepped rim and relatively high profile, but also for its incised and stamped decoration. It was found in Phase 3.

Cooking pot ware found parallels in form, decoration, and fabric in examples from medieval levels in the Keban region to the north of

---

[12] At Aşvan Kale, mica was found only occasionally, and lime never. At Taşkun Kale, lime (called "white grits" by McNicoll [*Taşkun Kale*]) and mica were found most often in cooking ware, and only occasionally elsewhere.

TABLE 3:26. COOKING POT DECORATION BY PHASE

Decorex	Phase							Total
	2	3	4	5	6	7	8	
Splash/drip-painted	2 20%	13 54%	14 48%	62 59%	29 56%	7 39%	3 60%	130 53%
Incised meander			1 3%	2 2%		1 6%		4 2%
Banded meander(s)				1 1%				1 0%
Incised reg. spaced lines						1 6%		1 0%
Reg. punctations		1 4%	6 21%	9 9%	6 12%	1 6%	1 20%	24 10%
Applied button(s)			1 3%	3 3%	1 2%			5 2%
Applied snake					1 2%			1 0%
Red-painted all over		1 4%				1 6%		2 1%
Crimped piecrust	1 10%	1 4%		3 3%	3 6%			8 3%
Splash/drip & reg. punctations		1 4%	4 14%	7 7%	1 2%			13 5%
Splash/drip with incised banded meander				2 2%				2 1%
Incised lines with applied buttons					3 6%	2 11%		5 2%
Painted line at rim		1 4%		1 1%	2 4%			4 2%
Reg. punctations on raised band		1 4%		3 3%		1 6%		5 2%
Reg. punctations, incised meander & splash/drip				1 1%				1 0%
Reg. incision, linear pattern	7 70%	5 21%	2 7%	11 10%	6 12%	4 22%	1 20%	36 15%
Banded zigzag			1 3%					1 0%

Gritille.[13] In addition, it resembled the cooking ware found closer by at Tille, Lidar, Samsat, and other sites in the Karababa basin.[14]

LIDS

Fabric color and temper of lids were tabulated by phase (Tables 3:27, 3:28). It may be possible to associate the 14 percent of the lid sample having a fabric color of gray-to-black with burning. Some 47 lid sherds, or 20 percent of the entire Gritille sherd corpus, had some marks of burning, likely the result of the cooking process. Many of the burned lid sherds were so completely burned that their fabric color changed too. Thus, the use, and not the manufacture, of these lids contributed to their fabric color as recovered.

A very wide range of decorative techniques appeared on lid surfaces (Table 3:29), more than on any other morphology type. Some are techniques used on jugs and pithoi—such as splash/drip painting and incised bands and meanders, punctation, and bands of regular incision—while others comprise a more random use of incision than seen on other types of pottery (Fig. 3:13A, H). There was also one handmade lid (Fig. 3:14E).

Mean lid diameters ranged from 16.4 centimeters for the flat-topped "no ripple" type (Fig. 3:13A, 23 examples, standard deviation of 3.387), to 18.8 centimeters for the grooved "small ripple" type (Fig. 3:14F, 28 examples, standard deviation of 2.653). The most numerous type by far was the "large ripple" type (Fig. 3:13E, G), in which the grooves were widely spaced and more highly raised. The mean diam-

eter for this type was 16.9 centimeters, with a standard deviation of 2.870 centimeters.

Of all lids, 60 percent were of this "large ripple" type, 20 percent were "small ripple," and 15 percent were flat or "no ripple." The small ripple type, unlike the other two, was found at medieval Gritille only in Phase 5 and subsequent phases.

What were these lids put on top of? The answer to this question has been hinted at in the discussion of burnt lids. Mean cooking pot rim diameters ranged from 19 to 21 centimeters, while lid diameters ranged from 16.4 to 19 centimeters. All cooking pot diameters were measured from the outside of the rim. Because most of these rims were everted, the vessel narrows before it expands to form the body of the pot. Lids must have rested on the pot just inside the rim or, in the case of stepped or grooved rims (Figs. 3:9F, 3:10G, 3:11A), in the groove or protrusion.

Lids, like the other major type categories at Gritille, were similar to lids found at sites in the Karababa basin as well as to the north in the Keban Dam basin.[15]

UNGLAZED BOWLS

Unglazed bowls formed a category noteworthy for its small size and consistency (Tables 3:30–3:32), constituting only 6 percent of the unglazed sample. Almost all (30 of 31) bowls were either orange or red-to-brown, and very few had vegetal inclusions (3 of 31) or lacked lime inclusions (1 of 31). As for decoration, splash/drip painting (Fig. 3:15F, G) and full-field red painting (Fig. 3:15B, H) constituted the alterna-

---

[13] Mitchell, *Aşvan Kale*, Fig. 96:110; McNicoll, *Taşkun Kale*, Fig. 81:280–281; Bakırer, "Medieval Pottery and Baked Clay Objects," Pl. 71 CW-6, -7.

[14] Moore (*Tille Höyük 1*, 71) isolates two types of cooking pots with differing chronological spans; examples of Tille cooking pots are Figs. 35–40. For Samsat, see Bulut, "Samsat İslami Devir Sırsız," Figs. 81–88; and Redford, "Medieval Ceramics from Samsat," Nos. Z, AA–EE. For Lidar, see Hauptmann, "Die Grabungen auf dem Lidar Höyük, 1979," Pls. 159:3, 162:3, 4. For Şaşkan Büyüktepe and other sites surveyed by Wilkinson, see Wilkinson, *Town and Country in Southeastern Anatolia*, Figs. B.25:42, 43, 51, and B.18:4, 5, 6, 10, 13, 18.

[15] McNicoll, *Taşkun Kale*, Figs. 71; 72:197; 73:204, 206, 207, 208–213; 82:291–294; Mitchell, *Aşvan Kale*, Fig. 105:1301, 1302; Bakırer, "Medieval Pottery and Baked Clay Objects," Pl. 72 CW 17; Hauptmann, "Die Grabungen auf dem Lidar Höyük, 1979," Pl. 162:7; Moore, *Tille Höyük 1*, Figs. 44–45; Bulut, "Samsat İslami Devir Sırsız," Figs. 113–123; Redford, "Medieval Ceramics from Samsat," Nos. FF–HH; Wilkinson, *Town and Country in Southeastern Anatolia*, Fig. B.18:15–16 (Site 23).

TABLE 3:27. LID FABRIC COLOR BY PHASE

Color				Phase				Total
	2	3	4	5	6	7	8	
Cream to tan					1	1		2
					4%	6%		1%
Orange	3	3	4	7	3	6	1	27
	23%	21%	21%	10%	12%	33%	50%	17%
Red to brown	3	2	3	2	3	3	1	17
	23%	14%	16%	3%	12%	17%	50%	11%
Brown	3	7	6	51	14	6		87
	23%	50%	32%	74%	54%	33%		54%
Dark brown	1	1	3			1		6
	8%	7%	16%			6%		4%
Gray to black	3	1	3	9	5	1		22
	23%	7%	16%	13%	19%	6%		14%

TABLE 3:28. LID TEMPER BY PHASE

Temper				Phase				Total
	2	3	4	5	6	7	8	
Vegetal, mineral		1		4	1	1		7
		8%		5%	3%	5%		4%
Vegetal, lime, mineral		6	9	40	14	11		80
		46%	47%	53%	42%	58%		46%
Lime, mineral	3	2	8	5	5	2	1	26
	23%	15%	42%	7%	15%	11%	50%	15%
Vegetal, lime, mica, mineral	1	3	1	9	3			17
	8%	23%	5%	12%	9%			10%
Lime, mica, mineral	8		1	11	9	3	1	33
	62%		5%	14%	27%	16%	50%	19%
Vegetal, lime	1	1		5	1	1		9
	8%	8%		7%	3%	5%		5%
Vegetal, mineral mica						1		1
						5%		1%
Vegetal, lime, grit				2				2
				3%				1%

TABLE 3:29. LID DECORATION BY PHASE

| Decorex | Phase | | | | | | | Total |
	2	3	4	5	6	7	8	
Splash/drip-painted		2 22%	1 7%	1 2%	7 27%	5 33%		16 11%
Bamded meander(s)					1 4%			1 1%
Reg. punctations		1 11%		1 2%		2 13%		4 3%
Red-painted all over				1 2%				1 1%
Crimped edge	8 62%	4 44%	9 64%	47 75%	14 54%	7 47%	1 100%	90 64%
Splash/drip, reg. punct & cr. edge		1 11%						1 1%
Splash/drip & reg. punctations			1 7%					1 1%
Incised & applied button(s)				1 2%	3 12%	1 7%		5 4%
Applied button(s)	1 8%			1 2%				2 1%
Reg. punctations on raised band				2 3%				2 1%
Stamped designs in rows				1 2%	1 4%			2 1%
Crimped edge & reg. punctations				2 3%				2 1%
Red paint & crimped band			1 7%					1 1%
Incised geom. design	1 8%			1 2%				2 1%
Reg. incised, linear design	3 23%	1 11%		4 6%				8 6%
Reg. punctations & geom. design				1 2%				1 1%
Reg. incised & crimped edge			1 7%					1 1%
Stamped & incised			1 7%					1 1%

TABLE 3:30. UNGLAZED BOWL FABRIC COLOR BY PHASE

Color	Phase						Total
	3	4	5	6	7	8	
Cream to tan			1 17%				1 3%
Orange	1 100%	1 100%	4 67%	4 100%	13 100%	4 67%	27 87%
Red to brown			1 17%			2 33%	3 10%

TABLE 3:31. UNGLAZED BOWL TEMPER BY PHASE

Temper	Phase						Total
	3	4	5	6	7	8	
Grit					1 8%		1 3%
Vegetal, lime, mineral			1 17%	1 25%	1 8%		3 10%
Lime, mineral			3 50%		4 31%	4 67%	11 35%
Lime, mica, mineral	1 100%		2 33%	3 75%	7 54%	2 33%	15 48%
Lime, mica, sand		1 100%					1 3%

TABLE 3:32. UNGLAZED BOWL DECORATION BY PHASE

Decorex	Phase						Total
	3	4	5	6	7	8	
Splash/drip-painted					4 33%		4 13%
Red-painted all over	1 100%	1 100%	5 100%	5 100%	7 58%	5 83%	24 80%
Painted line at rim					1 8%	1 17%	2 7%

TABLE 3:33. GLAZED EARTHENWARES BY FABRIC COLOR

Decor	Cream to tan	Orange	Color Red to brown	Brown	Dark brown	Total
Turquoise	2 2%					2 2%
Manganese	1 1%	2 2%				3 3%
Opacified green	9 10%	55 64%		1 1%		65 76%
Opacified yellow		1 1%				1 1%
Opacified brown	2 2%	4 5%	2 2%		1 1%	9 10%
Blue green		2 2%				2 2%
Dark brown		3 3%			1 1%	4 5%
Total	14 16%	67 78%	2 2%	1 1%	2 2%	86 100%

tives present in this sample. From other examples, we know that incision on the exterior of the bowl combined with full-field red painting (Fig. 3:15D, E, I) as did occasional burnishing (Fig. 3:15B).

Unglazed bowls were found in small numbers in every medieval phase at Gritille save the earliest (Phase 2). Splash/drip-painted bowls appeared only in Phase 7.

Parallels to the unglazed bowls found at Gritille came from Aşvan Kale, Taşkun Kale, Tille, and other sites in the Karababa basin.[16]

"PILGRIM FLASK" SHERDS

Five sherds of cream/tan, porous fabric ceramic with molded decoration were found in medieval levels at Gritille (Fig. 3:16K, L, M). These are fragments of so-called pilgrim flasks: molded, canteen-shaped vessels with two flat faces and a neck. At Gritille, this kind of ceramic was found only in Phases 7 and 8. In decoration, these pilgrim flask sherds conform to types known from northern Syrian workshops. Examples were also found at Samsat and Lidar.[17]

DIACHRONIC ANALYSIS OF GLAZED CERAMICS

GLAZED EARTHENWARES

All but five glazed indicator sherds of glazed earthenwares were from bowls. Four of these were handles: one each from Phases 2, 4, 5, and 7. One of these handles was frit. The fifth was the finely potted closed form fritware vessel depicted in Figure 3:15L, an import.

An examination of the fabric color of glazed earthenwares (Table 3:33) finds that 78 percent of

---

[16] Mitchell, *Aşvan Kale*, Figs. 93, 94, 101; McNicoll, *Taşkun Kale*, Figs. 62–64; Moore, *Tille Höyük 1*, Fig. 41:120, 121, 124; Bulut, "Samsat İslami Devir Sırsız," Figs. 95–112; Redford, "Medieval Ceramics from Samsat," Nos. KK–OO.

[17] Compare Figure 3:16L, M (this chapter) with Riis and Poulsen, *Hama*, Figs. 881, 1108a, b; see *Anadolu Medeniyetleri*, 54, Fig. D, for an example found at Samsat. See also Bulut, "Samsat İslami Devir Sırsız," Figs. 124–126; Öney, "Pottery from the Samosata Excavations," Pl. 283; Hauptmann, "Die Grabungen auf dem Lidar Höyük, 1979," Pl. 159:4.

TABLE 3:34. GLAZED EARTHENWARES BY PHASE

Decor				Phase				Total
	2	3	4	5	6	7	8	
Turquoise		1		1				2
		1%		1%				2%
Manganese					1		2	3
					1%		2%	3%
Opacified green			1	6	15	37	7	66
			1%	7%	17%	43%	8%	76%
Opacified yellow					1			1
					1%			1%
Opacified brown				4	1	3	1	9
				5%	1%	3%	1%	10%
Blue green				2				2
				2%				2%
Dark brown	3					1		4
	3%					1%		5%
Total	3	1	1	13	18	41	10	87
	3%	1%	1%	15%	21%	47%	11%	100%

these were orange. The homogeneity of glazed earthenwares extends to temper; inclusions were found in only 25 of the 86 sherds in this category. Only one of these had vegetal temper, and all but ten had lime as one of the inclusions.

Opacified green was by far the most common glaze used on glazed earthenwares, constituting over three-quarters of the total. Opacified brown was a distant second at 10 percent. Turquoise and blue-green should be viewed as existing on a continuum; even the brightest turquoise glazed earthenware did not approach the brightness of the turquoise found on frit-bodied ceramics.[18]

The distribution of glazed earthenware by phase (Table 3:34) shows that while there existed examples of glazed earthenwares in the earlier phases of the medieval sequence, it was not until Phase 7, marking the reoccupation of the mound, that this kind of ceramic came into widespread use. Phases 2 through 4 had three, one, and one examples each. Phases 5 and 6 had

15 and 21 percent of the total respectively, it is true, but this number rises to 47 percent in Phase 7. Interestingly, with a single exception found in Phase 4, the two largest glaze types, opacified brown and opacified green, commenced in Phase 5.

Representative shapes of this ware can be found illustrated in Figure 3:16. Typically, the exterior was glazed to a point below the rim (Fig. 3:16A, D), with the slip line still further down the body. Some examples had a carinated form resembling that of the unglazed earthenware bowls found in contemporary, as well as earlier, levels at Gritille (cf. Figs. 3:16B, D, E and 3:15G, H). Certain distinctive rim forms, too, were similar in both glazed earthenware bowls and unglazed bowls (cf. Figs. 3:15C and 3:16C).[19] Other shapes in both categories were most typically hemispherical.

The earthenware bowl with the upturned everted table rim shown in Figure 3:16G was unique. This shape, typical of fritwares, com-

---

[18] Bulut ("Samsat İslami Devir Sırsız," 38), without differentiating between artificial paste and earthenwares, noted the following percentages of monochrome glazed ceramics from medieval levels at Samsat: 60% green, 20% brown, 10% yellow, 5% manganese, and 5% turquoise.

[19] Rogers ("Mediaeval Pottery at Apamaea," 263), noted a similar coincidence of shape between "red ware" and sgraffiato bowls at Apamaea and Balis in Syria.

TABLE 3:35. SGRAFFIATO PER PHASE

Phase Value label	Value	Frequency	Percent	Valid Percent	CUM Percent
	5	4	15.4	15.4	15.4
	6	3	11.5	11.5	26.9
	7	13	50.0	50.0	76.9
	8	6	23.1	23.1	100.0
	Total	26	100.0	100.0	

Count	Value	One symbol equals approximately 0.40 occurrences
4	5.00	* * * * * * * * * *
3	6.00	* * * * * * * *
13	7.00	* *
6	8.00	* * * * * * * * * * * * * * *

```
        I.........I.........I.........I.........I.........I
        0         4         8         12        16        20
```
Histogram Frequency

Valid cases: 26
Missing cases: 0

bined with its manganese glaze, suggests it may have been an imitation of a fritware form. Another striking coincidence appears between a cooking pot form introduced at the same time as glazed earthenwares, and a glazed earthenware bowl shape (cf. Figs. 3:12:D and 3:16F). Both were introduced in Phase 5. This isomorphism seems to reinforce the point advanced earlier that cooking pots were also used as bowls to eat from.

Regarding firing methods, the glaze globules on the top of Figure 3:16A and the exposed clay spur on Figure 3:19I lead us to conclude that these pots were fired stacked upside down, with kiln furniture resting between vessels.[20]

We can attribute the relatively small quantity of earthenwares in Phases 5 and 6 to the spotty habitation of the mound at that time. Despite this paucity, we can surmise that the introduction of glazed earthenwares of a common cuprous green or brown coincided with the post-destruction levels of Phase 5.

Glazed earthenwares were found at all medieval sites in the Karababa basin and elsewhere in the region.[21]

SGRAFFIATO

The diachronic distribution of glazed sgraffiato earthenwares (Table 3:35; Fig. 3:19) reinforces the picture just drawn. The first instance of sgraffiato was encountered in Phase 5, but it is in Phase 7 that this ware was most prevalent: 50 percent of the total was found in that phase. This distribution parallels that of brown and green glazed earthenwares.

Denys Pringle has provided a manual of different styles of sgraffiato prevalent in the medieval eastern Mediterranean and, not surprisingly, the Gritille sgraffiato corresponds to his North Syrian category.[22] Since comparable sgraffiato has been found at sites throughout northern Syria and southeastern Turkey, and evidence for the manufacture of sgraffiato has been uncov-

---

[20] Cf. A. Lane, "Medieval Finds at Al Mina," 46; Bakırer, "Medieval Pottery and Baked Clay Objects," 196; also McNicoll, *Taşkun Kale*, Fig. 29:18; Mitchell, *Aşvan Kale*, Fig. 105:1298a, 1299. For kiln furniture found at Samsat, see Bulut, "Samsat İslami Devir Sırsız," 27, Figs. 166–168. See also Redford, "Medieval Ceramics from Samsat," Nos. WW, XX; and Moore, *Tille Höyük 1*, Fig. 51:301.

[21] Bulut, "Samsat İslami Devir Sırsız," Figs. 191–195, 202; Redford, "Medieval Ceramics from Samsat," Nos. UU, VV, YY, ZZ; Moore, *Tille Höyük 1*, Fig. 49:245–248, Fig. 50; Hauptmann, "Die Grabungen auf dem Lidar Höyük, 1979," Pl. 162:8–10; Wilkinson, *Town and Country in Southeastern Anatolia*, Fig. B.25:45, 48 (Şaşkan Büyüktepe).

[22] Pringle, "Medieval Pottery from Caesarea," 193.

TABLE 3:36. GLAZED FRITWARES/CALCAREOUS CLAY GLAZED EARTHENWARES BY PHASE

Decor	2	3	4	Phase 5	6	7	8	Total
Clear		1	4	16	15	3	1	40
	0%	0%	1%	5%	5%	1%	0%	13%
Cobalt blue				2	1			3
				1%	0%			1%
Turquoise		7	5	73	45	18	2	150
		2%	2%	24%	15%	6%	1%	50%
Manganese	1	2	5	51	25	4	1	89
	0%	1%	2%	17%	8%	1%	0%	30%
Celadon green				1				1
				0%				0%
Clear & cobalt				1				1
				0%				0%
Blue green			2	12				14
			1%	4%				5%
Total	1	10	16	156	86	25	4	298
	0%	3%	5%	52%	29%	8%	1%	100%

ered at Korucutepe and Aşvan Kale, two sites with small medieval settlements, it is time to shed the Port St. Symeon attribution assigned to it many years ago by Arthur Lane. It must be assumed that all cities and most towns manufactured their own sgraffiato and plain glazed earthenwares.[23]

FRITWARES AND CALCAREOUS CLAY GLAZED CERAMICS

Early on in our analysis, we formed a category for ceramics that were thought to have artificial paste bodies (i.e., fritwares). However, subsequent neutron activation analysis of a random sample of what were thought to be fritwares from Gritille revealed that approximately 22 percent actually had bodies of calcareous clay.[24] Since most of the calcareous clay sherds analyzed belonged to distinctive vessel types—

small cups with turquoise or blue-green glaze and beaded rims (see Figs. 3:15J and 3:16N)—it may be assumed that the percentage of calcareous clay vessels among the other "fritware" types discussed below was fairly low. For convenience sake, we will refer to all sherds below as "light-bodied glazed wares."

Table 3:36 is a cross-tabulation of all light-bodied wares with one or two glaze coverings. It excludes lusterware and underglaze painted ware, which will be treated separately. From this table we can see that manganese-glazed light-bodied ware was found in all phases. With the exception of Phase 2, clear-glazed and turquoise-glazed light-bodied ware were also found in all phases. Turquoise-glazed light-bodied ceramics occurred most frequently, constituting 50 percent of the sample. Manganese-glazed ceramics were second with 30 percent.[25] Other light-bodied ceramics—cobalt blue-

---

[23] See Allan, "Incised Wares of Iran and Anatolia," 16, 17, 19, for other sites in northwest Iran and Anatolia producing sgraffiato in the period of the 12th to 13th centuries. For examples of sgraffiato found at Samsat, see *Anadolu Medeniyetleri*, 49, D73, D74; Özgüç, "Sümeysat Definesi," Pl. 20; Redford, "Medieval Ceramics from Samsat," Nos. TT, WW, XX, AAA. For other sites in the Karababa basin, see Hauptmann, "Die Grabungen auf dem Lidar Höyük, 1979," Pl. 160:1; Wilkinson, *Town and Country in Southeastern Anatolia*, Fig. B.18:14 (Site 23). For Tille, see Moore, *Tille Höyük 1*, Figs. 33, 36:82–83, 37, 38, 39. For Harran, see Yardımcı, "Harran-1983," 90.

[24] Blackman and Redford, "Calcareous Clay Glazed Ceramics," 32.

[25] See Mitchell, *Aşvan Kale*, Fig. 43:585, for a manganese-glazed bowl from 11th-century levels (Medieval I) at Aşvan.

TABLE 3:37. UNDERGLAZE PAINTED SHERDS PER PHASE

Phase

Value label	Value	Frequency	Percent	Valid Percent	CUM Percent
	5	3	8.3	8.3	8.3
	6	8	22.2	22.2	30.6
	7	21	58.3	58.3	88.9
	8	4	11.1	11.1	100.0
	Total	36	100.0	100.0	

Count	Value	One symbol equals approximately 0.50 occurrences
3	5.00	* * * * * *
8	6.00	* * * * * * * * * * * * * * * *
21	7.00	* *
4	8.00	* * * * * * * *

```
        I.........I.........I.........I.........I.........I
        0         5        10        15        20        25
```
Histogram Frequency

Valid cases: 36
Missing cases: 0

glazed, clear-glazed with cobalt, blue-green, and a lighter green akin to celadon—also were present in small numbers.

This table demonstrates the constant, if small, presence of glazed light-bodied ceramics in all phases at medieval Gritille. It also shows that a relatively restricted range of glazes was used. This can be correlated to a restricted range of decorative techniques besides glazing. Of the glazed light-bodied ceramics, only four examples were glazed and incised (one each in Phases 5 and 7, two in Phase 8), and only four were glazed and molded (three in Phase 5 and one in Phase 7). These tended to be imported pieces such as the base of a clear-glazed Iranian vessel with an imitation of Chinese *an hua* decoration (Fig. 3:20E). Another piece (Fig. 3:15W) resembles Syrian imitations of this same ware.[26]

Unfortunately, the number of vessel profiles retrieved was too slight to allow for generalization on the basis of phase. However, one can note the presence of many profiles, from those seemingly echoing the profiles of earthenware bowls and their squared and beaded rims (Fig.

3:15S, X, Y) to those with shallower, straighter profiles and everted table rims (Figs. 3:15K, T, U; 3:17) closer to Syrian and Iranian fritwares.

In addition to all excavated sites in the Karababa basin, fritware was recovered from surface collection at the site of Şaşkan Büyüktepe.[27]

UNDERGLAZE PAINTED BLACK AND BLUE FRITWARE

Like sgraffiato and glazed earthenware, underglaze painted fritware was found only in Phase 5 and later phases at medieval Gritille (Table 3:37). Like these wares, too, it was found predominantly in Phase 7: 58 percent of all underglaze painted sherds were found in loci belonging to that phase.

This technique, in which the design was painted on the body of the vessel before the glaze was applied, was found infrequently at Gritille. Examples were black painted under turquoise glaze, black painted under clear glaze, and black and cobalt blue painted under clear glaze.[28]

---

[26] Pringle, "Medieval Pottery from Caesarea," 193.

[27] Wilkinson, *Town and Country in Southeastern Anatolia*, Fig. B.25:44, 47.

[28] Riis and Poulsen, *Hama*, date the beginning of manufacture of this type of fritware in Syria to the early 13th century. For examples found at Samsat, see *Anadolu Medeniyetleri*, 48, D 74; Redford, "Medieval Ceramics from Samsat," Nos. RR, SS; Özgüç, "Sümeysat Definesi," Pls. 16–19; Öney, "Pottery from the Samosata Excavations," Pls. 281, 282. For Lidar, see Hauptmann, "Die Grabungen auf dem Lidar Höyük, 1979," Pl. 160:2. For Tille, see Moore, *Tille Höyük 1*, Figs. 52, 53. For Harran, see Yardımcı, "1985 Harran Kazı ve Restorasyon Çalışmaları," 1:290–291, Figs. 13, 14.

TABLE 3:38. LUSTERWARE BY PHASE

Decor	Phase 2	3	4	5	6	7	8	Total
Green luster on white	1 1%			25 22%	10 9%	5 4%	1 1%	42 37%
Brown luster on white				3 3%	2 2%			5 4%
Green luster on manganese	1 1%	1 1%	1 1%	16 14%	12 11%	5 4%		36 32%
Ruby luster on turquoise				2 2%				2 2%
Green luster on turquoise				20 18%	4 4%	3 3%	1 1%	28 25%
Total	2 2%	1 1%	1 1%	66 58%	28 25%	13 12%	2 2%	113 100%

LUSTER

The term *luster* refers to a type of glazed ceramic (in this case fritware) painted with a metallic oxide that is affixed to the glaze by a second or third firing in a reduction kiln. The result of this firing is a design with a lustrous metallic sheen. In the Gritille sample, this technique was most often used as the sole means of decoration, although it was occasionally found combined with other techniques such as underglaze painting (Fig. 3:19B).[29]

The primary color of luster found at Gritille was called green although the actual color varied from a green tinged with yellow to a greenish gold color, depending on the preservation and the firing of the piece. Likewise, brown luster ranged in color from a dull, darkish brown to brownish gold.

Green luster accounted for all but 6 percent of the lusterware found at Gritille (Table 3:38). Green luster on a clear glaze accounted for 37 percent of the total, while green luster on manganese glaze was second with 32 percent. (Examples of these decorative types can be found in

Figs. 3:17 and 3:18.) Despite the closeness of the percentages, the distribution of these two most frequent types of lusterware was very different. With one exception found in Phase 2, all of the green luster on a clear glaze (as well as all of the green luster on a turquoise glaze, a category comprising 25% of the total) was found in Phase 5 and later. Green luster on manganese, by contrast, was found in all phases except the final one. This distribution paralleled that of plain manganese light-bodied ceramics observed in Table 3:36.

Noting a similarity between the profiles of lustered and unlustered manganese bowls, excavators proposed a local source of production for this fritware. A local source is possible as well for green-lustered clear-glazed fritwares. Although clear-glazed fritwares were found in every phase save Phase 2 (Table 3:36), the overwhelming majority of green luster on clear glaze sherds was found in the later phases of the sequence.

Lusterware was found at all excavated medieval sites in the Karababa basin and elsewhere in the vicinity.[30]

---

[29] This technique was also found at Tille. See Moore, *Tille Höyük 1*, 73, although luster is described as an underglaze technique, too.

[30] Öney, "Pottery from the Samosata Excavations," Pls. 278–279; idem, "1978–79 Yılı Samsat," Pls. 2, 3; Redford, "Medieval Ceramics from Samsat," Nos. PP, QQ, CCC; Moore, *Tille Höyük 1*, 72–73, Pl. 7; Hauptmann, "Die Grabungen auf dem Lidar Höyük, 1979," 262; N. Yardımcı, "1985 Harran Kazı ve Restorasyon Çalışmaları," 294.

DISCUSSION OF GLAZED WARES

Certainly, the settlement at Gritille in Phases 7 and 8 had at its disposal a wider range of glazed ceramics than did earlier settlements at the site. Monochrome glazed and sgraffiato wares were found together with green-on-white and green-on-manganese lusterware, monochrome glazed fritware, monochrome glazed calcareous clay earthenwares, as well as underglaze painted bowls. F. Waagé noted the coexistence of glazed fritwares and earthenwares at medieval Antioch, but there the longer sequence in the thirteenth century led to "the supersession of the types with opaque glaze on argillaceous body by those with colorless glaze on sandy body."[31] Nevertheless, he noted the continued popularity of green glazed earthenwares.

At Gritille, we can note the continued use of earthenware glazed in strong greens, browns, and yellows in the pottery from smaller outlying settlements that postdate Gritille in the medieval period, and few if any frit or calcareous clay examples.[32] This trend applied also at the late thirteenth- and early fourteenth-century levels at Aşvan Kale, Taşkun Kale, and Korucutepe, where sgraffiato and other earthenwares were by far and away the most frequently encountered glazed wares. In fact, as noted above, glazed earthenwares were manufactured at two of these three sites, as well as at Antioch and its port, al-Mina.[33] In an earlier medieval level of Aşvan, however, only one sgraffiato sherd was found.

Present in both early and late medieval levels at Aşvan were sherds of small vessels with a particulate yellowish body covered with blue or manganese glaze. This vessel type was also recovered at Tille and Samsat.[34] Although some bear different decoration, similarity in size, glaze, and shape link these with Gritille examples found to have calcareous clay bodies.[35] The continued exploitation of calcareous clays for ceramic production in the thirteenth century is evidence of continuity in glazed ceramic production concurrent with the explosion of artificial paste bodied ceramics in the later twelfth and thirteenth centuries throughout the Near East. In this border region, calcareous clay vessels seem to have been restricted to these small cups. However, they appear to have been produced as part of a continuum of glazed ceramic production that used the same white clays for these as well as artificial paste bodied ceramics.[36]

Ankara University excavations uncovered evidence of glazed pottery production at Samsat.[37] Only full publication of the wasters, kiln furniture, and other finds, however, will tell us if this included fritware and lusterware production.

Instrumental neutron activation analysis of 131 sherds of fritware from medieval levels at Gritille complicated a simple model of regional production of certain vessel types and decorative techniques coexisting with rare, finely potted, and decorated imported wares.[38] This sample produced nine different groups as determined by chemical analysis. The harder, whiter fabrics were found most often in three groups, the softer, more yellowish fabrics in three others, including the largest groups. Despite this general division, there was no restriction of one glaze color, decorative technique, or vessel shape to any one chemical group, nor was there a strong chronological grouping of any one group. This strongly suggests that multiple workshops were in operation over the length of the medieval sequence at Gritille, rather than that different sources of raw materials were exploited by one

---

[31] Waagé, *Antioch on-the-Orontes*, 103.

[32] See Chapter 7, this volume, for Gil Stein's presentation of this material.

[33] A. Lane, "Medieval Finds at Al Mina," 45–46; Waagé, "The Glazed Pottery," in idem, *Antioch-on-the-Orontes*, Vol. 4, Pt. 1:101, Fig. 92. In addition to kiln furniture and wasters found at Antioch, Waagé identified a certain type of sgraffiato as "local Antiochene ware."

[34] Bulut, "Samsat İslami Devir Sırsız," Figs. 205–207; Moore, *Tille Höyük 1*, Fig. 49:220–242.

[35] See Blackman and Redford, "Calcareous Clay Glazed Ceramics," Fig. 1.

[36] See Redford and Blackman, "Luster and Fritware Production," Fig. 11 and its discussion.

[37] Bulut, "Samsat İslami Devir Sırsız," 285: "In the excavations, in the Seljuk-Artuqid and Ayyubid levels, in the same place where pottery was recovered, the retrieval of kilns, basins (*havuzlar*) for ceramics, refuse pits, kiln furniture tripods, pieces stuck together as the result of manufacturing mistakes, and half-finished decorated but unglazed pieces indicate the presence of regional pottery production at Samsat."

[38] Redford and Blackman, "Luster and Fritware Production," passim.

workshop over time. One or more of these ceramic workshops must have been in Samsat, but it is obvious that Samsat was not the only fritware production center in the border regions between northern Syria and southeastern Anatolia. As with sgraffiato and other glazed earthenwares, fritwares, including those decorated with the relatively more expensive and technically sophisticated techniques of luster and underglaze painting, must have been produced in other towns of the region and farther south in northern Syria.

General conclusions based on the ceramic evidence are reached in Chapter 8.

POTTERY CATALOG

BASINS (FIGURES 3:1–3:2)

FIGURE 3:1. BASINS.

A. GT 16067. Orange fabric; chaff, lime, sand, and mica inclusions. Handmade. Diameter 36 cm.

B. GT 15599. Red/brown fabric; chaff, sand, and lime inclusions. Handmade. Tool-incised decoration on exterior. Irregular diameter, approximately 45 cm.

C. GT 17053. Leached orange fabric; chaff, sand, lime, and mica inclusions. Exterior: gouged and molded bands. Interior surface smoothed. Diameter 43 cm.

D. GT 8085. Orange fabric; mica, sand, and lime inclusions. Incised meander at top of rim. Diameter 41 cm.

E. GT 17111. Brown fabric; pebble, chaff inclusions. Handmade. Finger indentations, tool marks on interior and exterior. Incised meander on top of rim. Diameter 36 cm.

F. GT 17833. Leached fabric; sand, lime, and mica inclusions. Incised meander on top of rim. Diameter 50 cm.

G. GT 17683. Brown fabric; sand and mica inclusions. Exterior and small area of interior red slip-painted. Incised line on exterior just below rim. Diameter 34 cm.

H. GT 3030. Brown fabric; mica, sand, and lime inclusions. Diameter 33 cm.

I. GT 17096. Orange fabric. Faded traces of splash/drip painting on interior and exterior (not shown). Exterior has two modeled bands. Incised meander on top of rim.

J. GT 16288. Orange fabric; lime, sand, and mica inclusions. Incised meanders on exterior and top of rim.

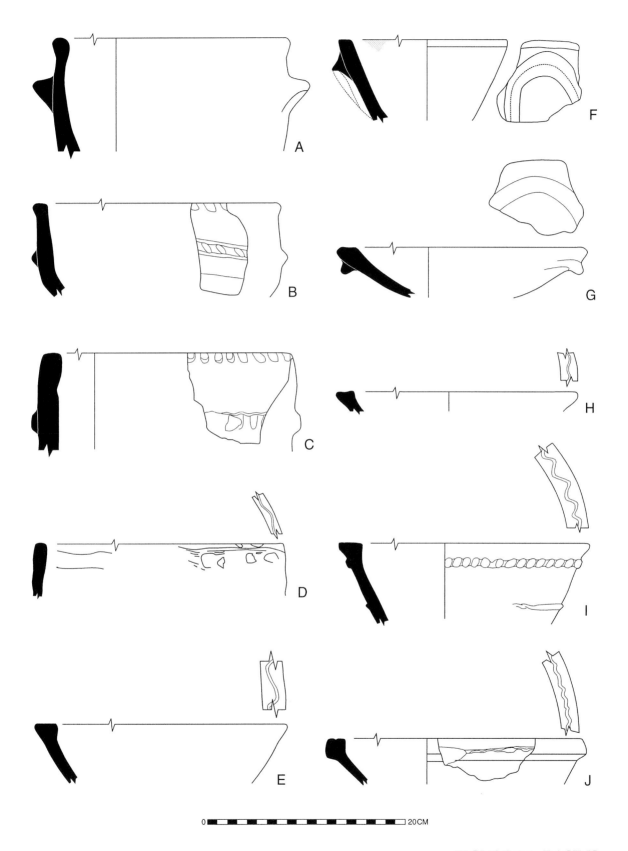

FIGURE 3:1. BASINS

FIGURE 3:2. BASINS.

A. GT 18592. Orange fabric; lime, grit, and sand inclusions. Exterior burnt; punctations on lug. Diameter 34 cm.

B. GT 15599. Orange fabric; chaff inclusions. Interior splash/drip-painted. Diameter 47 cm.

C. GT 15560. Red/brown fabric; grit and mica inclusions. Diameter 48 cm.

D. GT 15316. Orange fabric; grit, lime, mica, and sand inclusions. Red-painted line at rim. Diameter 38 cm.

E. GT 17442. Red/brown fabric; lime, sand, and mica inclusions. Incised lines on exterior.

F. GT 18578. Red/brown fabric; grit, lime, mica, and sand inclusions. Incised line on exterior. Diameter 44 cm.

G. GT 16091. Red/brown fabric; mica, sand, and lime inclusions. Incised lines on exterior. Diameter 48 cm.

H. GT 7105. Orange fabric; sand, mica, and lime inclusions. Diameter 44 cm.

I. GT 16070. Brown fabric; grit and chaff inclusions. Handmade. Diameter 33 cm.

J. GT 16709. Orange fabric. Diameter 32 cm.

K. GT 1449. Red/brown fabric; chaff, gravel, and lime inclusions. Handmade. Burnt exterior. Lime flecks stuck to interior; interior also bears scraping striations.

L. GT 17824. Leached and burnt fabric; chaff, mica, sand, and lime inclusions. Handmade. Diameter 38 cm.

M. GT 16100. Brown fabric; grit and chaff inclusions. Diameter 32 cm.

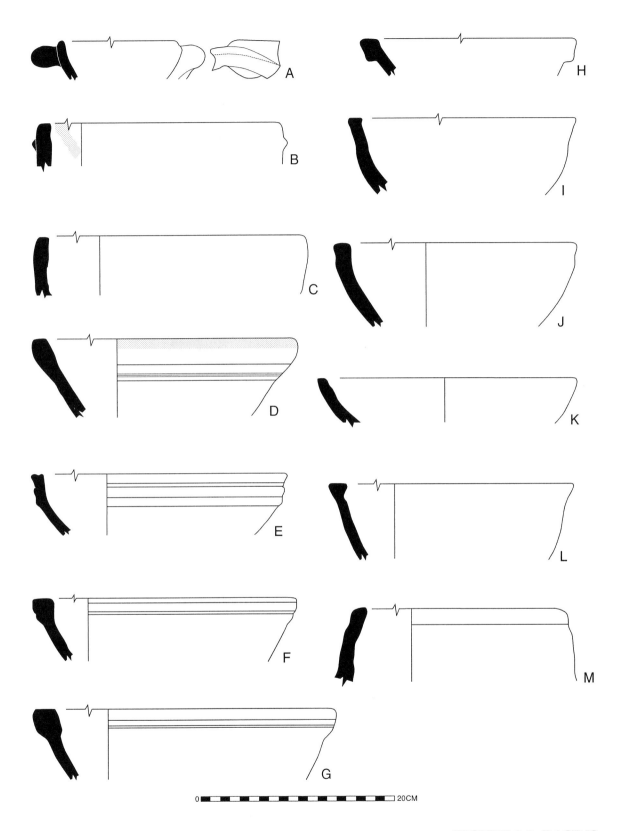

FIGURE 3:2. BASINS

PITHOI (FIGURES 3:3–3:4)

FIGURE 3:3. PITHOI.

A. GT 17058. Red/brown fabric; sand and lime inclusions. Impressed band on exterior.

B. GT 18816. Orange fabric; lime, mica, grit, and sand inclusions. Modeled and cloth-impressed band on exterior.

C. GT 19223. Red/brown fabric; pebble, sand, gravel, and lime inclusions. Impressed scalloped bands on exterior.

D. GT 18667. Red/brown fabric; lime, sand, and mica inclusions. Red slip-painted interior and exterior.

E. GT 17313. Orange fabric; mica, sand, and lime inclusions. Incised lines on exterior.

F. GT 3115. Orange fabric; mica, sand, and lime inclusions. Incised marks on interior. Rim thrown separately, attached to body at thickened spot on shoulder. Exterior shows rough tooling marks. Diameter 42–44 cm.

G. GT 16930. Orange fabric with tan core; sand and mica inclusions. Diameter 27 cm.

H. GT 17098. Orange fabric; grit, sand, and lime inclusions. Exterior: modeled and incised meander band, splash/drip painting.

I. GT 17715. Orange fabric; lime, sand, and mica inclusions. Impressed band on exterior.

J. GT 16747. Orange fabric; mica, sand, and lime inclusions. Exterior red slip-painted and incised with line and meander.

K. GT 1449. Red/brown fabric; sand and mica inclusions. Exterior red slip-painted and burnished.

L. GT 16718. Orange fabric; sand and lime inclusions. Diameter 38 cm.

M. GT 2316. Brown fabric; lime, sand, and grit inclusions. Diameter 34 cm.

N. GT 18066. Red/brown fabric; mica, lime, and sand inclusions. Red slip-painted exterior; interior rim red slip-painted.

O. GT 16699. Orange fabric with black core; sand and mica inclusions.

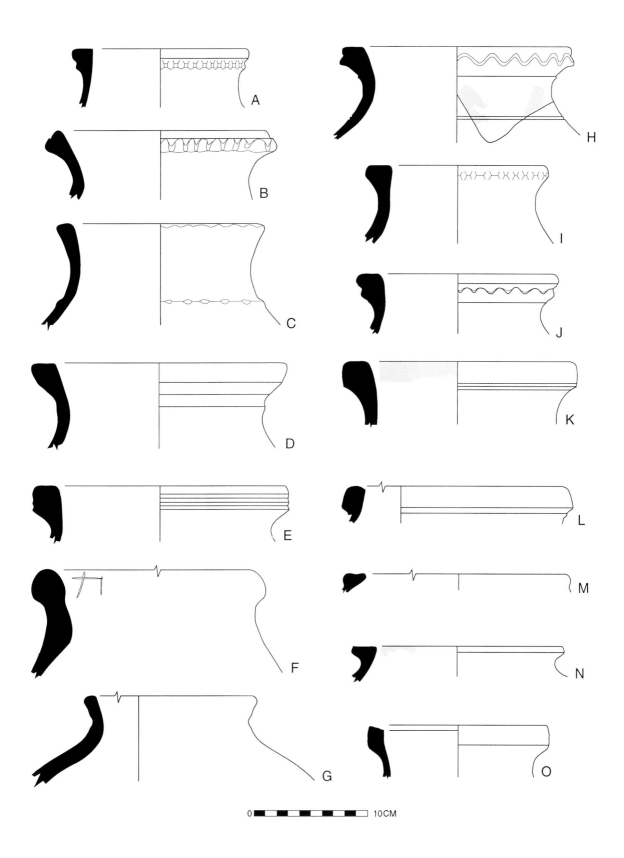

FIGURE 3:3. PITHOI

FIGURE 3:4. PITHOI.

A. GT 16070. Orange fabric; mineral inclusions. Exterior: rows of stamped decoration under red slip paint.

B. GT 16091. Orange fabric; mineral inclusions. Exterior: rows of stamped decoration under red slip paint.

C. GT 1977. Orange fabric; sand and lime inclusions. Exterior: rows of stamped decoration.

D. GT 5065. Orange fabric; lime, sand, and mica inclusions. Exterior: rows of stamped decoration under full-field burnished red slip painting.

E. GT 18698. Orange fabric; lime and sand inclusions. Exterior: rows of stamped decoration under red slip paint.

F. GT 22385. Orange fabric; mineral inclusions. Incised banded meander and splash/drip red-painted decoration.

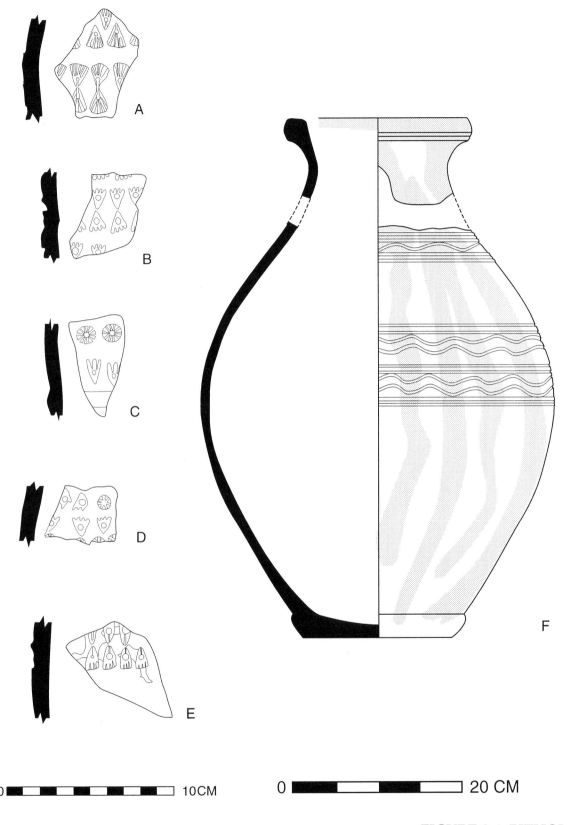

FIGURE 3:4. PITHOI

0 ▪▪▪▪▪▪ 10CM

0 ▪▪▪▪▪▪ 20 CM

JUGS (FIGURES 3:5–3:8)

FIGURE 3:5. JUGS.

A. GT 16093. Red-to-brown fabric; grit and sand inclusions. Incised line on exterior.

B. GT 16090. Orange fabric; mica, sand, and lime inclusions.

C. GT 1303. Orange fabric; mica, sand, and lime inclusions.

D. GT 18969. Brown fabric; sand, lime, and mica inclusions. Red-painted line at rim on exterior.

E. GT 691. Orange fabric; sand and lime inclusions. Red-painted at rim interior and exterior.

F. GT 2336. Orange fabric; sand, lime, and mica inclusions. Red-painted at rim exterior.

G. GT 16100. Orange fabric; sand inclusions. Red-painted exterior and interior as indicated.

H. GT 16091. Orange red fabric; mineral inclusions.

I. GT 16757. Orange fabric; sand and lime inclusions. Splash/drip-painted on exterior.

J. GT 18698. Light brown fabric; mineral inclusions. Exterior and interior: red paint at rim.

K. GT 18057. Cream-to-tan fabric.

L. GT 1041. Orange fabric; mica and lime inclusions.

M. GT 18698. Orange fabric; mica, sand, and lime inclusions. Exterior splash/drip-painted.

N. GT 1260. Orange fabric; sand inclusions. Splash/drip-painted on exterior.

O. GT 18065. Orange fabric; sand, lime, and mica inclusions.

P. GT 17054. Orange fabric; sand, lime, and mica inclusions. Incised line on exterior.

Q. GT 16718. Orange fabric; mica, sand, and lime inclusions.

R. GT 7184. Orange fabric; mica and lime inclusions.

S. GT 17840. Orange fabric; lime and sand inclusions.

T. GT 18860 + 18534. Leached fabric; sand and mica inclusions. Incised lines on exterior; handle imprint.

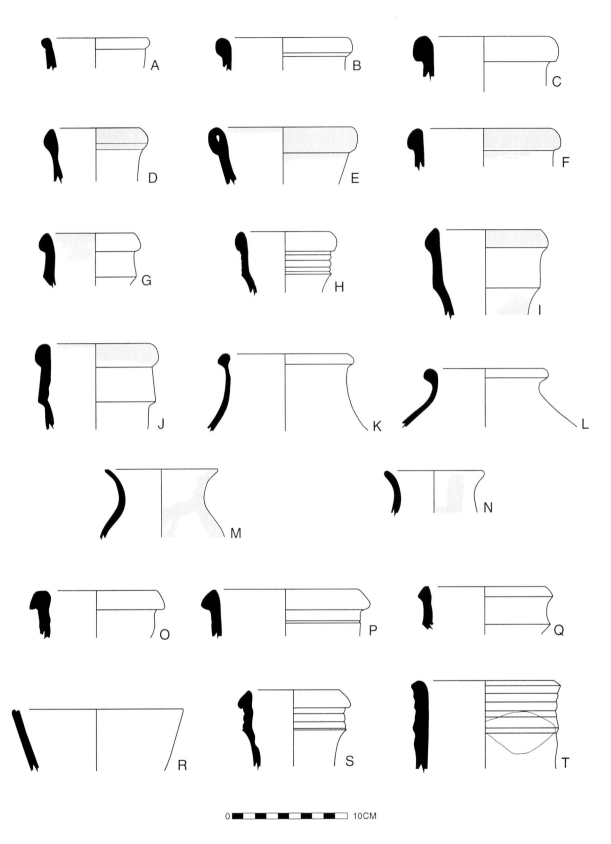

FIGURE 3:5. JUGS

FIGURE 3:6. JUGS.

A. GT 15953. Leached fabric; lime, mica, and sand inclusions.

B. GT 17740. Leached fabric; lime, mica, and sand inclusions.

C. GT 17094. Leached fabric; lime and sand inclusions.

D. GT 15978. Orange fabric.

E. GT 14596. Orange fabric; lime, mica, and sand inclusions.

F. GT 548. Orange fabric. Splash/drip-painted on exterior.

G. GT 15978. Orange fabric; mica, lime, and sand inclusions. Incised band on exterior.

H. GT 17053. Leached orange fabric; grit, sand, lime, and chaff inclusions.

I. GT 17436. Orange fabric; lime and sand temper. Punctated band on exterior.

J. GT 18858. Leached fabric; sand and lime inclusions. Rope-impressed band on exterior.

K. GT 18543. Brown fabric; mica, lime, and sand inclusions. Tool-impressed band on exterior.

L. GT 15585. Leached brown fabric; grit, chaff, mica, and sand inclusions. Irregular impressed band on exterior.

M. GT 16911. Orange fabric; lime, mica, and sand inclusions. Splash/drip-painted on exterior.

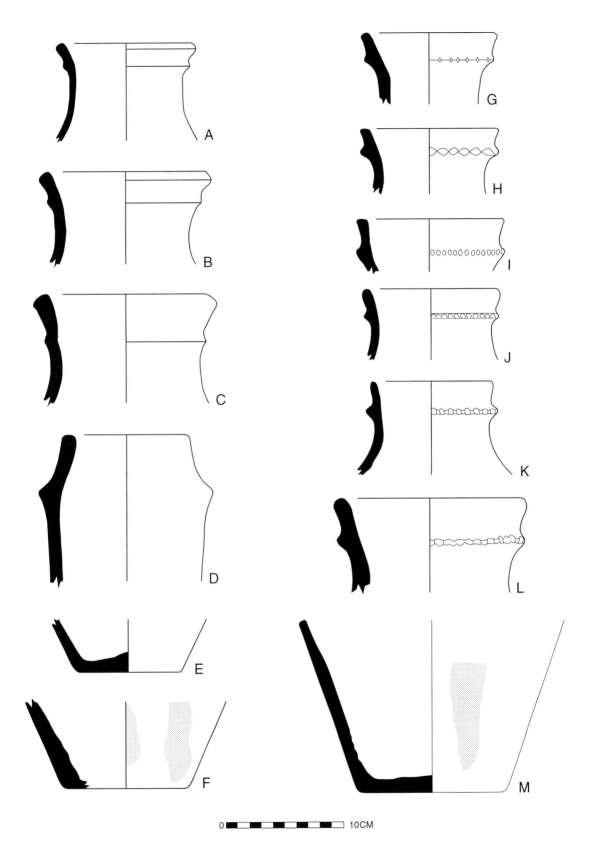

FIGURE 3:6. JUGS

FIGURE 3:7. JUGS.

A. GT 15898. Orange fabric; mineral inclusions. Exterior splash/drip brown-painted. Burnt.

B. GT 5518. Orange fabric; mineral inclusions.

C. GT 16097. Orange fabric. Splash/drip-painted on interior and exterior.

D. GT 15174. Orange fabric; mineral inclusions. Exterior splash/drip brown-painted, incisions on top of handle.

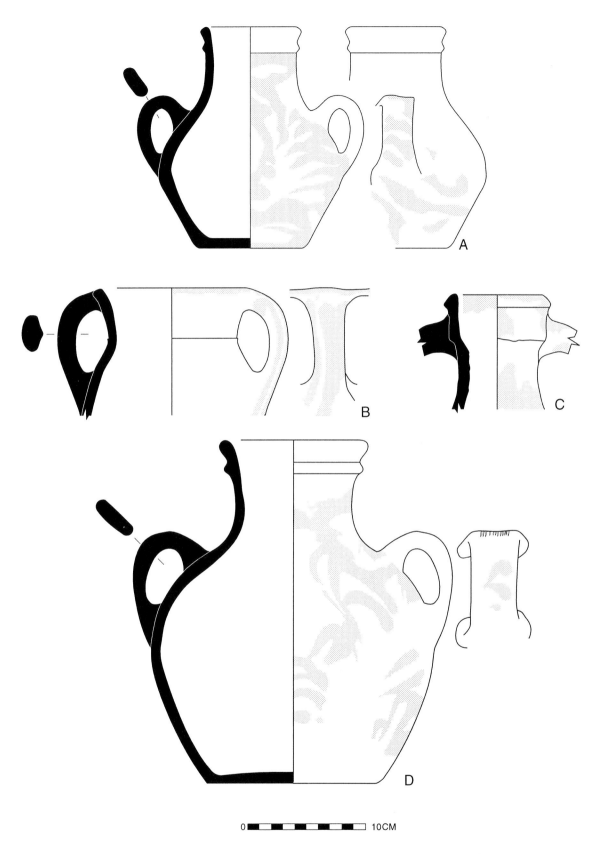

FIGURE 3:7. JUGS

FIGURE 3:8. JUGS.

A. GT 5544. Orange fabric; mineral inclusions. Exterior red splash/drip-painted.

B. GT 18591. Orange fabric; mineral inclusions. Exterior: leached splash/drip-painted (not shown). Pinched spout with applied pieces over rim.

C. GT 236. Orange fabric; mineral inclusions. Exterior: applied band with impressed decoration. Handle tool-incised.

D. GT 15166. Dark brown fabric; sand and mica inclusions. Part of double-chambered pinched spout. Applied clay strap between chambers.

E. GT 4264. Orange fabric; mineral inclusions.

F. GT 651. Orange fabric; mineral inclusions. Exterior full-field red slip-painted.

G. GT 19852. Orange fabric. Exterior full-field red-painted; interior red-painted as indicated.

H. GT 5243. Orange fabric; mineral inclusions. Exterior and handle: splash/drip-painted.

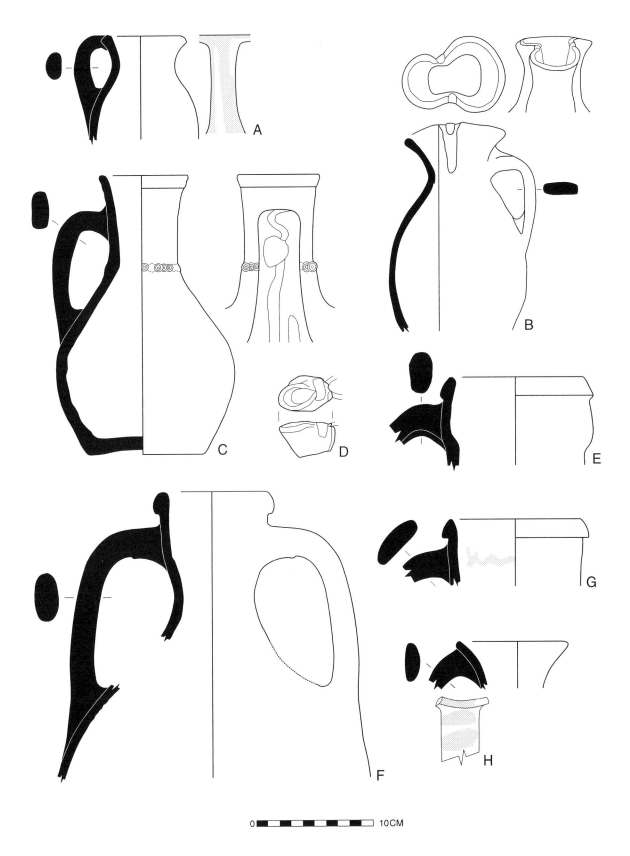

FIGURE 3:8. JUGS

COOKING POTS (FIGURES 3:9–3:12)

FIGURE 3:9. COOKING POTS.

A. GT 12414. Brown fabric, mineral inclusions. Exterior: faded splash/drip red-painted (not shown), incision and applied "snake" thumbstop; incision on rim. Interior: splash/drip red-painted at rim.

B. GT 15600. Dark brown fabric; grit, lime, sand, and mica inclusions. Splash/drip-painted interior and exterior. Applied "snake" on exterior.

C. GT 18697. Orange fabric; sand and mica inclusions. Splash/drip-painted on exterior. Punctation on handle. Join marks at neck and apex of body.

D. GT 18087. Brown fabric; mineral inclusions. Incised lines and meander on exterior.

E. GT 17680. Orange fabric; mineral inclusions. Exterior: splash/drip red-painted decoration. Interior: red-painted rim. Splash/drip-painted ribbed handle.

F. GT 18087. Brown fabric; mineral inclusions. Exterior: incised and punctated decoration. Applied "snake" thumbstop.

G. GT 17429. Dark brown body; mineral inclusions. Exterior: splash/drip brown-painted, applied ridges with punctate decoration. Interior: rim painted brown. Burnt.

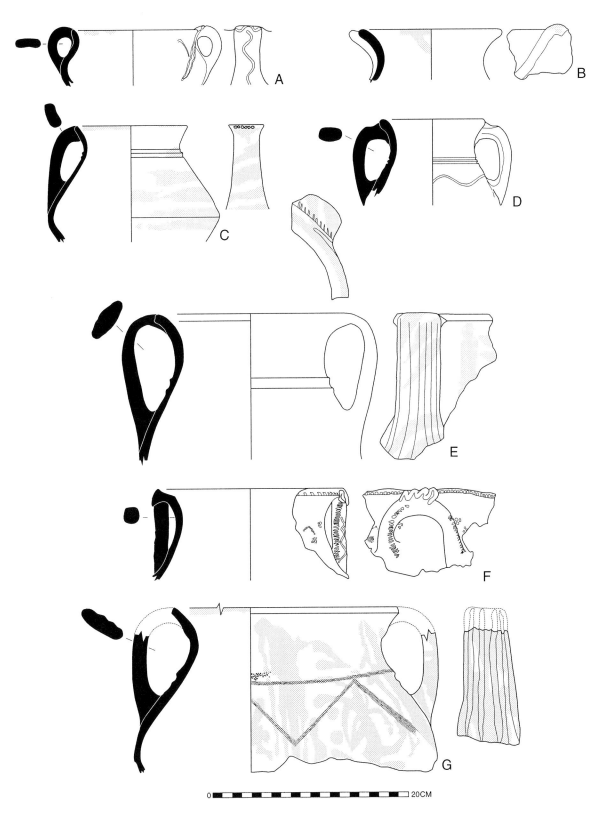

FIGURE 3:9. COOKING POTS

FIGURE 3:10. COOKING POTS.

A. GT 18057. Orange fabric; mica, sand, and lime inclusions. Incised decoration on exterior.

B. GT 19247. Black fabric; grit inclusions. Burnt interior and exterior.

C. GT 2414. Orange fabric; mica and grit inclusions. Burnt interior.

D. GT 10857. Brown fabric; mineral inclusions. Exterior: punctated and impressed decoration.

E. GT 16100. Orange fabric; grit and sand inclusions. Splash/drip-painted exterior.

F. GT 17442. Dark brown fabric; lime, sand, and mica inclusions. Exterior splash/drip-painted and punctated.

G. GT 18507. Brown fabric; mineral inclusions. Exterior and interior: reddish splash/drip-painted.

H. GT 17705. Leached dark brown fabric; lime, mica, and sand inclusions. Incised lines on exterior.

I. GT 16100. Orange fabric; grit inclusions. Burnt exterior and interior.

J. GT 2283. Dark brown fabric; lime, mica, and sand inclusions. Diameter 26 cm.

K. GT 17084. Brown fabric; mineral inclusions. Exterior: punctated and splash/drip-painted decoration. Burnt.

L. GT 19693 + 18856. Orange fabric; sand, mica, and lime inclusions.

M. GT 17402. Brown fabric, mineral inclusions. Exterior: splash/drip-painted, punctation. Burnt.

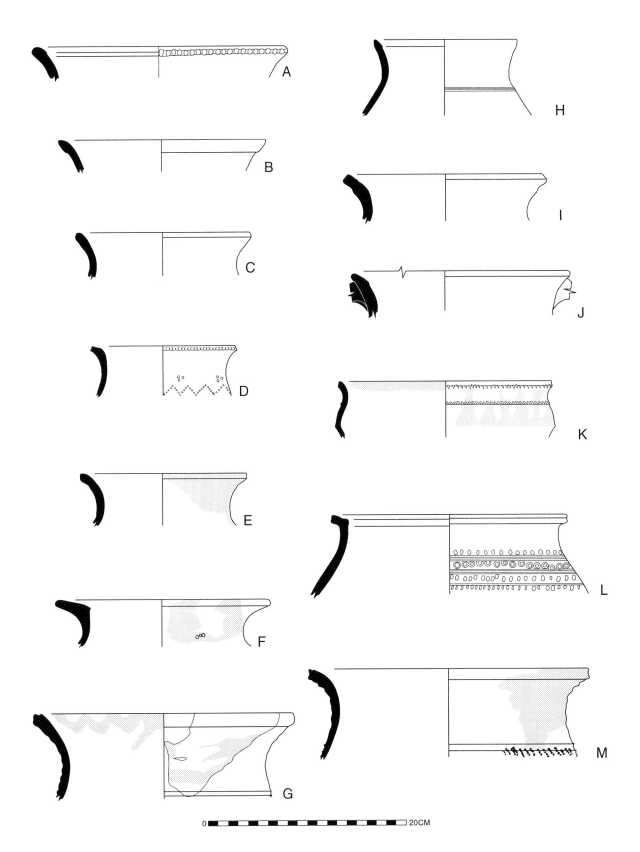

FIGURE 3:10. COOKING POTS

FIGURE 3:11. COOKING POTS.

A. GT 682. Dark brown fabric; grit, lime, sand, and mica inclusions. Incised lines and punctation on exterior. Exterior burnt.

B. GT 5739. Brown fabric; mineral inclusions. Exterior: incised lines and meander. Ribbed handle with two applied thumbstop buttons.

C. GT 17817. Dark brown fabric; sand and mica inclusions. Faded splash/drip painting on exterior (not shown).

D. GT 17719. Orange fabric; lime, sand, grit, and mica inclusions. Punctations and incised line on exterior. Burnt exterior and interior.

E. GT 18858. Dark brown fabric; lime, mica, and sand inclusions. Exterior: splash/drip-painted, punctated, and comb-incised.

F. GT 16757. Black fabric; mica, sand, grit, and lime inclusions. Burnt exterior and interior.

G. GT 19713. Dark brown fabric; mica, sand, grit, and lime inclusions.

H. GT 18856. Orange fabric; lime and sand inclusions. Stamped exterior.

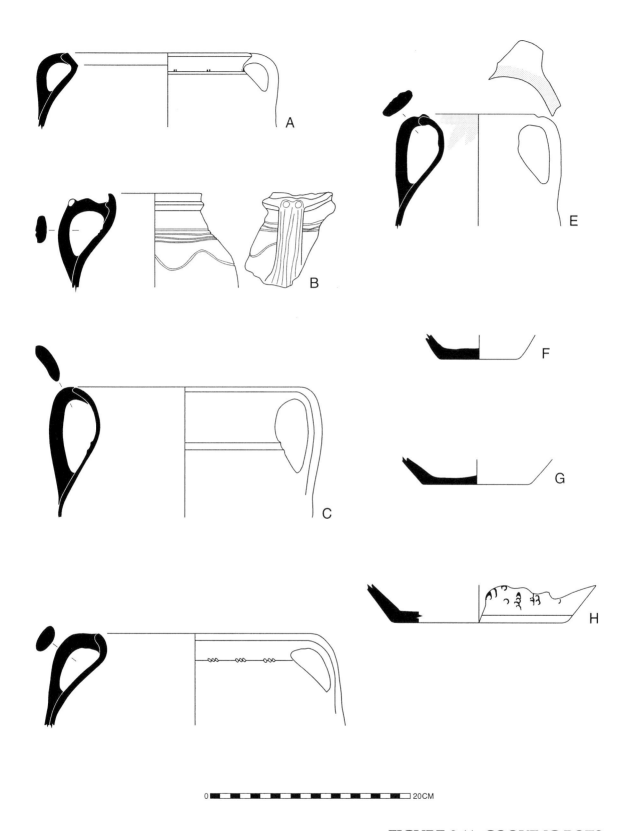

FIGURE 3:11. COOKING POTS

FIGURE 3:12. COOKING POTS.

A. GT 18856. Orange fabric; lime, sand, and mica inclusions. Incised and stamped decoration on exterior.

B. GT 17698. Dark brown fabric; grit, lime, and sand inclusions. Splash/drip-painted on interior rim and exterior. Punctations on top of handle. Incised lines on exterior. Diameter 28 cm.

C. GT 16744. Brown fabric; mineral inclusions. Three applied thumbstop buttons on top of handle.

D. GT 16067. Orange fabric; sand, grit, and lime inclusions. Incision on handle.

E. GT 16744. Orange fabric. Splash/drip-painted on exterior. Punctations on handle.

F. GT 18838. Dark brown fabric; lime, mica, grit, and sand inclusions. Applied "snake" thumbstop on handle.

G. GT 16061. Dark brown fabric; lime, grit, and sand inclusions. Exterior and interior rim splash/drip-painted; punctation at handle top.

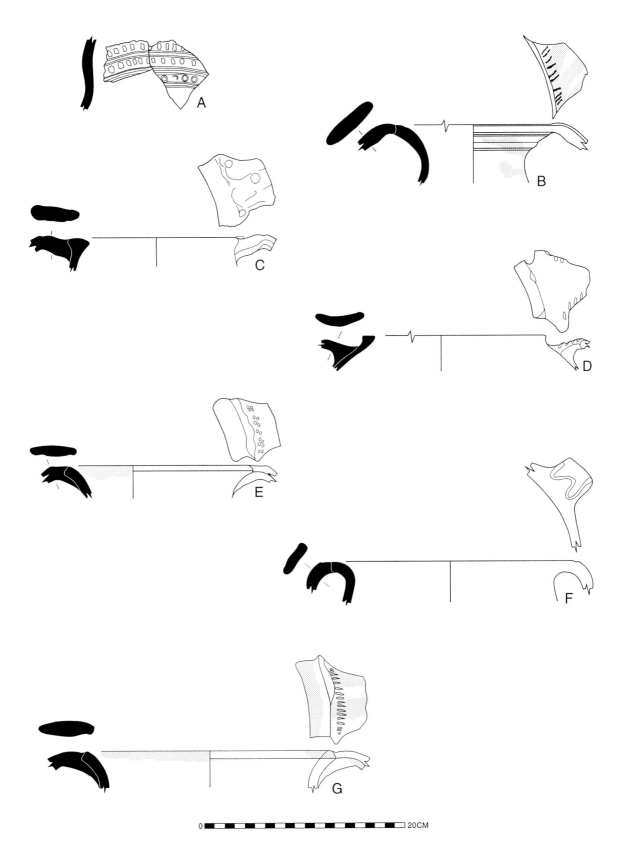

FIGURE 3:12. COOKING POTS

LIDS (FIGURES 3:13–3:14)

FIGURE 3:13. LIDS.

A. GT 18083. Brown fabric; sand, lime, and mica inclusions. Incised and gouged decoration.

B. GT 20986. Orange fabric; mineral inclusions. Punctations around edge, stamped geometric roundels and splash/drip red-painted decoration.

C. GT 16097. Orange fabric; sand and lime inclusions. Incised banded meanders with splash/drip painting.

D. GT 15963. Orange fabric; mineral inclusions. Incised linear decoration, splash/drip red-painted.

E. GT 8093. Orange fabric; mineral inclusions. Punctations, splash/drip red painting, and modeled piecrust edge. Hollow pierced central knob.

F. GT 16100. Leached fabric; color unclear, mineral inclusions. Pinched piecrust edge.

G. GT 5708. Orange fabric; mineral inclusions. Incision, pinched piecrust edge.

H. GT 17108. Orange fabric; mineral inclusions. Incised linear pattern, pinched piecrust edge.

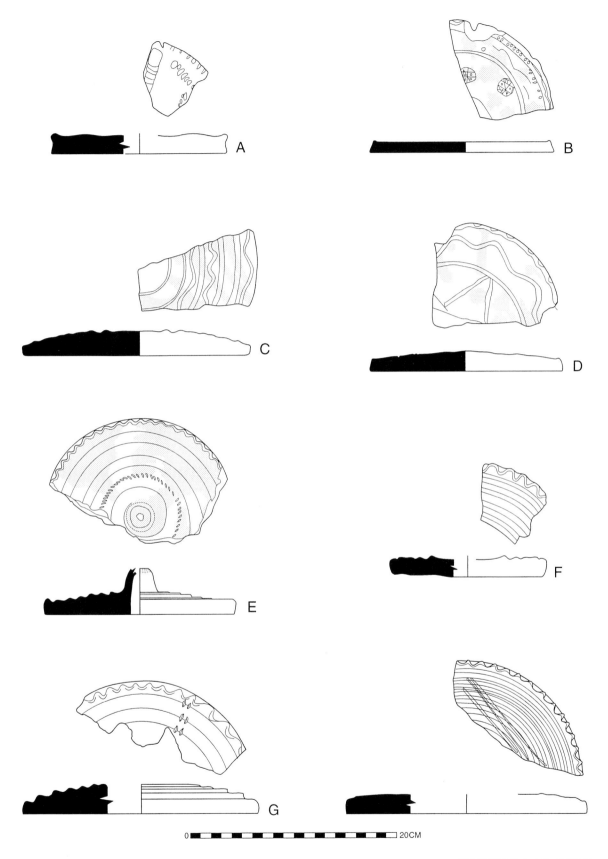

FIGURE 3:13. LIDS

FIGURE 3:14. LIDS.

A. GT 15246. Dark brown fabric; sand, mica, pebble, chaff inclusions. Incised radiating broken linear decoration. Burnt. Piecrust edge created with blunt-edged tool.

B. GT 15057. Light brown fabric; mineral inclusions. Burnt. Incised and punctate decoration with pinched piecrust edge.

C. GT 15587. Light brown fabric; mineral inclusions. Pinched piecrust edge.

D. GT 19587. Orange fabric; mineral inclusions. Incised linear decoration and applied "snake" thumbstop on handle.

E. GT 13829. Brown fabric; sand, mica, lime, and chaff inclusions. Bottom burnt. Pinched and smoothed rings; punctation on ring ridges. Edge incised.

F. GT 16097. Brown fabric; mica, sand, and lime inclusions.

G. GT 18667. Orange fabric; mineral inclusions. Splash/drip red-painted, pinched edge, central knob.

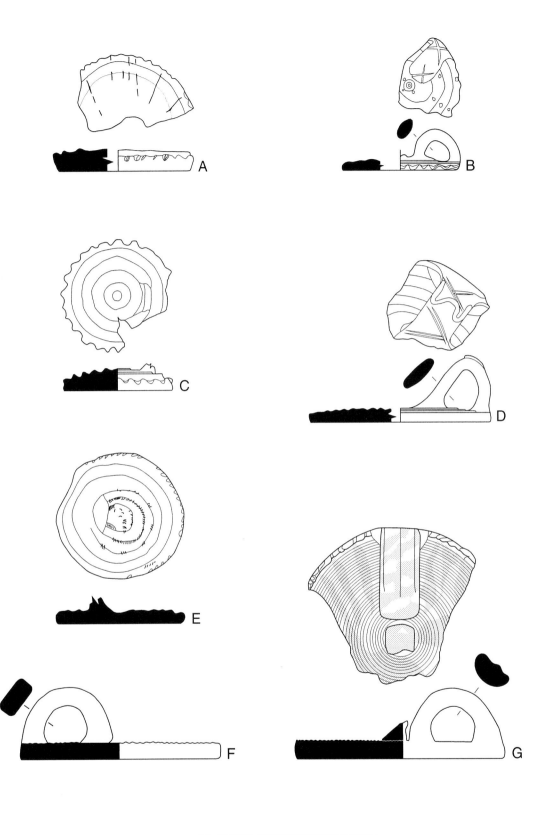

FIGURE 3:14. LIDS

UNGLAZED AND MONOCHROME GLAZED FRIT AND CALCAREOUS CLAY BOWLS (FIGURE 3:15)

FIGURE 3:15A–I. UNGLAZED BOWLS.

A. GT 18888. Orange fabric; mica, sand, and gross lime inclusions.

B. GT 15559. Cream/tan fabric. Red-painted interior and exterior. Exterior burnished.

C. GT 16747. Leached orange fabric.

D. GT 964. Orange fabric. Red-painted and smoothed on exterior and interior. Incised meander on exterior.

E. GT 2501. Cream/tan fabric; grit and chaff inclusions. Red-painted interior and exterior. Modeled indentations on exterior rim.

F. GT 16940. Orange fabric; sand and mica inclusions. Splash/drip-painted on interior and exterior.

G. GT 700. Orange fabric. Splash/drip-painted on interior and exterior.

H. GT 15559. Orange fabric. Red-painted interior and to line indicated on exterior.

I. GT 16709. Orange fabric. Red-painted interior and exterior. Incised and banded meander on exterior.

FIGURE 3:15J–Y. MONOCHROME GLAZED FRITWARE AND CALCAREOUS CLAY VESSELS.

J. GT 15738. Fine white frit fabric. Incisions on rim. Turquoise glaze on interior, rim.

K. GT 19684. Particulate cream/tan fabric with sand inclusions. Manganese glaze on interior and exterior to line indicated.

L. GT 19675. White frit fabric. Clear glaze on interior and exterior. Exterior flecked with cobalt glaze. Closed form. Base potted separately.

M. GT 17053. Coarse tan/beige fabric with lime and sand inclusions. Manganese glaze on interior.

N. GT 16728. White frit fabric. Clear glaze on interior and exterior. Incised ring on interior.

O. GT 17680. Cream/tan particulate fabric with sand inclusions. Manganese glaze on interior and dripped on exterior.

P. GT 16757. Fine white frit fabric. Manganese glaze on interior.

Q. GT 16716. White frit fabric. Turquoise glaze interior and exterior.

R. GT 18667. Cream/tan particulate fabric. Brownish pocked manganese glaze on interior.

S. GT 16718. White frit fabric. Turquoise glaze on interior and to line indicated on exterior.

T. GT 18847. Fine white frit fabric. Clear glaze on interior and exterior.

U. GT 18089. Coarse cream/tan fabric with mica inclusions. Brown manganese glaze on interior and exterior.

V. GT 17843. Coarse, soft cream/tan fabric. Manganese glaze on interior and exterior.

W. GT 17442. White frit fabric. Clear glaze on interior and exterior.

X. GT 16718. White frit fabric. Turquoise glaze on interior and to line indicated on exterior.

Y. GT 16757. Fine white frit fabric. Manganese glaze on interior and dripped on exterior.

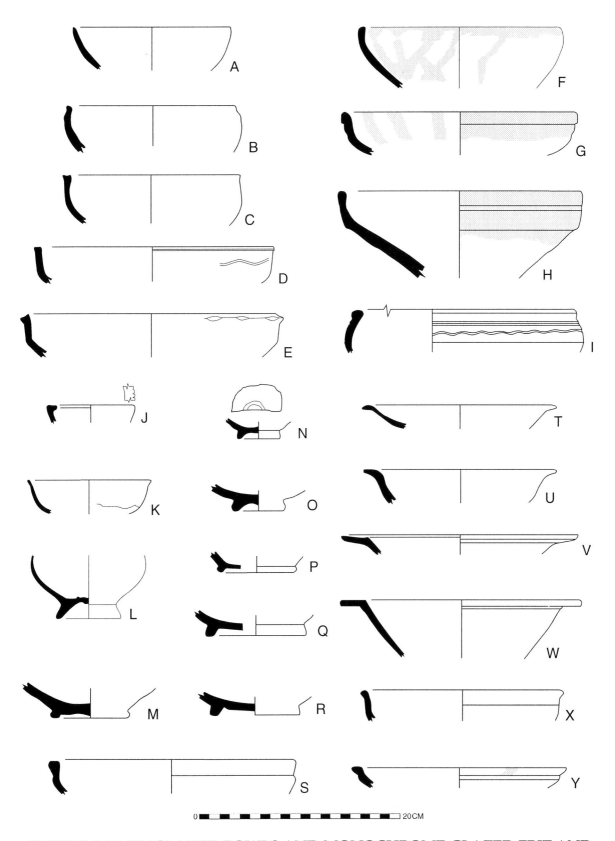

FIGURE 3:15. UNGLAZED BOWLS AND MONOCHROME GLAZED FRIT AND
CALCAREOUS CLAY BOWLS

MONOCHROME GLAZED EARTHENWARE AND CALCAREOUS CLAY BOWLS, PILGRIM FLASKS, AND LAMPS (FIGURE 3:16)

FIGURE 3:16A–J. MONOCHROME GLAZED EARTHENWARE AND CALCAREOUS CLAY BOWLS.

A. GT 17734. Orange fabric. White slip on interior and exterior to lower line indicated. Yellow/brown glaze on interior and exterior to upper line indicated. Glaze beads on rim indicate that bowl was fired upside down.

B. GT 16097. Orange fabric; lime inclusions. White slip on interior and exterior to line indicated. Green glaze on interior and exterior rim.

C. GT 101. Orange fabric. White slip on interior and exterior. Green glaze on interior and exterior rim.

D. GT 4258. Orange fabric. White slip on interior and exterior to lower line indicated. Green glaze on interior and exterior to upper line indicated.

E. GT 1102. Orange fabric. White slip on interior and to line indicated on exterior. Green glaze on interior and exterior rim.

F. GT 18966. Orange fabric. White slip on interior and exterior. Green glaze on interior and exterior.

G. GT 15209. Orange fabric. Manganese glaze on interior and exterior.

H. GT 548. Orange fabric. Green glaze, slip on interior. Green glaze to line indicated on exterior. Diameter 30 cm.

I. GT 17053. Orange fabric. Turquoise glaze on interior.

J. GT 16100. Leached earthenware fabric. Turquoise glazed interior.

FIGURE 3:16K–M. PILGRIM FLASK SHERDS.

K. GT 528. Cream/tan fabric. Molded spiral relief decoration (worn). Underside outside edge bears traces of pinching; indication of area of join and therefore vessel edge.

L. GT 2302. Cream/tan fabric. Molded relief decoration. Central rosette with obscured guilloche design.

M. GT 1785. Cream/tan fabric. Molded relief (epigraphic?) decoration. Smoothing marks on edge and underside.

FIGURE 3:16N–Q. MONOCHROME GLAZED EARTHENWARE AND CALCAREOUS CLAY BOWLS.

N. GT 2283. Cream/tan fabric. Green-blue glaze on interior and splashed over rim on exterior as indicated.

O. GT 4985. Cream/tan fabric with sand, lime, pebble inclusions. Blue-green glaze on interior.

P. GT 16728. Cream/tan fabric; lime, mica, and sand inclusions. Manganese glaze on interior.

Q. GT 19109. Cream/tan fabric. Turquoise glaze on interior and exterior.

FIGURE 3:16R–V. LAMPS.

R. GT 18687. Orange fabric; sand and mica inclusions. Interior: incised meander, punctations, and faded splash/drip painting (not shown).

S. GT 16718. Brown fabric; mineral inclusions.

T. GT 19246. Brown fabric; sand and mica inclusions. Made in three pieces: bottom, reservoir, and sides. Wick hole cut through reservoir wall. Spout burnt inside and out.

U. GT 19704. Dark brown fabric; grit inclusions. Burnt at base of handle and spout. Lime encrustations on bottom. Handmade.

V. GT 1992. Orange fabric; sand, lime, and mica inclusions. Spout fire-blackened on interior and exterior.

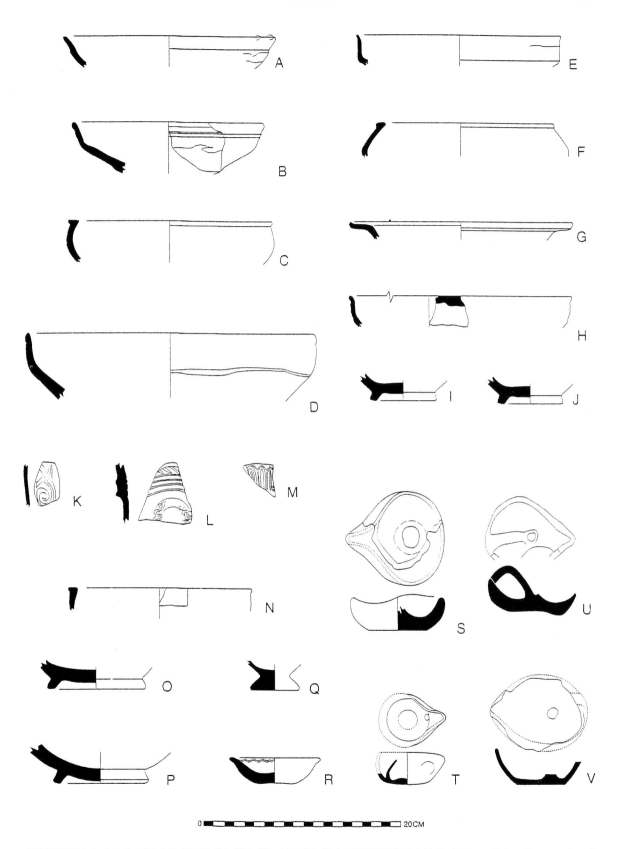

FIGURE 3:16. MONOCHROME GLAZED EARTHENWARE AND CALCAREOUS
CLAY BOWLS, PILGRIM FLASKS, AND LAMPS

LUSTERWARE BOWLS (FIGURES 3:17–3:18)

FIGURE 3:17. LUSTERWARE BOWLS.

A. GT 17420. White frit fabric. Clear glaze on interior and exterior. Curvilinear design in green luster on interior.

B. GT 77. White frit fabric. Exterior: clear glaze. Interior: reserve-painted curvilinear design in green luster on clear glaze. "Tell Minis."

C. GT 16070. White frit fabric. Exterior: manganese glaze. Interior: curvilinear design in green luster on manganese glaze.

D. GT 18369. White frit fabric. Clear glaze on interior and exterior. Curvilinear design in green luster on interior.

E. GT 18654. White frit fabric. Exterior: turquoise glaze. Interior: curvilinear design in green luster on turquoise glaze.

F. GT 13829. White frit fabric. Manganese glaze on interior and exterior. Curvilinear design in green luster on interior.

G. GT 2929. White frit fabric. Exterior: manganese glaze. Interior: curvilinear design in green luster on manganese glaze.

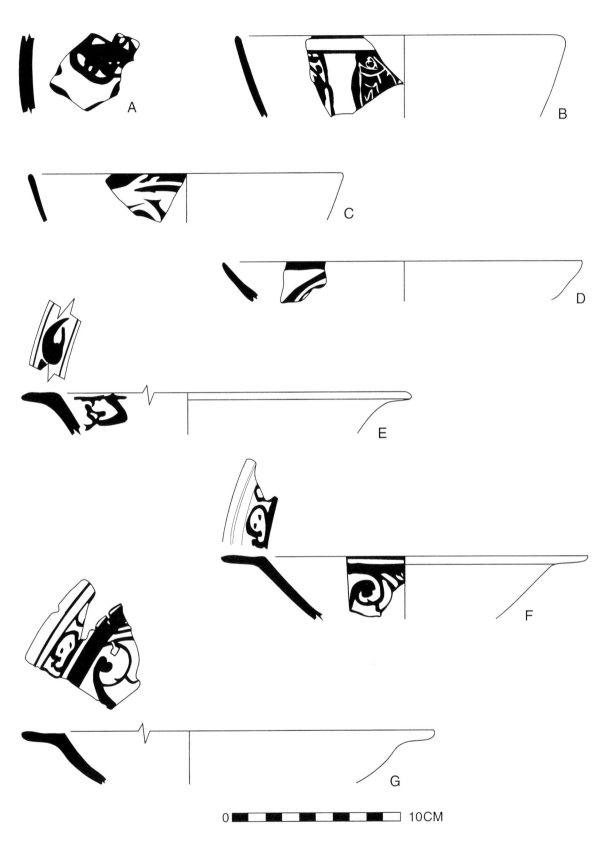

FIGURE 3:17. LUSTERWARE BOWLS

FIGURE 3:18. LUSTERWARE BOWLS.

H. GT 1784. Frit fabric. Exterior: clear glaze. Interior: centriform reserve-painted curvilinear design in green luster on clear glaze.

I. GT 15554. Off-white frit fabric with sand inclusions. Exterior: clear glaze. Interior: curvilinear design in brown luster on clear glaze.

J. GT 18059. Frit fabric. Manganese glaze on interior and exterior. Interior has reserve-painted curvilinear design in green luster.

K. GT 19094. Off-white frit fabric with sand inclusions. Exterior: manganese glaze. Interior: centriform curvilinear design in green luster on manganese glaze.

L. GT 19073. White frit fabric. Exterior: manganese glaze. Interior: banded radiating curvilinear design in green luster on manganese glaze.

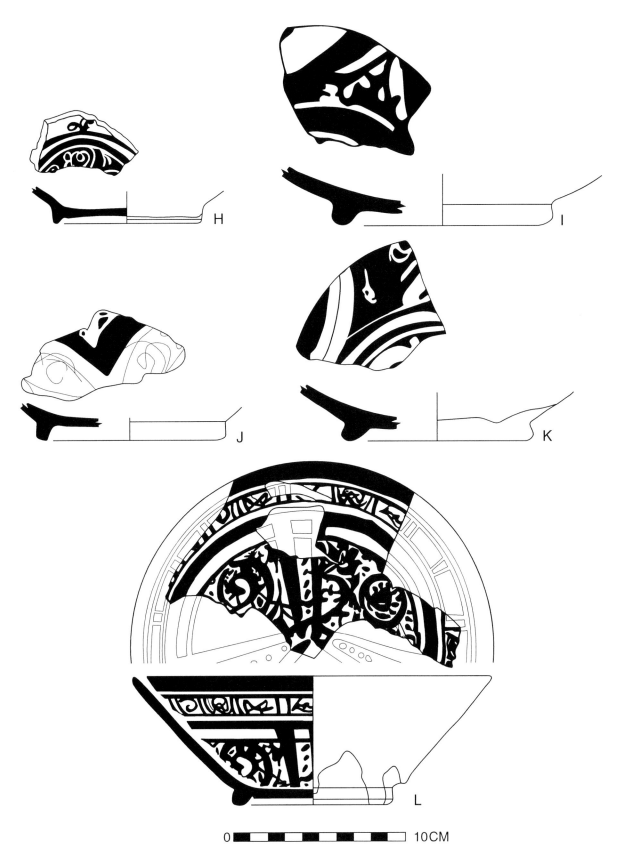

FIGURE 3:18. LUSTERWARE BOWLS

UNDERGLAZE PAINTED, SGRAFFIATO, AND OTHER BOWLS (FIGURE 3:19)

FIGURE 3:19. UNDERGLAZE PAINTED, SGRAFFIATO, AND OTHER BOWLS.

A. GT 692. Frit fabric. Body sherd. Interior and exterior: underglaze-painted black design under turquoise glaze.

B. GT 16792. Frit fabric. Interior: clear glaze with striped radial design of underglaze-painted cobalt blue stripe flanked by green luster lines.

C. GT 1102. Orange fabric. White slip and dark green glaze on interior. Sgraffiato design on interior.

D. GT 975. Cream/tan fabric. White slip, dark green glaze, and curvilinear sgraffiato design on interior

E. GT 1266. Frit fabric. Exterior: clear glaze. Interior: underglaze-painted curvilinear design in black and cobalt blue under clear glaze.

F. GT 1947. Orange fabric. White slip on interior. Interior: light green glaze splashed with green and brown in incised areas. Sgraffiato design.

G. GT 13230. Frit fabric. Lamp base. Turquoise glaze on interior. Bottom burnt.

H. GT 969. Orange fabric; sand and mica inclusions. Yellow glaze with sgraffiato line (not shown) on interior; flecks of green glaze on exterior.

I. GT 1187. Orange fabric. White slip on interior. Interior: pale green glaze with splatterings of brown and green, linear sgraffiato decoration, and point of exposed body fabric from kiln furniture.

J. GT 1303. Orange fabric with mineral temper. Exterior: plain. Interior: white slip, incised lines with brown glaze, green glaze over incisions (green glaze indicated by shading).

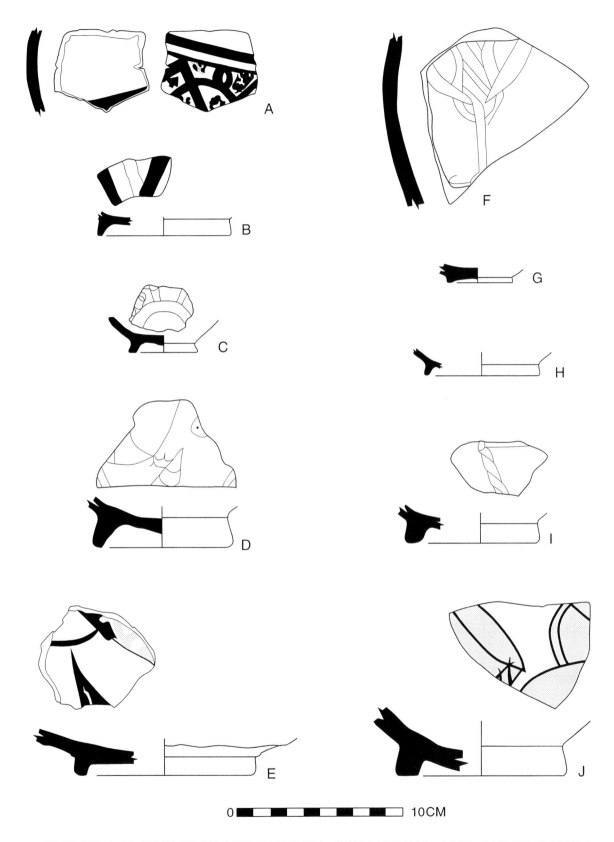

FIGURE 3:19. UNDERGLAZE PAINTED, SGRAFFIATO, AND OTHER BOWLS

MOLDED AND MOLDED AND INCISED BOWLS (FIGURE 3:20)

FIGURE 3:20. MOLDED AND MOLDED AND INCISED BOWLS.

A. GT 16100. White frit fabric. Exterior: turquoise glaze over molded vertical panels. Interior: turquoise glaze.

B. GT 15600. White frit fabric. Exterior: molded basketweave pattern under turquoise glaze. Interior: turquoise glaze.

C. GT 17090. Off-white frit fabric with sand inclusions. Exterior: manganese glaze to line indicated. Interior: molded (figural?) design under manganese glaze. May belong to same vessel as D.

D. GT 17090. Off-white frit fabric with sand inclusions. Exterior: manganese glaze. Interior: molded design under manganese glaze.

E. GT 19226. Fine frit body. Clear glaze interior and exterior with underglaze cobalt blue drip on interior. Interior has incised and molded *an hua* design.

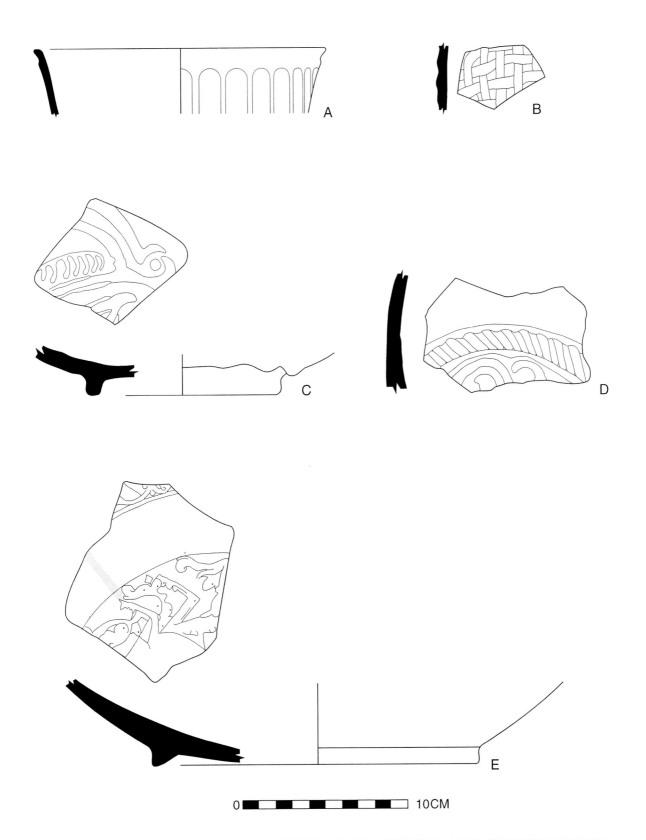

FIGURE 3:20. MOLDED AND MOLDED AND INCISED BOWLS

IV

COINS AND SMALL FINDS

This chapter describes both representative and exceptional objects recovered during the four seasons of excavation in medieval levels at Gritille. Islamic, Byzantine, and Crusader coins are detailed, followed by descriptions of objects in metal, glass, and stone. Relevant comparative material from other excavated sites in both Anatolia and Syria is incorporated in the discussion.

NUMISMATIC EVIDENCE FOR THE DATING OF MEDIEVAL LEVELS AT GRITILLE

While the dating of Phase 2 at Gritille has been proposed on analogy with that of Lidar, the dating of Phase 3 is aided by the discovery of the hoard of Crusader silver coins, a find that helps date this level to sometime during the reign of the County of Edessa. Although the city of Urfa fell in 1144, Samsat remained in Crusader hands until the end of the fifth decade of the twelfth century.

No coins were found in Phase 4, but two groups came from loci in the middle of Phase 5. The first group comprises five Byzantine eleventh- or twelfth-century *folles* with countermarks (GT 16702a, b, GT 16703, and GT 16705a, b). One of these reads *Sayf al-Dīn*, the rest *Badr*. These countermarks are known for this region in the twelfth century, but they have been attrib-

uted to Akhlat farther east.[1] Because of their find locations, however, Lowick proposed that they are countermarks of the local Artuqid governors of Samsat.[2] Unfortunately, those governors' names that have come down to us do not match these. This may be due to the multiplicity of names borne by Muslim rulers in this period. As noted in the first chapter, Artuqid governors ruled Samsat from 1150 to 1182–83, when the Ayyubids took over the region.

The second set from Phase 5 consists of three copper *fulūs* of Najm al-Dīn Alpī, Artuqid ruler of Mardin and of the Samsat region after 1152 (GT 5704, 5731, and 5732). Consequently, Phase 5 can be dated to the Artuqid era.

Phase 7, which marked the reoccupation of the mound and the laying of the second street, can be dated to the middle of Ayyubid hegemony over this region. A small hoard of Ayyubid copper *fulūs* (GT 434a–h) found at the end of Phase 7 levels in Operation 10 date this level to the 1220s or 1230s. Of the eight coins found, one, struck in Aleppo in 621 A.H./A.D. 1224–25, provides a *terminus pro quem* for Phase 8 at Gritille.

Since al-Malik al-Afḍal died in 1225, the end of this phase may coincide with the installation of an Ayyubid governor, or a Rum Seljuk vassal at Samsat. The final phase probably extends the medieval occupation at Gritille well into the next (fourth) decade of the thirteenth century.

---

[1] Lowick, Bendall, and Whitting, *The "Mardin" Hoard*, 35–36, 43–44.
[2] Private correspondence, July 3, 1986.

THE COIN CATALOGUE

Of the 111 coins recovered from medieval levels at Gritille, it was possible to identify 48 coins partially or wholly. The following identifications and commentary were prepared by Dr. Michael Bates, Curator of Islamic Coins, and Dr. Alan Stahl, Curator of Medieval Coins, at the American Numismatic Society, New York. In addition, the late Dr. Nicholas Lowick, Curator of Islamic Coins at the British Museum, examined the countermarks on Byzantine or Crusader copper coinage listed under Byzantine coinage.

Coins are listed by their field numbers. In 1981 this number was prefaced by GR-81, in subsequent years by GT. This number is then followed by findspot information.

ISLAMIC COINAGE

Abbreviations are to the following reference works: Balog = Paul Balog, *The Coinage of the Ayyubids*, Royal Numismatic Society Special Publication Number 12 (London: Royal Numismatic Society, 1980); and BM = Stanley Lane-Poole, *Catalogue of Oriental Coins in the British Museum*. Volume 3: *The Coins of the Turkumän Houses of Seljook, Urtuk, Zengee, etc.* (London: British Museum, 1872).

GR-81: 13. OPERATION 1, LOCUS 4, LOT 9

Syria, Aleppo. AE fals. Under Ayyubid king al-ʿAzīz Muḥammad (1216–1236), with uncertain caliph, most probably al-Nāṣir (1180–1225). Date not legible, most probably 613–622 A.H. (A.D. 1216–1225), possibly 613–623 A.H. (A.D. 1216–1226). Balog 708–719, probably Balog 713.

Obverse:	al-Malik
	al-ʿAzīz
Reverse:	al-Imām
	al-Nāṣir (?)

Both in octalobe of points in linear octalobe (the lobes are so shallow on this example as to appear rectilinear; this characteristic of this series is seen especially in the year 622 A.H./A.D. 1225). Marginal inscriptions illegible.

GR-81: 26. OPERATION 3, LOCUS 8

Unknown mint. Under Rum Seljuk Sultan Kay Kāʾūs, b. Kay Khuṣraw (A.D. 1245–1257), with Caliph al-Mustaʿṣim. Mint name not on coin, undated. BM, 244 var.

Obverse:	al-Sulṭān al-
	Aʿẓam ʿIzz a
	l-Dunya . . .
Reverse:	al-Imām
	al-Mustaʿṣim billāh
	Amīr al-muʾminīn

Both sides in square of points within outer circle of points; six-rayed stars in segments between square and circle.

GR-81: 48. OPERATION 2, LOCUS 19, LOT 38

Possibly Syria, Aleppo. AE fals. Possibly al-Nāṣir Yūsuf with Caliph al-Mustaʿṣim, thus 1242–1258. Balog 781 (?).

Obverse:	Illegible
Reverse:	al-Imām . . .

Both sides in linear hexagram within hexagram of points.

GR-81: 49. OPERATION 2, LOCUS 19, LOT 39

Obverse:	. . . al-Malik al-Nāṣir
	ibn Muḥammad
Reverse:	al-Imām al-M
	. . . l-Ḥalab

GR-81: 69. OPERATION 2, LOCUS 23, LOT 65

al-Jazīra. Mārdên. AE fals. Under Artuqid King Nāṣir al-Dīn Artuq-Arslān (A.D. 1200–1239), with Ayyubid al-ʿĀdil (1200–1218) as overlord. Mint name not on coin, but Mārdīn is to be presumed. Date not fully legible, but issue is only from 611 A.H./A.D. 1214–1215. BM 443.

Obverse: Laureate head, left.
Marginal inscription:

	Nāṣir al-Dunyā waʾl-Dīn
	Artuq Arslān Malik Diyār Bakr.
Reverse:	Abu al-ʿAbbās Aḥmad
	al-Nāṣir li-Dīn Allāh
	Amīr al-Muʾminīn

al-Malik al-'Ādil abu
[Bakr bin] Ayyūb.
Right margin: [Iḥdā 'ashar].
Left margin: wa ṣitta mǐa.

GT 90. OPERATION 9, LOCUS 3, LOT 3

Fals. Ḥamāh (?), 641 (?) under al-Ṣāliḥ
Ayyūb. Much like Balog 566, of that date and
mint.

GT 434. OPERATION 10, LOCUS 10, LOT 7

This number consisted of a hoard of eight
coins.
GT 434a. Fals. Aleppo, dated 621 A.H., under
al-'Azīz Muḥammad (613–634) and Caliph al-
Nāṣir (575–622 A.H.) Balog 712.
GT 434b. Fals. Aleppo (legible on coin), under ruler al-'Azīz (613–634 A.H.) and Caliph al-
Nāṣir (575–622); early type, Balog 708–714.
GT 434c. Fals. Damascus, date 594 or 595,
under ruler al-'Azīz 'Uthmān. Balog 222–223.
(Century is clearly not present on this coin.)
GT 434d. Fals. al-Ruhā, type of 602–605 A.H.,
under ruler al-'Ādil Abu Bakr (596–615). Balog
349–52, especially Balog 352 of 605 A.H. (same
ornamentation).
GT 434e. Fals. Same type as GT 434b; struck
twice.
GT 434f. Fals. Probably Aleppo, probably
same type as GT 434b and e, but may be from
last years of al-Ẓāhir Ghāzī (d. 613 A.H.) or from
early years of his son's reign.
GT 434g. Seems Ayyubid, but effaced.
GT 434h. Fals. al-Ruhā, under al-'Ādil.
Balog 353–357.

GT 517. OPERATION 9, LOCUS 8, LOT 20

Fals, Aleppo. Same as GT 434b, etc. Date
illegible.

GT 739. OPERATION 10, LOCUS 22, LOT 21

Fals. Under Rum Seljuk Sultan Kay-
Khusraw, b. Kay Qubādh (634–644). BM III no.
232, also with mint and date illegible.

GT 972. OPERATION 10, LOCUS 28, LOT 32

Fals. Probably Aleppo, but apparently without date or mint, under al-Nāṣir Yūsuf (634–658

A.H.) and Caliph al-Musta'ṣim (640–656 A.H.).
Could be from Aleppo, 640–656 A.H., or any-
where in northern Syria, 648–656. Balog 783.

GT 1431. OPERATION 10, LOCUS 47, LOT 41

Fals. Damascus, type of 631–633 A.H., under
al-Kāmil. Struck twice; undertype perhaps different. Balog 464–465.

GT 4879. OPERATION 25, LOCUS 37, LOT 43

Fals. Aleppo, under al-Ẓahir Muḥammad.
Balog 670–679, of 603–612 A.H.

GT 5704. OPERATION 11, LOCUS 15, LOT 25

Fals (or copper "dirham"). Probably Mārdīn, under Najm al-Dīn Alpī (547–572 A.H.), with
caliph's name illegible (either al-Mustanjid bil-
lāh, d. 566 A.H., or his successor al-Must'aḍī bi-
amr Allāh). BM 380–385.

GT 6349. OPERATION 25, LOCUS 49, LOT 82

Fals. Aleppo, under al-'Azīz Muḥammad
with Caliph al-Ẓāhir (622–623 A.H.). Balog
715–717.

GT 18568. OPERATION 26/27, LOCUS 36, LOT 73

Atabeg.

BYZANTINE COINAGE

GR-81:48. OPERATION 3, LOCUS 1, LOT 1

Justinian the Great.

GR-81:122. OPERATION 1, LOCUS 19, LOT 32

Anonymous folles, 1050s.

GT 16277. OPERATION 43, LOCUS 16, LOT 18

Haloed figure with Greek cross, Arabic
counterstamp, possibly *lillāh*.

GT 16702A. OPERATION 9, LOCUS 12, LOT 36

Byzantine folles with Arabic counterstamp:
Badr.

GT 16702B. OPERATION 9, LOCUS 12, LOT 36

Byzantine folles with Arabic counterstamp: *Sayf al-Dīn.*

GT 16703. OPERATION 9, LOCUS 12, LOT 36

Crusader or Byzantine fabric. Counterstamp: *Badr.*

GT 16705A. OPERATION 9, LOCUS 12, LOT 36

Crusader or Byzantine fabric. Counterstamp: *Badr.*

GT 16705B. OPERATION 9, LOCUS 12, LOT 36

Crusader or Byzantine fabric. Counterstamp: *Badr.*

GT 18577. OPERATION 26/27, LOCUS 39, LOT 75

"North Syrian 12th century fabric" (Lowick). Counterstamp illegible.

GT 23001 AND 23002. OPERATION 37

No other context information available. These coins were discovered and pocketed by a workman on the excavation and only recovered subsequently. They can be assigned to the later medieval occupation levels (6–8).

Gold solidus, Emperor Michael VII Doukas, reg. 1071–1078.

CRUSADER COINAGE

The following coins were first identified by Dr. Stahl. The hoard was published by D. M. Metcalf ("The Gritille Hoard of Coins of Lucca and Valence," *The Numismatic Chronicle* 147 [1987], 92–95). Information given below is reproduced from Metcalf's article.

GR-81: 10. OPERATION 4, LOCUS 2, LOT 2

Denier of Valence.
Obverse: Cross pommee, with annulet in fourth quarter. +SAPOLLINARS
Reverse: Winged angel or eagle standing facing. VRBS VALENTIAI
This coin was incorrectly published as copper.[3]

GT 20051 = GR 342. OPERATION 45, LOCUS 23, LOT 31

Denier of Valence.

GT 20052 = GR 343. OPERATION 45, LOCUS 23, LOT 31

Denier of Valence.

GT 20053 = GR 344. OPERATION 45, LOCUS 23, LOT 31

Denier of Valence.

GT 20054 = GR 345. OPERATION 45, LOCUS 23, LOT 31

Denier of Valence.

GT 20055 = GR 346. OPERATION 45, LOCUS 23, LOT 31

Denier of Valence.

GT 20056 = GR 347. OPERATION 45, LOCUS 23, LOT 31

Denier. Lucca. Neat style.
Obverse: Debased OTTO monogram. +IHPERATOR
Reverse: LVCA cross-wise around central pellet. +ENRICVS

GT 20057 = GR 348. OPERATION 45, LOCUS 23, LOT 31

Denier. Lucca. Neat style.

GT 20058 = GR 349. OPERATION 45, LOCUS 23, LOT 31

Denier. Lucca. Rough style.

GT 20059 = GR 350. OPERATION 45, LOCUS 23, LOT 31

Denier. Lucca. Neat style.

GT 20060 = GR 351. OPERATION 45, LOCUS 23, LOT 31

Denier. Lucca. Neat style.

---

[3] Ellis and Voigt, "1981 Excavations at Gritille," Fig. 17.

GT 20061 = GR 352. OPERATION 45, LOCUS 23, LOT 31

Denier. Lucca. Neat style.

GT 20062 = GR 353. OPERATION 45, LOCUS 23, LOT 31

Denier. Lucca. Neat style.

GT 20063 = GR 354. OPERATION 45, LOCUS 23, LOT 31

Denier. Lucca. Neat style. The reverse is off center.

GT 20064 = GR 355. OPERATION 45, LOCUS 23, LOT 31

Denier. Lucca. Rough style.

GT 20065 = GR 356. OPERATION 45, LOCUS 23, LOT 31

Denier. Lucca. Rough style.

SMALL FINDS

IRON OBJECTS

Like other medieval sites in the region, Gritille yielded many objects of iron (Figs. 4:1–4:4). Evidence of iron metallurgy was uncovered at two nearby sites, Horis Kale and Lidar, as well as at Korucutepe to the north.[4] This leads to the supposition that implements for farming, hunting, building, and war were produced locally throughout the region. The variety of shapes of the three most commonly recovered metal objects—nails, blades and projectile points—may also be explained by a variety of local manufactories as small as the lone pyrotechnic feature associated with metallurgy at Lidar.

Efforts to classify and quantify iron objects were frustrated by corrosion. Examples shown here were exceptionally well preserved; still, only the general shapes of many pieces were readily distinguishable.

Nevertheless, one observation can be made in reference to the quantities of iron objects recovered: the most commonly recovered iron object was undoubtedly the nail, found in all contexts and in a wide variety of shapes and sizes. In an architectural ensemble characterized by mudbrick walls on stone footings, the ubiquity of nails implies an extensive use of wood in the buildings of medieval Gritille. Chunks of charred wood recovered from Phase 3 levels in the West End indicate the use of wood as a roofing material; and the incidental use throughout the medieval settlement of stone bases like that illustrated in Figure 4:6E, F means that wood was also used for support posts. This stands in contrast to the spare use of wood in 1980s mudbrick village houses in the Karababa basin, where wood (poplar) was used structurally only for rafters. Nails were also undoubtedly commonly used for equid shoes.

Iron scythes, saws, cooking utensils, nails, bolts, hinges, doorstops, hooks, projectile points, scale-armor fragments, and iron sheets were recovered from medieval levels at Samsat.[5] Similar iron objects were recovered at Tille, Lidar (knife blades, scythes, shovels, spatulas, and projectile points), Horis Kale (knife blades, projectile points, and scissors), Arsameia (Eski Kâhta), Aşvan Kale, Korucutepe, and Taşkun Kale, as well as at Hama in central Syria.

---

[4] H. Hauptmann ("Die Grabungen auf dem Lidar Höyük, 1979," 261, Pl. 157:2) found metal slag associated with a pyrotechnic feature at Lidar; Baki Öğün ("Horis Kale Kazıları, 1978–1979," 147) reported that iron slag and other debris was discovered in medieval levels there. With so many iron implements (arrowheads, knives, and scissors) recovered from medieval levels at Horis Kale, the author posited their manufacture on site. At Korucutepe, excavators found iron slag associated with one pyrotechnic feature in medieval levels; see van Loon, *Korucutepe*, 2:43.

[5] Goell, "Samosata Archaeological Excavations," 98. These objects were not illustrated, nor have the small finds from Ankara University excavations at Samsat been published.

KNIFE BLADES

Knife blades were found at Gritille with and without tangs and rivet holes. The following correspondences with other sites can be seen.[6]

> Tangs: Cf. Gritille Figure 4:1B, C and Tille Figure 67:92, 93.

> Rivets: Cf. Gritille Figure. 4:1I and Tille Figure 67:91, though the latter had additional discovery of traces of wood on them.

> Cf. Gritille Figure 4:1K and Aşvan Kale Figure 118:37.

> Cf. Gritille Figure 4:1M and Aşvan Kale Figure 118:38.

> Cf. Gritille Figure 4:1L and Tille Figure 57:93.

Comparable examples can also be seen in Hama Figures 21:8, 22:10 (with tang), and 22:12 (with three rivet holes).

PROJECTILE POINTS

Projectile points were found in a great variety of shapes and sizes. Although corrosion made it hard to distinguish this consistently, it appears that there was a qualitative difference among the points, probably owing to the presence of imported mass-produced arrowheads (e.g., Fig. 4:2A, E) alongside locally produced examples.

The following correspondences with other sites can be seen.

> Cf. Gritille Figure 4:1D with Taşkun Kale Figure 90:32 and Aşvan Kale Figure 119:49.

> Cf. Gritille Figure 4:1E and Taşkun Kale Figure 90:29.

> Cf. Gritille Figure 4:2B and Taşkun Kale Figure 90:25.

> Cf. Gritille Figure 4:2D and Korucutepe Plate 116F.

> Cf. Gritille Figure 4:2E with Lidar Plate 161:1–5, Taşkun Kale Figure 90:30, Korucutepe Plate 116G, and Tille Figure 70:154.

> Cf. Gritille projectile points and Hama Figure 21:1.

No barbed arrowheads were found at Gritille, although they were recovered elsewhere. Barbed arrowheads are sometimes associated with warfare (as opposed to hunting), although they have also been associated with fishing.[7] Gritille's intimate relation to the Euphrates is assured by its riverside location, and fishbones were recovered in several ovens and hearths, but two fishhooks were recovered from medieval levels. Both were made of copper/bronze (Fig. 4:4C; Pl. 4:1); they were not paralleled in published reports from other sites. Only one spearpoint (Fig. 4:2P; Pl. 4:2) was found.

NAILS

The number and variety of nails found has been linked to the use of wood in the buildings of Gritille and the presence of local smithies.

The following correspondences with other sites can be seen.

> Cf. Gritille nails (Fig. 4:2H, K, Q, R, S; Pls. 4:3–4:5) with Tille Figure 72; Hama Figure 23:6; and all other medieval sites.

> Cf. Gritille Figure 4:2J (a stud for a leather garment or bag) with Korucutepe #257 and Arsameia Plate 75:20, 21.

MISCELLANEOUS SMALL IRON FINDS

The following correspondences with other sites in the region can be seen.

> Cf. equid shoes from Gritille in Figure 4:3A–C; Plate 4:6 with Arsameia Plate 75:23; and Hama Figures 22: 2 and 23:1. Figure 67:96 at Tille also resembles a shoe.

> Cf. an adze from Gritille in Figure 4:3D and Plate 4:7 with Tille Figures 69:100 and

---

[6] The references given in the text following are to the following works. Tille: Moore, *Tille Höyük 1*; Lidar: Hauptmann, "Die Grabungen auf dem Lidar Höyük, 1979"; Horis Kale: Öğün, "Horis Kale Kazıları, 1978–1979"; Arsameia: Stronach, "Metallfunde in Arsameia am Nymphaios," 275–281, Pls. 72–75; Aşvan Kale: Mitchell, *Aşvan Kale*; Korucutepe: van Loon, "The Other Medieval Objects," in idem, *Korucutepe*, 3:251–267; Taşkun Kale: McNicoll, *Taşkun Kale*; Hama: Ploug et al., *Hama. Fouilles et recherches 1931–38*.

[7] Mitchell, *Aşvan Kale*, 229.

70:104, Aşvan Kale Figure 118: 35, and Hama Figure 23:5.

A shackle from Gritille (Fig. 4:3E ; Pl. 4:8) is without published parallel.

Cf. buckles from Gritille in Figure 4:4A, B and Plate 4:10 with Tille Figure 63:71, 72, and Korucutepe, #238.

Cf. the iron ring from Gritille in Figure 4:4E and Taşkun Kale Figure 90:20.

Cf. the large and small sickles from Gritille in Figure 4:4F, G, and Plate 4:11, with Tille Figures 67:94, 95, and 59:30a.

Agricultural implements similar to those found at Gritille were used in the Byzantine realm. There, too, iron seems to have been widely available in the twelfth and thirteenth centuries and extensively used for tools of all sorts.[8]

COPPER/BRONZE OBJECTS

The following objects were made of copper or copper alloy: pins (Figs. 4:2G, 4:2M; Pls. 4:12, 4:13), rings (Figs. 4:2I, 4:4D), a pair of tweezers (Pl. 4:9), a fishhook (Fig. 4:3C), and various vessels and crosses (Fig. 4:5). The following correspondences with other sites can be seen.

Cf. Gritille Figure 4:2G/Plate 4:12, identified as a pin, with similar Hama objects identified as spatulas and mascara appliers.

Cf. Gritille "pin" in Figure 4:2M with Hama Figure 24:6, 7 (decorated spatulas/mascara appliers) and Korucutepe #259 (called pins or awls). Similar objects were also recovered from Harran.[9]

Copper/bronze rings were found at Aşvan (Aşvan Kale Fig. 120: 50–57), including one with incised or chased patterns (Aşvan Kale Fig. 121: 62), at Korucutepe (#260) and at Harran.[10] Rings with bezels, although not exactly like the Gritille example seen in Plate 4:D, were recovered at Hama (Hama Fig. 30: 1, 4, 5).

SPINDLE WHORLS

Spindle whorls in stone (Fig. 4:3F, I) and bone (Fig. 4:3H) were found at Gritille, as was an unpierced clay disk of unknown function (Fig. 4:3G). Correspondences with other sites include the following.

Cf. stone spindle whorls from Gritille (Fig. 4:3I) with Aşvan Kale Figure 116:26.

Cf. stone spindle whorl from Gritille (Fig. 4:3F) with Tille Figure 77:166, 170–74.

Cf. bone spindle whorl from Gritille (Fig. 4:3H) with Tille Figure 75:148–52, and examples recovered at Harran.[11]

Cf. stone and bone spindle whorls from Gritille with Hama's stone (Hama Fig. 39:8–11) and bone (Hama Fig. 44:10–16) examples, which were classified into three forms: flat conical, thick to sphero-conical, and disc-shaped.

COPPER/BRONZE VESSEL AND LAMPS

A single copper vessel was recovered from Gritille (Fig. 4:5E; Pl. 4:14). It compares with a weighing pan found at Hama (Hama Fig. 9:12), but the Gritille vessel had only one hole pierced in its side, making it unlikely that it served the same purpose as the Hama vessel.

Vessels of copper or copper alloy were recovered also from Tille, including a plate (Tille Fig. 60), a gilded bronze cup (Tille Fig. 64:75), and weighing pans and other balance equipment, which were found as well at Hama, as noted above. Lidar also produced some copper vessels.[12]

Two copper/bronze lamps were recovered at Gritille (Figs. 4:5F, G; Pls. 4:15, 4:16). These are grander than the glazed and unglazed ceramic lamps commonly found at Gritille, but much less elaborate than the large twin-spouted copper alloy lamps recovered at Tille (Tille Figs. 57:28, 58:29). The Gritille lamp in Figure 4:5G finds an almost exact parallel from al-Mina, which, however, was thought to be "Coptic

[8] Harvey, *Economic Expansion*, 124–125.

[9] Yardımcı, "1985 Harran Kazı ve Restorasyon Çalışmaları," 1:295.

[10] Yardımcı, "1987 Dönemi Harran Kazı ve Restorasyon Çalışmaları," Vol. 1, Pl. 26, 306.

[11] Ibid., Pl. 22.

[12] Hauptmann, "Die Grabungen auf dem Lidar Höyük, 1979," 262.

5–6th centuries,"[13] clearly not the case with the Gritille objects. Because of their recovery at a rural site such as Gritille, it also seems unlikely that these objects were cupping vessels, as is maintained on a label for a similar object in the Islamic galleries in the British Museum, London.

CROSSES

Several crosses were found at Gritille. One (Fig. 4:5A, Pls. 4:17, 4:18) was a historiated phylactery. Consisting of two independently fashioned pieces hinged at the top, it was intended to house a relic, amulet, or holy souvenir. It was found in Level 2, the period most likely associated with Byzantine occupation of this region in the eleventh century. Vikan has noted the conscious revival of the pilgrimage trade in Byzantium after the conquest of Antioch, a trade that had lain dormant since the Arab conquest of the Holy Land.[14] With pilgrimage came the paraphernalia of flasks and other receptacles for holy water, oil, and souvenirs. This cross is most likely an example from that era.

This cross depicts the Crucifixion (obverse) and the Virgin holding the Christ Child (reverse). In the arms of the cross are busts of saints; corrosion has prevented further identification. The historiated phylactery from Gritille is typologically closest to a group of crosses identified by a Hungarian scholar as produced in Kiev in the twelfth and thirteenth centuries.[15] These crosses, according to the author, were based on Byzantine prototypes rather than on those produced for the pilgrimage trade in the Holy Land. If this is correct, then the Gritille phylactery must be an example of the Byzantine prototype.

Other crosses include two with traces of incised depictions of Christ on the cross (Fig. 4:5C, D; Pl. 4:19). Smaller, lobed crosses are illustrated in Figure 4:5B and Plates 4:20 and 4:21.

Pectoral crosses were found at Lidar,[16] Tille (Tille Fig. 64:73, 74), Taşkun Kale (Taşkun Kale Fig. 89:8) and Hama (Hama Fig. 31:21, 22). All were copper/bronze with the exception of one cross from Tille and the cross from Taşkun, which were silver. This last most resembles the Gritille cross in Figure 4:5B in size and shape.

LARGE STONE OBJECTS

Fragments of stone vessels were uncovered at Gritille. One (Fig. 4:6A) was the base of a large stone vessel; another (Fig. 4:6C) appears to be the edge fragment of a quernstone.[17] Large basalt stone vessels like these were found at Tille (Tille Fig. 80:191–93) and Lidar. Two grindstones were also recovered (Pls. 4:22, 4:23).

Other stone artifacts found included architectural elements made of local limestone: post supports (Fig. 4:5E, F), door sockets, and large hollowed stones likely used for the pounding of wheat to make bulgur (Pl. 4:24). None of the last was drawn because they were too heavy to transport to the dig house; when, as a consequence, they were left on site, they disappeared, put to the purpose advanced above.

Two other stone artifacts (Fig. 4:5B, D; Pls. 2:33, 2:34) are not as easy to identify. These were found in secondary reuse, built into the walls of the Phase 4 North End, where they may have served as post bases. They are almost identical to the top elements of an olive press; such a use would have them placed on end, yoked together and attached to a stout trunk, and turned by human or animal power in a large, shallow, circular trough over the olives. Despite this similarity to an olive press, however, the absence of olive growing in the region at present and in the written and archaeobotanical records makes it highly unlikely that these elements were used to crush olives. Given the agricultural economy of the region, it is much more likely that they were used for pressing grapes, either to make wine or *pekmez*, a grape syrup traditional to the eastern Mediterranean.

Also represented from Gritille is part of a stone chancel screen, tentatively dated to the fifth to sixth centuries (Pls. 4:25, 4:26). It was found in a field to the south of Biriman village by Gil Stein's survey team. No other architectural remains were found with it.

---

[13] A. Lane, "Medieval Finds at Al Mina," Fig. 14:A.

[14] Vikan, *Byzantine Pilgrimage Art*, 40.

[15] Lovag, "Byzantine Type Reliquary Crosses," Fig. 4, also p. 158.

[16] Hauptmann, "Die Grabungen auf dem Lidar Höyük, 1979."

[17] Personal communication from Prof. Harald Hauptmann.

GLASS

In common with Harran, Tille, Arsameia, Lidar, Samsat, and most other medieval sites in the Near East, glass bangles or bracelets were found in large quantities at Gritille. Bracelets were fashioned out of monochrome glass (Fig. 4:7A, B, C), twisted with or without threads of a different colored glass (Fig. 4:7D–G), and had applied decoration, either a thread (Fig. 4:7H) or marvered threads and prunts (Fig. 4:7N).

Fragments of glass vessels were also found at Gritille. In general, they were of transparent glass, although examples were also found with applied colored threads. Figure 4:7W is the most complete example of a typical form, the cup, underscoring the popularity of this vessel type to medieval Islamicate society as depicted in art and described in poetry and history. Commonly, cups were paired with bottles, of which no examples were recovered from Gritille.

Correspondences with other sites include the following.

Cf. Gritille Figure 4:7W with Tille Figure 93:251 and Samsat.[18]

Cf. Gritille Figure 4:7AA with Samsat Figure 13.

Cf. Gritille Figure 4:7BB with Samsat Figure 12, as well as Tille Figure 93:251.

Cf. Gritille Figure 4:7Y with Tille Figure 92:243 and Samsat Figure 30.

Cf. Gritille Figure 4:7X with Samsat Figure 32.

Cf. Gritille Figure 4:7T with Samsat Figure 20.

Cf. the folded rim of Gritille Figure 4:7U with a parallel at Tille (Tille Fig. 91: 234, 236, and 238).

No doubt the range of comparanda will expand as more glass from sites in the region is published.

Vessels found at Gritille were decorated with threads of glass (Fig. 4:7K, P, U, V, X), prunts (Fig. 4:7S), enamel (Fig. 4:7Q, R), and enameled and gilded decoration (Fig. 4:7O). Enameled and gilded cups and other glassware forms are well-known features of the luxury glass production of late twelfth- and thirteenth-century Syria. Other examples of cups and bottles with similar decoration have been recovered from Harran,[19] Lidar (Lidar Pl. 160: 3), and Samsat (Samsat Figs. 4, 28). Although rare, the domestic context of both the Harran and Gritille finds calls into question the scarcity of these finely decorated vessels and their cost. Presumably, gilded and enameled vessels were available, albeit seldom, even to residents of small provincial sites.

Small clear glass rods (Fig. 4:7I, J) of unclear function were unearthed at Gritille. They were also found at Tille (Tille Fig. 93:244–247) and Harran.[20]

---

[18] Redford, "Ayyubid Glass from Samsat, Turkey," Figs. 24–26 (cup bases). All other references to Samsat in this section refer to this same article.

[19] Yardımcı, "1987 Dönemi Harran Kazı ve Restorasyon Çalışmaları," Pl. 19.

[20] Ibid., Pl. 18.

SMALL FINDS CATALOG

FIGURE 4:1 IRON OBJECTS.

A. GT 5091. GR83-156. Iron implement.

B. GT 15958. GR84-78. Iron blade with haft.

C. GT 786. GR82-90. Iron blade with haft. Broken at top.

D. GT 8091. GR83-347. Iron projectile point.

E. GT 16099. GR84-101. Iron blade with haft.

F. GT 3914. GR83-63. Iron blade base with two rivets in rivet holes.

G. GT 8560. GR83-355. Iron blade base with one rivet in rivet hole.

H. GT 18200. GR84-240. Iron blade base.

I. GT 16071. GR84-84. Iron blade. Top broken. Base has two rivets in rivet holes.

J. GT 15241. GR84-119. Iron blade. Top and bottom broken.

K. GT 824. GR82-98. Iron blade. Beginning of haft present.

L. GT 15551. GR84-36. Iron blade with intact haft and pommel.

M. GT 19726. GR84-336. Iron blade. Top and bottom broken.

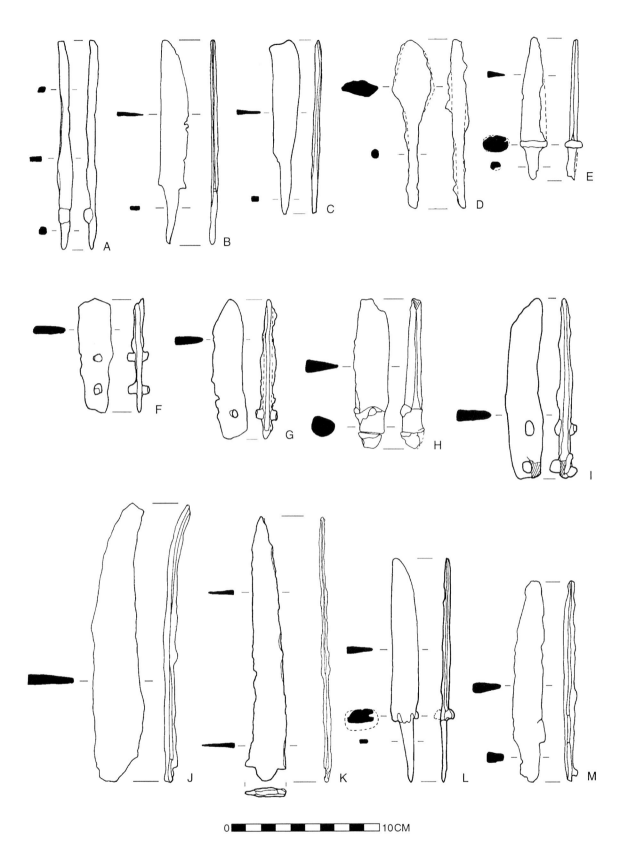

FIGURE 4:1. IRON OBJECTS

FIGURE 4:2. METAL OBJECTS.

A. GT 3554. GR83-9. Iron projectile point.

B. GT 4324. GR83-107. Iron projectile point.

C. GT 19694. GR84-379. Iron projectile point. Point broken.

D. GT 7341. GR83-292. Iron projectile point.

E. GT 1310. GR82-256. Iron projectile point. Point broken.

F. GT 4846. GR83-127. Iron projectile point.

G. GT 15190. GR 84-56. Bronze pin.

H. GT 77. GR81-27. Iron nail.

I. GT 2440. GR82-240. Copper/bronze ring. Detail at right shows chased herringbone pattern to either side of join.

J. GT 748. GR82-85. Iron leather fastener.

K. GT 6229. GR83-225. Iron nail.

L. GT 749. GR82-291. Iron nail or implement.

M. GT 17080. GR84-163. Copper/bronze pin.

N. GT 16165. GR84-85. Iron needle. Detail of eye at left.

O. GT 124. GR81-30. Iron nail or spike.

P. GR 81-88 Iron spear point.

Q. GT 449. GR82-72. Iron nail or spike.

R. GT 2300. GR82-271. Iron nail.

S. GT 505. GR82-44. Iron nail.

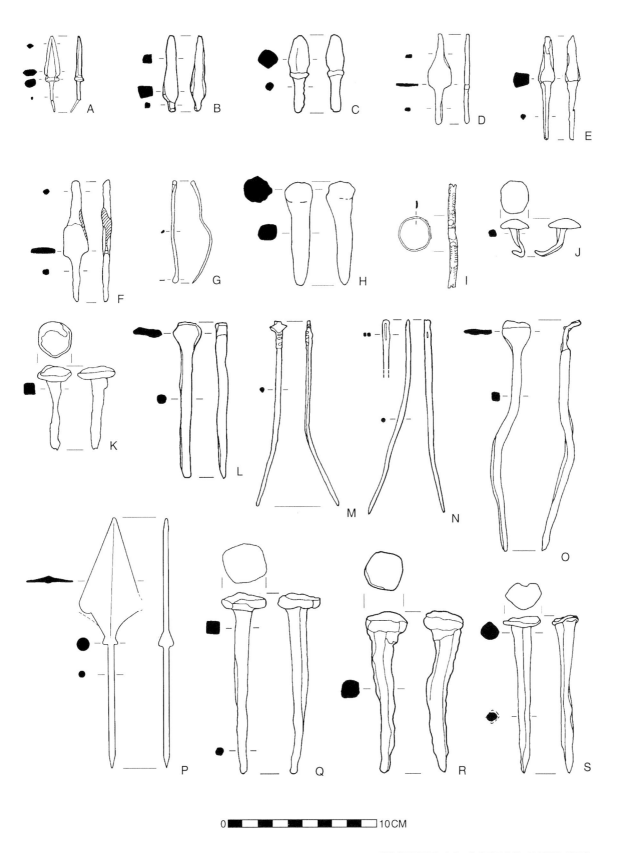

FIGURE 4:2. METAL OBJECTS

FIGURE 4:3. METAL OBJECTS AND SPINDLE WHORLS.

A. GT 8653. GR83-366. Iron animal shoe. Two nail holes.

B. GT 18216. GR84-238. Iron animal shoe. Two nail holes.

C. GT 18358. GR84-244. Iron animal shoe. Three nail holes.

D. GT 274. GR81-73. Iron adze.

E. GT 20070. GR84-371. Iron shackle.

F. GT 15328. GR84-46. Stone whorl.

G. GT 16661. GR84-110. Clay disc. Incised lines.

H. GT 19733. GR84-334. Bone whorl.

I. GT 15589. GR84-62. Stone whorl.

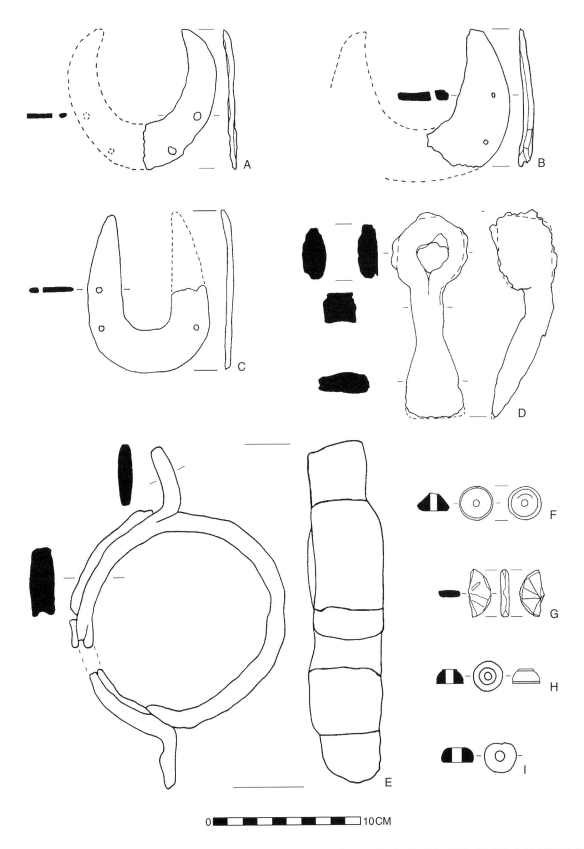

FIGURE 4:3. METAL OBJECTS AND SPINDLE WHORLS

FIGURE 4:4. METAL OBJECTS.

A. GT 15187. GR84-53. Iron buckle.

B. GT 17723. GR84-219. Iron buckle.

C. GT 110. GR82-51. Copper/bronze fish hook.

D. GT 17693. GR84-197. Copper/bronze ring with bezel.

E. GT 18865. GR84-299. Iron ring.

F. GT 2662. GR82-233. Iron knife or small sickle blade. Two rivet holes.

G. GT 3147. GR82-335. Iron sickle blade.

H. GT 9018. GR83-426. Iron ladle. Detail at left shows raised spiral decoration at handle tip.

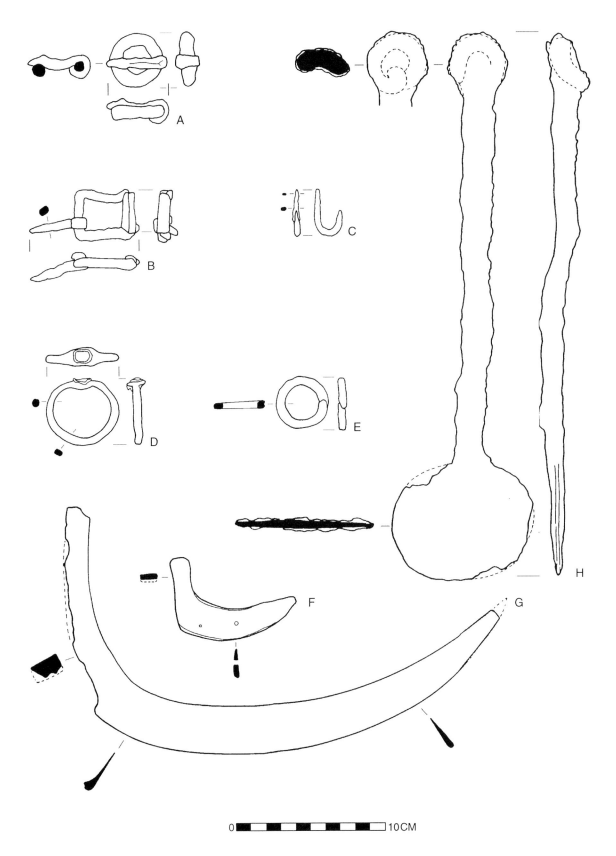

FIGURE 4:4. METAL OBJECTS

FIGURE 4:5. COPPER/BRONZE VESSELS AND CROSSES.

A. GT 2440. GR 82-370. Copper/bronze historiated phylactery.

B. GT 3423. GR 82-369. Copper/bronze pectoral cross.

C. GT 2842. GR 82-311. Copper/bronze pectoral cross with incised crucifixion on obverse.

D. GR 81-106. Iron cross with traces of incised circle (head?) at top. Left arm of cross missing.

E. GT 18657. GR84-243. Copper/bronze bowl.

F. GT 19857. GR84-365. Copper/bronze lamp.

G. GT 15186. GR84-52. Copper/bronze lamp.

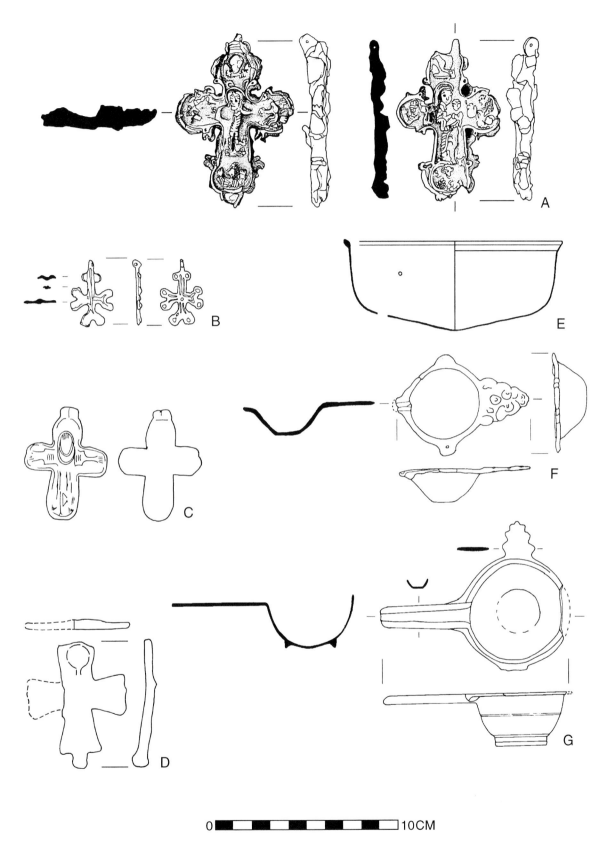

FIGURE 4:5. COPPER/BRONZE VESSELS AND CROSSES

FIGURE 4:6. STONE OBJECTS.

A. GT 6980. GR83-260. Basalt groundstone vessel base.

B. GT 20109. Basalt press element.

C. GT 13740. Basalt grinding stone fragment.

D. GT 20110. Basalt press element.

E. GT 18972. GR84-305. Limestone column or post base.

F. GT 18971. GR84-304. Limestone column or post base.

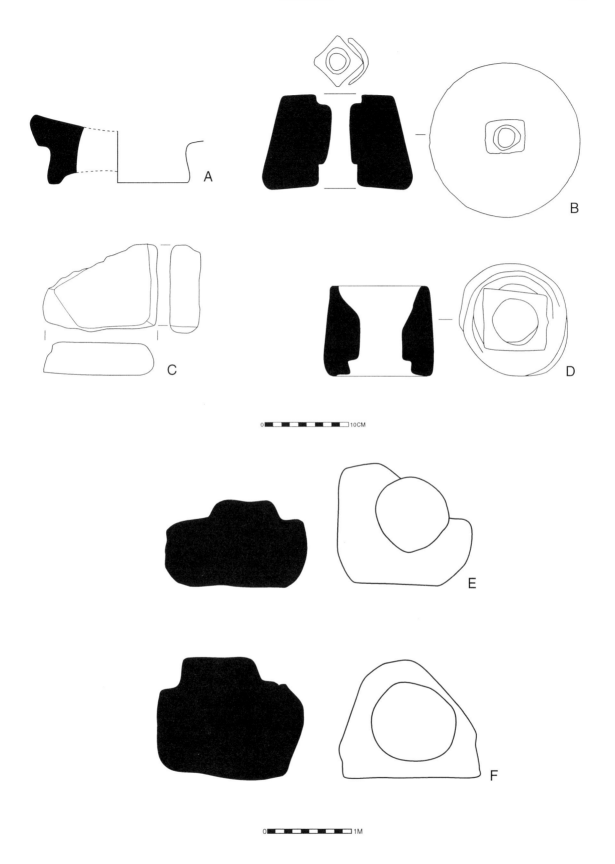

FIGURE 4:6. STONE OBJECTS

FIGURE 4:7. GLASS OBJECTS.

A. GT 5719. Bangle. Dark blue to black fabric. Details show three raised ridges at join and join line. Diameter 6 cm.

B. GT7171. Bangle. Black fabric. Join shown at left. Diameter 7 cm.

C. GT 16265. Bangle. Fabric color unrecorded. Diameter 6 cm.

D. GT 554. Bangle. Dark fabric twisted with applied red-purple threads (shown in black on drawing). Diameter 7 cm.

E. GT 1378. Bangle. Amber fabric. Twisted. Join marked by impressed area on exterior of bangle at bottom of drawing. Diameter 7.5 cm.

F. GT 554. Bangle. Blue fabric twisted with applied red threads (shown in black on drawing). Diameter 7 cm.

G. GT 7379. Bangle. Green fabric. Twisted. Diameter 8 cm.

H. GT 7379. Bangle. Dark brown fabric. Applied yellow stripe on exterior (shown in black on drawing). Diameter 7 cm.

I, J. GT 4862. Rods. Clear fabric.

K. GT 8143. Body sherd. Clear fabric with applied raised threads of turquoise (top line, indicated in black) and clear glass.

L. GT 7110. Bead. Blue fabric with yellow thread marvered flat into surface.

M. GT 15181. GR84-45. Vial. Clear fabric.

N. GT 4372. Bangle. Dark blue fabric. Light green prunts applied to exterior on top of marvered decoration in turquoise, red, and yellow. Diameter 7.5 cm.

O. GT 1432. Body sherd. Clear fabric. Gilded Arabic inscription (possibly al-Muẓaffar) and lower curvilinear design, and white enamel dotted border framed by red painted lines.

P. GT 4124. Body sherd. Clear fabric. Gold band with red painted lines to either side.

Q. GT 1552. Body sherd. Clear fabric. Cobalt blue enamel dots on a cobalt blue enamel band. This band is flanked by gold bands flanked by thin red lines.

R. GT 689. Body sherd. Clear fabric. White enamel dots on a cobalt blue band flanked by thin red lines.

S. GT 1832. Body sherd. Clear fabric. Applied clear glass thread (at top) and clear prunts on an enameled blue meander design.

T. GT 6268. Rim sherd. Clear fabric. Diameter 11 cm.

U. GT 7108. Rim sherd. Clear fabric. Folded rim. Diameter 7 cm.

V. GT 5992. Rim sherd. Clear fabric. Turquoise glass line at rim. Diameter 10 cm.

W. GT 685. Rim and base of cup. Clear fabric. Rim diameter 11 cm; base diameter 5 cm. Positioning approximate.

X. GT 2461. Rim sherd. Clear fabric with applied turquoise threads at rim and upper body. Diameter 6 cm.

Y. GT 685. Rim sherd. Clear fabric. Rim diameter 11 cm.

Z. GT 6964. Base sherd. Clear fabric. Irregularity of base shown in detail. Diameter approximately 3.5 cm.

AA. GT 4959. Base sherd. Clear fabric. Diameter 5 cm.

BB. GT 1775. Base sherd. Clear fabric. Diameter 6.5 cm.

CC. GT 7393. Base sherd. Clear fabric. Diameter 8 cm.

DD. GT 7393. Base sherd. Clear fabric. Diameter 8 cm.

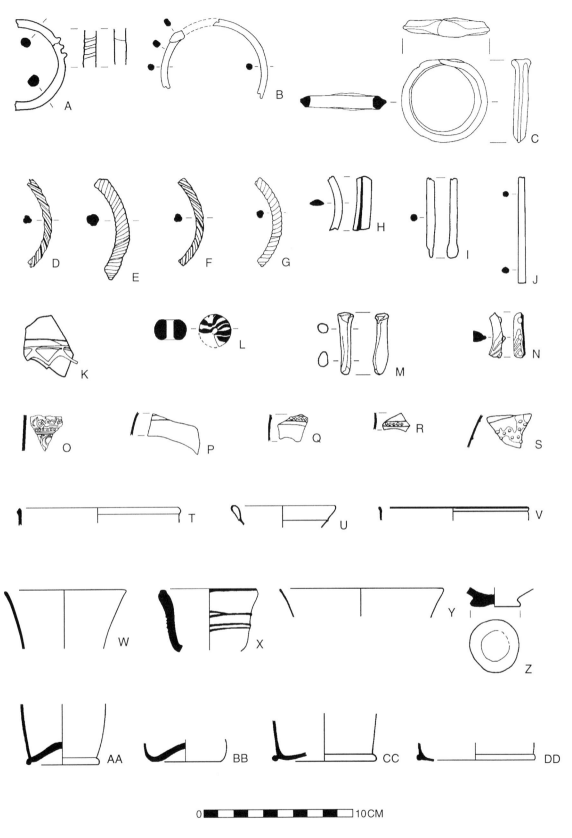

FIGURE 4:7. GLASS BANGLES, VESSELS, AND OBJECTS

V

MEDIEVAL PASTORAL PRODUCTION SYSTEMS AT GRITILLE

Gil J. Stein

The faunal remains from Gritille provide important information about the organization of medieval herding systems in southeast Anatolia. This chapter has three parts. The first section presents an overall description of the medieval sample and the analytical procedures followed in the examination of this data set. The second part evaluates the effects of potential biases on sample composition, with particular attention paid to preservational factors, recovery procedures, and the effects of intrasite variability. After establishing that these factors have not overly biased the representativeness of the Gritille medieval sample, the final section reconstructs the twelfth- to thirteenth-century pastoral production system at this rural settlement in the Euphrates valley.

ANALYTICAL PROCEDURES AND SAMPLE DESCRIPTION

Four seasons of excavation at Gritille exposed over 1,100 square meters of medieval deposits, mainly in three areas at the top of the mound. Medieval animal bone remains were recovered in two ways: directly in the course of excavation, and through dry sieving (using a 0.5 cm mesh) of 20 percent (by volume) of excavated sediments from selected contexts. Sieving focused on the most reliable stratigraphic contexts such as floor deposits, intact floor features (e.g.,

ovens, hearths, or bins), and dense trash deposits associated with habitation floors. In any given context, bones recovered by dry sieving were bagged separately from the bone recovered in the course of excavation. This permits a controlled comparison of recovery rates between the composition of the faunal sample found in the course of excavation with the faunal material recovered in the sieving of those same sediments.

The Gritille bone coding system recorded 44 variables for each specimen. In addition to the standard anatomical information (species, element, fusion, etc.), coding variables also included detailed information on recovery procedures, stratigraphic provenience, chronological phasing, and the type of archaeological deposit. Archaeological deposits were classified as "primary" (in situ), "secondary" (redeposited, e.g., midden or trash in pits), or "tertiary" (redeposition of a secondary deposit, e.g., midden used in mud bricks, or mudbrick wash). In a secondary classification, bones were coded for the type of context in which they were found, such as interior floor, exterior surface, oven, mudbrick wash, wall collapse, and the like.

Each bone was weighed to the nearest 0.5 gram. Bones in association, such as articulated limbs or a set of teeth in the same mandible, were coded as deriving from the same individual. When sufficiently complete, selected teeth or bones were measured, following standardized measurements suggested by von den Driesch, Hole et al., and Speth.[1] Schematic drawings were made of all examples of butchery, showing the locations and orientations of chop and cut marks. Faunal identifications were made using comparative collections in zooarchaeology laboratories at the British Institute of Archaeology in Ankara, the University of Michigan Museum of Anthropology, and the Museum Applied Science Center for Archaeology (MASCA) at the University of Pennsylvania. Statistical analyses were conducted using the SAS software package.

Although all recovered fragments were saved, the massive volume of recovered animal bones required the use of some form of sampling to analyze this assemblage. Three criteria guided the selection of excavation areas from which bone was analyzed: (1) the degree of stratigraphic control; (2) the detail of recording; and (3) the horizontal coverage of different parts of the mound to insure that the sample represented a wide range of socially and/or functionally discrete areas of the medieval settlement. On this basis, material was analyzed from fourteen excavation areas exposed in the 1982–1984 field seasons. These excavation areas comprise approximately 600 of the 1,100 square meters of medieval exposure, providing representative coverage of the north, west, and east-central parts of the settlement (Fig. 5:1). Medieval exposures on the south end of the mound were omitted from this study because these excavation units focused mainly on tracing the settlement's fortification wall rather than on the recovery of habitation areas. The 600 square meter exposure of predominantly habitation areas and associated streets provides a faunal sample of 23,597 specimens from 4 percent of the area of the 1.5 hectare medieval mound.

Redford (Chapter 2, this volume) divides the two-century-long medieval occupation of Gritille into nine phases extending from the late eleventh through the mid-thirteenth centuries A.D. (Table 5:1). The majority of the analyzed sample derives from the post-Crusader medieval occupation overlying Phase 3 (the "Burnt Level"). Of the 23,597 analyzed specimens (Table 5:2), 6,799 fragments (28.81%) remained unidentified, while an additional 8,455 (35.83%)

TABLE 5:1. GRITILLE MEDIEVAL PHASES AND FAUNAL SAMPLES

Phase*	Size of analyzed faunal sample
0 (indeterminate)	5701
1	31
2	32
3	217
4	503
(4 or 5)	660
5	3932
(5 or 6)	2395
6	2441
(6 or 7)	596
7	3761
(7 or 8)	1922
8	1245
(8 or 9)	161
9	0

* Subphase 1 = earliest, 9 = latest

could only be identified in relatively general terms such as "large mammal" (cattle-horse-camel size range), "medium mammal" (sheep-goat-pig-dog size range), and "small mammal" (e.g., hedgehog, hare). The remaining 8,343 bones, comprising 35.36 percent of the analyzed medieval assemblage, were identified with greater precision to genus or species. In evaluating sample reliability, the following discussion generally treats the medieval fauna as a unit, combining all phases because of the relatively short timespan represented.

THE MEDIEVAL SAMPLE

Pigs predominate in the fragment counts, forming 44.97 percent of the identified medieval bone. Caprines (sheep and goats) take second place, comprising 29.62 percent of the identified fragments. When the distinction between *Ovis* (sheep) and *Capra* (goat) could be made, goat

---

[1] von den Driesch, *Guide to the Measurement of Animal Bones*; Hole et al., *Prehistory and Human Ecology*; Speth, *Bison Kills and Bone Counts*, Figs. 37–60.

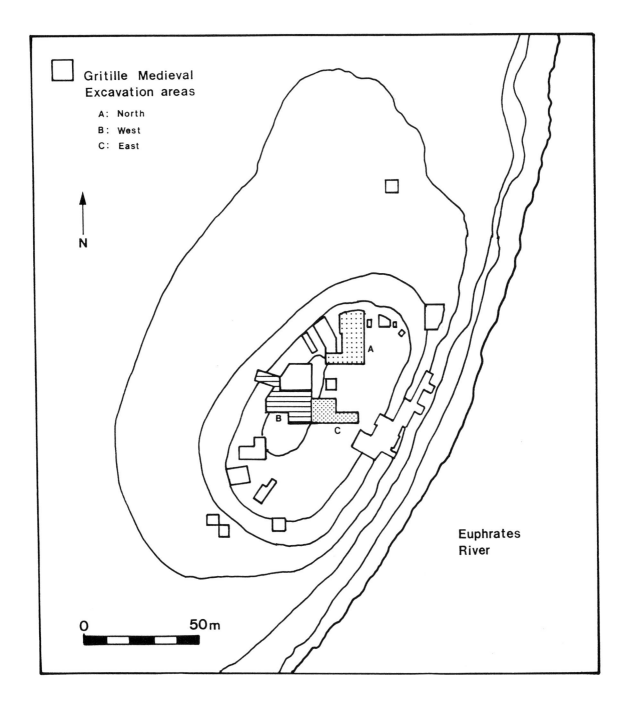

Figure 5:1. Gritille medieval excavation areas.

TABLE 5:2. FRAGMENT COUNTS (NISP) OF GRITILLE MEDIEVAL FAUNA, ALL PHASES

Identification	Fragment count (NISP)
Unidentified	6799
Large mammal	3386
Medium mammal	4482
Small mammal	97
Bovid	3
Ovis/Capra/Gazella	2
Ovis/Capra	1998
Ovis (sheep)	160
Capra (goat)	313
Gazella	1
Bos (cattle)	1609
Cervid	34
Capreolus (roe deer)	6
Cervus (red deer)	251
Dama (fallow deer)	22
Sus (pig)	3752
Equid	144
Equus asinus/hemionus	31
Equus caballus	6
Large carnivore	2
Medium carnivore	2
Small carnivore	2
Felis (cat)	10
Large canid	1
Small canid	4
Canis sp.	4
Erinaceus	20
Rodent	81
Microtus	96
Spalax	45
Lepus (hare)	9
Gallus	3
Potamon	1
Large bird	18
Medium bird	189
Small bird	8
Testudo	18
Bufo	1
Total	23597

bone outnumbered sheep bone by a ratio of almost 2 to 1, a somewhat surprising reversal of the sheep-to-goat proportions present in the earlier Neolithic and Early Bronze Age levels at the site.[2] Cattle are the third most common taxon, making up 12.29 percent of the identified fragments. Hunted wild animals, especially red deer (*Cervus elaphus*), appear with a surprising frequency as the fourth most common identified taxon (3.01 percent).

Minimum numbers of individuals (MNI) were also calculated for the medieval sample, making separate estimates for postcranial remains and teeth. Postcranial MNI calculations selected the most commonly occurring element (e.g., distal humerus or proximal metacarpal) for each taxon. These fragments were then sorted by side (left versus right) and fusion status (fused, fusing, unfused). Within each of these fusion categories, bones were counted from whichever side occurred most frequently; the sum of these three numbers forms the postcranial MNI for each animal (Table 5:3). MNI figures were also calculated from tooth counts for the most commonly occurring taxa: pigs, caprines, cattle, and red deer. This procedure examined deciduous fourth premolars (dp4) and adult molars 1 to 3 from both the upper and lower jaws. These calculations selected the most common side of the most frequently occurring tooth number (Table 5:4). Final MNI determination is based on comparison between the tooth-based and postcranial-based MNI results for each taxon, selecting whichever method gave the larger number.

Table 5:5 shows the high degree of agreement between MNI values and fragment counts (NISP = number of identified specimens) in describing the composition of the identified medieval sample. Both measures yield the same rank-ordering of pig as the most abundant taxon, followed by caprines, cattle, and red deer. Linear regression reveals a high correlation between fragment counts and MNI (correlation = .95, r^2 = .91) for the 20 identified taxa in the medieval sample. This type of correlation suggests that fragment counts provide a good predictor of MNI in the Gritille assemblage.[3] As a result, either fragment counts or MNI values can be used as a valid measurement in the following discussions of sample composition and inferences about economic organization in the medieval settlement.

---

[2] Stein, "Village Level Pastoral Production"; idem, "Regional Economic Integration"; idem, "Strategies of Risk Reduction," 87–97.

[3] Grayson, *Quantitative Zooarchaeology*, 62–63.

TABLE 5:3. MINIMUM NUMBER OF INDIVIDUALS (MNI) FROM POST-CRANIAL DATA, GRITILLE MEDIEVAL IDENTIFIED FAUNA, ALL PHASES

Taxon	Most frequent element	(A) Unfused	(B) Fusing	(C) Fused	(A+B+C) MNI
Ovis/Capra	Distal tibia	6 (R)	0	11 (R)	17
Ovis	Astragalus**	0	0	14 (L)	14
Capra	Astragalus**	0	0	15 (R)	15
Gazella	-	-	-	-	1*
Bos	Distal tibia	5 (R)	1	15	21
Sus	Temporal	24 (L)	13 (R)	9 (L)	46
Cervus	Astragalus**	0	0	8 (L)	8
Dama	Distal humerus	0	0	1 (L)	1
Capreolus	Distal tibia	0	0	1 (R)	1
E. asinus/hemionus	Distal metacarpal 3	1 (L)	0	2 (L)	3
E. caballus	Distal femur	0	0	1 (L)	1
Felis catus	Mandible	1 (L)	0	0	1
Canis	Mandible	1 (L)	0	0	1
Lepus	Distal humerus	0	0	2 (L)	2
Microtus	-	-	-	-	1*
Spalax	Maxilla	1 (L)	0	0	1
Erinaceus	-	-	-	-	1*
Testudo	-	-	-	-	1*
Gallus	Distal femur	0	0	1 (R)	1
Potamon	-	-	-	-	1*
Bufo	-	-	-	-	1*

(R) = Right side   (L) = Left side

* Estimated MNI: MNI must be at least 1 since some bone is present from this taxon. However, standard MNI calculations could not be made in the absence of side and/or fusion data.

** Non-fusing element.

TESTS FOR POTENTIAL SAMPLE BIASES

To insure the reliability of faunal-based reconstructions of the medieval economy, the Gritille sample was examined to determine the extent to which the species and age composition were subject to distortion by preservational factors, intrasite variability in activities or social status, and recovery biases. These analyses of sample composition are presented in detail elsewhere;[4] the results are summarized below. These potential biases commonly affect archaeofaunal samples, often leading to the underrepresentation of juveniles and the overrepresentation of denser boned taxa such as cattle and pigs.

PRESERVATIONAL BIASES

Three forms of potential sources of preservational bias were investigated: carnivore gnawing, burning, and the form of archaeological deposit (primary, secondary, and tertiary). Only 4.5 percent of the medieval sample showed signs of carnivore gnawing. The primary effect of carnivore gnawing appears to have been to alter species and age composition of the gnawed material by damaging, rather than destroying, bone, resulting in fewer bones identifiable to the genus or species level, and a corresponding increase in bones identified more generally as "medium mammal" and "fusion indeterminate." Burning, the second potential source of preservational bias, affected only 2.12 percent of the sample. Burning shattered the bone of medium mammals more than large mammals, but did not selectively destroy any particular species or age group.

Preservational biases can also arise from the type of archaeological deposit from which the fauna derived. As a general principle, one would expect a better representation of juve-

---

[4] Stein, "Pastoral Production in Complex Societies."

niles and fragile boned taxa in primary (in situ) deposits, and an increasing bias toward larger, older, denser-boned specimens in the progression from primary to secondary (trash) to tertiary (wash, mudbrick) deposits. Some 96.72 percent of the medieval bone derives from secondary or tertiary deposits. Examination of the Gritille material showed that these two types of archaeological deposits have virtually identical composition (Table 5:6). The main difference in sample composition occurs between secondary/tertiary deposits on the one hand, and the much rarer primary deposits, on the other. The former have lower percentages of caprine bones and higher percentages of pigs than in situ materials. Except for cases of sudden site destruction, primary and secondary deposits form complementary assemblages in which the primary deposits contain debris overlooked in housekeeping, while the vast bulk of bone from domestic consumption ends up in secondary/tertiary deposits, rather than in its original place of use.

INTRASITE VARIABILITY

After preservational factors, intrasite variability in activities or social status forms the second main class of potential biases in faunal samples. In the simplest terms, we are trying to determine whether the composition of the medieval sample reflects activities at the settlement as a whole, or if the sample is biased by representing only a limited range of activities and groups at the site.

Intrasite variability can arise through differences in the spatial distribution of activities and their associated functional contexts. If all functional contexts contain more or less similar faunal material, then the medieval sample is not biased by small-scale intrasite variability. Table 5:7 compares the percentages of caprines, cattle, and pigs in different functional contexts of the medieval settlement. Most of the functional contexts with sample sizes over 100 fragments showed a close similarity in the representation of caprines (9–12%), cattle (5–8%), and pigs (16–19%). This similarity seems to derive from

TABLE 5:4. TOOTH-BASED MINIMUM NUMBER OF INDIVIDUALS (MNI) FOR CAPRINES (SHEEP/GOAT), CATTLE, AND PIGS IN GRITILLE MEDIEVAL IDENTIFIED FAUNA, ALL PHASES

(A) CAPRINES: COMBINED SHEEP AND GOATS

TOOTH		Upper dp4	Lower dp4	Upper M1	Lower M1	Upper M2	Lower M2	Upper M3	Lower M3
SIDE	Left:	11	14	30	46	32	40	22	32
	Right:	16	23	27	45	32	43	29	37

Tooth-based Caprine MNI = 46 (Left lower M1)

(B) *BOS*: CATTLE

TOOTH		Upper dp4	Lower dp4	Upper M1	Lower M1	Upper M2	Lower M2	Upper M3	Lower M3
SIDE	Left:	8	5	14	15	8	18	7	18
	Right:	12	1	13	4	13	10	10	7

Tooth-based Bos MNI = 18 (Left lower M2)

(C) *SUS*: PIG

TOOTH		Upper dp4	Lower dp4	Upper M1	Lower M1	Upper M2	Lower M2	Upper M3	Lower M3
SIDE	Left:	19	24	55	43	55	44	41	25
	Right:	17	24	52	52	53	41	41	29

Tooth-based Sus MNI = Tooth-based MNI = 55 (Left upper M1)

TABLE 5:5. COMPARISON OF FRAGMENT COUNTS (NISP) AND MINIMUM NUMBER OF INDIVIDUALS (MNI) COMBINED FROM TOOTH AND POST-CRANIAL DATA FROM THE GRITILLE MEDIEVAL IDENTIFIED FAUNA, ALL PHASES

Taxon	Fragment count (NISP)	Percent	MNI (combined)	Percent
Ovis/Capra	1998	23.95	46	31.08
Ovis	160	1.92	14	*
Capra	313	3.75	15	*
Gazella	1	.01	1	0.68
Bos	1609	19.29	21	14.19
Sus	3752	44.97	55	37.16
Cervus	251	3.01	8	5.41
Dama	9	0.11	1	0.68
Capreolus	6	0.07	1	0.68
E. asinus/hemionus	31	0.37	3	2.03
E. caballus	6	0.07	1	0.68
Felis catus	10	0.12	1	0.68
Canis	4	0.05	1	0.68
Lepus	9	0.11	2	1.35
Microtus	96	1.15	1	0.68
Spalax	45	0.54	1	0.68
Erinaceus	20	0.24	1	0.68
Testudo	18	0.22	1	0.68
Gallus	3	0.04	1	0.68
Potamon	1	0.01	1	0.68
Bufo	1	0.01	1	0.68
Total	8343	100.00	148	100.00

*Omitted from MNI calculations to maintain mutual exclusivity of categories.

the nature of the most common functional contexts (collapse, wash, trash, road/street, and exterior surfaces) as areas of trash deposition or redeposition. The overall uniformity of trash deposition (or redeposition) suggests that most of the Gritille medieval fauna do not represent the remains of specific activities, but represent instead a wide variety of activities whose debris was mixed and spread out over much of the settlement.[5] A few functional contexts, such as ovens, shaped pits, and in situ surface deposits, had different faunal compositions, most notably a lower representation of pigs.

These "anomalous" contexts form only a small part of the total faunal assemblage. However, the potential sampling problems of small scale differences between functional contexts become apparent in larger scale comparisons of the fauna between different parts of the medieval settlement. The following discussion compares the North (Operations 33, 43, 44, 47, 54), West (Operations 8, 9, 10, 11, 25) and East-Central (Operations 26, 27, 31) areas of Gritille in Phases 5/6 and 7/8, the two chronological divisions from which the largest faunal samples are available. Redford (Chapter 2, this volume) suggests that, in Phases 5/6, the North area was a domestic quarter, the West area served some kind of industrial purpose (perhaps lime manufacturing), and the East area was used as an open area trash dump. Subsequently, all three parts of the site served as domestic quarters during Phases 7/8. Given these changes in function, we might expect to see greater intrasite variability in Phases 5/6 (when each area served a different purpose), and less variability in Phases 7/8, when all three parts of the site functioned as residential areas.

A comparison of the percentages of the main taxa from the three areas of Gritille in Phases 5/6 and 7/8 (Table 5:8) shows the ways in which small samples can create a misleading

[5] See also Boone, "Defining and Measuring Midden Catchment," 336–345.

impression of intrasite differences in faunal composition. In Phases 5/6, all three areas show virtually identical percentages of caprines and cattle. However, the North area has markedly lower percentages of pigs (6.37%) than do the West (14.12%) and East-Central (16.01%) areas. This anomaly seems to have been caused by the effects of "atypical" functional contexts (described above) on a small sample. In the numerically small (*n* = 424) sample from the North residential area, more than a third of the animal

bones come from ovens and shaped pits. These functional contexts characteristically have lower percentages of pigs, regardless of area in the medieval settlement (see Table 5:7). In a larger sample (e.g., the West or East-Central area), these atypical functional contexts would have little effect on overall sample composition, because they would be far outnumbered by more typical trash-filled functional contexts. However, in the relatively small sample from the Phase 5/6 North area, the atypical bones from contexts

TABLE 5:6. COMPARISON OF TAXONOMIC ABUNDANCES (NISP) IN PRIMARY, SECONDARY, AND TERTIARY DEPOSITIONAL CONTEXTS OF THE GRITILLE MEDIEVAL FAUNA, ALL PHASES

Identification	Primary contexts		Secondary contexts		Tertiary contexts	
	Count	Percent	Count	Percent	Count	Percent
Unidentified	353	52.8	2469	30.2	2555	25.6
Large mammal	34	5.1	1086	13.2	1548	15.5
Medium mammal	131	19.6	1342	16.4	2038	20.4
Small mammal	1	0.1	23	0.3	38	0.4
Bovid	0	0.0	1	*	2	0.1
Ovis/Capra/Gazella	0	0.0	0	0.0	1	*
Ovis/Capra	54	8.1	741	9.1	824	8.3
Ovis (sheep)	4	0.6	45	0.5	69	0.7
Capra (goat)	1	0.1	87	1.1	150	1.5
Gazella	1	0.1	0	0.0	0	0.0
Bos (cattle)	13	1.9	520	6.4	710	7.1
Cervid	1	0.1	12	0.1	18	0.2
Capreolus (roe deer)	1	0.1	1	*	3	*
Cervus (red deer)	2	0.3	104	1.3	113	1.1
Dama (fallow deer)	1	0.1	1	*	2	*
Sus (pig)	54	8.1	1390	17.0	1702	17.1
Equid	0	0.0	124	1.5	11	0.1
Equus asinus/hemionus	0	0.0	0	0.0	27	0.3
Equus caballus	0	0.0	2	*	1	*
Large carnivore	0	0.0	0	0.0	2	*
Medium carnivore	0	0.0	0	0.0	2	*
Small carnivore	0	0.0	0	0.0	1	*
Felis (cat)	0	0.0	0	0.0	1	*
Large canid	0	0.0	0	0.0	1	*
Small canid	0	0.0	0	0.0	4	*
Canis sp.	1	0.1	0	0.0	3	*
Erinaceus	0	0.0	20	0.2	0	0.0
Rodent	1	0.1	5	0.1	57	0.6
Microtus	0	0.0	82	1.0	14	0.1
Lepus (hare)	0	0.0	2	*	2	*
Gallus	0	0.0	1	*	1	*
Large bird	0	0.0	5	0.1	9	0.1
Medium bird	16	2.4	101	1.2	49	0.5
Small bird	0	0.0	4	*	3	*
Testudo	0	0.0	8	0.1	3	*
Total	669	100	8176	100	9964	100

TABLE 5:7. BREAKDOWN OF GRITILLE MEDIEVAL FAUNA, MAIN TAXA, BY FUNCTIONAL CONTEXT

Functional context	n (All bone)	Caprine %	Cattle %	Pigs %
Collapse	6005	10.54	7.16	17.55
Wash	2631	9.96	7.22	19.23
Trash	2486	11.54	7.28	19.75
Road/street	1555	11.25	8.36	19.61
Exterior surface	1248	12.50	6.09	16.35
Shaped pit	1102	9.89	2.54	8.44
Wall	1047	12.03	7.83	11.84
Surface (indeterminate)	1045	6.41	3.06	12.73
Floor (interior)	803	11.21	5.98	18.80
Oven	370	9.46	1.89	9.46
Ash	304	6.25	8.22	14.47
In situ surface deposit	167	5.39	1.20	11.38
Curb wall	42	4.76	2.38	0.00
Drain	35	5.71	0.00	8.57
Hearth	16	0.00	0.00	0.00
Foundation trench	9	33.33	0.0	11.11
Irregular pit	1	100.00	0.0	0.00

Note: "Indeterminate," "mixed," and "plow zone" contexts and associated fauna omitted from table.

such as ovens and shaped pits can create serious distortions of the faunal inventory. A similar sampling problem also seems to have affected the representation of cattle and pigs in the North area sample from subsequent Phases 7/8.

In short, the observed differences among the North, West, and East-Central parts of Gritille in Phases 5/6 and 7/8 can be explained by the effects of functional context on small subsamples. These biases arise only when the medieval sample from a given phase is further divided into a large number of spatial units for analysis. This suggests that the North, West, and East-Central areas at Gritille should be combined to provide the most accurate analysis of medieval faunal economy at the level of the settlement as a whole.

RECOVERY PROCEDURES

Recovery procedures form the third main class of potential biases which might have affected the composition of the Gritille medieval sample. Unscreened or unsieved faunal samples can underrepresent smaller mammals, such as caprines, relative to larger mammals such as

TABLE 5:8. PERCENTAGE COMPARISONS OF MAIN TAXA REPRESENTED IN THE NORTH, WEST, AND EAST-CENTRAL AREAS FOR PHASES 5/6 AND 7/8 OF THE GRITILLE MEDIEVAL FAUNA

PHASES 5/6

Area	Sample size*	Caprines	Cattle	Pigs
North	424	10.85	4.72	6.37
West	5855	11.50	6.88	14.12
East-Central	1661	13.90	6.38	16.01

PHASES 7/8

Area	Sample size*	Caprines	Cattle	Pigs
North	130	7.69	1.54	39.23
West	3016	8.59	9.55	14.72
East-Central	3355	7.93	6.53	18.84

*Total number of unidentified and identified fragments.

pigs or cattle as well as juveniles relative to adults. Dry sieving sediments through a 0.5 centimeter mesh recovers the majority of medium and large mammal bone which might otherwise be missed in the course of excavation.[6]

Excavators were requested to sieve 100 percent of the excavated matrix from each floor deposit, and at least 20 percent of the matrix from other deposits. Unfortunately, owing to the salvage nature of the fieldwork, the pace of excavation did not always permit these procedures to be followed. Consequently, sieved samples are available from only a small number of medieval contexts. Material recovered by dry sieving forms 6.40 percent (1,499 fragments of the total medieval sample). Sieving procedures were as follows. Workmen inspected the excavated sediments, bagging all bone found at the time. After this initial inspection, the excavators dry sieved 20 to 100 percent (by volume) of the excavated sediments from that deposit through a 0.5 centimeter mesh. Since the excavated matrix was sorted through before sieving, the sieved sample consisted of those fragments that were missed in the course of excavation. Thus the sieved and unsieved samples from any given context must be considered complementary. By comparing the composition of the sieved and unsieved samples, one can identify the differences between the two recovery techniques in the taxa, age groups, or body parts represented. From this information, we can estimate the information lost due to recovery biases in unsieved contexts. Sieved material is available from medieval Operations 25, 26, 27, 31, and 42. Table 5:9 compares the taxa recovered from sieved and unsieved samples from only those contexts in which 100 percent of the excavated sediments were dry sieved. This provides the most accurate estimate of the information lost in those contexts where no sediments were sieved.

The species composition of the dry sieved sample differs markedly from the fauna recovered in the course of excavation (i.e., the unscreened sample). Although pigs outnumber caprines by a ratio of almost 2 to 1 in the unsieved sample, caprines outnumber pigs in the sieved sample. Cattle appear only rarely in the sieved sample (0.93%), since these large bones are almost all recovered in the course of excava-

tion. In other words, these data conform to our expectation that the unsieved sample overrepresents pigs and especially cattle relative to caprines.

The evidence from sieved contexts suggests that caprines are probably underrepresented in other (unsieved) medieval deposits as well. However, correction factors derived from the above unsieved-to-sieved comparisons allow us to estimate the changes to be expected in overall medieval fragment counts if sieved material were available from all contexts. Following Thomas's method of calculation,[7] a sieving correction factor X for each taxon can be defined as the number of fragments of that taxon in the sieved sample, divided by the number of fragments in the unsieved sample. This number will be different for each taxon. This correction factor can then be applied to the overall medieval assemblage. The following formula estimates the frequency of each taxon if all medieval deposits had been dry sieved:

$$C = U + X(U)$$
where
C = the corrected fragment count for each taxon
U = the number of fragments of that taxon from unsieved contexts
X = the correction factor for that taxon (from Table 5:9 column F)

Since preservational factors and recovery procedures can be expected to vary from site to site, values of the taxon-specific correction factor X must be considered as unique to each faunal assemblage and should be calculated independently for each sample, before applying the formula to unsieved material from other sites.

When the correction factors derived from the sieved medieval material were applied to the unsieved portion of the Gritille fauna, sample size increased from an uncorrected total of 23,597 fragments to a corrected estimate of 38,638. In other words, if these contexts had been sieved, sample size would have been an estimated 63.7 percent larger. Most of this increase occurs in the unidentified and medium mammal categories. The number of pigs declines from 15.90 percent of the total (i.e., identified

---

[6] Meadow, "Animal Bones"; Thomas, "Great Basin Hunting Patterns," 392–401.

[7] Ibid., 396.

TABLE 5:9. DERIVATION OF CORRECTION FACTORS FOR SIEVING RECOVERY OF THE GRITILLE MEDIEVAL FAUNA

(A) Taxon	(B) Sieved count	(C) Sieved percent	(D) Unsieved count	(E) Unsieved percent	(F) Correction factor (X = B/D)
Unidentified	580	53.95	525	32.13	1.10
Large mammal	44	4.09	204	12.48	0.22
Medium mammal	301	28.00	300	18.36	1.00
Small mammal	0	0.00	1	0.06	0.00
Ovis and *Capra*	66	6.14	143	8.75	0.46
Bos	10	0.93	168	10.28	0.06
Cervid	0	0.00	1	0.06	0.00
Cervus	1	0.09	2	0.12	0.50
Sus	59	5.49	268	16.40	0.22
Equid	0	0.00	1	0.06	0.00
Canis	0	0.00	1	0.06	0.00
Rodent	1	0.09	0	0.00	0.00
Lepus	0	0.00	1	0.06	0.00
Potamon	0	0.00	1	0.06	0.00
Large bird	0	0.00	1	0.06	0.00
Medium bird	12	1.12	15	0.92	0.80
Small bird	1	0.09	2	0.12	0.50
Totals	1075	100.00	1634	100.00	

plus unidentified fragments) uncorrected sample to 11.85 percent of the total corrected sample. However, the ranking of the main taxa remains unchanged, so that pigs are still the most numerous, with caprines second, and cattle third in both the uncorrected and sieving-corrected samples (Fig. 5:2).

The analysis of potential recovery biases also tested whether juveniles are underrepresented relative to adults in unsieved faunal samples. This was done by comparing epiphyseal fusion patterns and deciduous versus adult teeth between the unsieved and sieved samples from Operations 25, 26, 27, 31, and 42. If unsieved samples underrepresent juveniles, then one would expect to see the predominance of fused bones and adult teeth in the unsieved material, while most of the unfused bone and deciduous teeth should appear in the sieved sample (since the latter represents the material missed in the course of excavation). This in fact turns out to be the case. Fused (i.e., adult) bone outnumbers unfused bone by a ratio of about 3 to 2 in the unsieved sample; however, unfused bone predominates in the sieved sample. In contrast with bone fusion, teeth seem to suffer much less from the effects of recovery procedures. In unsieved samples, adult teeth outnumber deciduous teeth by a ratio of about 5 to 1; adult teeth still

predominate in the sieved sample, but by a smaller ratio of 3.36 to 1. In short, both bone fusion and tooth data suggest that unsieved medieval samples underrepresent juveniles, although teeth are only slightly affected by this recovery bias.

Overall, analysis of the bone recovered by dry sieving suggests that the unsieved majority of the Gritille sample slightly underrepresents caprines relative to pigs. However, despite this problem, the unsieved sample correctly reflects the general importance of pigs in the medieval assemblage; even after the application of sieving correction factors, our estimates of the overall assemblage still show that pigs predominate, with caprines second, and cattle third. In other words, recovery biases have not significantly distorted the relative abundance of different taxa in the medieval assemblage. The unsieved postcranial bone sample seems to underrepresent juvenile caprines and pigs, although unsieved teeth provide a more representative picture of the relative importance of different age groups. In sum, although recovery procedures have undoubtedly affected the composition of the medieval sample, the limited and quantifiable scope of these problems means that they need not prevent us from using the Gritille fauna as a source for economic inferences.

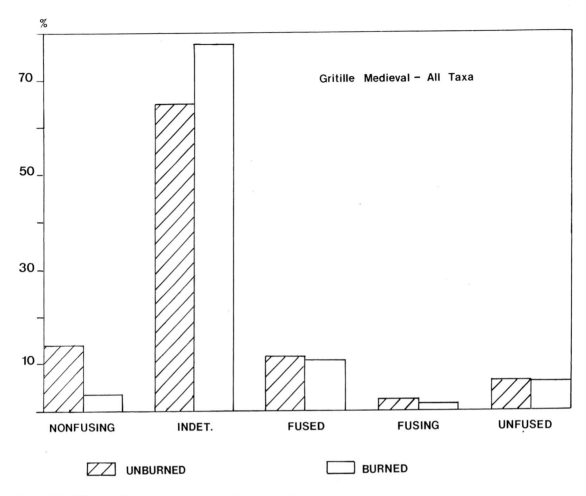

Figure 5:2. Effects of burning on preservation of fused and unfused bone.

SUMMARY OF TESTS FOR POTENTIAL SAMPLE BIASES

Although some biases exist in the medieval faunal assemblage, the analyses presented here indicate that preservation, intrasite variability, and recovery procedures have had a relatively limited and quantifiable impact on overall sample composition. In particular, the unexpectedly high percentage of pigs in the faunal sample cannot simply be dismissed as a mere byproduct of recovery biases or the type of archaeological deposit. Instead, pigs appear to have played a fairly important role in the medieval faunal assemblage. The data strongly suggest that the observed patterning in the Gritille fauna reflects the patterning of ancient trash disposal, which in turn reflects economic activities, rather than the sampling problems connected with site for-mation processes. As a result, we can use the population composition of the faunal remains to reconstruct pastoral strategies in the medieval settlement.

MEDIEVAL PASTORAL PRODUCTION AT GRITILLE

Material from Phases 5/6 and 7/8 forms about two-thirds of the 23,597 analyzed bones and teeth from medieval Gritille. These phases span a period of less than 100 years, from the mid-twelfth through early thirteenth centuries A.D. Close comparison shows a high degree of similarity between the two assemblages.[8] Analyses of intrasite variability presented above showed only minor differences (related to sample size) in the faunal samples from the North, West, and East-Central areas of the site in these

[8] Stein, "Pastoral Production in Complex Societies," 307–312.

phases. Ideally, it would be desirable to analyze each phase as a discrete unit. Unfortunately, the available sample sizes make this approach impractical. However, given the overall similarity in sample composition and taxonomic abundance for Phases 5/6 and 7/8, it seems reasonable to combine the faunal material from these units in the following analyses of late medieval pastoral production strategies at Gritille.

Pigs: Herd Composition and Production Strategies

Pigs were the most frequently slaughtered animals throughout the Gritille medieval sequence, comprising 44.90 percent of all identified fragments (and 37.50% of MNI) in Phases 5 through 8 (Table 5:10). Tooth eruption and epiphyseal fusion patterns in postcranial bone both provide estimates of the ages at which pigs were slaughtered.

To estimate age composition from epiphyseal fusion patterns, the bones in the pig skeleton were first divided into four groups, based on the age at which bone shafts and epiphyses fuse in modern pigs: one year, two years, two and a half years, and three and a half years.[9] The Gritille pig bones from each age group were then classified as "fused," "fusing," or "unfused." Survivorship was defined as the percentage of fused bones among the total number of fused, fusing, and unfused bones from that particular age group.[10] Table 5:11 summarizes the postcranial fusion data for late medieval pigs (*n* = 222 fragments). The fusion percentages suggest that about two-thirds (67.31%) of all pigs survived past the age of one year. The major culling period seems to have taken place between one and two years; only 29.63 percent of the pigs survived beyond this point. The fusion data suggest that very few adults (2.17%) were retained beyond three and a half years as breeding stock (Fig. 5:3).

Pig age estimates from patterns of tooth eruption and wear provide an independent check on the postcranial fusion survivorship data. The known eruption ages for modern pig teeth were applied to both mandibles and maxillae to establish ages at death of late medieval pigs.[11] Pig teeth provide relatively accurate age data up to 17 to 22 months, the age at which the third molar erupts. Beyond this age, patterns of tooth wear can provide age estimates.[12] For those specimens from which the actual teeth were missing, it was often possible to determine whether or not the tooth had erupted by examining the shape of the alveolar cavity inside the mandible or maxilla. When left and right mandibles or maxillae having identical tooth eruption patterns were found in the same archaeological context, they were assumed to have belonged to the same individual; in these cases, only one specimen was counted in the age analysis. Mandibles or maxillae yielding imprecise age data (because of missing or damaged teeth) were also excluded. These procedures reduced the sample from 275 to 159 mandibles and maxillae. These 159 specimens were then sorted into four age groups based on observed eruption patterns for deciduous fourth premolars, permanent fourth premolars, along with the first, second, and third molars (Table 5:12). The tooth-based survivorship data show that about 50 percent of all pigs were slaughtered between the ages of one and two years (Fig. 5:4). Apparently, only 16.98 percent of the pigs survived beyond 22 months, the age at which most sows begin to breed.[13] These results agree closely with the fusion-based survivorship data.

Reconstruction of pig culling patterns and herding strategies requires information on both age patterning and sex ratios. Calculation of sex ratios for pigs relies on morphological differences between the upper canines (tusks) of boars and sows.[14] The known ages at which pig teeth erupt can then indicate whether males and females were slaughtered at different ages. Where the canine was missing from a particular mandible or maxilla, it was often possible to infer the sex of the animal from the shape of the alveolar cavity which had held the tooth.

Sex could be determined for 56 late medieval pig canines. The sample shows an even sex

---

[9] Silver, "Ageing of Domestic Animals," 285–286.

[10] Hole et al., *Prehistory and Human Ecology*, 284.

[11] Silver, "Ageing of Domestic Animals," 298–299.

[12] Grant, "Use of Tooth Wear as a Guide," 91–108; Higham, "Stock Rearing," 84–103.

[13] Grigson, "Porridge and Pannage," 298.

[14] Schmid, *Atlas of Animal Bones*, 81.

TABLE 5:10. FRAGMENT COUNTS (NISP) AND MINIMUM NUMBER OF INDIVIDUALS (MNI) OF THE GRITILLE MEDIEVAL IDENTIFIED FAUNA, PHASES 5–8

Taxon	Fragment count (NISP)	Percent	MNI	Percent
Ovis/Capra/Gazella	1	0.02	*	
Ovis/Capra	1297	23.02	34	30.36
Ovis	90	1.60	*	
Capra	198	3.53	*	
Bos	1160	20.60	15	13.39
Cervus/Dama	22	0.39	*	
Capreolus	2	0.04	1	0.89
Cervus	112	1.99	5	4.46
Dama	4	0.07	1	0.89
Sus	2528	44.90	42	37.50
E. asinus/hemionus	30	0.53	2	1.79
E. caballus	3	0.05	1	0.89
Felis catus	10	0.18	1	0.89
Canis	1	0.02	1	0.89
Erinaceus**	20	0.36	1	0.89
Microtus**	82	1.46	1	0.89
Spalax**	45	0.80	1	0.89
Lepus	8	0.14	2	1.79
Gallus	1	0.02	1	0.89
Potamon	1	0.02	1	0.89
Testudo	14	0.25	1	0.89
Bufo	1	0.02	1	0.89
Totals	5630	100.00	112	100.00

*   Omitted to maintain mutual exclusivity of categories.
**   Articulated skeleton of single individual.

ratio of 29 males to 27 females. Culling patterns for males and females appear to have been strikingly similar. The vast majority of both males (22) and females (20) were slaughtered between the ages of one and two years. The sexed sample suggests that very few sows were kept alive as a breeding population; in fact, only 4.35 percent of the females seem to have survived beyond 17 to 22 months.

Late medieval pig herding at Gritille apparently followed a nonintensive herding strategy known as *pannage*, rather than the more modern system of sty husbandry. These two systems differ markedly in the degree of human control over the animals. Sty husbandry is an intensive management strategy in which pigs are kept in pens and fed directly by their keepers. By contrast, the term *pannage* refers to a widespread traditional practice of nonintensive husbandry

in which pigs range freely, foraging on acorns, bracken, and other forest resources, with relatively little supplemental feeding by humans (this practice is the origin of the expression "to run *hog wild*"). Under a pannage system, adult pigs generally spend very little time in the settlements—usually only in the late winter/early spring, when the sows give birth and nurse their newborn litters.[15] Unfortunately, almost no research to date has focused on the archaeological evidence for pannage versus the more intensive sty husbandry system.[16] The pig age structure at Gritille is consistent with a pannage system similar to that practiced in the contemporaneous settlements of medieval England; the latter sites, where we know from historical sources that pannage was practiced, are characterized by a predominance of juvenile pigs.[17] If such a system were practiced at medieval Gritille, this would

[15] Grigson, "Porridge and Pannage," 304–305.
[16] Biddick, "Pig Husbandry on the Peterborough Abbey Estate," 168; see also Redding, "Role of the Pig," 20–30.
[17] Noddle, "Comparison of the Animal Bones," 250, 255.

TABLE 5:11. EPIPHYSEAL FUSION DATA (*n* = 222) FOR GRITILLE MEDIEVAL PIGS, PHASES 5–8

Element	Fusion age (Mos.)	Fused	Fusing	Unfused
1 Year				
Dist. scapula	12	26	0	7
Prox. second phalanx	12	1	0	1
Dist. humerus	12	23	1	22
Prox. radius	12	20	1	2
2 Years				
Dist. metacarpals 3-4	24	7	0	12
Prox. first phalanx	24	0	0	4
Dist. tibia	24	9	2	20
2.5 Years				
Dist. metatarsals 3-4	27	3	2	8
Calcaneum	24-30	0	0	2
Dist. fibula	30	0	0	3
3.5 Years				
Prox. ulna	36-42	1	0	10
Dist. radius	42	0	0	6
Prox. humerus	42	0	0	7
Prox. femur	42	0	0	7
Dist. femur	42	0	0	7
Prox. tibia	42	0	0	8

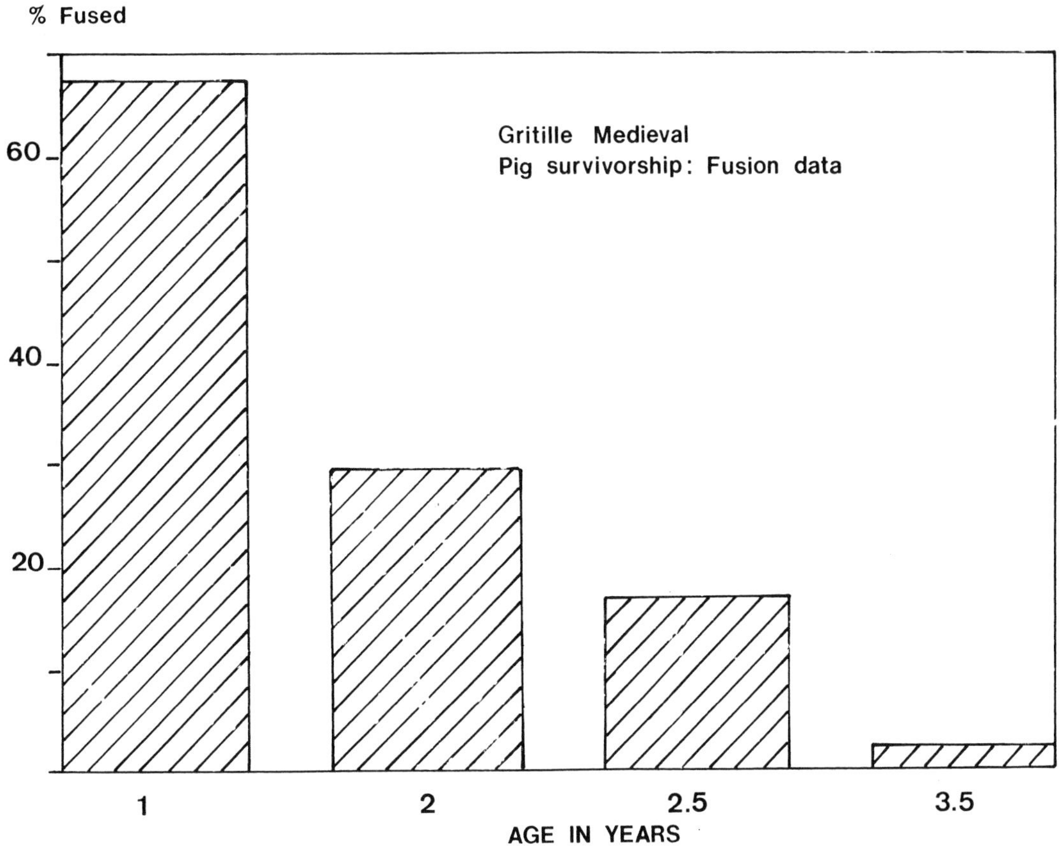

Figure 5:3. Gritille medieval pig survivorship: epiphyseal fusion data.

TABLE 5:12. AGE DATA FROM MANDIBULAR AND MAXILLARY TOOTH ERUPTION OF GRITILLE MEDIEVAL PIGS, PHASES 5-8

Age group Age	Number of specimens
13 months	
Younger than 2 months	2
Younger than 4–6 months	4
4–6 months	7
8–12 months	2
4–13 months	22
7–13 months	11
16 months	
1–16 months	1
4–16 months	7
7–16 months	4
12-16 months	3
22 months	
7–22 months	1
12–22 months	16
17–22 months	52
Older than 17–22 months:	27
Total	159

Note: Age estimates derived from pig tooth eruption ages in Silver, "Ageing of Animals," Table G.

have generated a pattern in which young males and females were consumed in the settlement, while the free ranging adults tended to be spared. Given the great fecundity of pigs, only a small number of adults could generate consistently large supplies of meat.

The large numbers of pig bones in the late medieval settlement do not necessarily prove that pigs were preeminent in the Gritille animal economy. Instead, the frequency of pig bone simply reflects the cross-culturally valid principle that the main economic value of pigs is as a source of meat. For this reason, the productive life of pigs extends only up to an age of two to three years, that is, the point when their growth curve begins to level off at or near their maximum meat weight. In contrast, sheep, goats, and cattle generally have a much longer productive life span of six to eight years, owing to their additional economic value as sources of fiber, dung, traction, and milk. This difference in productive lifespan means that pigs would have been cycled through the economic system at a faster rate than caprines or cattle.

Even if the medieval inhabitants of Gritille had kept equal proportions of live cattle, cap-

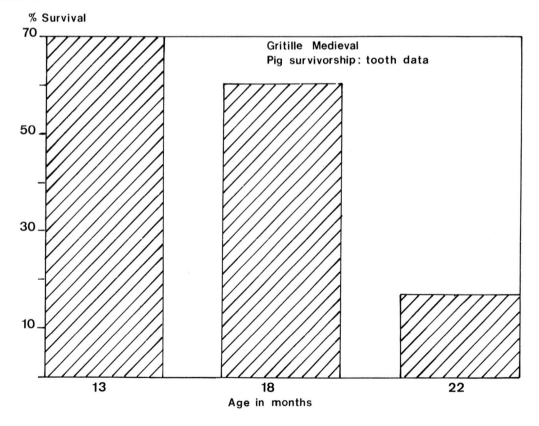

Figure 5:4. Gritille medieval pig survivorship: tooth eruption data.

rines, and pigs at any single point in time, pigs would still appear in the archaeological record more often than caprines or cattle simply because they were killed more often. Thus four generations of pigs might be born, raised, and slaughtered during the productive lifespan of a single generation of cattle. The rapid rates of both pig consumption and population replenishment, through short gestational periods, large litters, and speedy growth, suggest that late medieval pig production provided the inhabitants of Gritille with a meat diet based on "fast food."

CAPRINES: HERD COMPOSITION AND PRODUCTION STRATEGIES

Sheep and goats form the second largest component of the late medieval faunal assemblage, accounting for 28 percent of all identified fragments and 30 percent of MNI in Phases 5 through 8 (Table 5:10). Information on the sheep-to-goat ratio, sex ratios, and ages at death provide the basis for reconstructing caprine production strategies at Gritille. Of the 1,585 late medieval caprine bones, the majority (1,297 fragments) were identified generally as "sheep/ goat." However, on those bones for which the species could be determined, 198 were identified as goat and 90 as sheep. Goats outnumber sheep in virtually every skeletal element for which the distinction could be made (Table 5:13). The predominance of goats contrasts markedly with the dominance of sheep in the earlier third millennium B.C. and neolithic herding systems at Gritille.[18] Several economic and ecological factors may account for the high frequency of goats in the late medieval assemblage. Sheep and goats differ in both the quality and quantity of their secondary products. Both sheep meat and milk have higher fat content than the equivalent products of goats.[19] However, what goats lack in quality, they make up for in quantity. Goats not only produce more milk than sheep per milking; they also lactate for a longer time, continuing to produce even in the summer months after the sheep milk production has ceased.[20] Goats also tend to produce

TABLE 5:13. SHEEP-TO-GOAT RATIOS COMPARED BY SKELETAL ELEMENT, GRITILLE MEDIEVAL CAPRINES, PHASES 5-8

Element	Sheep	Goat
Parietal	1	3
Frontal	2	10
Petrous	1	2
Squamous-temporal	0	1
Mandible	3	4
Tooth	9	18
Horn core	7	51
Axis	0	3
Scapula	2	2
Humerus	7	12
Radius	8	11
Ulna	2	8
Radial carpal	0	1
Intermediate carpal	0	2
Metacarpal 3-4	4	9
Innominate	4	3
Femur	0	1
Tibia	11	16
Lateral malleolus	0	1
Astragalus	16	19
Calcaneum	3	4
Central-fourth tarsal	1	0
Metatarsal 3-4	2	1
Metapodial 3-4	0	1
First phalanx	5	10
Third phalanx	2	4
2+3 tarsal	0	1
Total	90	198
Total (horn cores omitted)*	83	147

*Horn cores are omitted in the second set of totals because horns are present in both male and female domesticated goats, while they are absent in female domesticated sheep.

more meat, since they have twins more frequently than do sheep.[21] Thus a pastoral economy concerned with a high level of output (rather than the maximization of nutritional value) might emphasize the production of goats instead of sheep.

Ecological factors might also have favored a

[18] Stein, "Regional Economic Integration"; idem, "Herding Strategies at Neolithic Gritille," 35–42; idem, "Strategies of Risk Reduction."

[19] Dahl and Hjort, *Having Herds*, 216.

[20] Redding, *Decision Making*, 110.

[21] Dahl and Hjort, *Having Herds*, 93.

late medieval emphasis on goat production. Goats can exploit arid and/or degraded range conditions better than sheep. Over the course of the summer, forage grasses dry out, losing their nutritional value at a faster rate than woody shrubs and trees. The ability of goats to shift from grazing grasses to browsing shrubs allows them to remain healthy even in particularly arid conditions, when the grasses have lost much of their nutritional value. By contrast, the exclusive reliance of sheep on grazing means that they undergo more nutritional stress late in the summer or in especially dry years.[22] The ability of goats to consume (and like) a wide variety of plant resources allows them to flourish in deforested or otherwise degraded pasture land. Palynological, geomorphological, and paleobotanical evidence suggests that progressive deforestation may have taken place in this part of southeast Anatolia during the third millennium B.C.[23] Such conditions might have encouraged a long-term shift from sheep to goats as the caprine of choice in this region. At present we are limited to educated guesses in attempting to specify the reasons for the late medieval focus on goats. However, the economic and ecological factors discussed here may have acted together to encourage a heavier reliance on goats in the twelfth to thirteenth centuries A.D.

Differences in culling patterns of males and females can help us reconstruct production strategies for sheep and goats. Although herders usually spare all reproductively active females, they tend to cull males much more freely, because only a small number of rams or bucks are necessary to maintain a viable breeding population. Sexual dimorphism in the pelvis (especially the pubis) and horn cores serves to distinguish male and female caprines. The pubis of male sheep and goats tends to be more massive and rounded in cross-section, while females have a thinner, flatter pubis with a more sharply protruding pecten ossis pubis.[24] Horn core morphology was mainly used to determine sex for goats. The horn cores of males have a very flat medial surface, a sharp anterior keel, and a high degree of helical twisting. By contrast, the horn cores of females have a slightly rounded medial surface, a more rounded anterior keel, and only slight helical twisting.[25]

Using these criteria, 32 of the 1,585 medieval caprine bone fragments were identified by sex. Females slightly outnumber males (18 to 14), but this is probably a product of the small sample size. Fusion patterns for the sexed caprine bones suggest possible differences in the treatment of young males versus females. Both sexes are commonly represented in the fused bones of adults. However, the fact that all unfused (juvenile) bones in the sample were males may support the idea that herders at Gritille allowed the female caprines to live until they had fulfilled their reproductive potential as breeding adults.

Given the small size of the sexed sample, age data form the main source of information concerning late medieval production strategies for sheep and goats. Epiphyseal fusion data and mandibular tooth eruption/wear provide complementary profiles of caprine mortality. Fusion estimates are based on data from 173 caprine bone fragments; of these, 92 were identified as *Ovis/Capra* (i.e., either sheep or goat), 32 as sheep, and 49 as goats (Table 5:14). The fusion data suggest that the major culling took place between the ages of one and two years, when survivorship drops by 28.49 percent (Fig. 5:5). Half of all caprines survive beyond three years, dropping off to 36 percent after three and a half years. Caprines in these latter two age groups probably represent a predominantly female population.

These figures represent the combined fusion-based survivorship data for a population in which goats outnumber sheep by a ratio of 1.77 to 1. Did the medieval inhabitants of Gritille cull their sheep and goats at the same ages? Although identified sheep and goats make up less than half of the overall caprine postcranial material, one can still make a limited comparison of survivorship for these two taxa. Figure 5:6 shows similar survivorship percentages for sheep and goats in the first year of life. However, in the second year,

---

[22] Redding, *Decision Making*, 49–50.

[23] van Zeist et al., "Studies of Modern and Holocene Pollen," 19–39; Wilkinson, "Environmental Change and Local Settlement History," 38–46; Willcox, "History of Deforestation," 117–133.

[24] Boessneck, "Osteological Differences," 345.

[25] Sebastian Payne, personal communication. For an illustration comparing male and female horn core morphology, see Boessneck and von den Driesch, "Tierknochenfunde vom Korucutepe," 1:79, Pls. 5, 6.

TABLE 5:14. EPIPHYSEAL FUSION DATA FOR GRITILLE MEDIEVAL CAPRINES, PHASES 5-8

Element	Fusion age (mos.)	Fused	Fusing	Unfused
1 Year				
Dist. scapula	6-8	14	0	2
Prox. radius	10	20	0	0
Dist. humerus	10	27	1	2
2 Years				
Prox. second phalanx	13-16	1	0	0
Prox. first phalanx	13-16	1	0	0
Dist. tibia	18-24	28	4	8
Dist. metacarpal 3-4	18-24	8	0	9
Dist. metatarsals 3-4*	20-28	1	0	1
3 Years				
Prox. ulna	30	0	0	1
Calcaneum	30-36	0	0	2
Prox. femur	30-36	3	0	5
Dist. radius	36	5	0	2
3.5 Years				
Prox. tibia	36-42	3	0	4
Dist. femur	36-42	5	0	2
Prox. humerus	36-42	0	2	6

NOTE: Includes fragments identified as *"Ovis/Capra"* (*n* = 92), *"Ovis"* (*n* = 32), and *"Capra"* (*n* = 49). Total sample size *n* = 173.

*Distal metatarsal fusion age overlaps between the two- and three-year age groups. It was included in the two-year age group because of its similarity to the distal metacarpal.

goat survivorship drops by about 40 percent, an attrition rate almost double that of sheep. Unfortunately, we cannot make accurate comparisons beyond the age of two; survivorship data for the three-year-old age group are misleading because of the tiny available sample of identified sheep and goat bones which fuse at this age (sheep: *n* = 2; goats: *n* = 5). In short, the fusion data suggest a tendency to cull goats at a younger age than sheep. If this interpretation is correct, then the relative proportion of sheep to goats probably varied with age. Thus sheep may well have predominated in the adult population of caprines older than three years, even if the goats were originally more numerous in the juvenile population.

Eruption and wear patterns on caprine teeth provide more accurate age information than does epiphyseal fusion, despite the difficulty in distinguishing the mandibles of sheep from those of goats. The caprine mandibles, individual deciduous fourth premolars (dp4), and individual third molars (M3) were sorted into age stages from birth to ten years, using Payne's coding system for tooth eruption and wear.[26] When left and right mandibles of identical size and wear stages occurred in the same excavation unit, it was assumed that they belonged to the same individual, and only one of the pair was used in age calculations. Otherwise, this analysis used all available mandibles, individual dp4 and M3 teeth to which age stages could be assigned. The sample consists of 57 caprine mandibles and one individual third molar (Table 5:15). Experimental studies have demonstrated that a randomly selected aged sample of this size is sufficiently large to represent mortality patterns in the larger population from which it was drawn.[27]

---

[26] Payne, "Kill-Off Patterns," 281–303.
[27] Lyman, "Analysis of Vertebrate Mortality Profiles," 125–142.

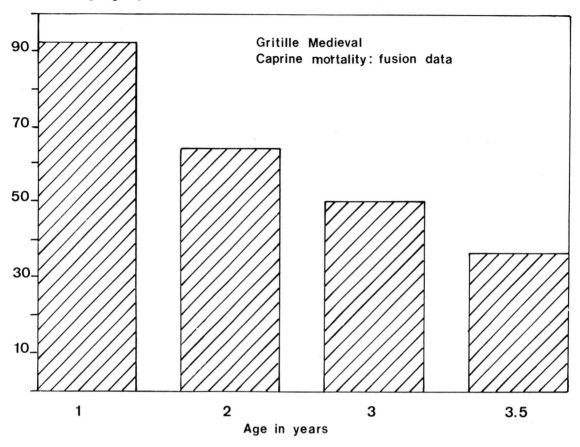

Figure 5:5. Gritille medieval caprine mortality: epiphyseal fusion data.

TABLE 5:15. GRITILLE MEDIEVAL CAPRINE MORTALITY PATTERNS FROM MANDIBULAR TOOTH ERUPTION AND WEAR

Wear stage	Age	Raw count	Corrected count*	Corrected %	Cumulative %
Birth	0 mo.				100.00
A	0–2 mos.	1	1	1.72	98.28
B	2–6 mos.	3	4	6.90	91.38
C	6–12 mos.	8	9	15.52	75.86
D	1–2 yrs.	10	13	22.41	53.45
E	2–3 yrs.	3	3	5.17	48.28
F	3–4 yrs.	9	11	18.97	29.31
G	4–6 yrs.	6	12	20.69	8.62
H	6–8 yrs.	1	2	3.45	5.17
I	8–10 yrs.	3	3	5.17	0.00
Totals		44	58	100.00	

*Corrected counts assign most probable age attributions to wear stages following Payne's ("Kill-Off Patterns") system of proportional allocation.

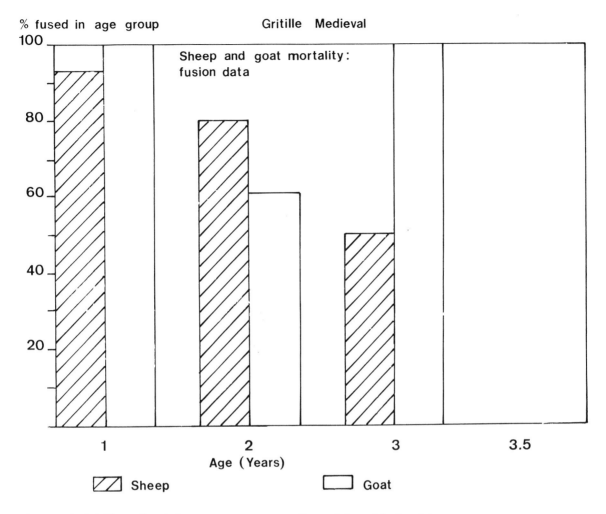

Figure 5:6. Gritille medieval sheep versus goat mortality: epiphyseal fusion data.

Mortality patterns in the Gritille mandibles show two peak culling periods (Fig. 5:7). The first, at the age of one to two years, reduces herd size by 22.41 percent and probably reflects the culling of young males. The second culling peak removes 20.69 percent of the herd in the four- to six-year age range, when the reproductive capacities of the females begin to decline. When converted into cumulative survivorship data, the tooth-based ages largely agree with the fusion data in showing that about half the herd lived past the age of three years. However, the mandibular eruption and wear patterns show that caprines younger than one year were culled at a much higher rate (24%) than had been indicated by the fusion patterns (8%). The mandibular data are almost certainly more accurate, reflecting the better preservation of teeth over

the unfused postcranial bones of lambs or kids younger than one year.

In order to reconstruct the late medieval caprine herding system, the Gritille mandibular age distributions were compared with the expected culling patterns for two contrasting sets of pastoral production strategies: (1) specialized, surplus-oriented systems such as dairy production, wool production, and the intersite transport of animals; and (2) generalized systems focusing on either meat production for local consumption or herd security as a primary goal. The optimum form of herd composition differs for each of these strategies; consequently, the associated culling pattern will also vary, as herders attempt to attain the most desirable proportions of different ages and sexes for that particular production goal.

No. of cases

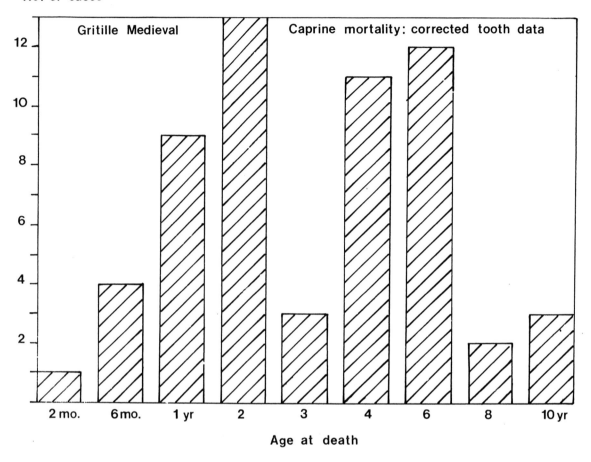

Figure 5:7. Gritille medieval caprine mortality: mandibular tooth eruption and wear data.

Specialized herding systems emphasizing dairy production cull almost all males before the age of one year,[28] because males compete with females for pasture but produce no milk. Late medieval caprine culling patterns at Gritille do not match the profile expected for dairy production (Fig. 5:8). The Gritille data were then compared with the model culling patterns for specialized fiber (wool or goat hair) production. This latter production strategy contrasts markedly with dairy production in that males have substantial value as wool producers. In fact, wethers (castrated males) are often the animal of choice in traditional wool producing economies,

because they have a greater resistance to disease than do breeding ewes, while producing almost twice as much fleece as the females.[29] For this reason, herders emphasizing wool or goat hair production would be expected to castrate and retain their rams and bucks, rather than to cull or sell them at an early age. This strategy would generate a survivorship curve in which a relatively high percentage of all animals would survive into adulthood.[30] The Gritille caprine culling data do not fit the expected profile for a specialized herding system geared toward wool or goat hair production (Fig. 5:9). This result corresponds well with the sheep-to-goat ratio for the

[28] Payne, "Kill-Off Patterns," 283, Fig. 2; D. Bates, *Nomads and Farmers*, 147–148.
[29] Killen, "Wool Industry of Crete," 5.
[30] Payne, "Kill-Off Patterns," Fig. 3.

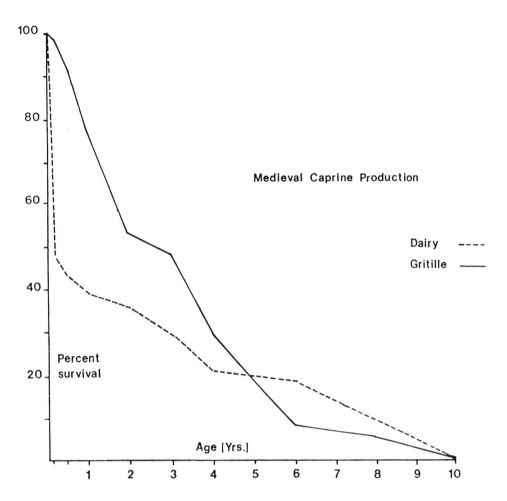

Figure 5:8. Gritille medieval caprine survivorship compared with expected survivorship pattern for dairy production.

late medieval. If wool production had been a primary economic focus, then one would expect to see a heavier emphasis on sheep; instead, goats predominate in the caprine assemblage.

The Gritille caprines were then compared with the expected survivorship patterns for a specialized herding strategy emphasizing inter-site exchange, that is, rural production of animals that were then delivered to larger centers for consumption. Under this system, the rural production areas would be expected to retain the youngest animals and the older animals as breeding stock, while the centers or areas of consumption would have those prime aged animals (aged 2–3 years) in greatest demand as meat sources.[31] This production strategy would generate a convex survivorship curve for those sites

that were consuming animals, and a concave-convex curve for the producing sites (Fig. 5:10). The Gritille late medieval survivorship data do not fit either the producers' or consumers' model survivorship curves for specialized inter-site exchange.

The Gritille caprines were then compared with the survivorship patterns expected for two generalized, subsistence-oriented pastoral production strategies: (1) meat production for local consumption, and (2) maintenance of herd security as a primary goal.[32]

In a subsistence-oriented strategy emphasizing meat production for local consumption, caprines are culled when their growth curve levels off as they approach their full adult body weights after two years.[33] Since the average

---

[31] Mudar, "Early Dynastic III Animal Utilization," 26; Zeder, *Feeding Cities.*

[32] Payne, "Kill-Off Patterns," 281; Redding, *Decision Making*, 93, 96.

[33] Redding, *Decision Making*, 89–97.

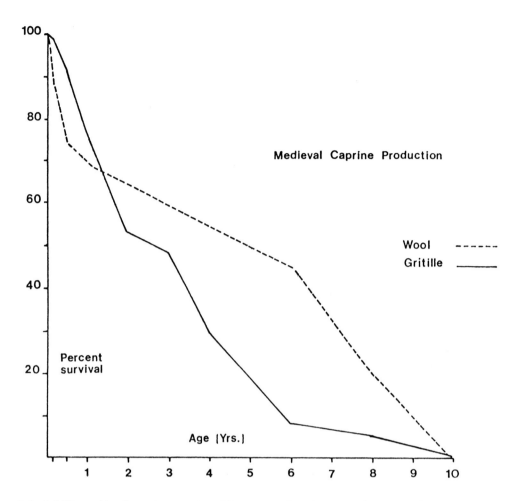

Figure 5:9. Gritille medieval caprine survivorship compared with expected survivorship pattern for wool production.

weight of an adult male sheep or goat is almost twice that of an adult female, herders emphasizing meat production for local consumption would be expected to cull males at or close to an age of two years, instead of the first-year culling associated with dairy production.[34] Females, of course, would be retained as breeding stock until their reproductive capacities declined, usually after an age of six years.[35] The expected survivorship curve would therefore show two peak culling periods: the male cull at two to three years, and the female cull beginning at about six years.

In caprine production strategies emphasizing herd security, males are culled only when the herders can be sure that their consumption would not create any risks for the future viability of the herd. For that reason, herders would refrain from culling young males until they had assessed the size and survival potential of the newly born crop of lambs and kids.[36] A herd security production strategy would extend the culling period of young males from one-half to three years, compared with a culling period of two to three years under a strategy of meat production for local consumption.[37] However, despite the difference in the length of the culling period for young males, these two generalized, subsistence-oriented production strategies are so similar that herders emphasizing one goal would automatically emphasize the other as well.

---

[34] Ibid., 93, 96; Payne, "Kill-Off Patterns," Figs. 1, 2.
[35] Dahl and Hjort, *Having Herds*, 91; Koster, "Ecology of Pastoralism," 235–237; Redding, *Decision Making*, 70.
[36] Ibid., 204.
[37] Ibid., Table X-3.

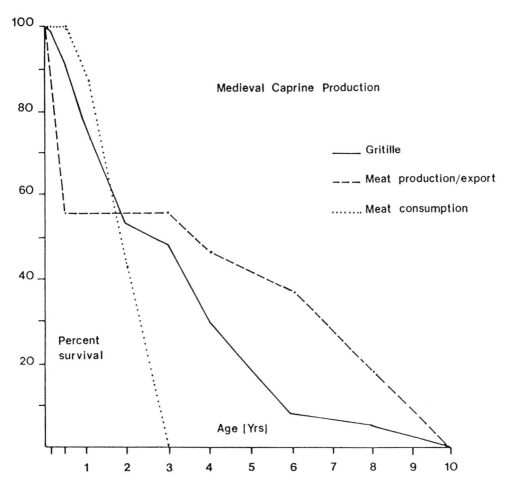

Figure 5:10. Gritille medieval caprine survivorship compared with expected survivorship pattern for intersite exchange of animals (with separate curves for centers of production and consumption).

Survivorship patterns for the Gritille caprines show a close fit with the model survivorship patterns associated with both herd security and meat production for local consumption (Fig. 5:11). This evidence strongly suggests that caprine herding at the late medieval settlement followed generalized, subsistence-level herding strategies oriented toward local autonomy, rather than the production of surplus animals or animal products for exchange.

CATTLE: HERD COMPOSITION AND PRODUCTION STRATEGIES

Cattle form the third largest component of the late medieval assemblage, with 1,160 specimens forming 20.60 percent of the identified fragments and 13.39 percent of MNI. Because sex could only be determined for six cattle innominate bones, reconstructions of cattle herding strategies at Gritille relied exclusively on age

data derived from epiphyseal fusion and tooth eruption/wear.

Epiphyseal fusion data from 159 postcranial bone fragments provides age information for late medieval cattle (Table 5:16). The fusion data show very low mortality among juveniles, with 92.11 percent of cattle surviving past the age of one and a half years. In fact, more than 66 percent of the cattle seem to have survived well into adulthood, past the age of four years. Mandibular tooth eruption forms the second source of information on age-related patterns of cattle mortality (Fig. 5:12). The high survivorship rate for both juveniles and young adults (the age at which males are most often culled) suggests that males and/or castrates formed a significant part of the adult population.

The Gritille data can be compared with three models of the culling patterns expected if cattle are being raised to produce meat, dairy products, or traction. Under meat production,

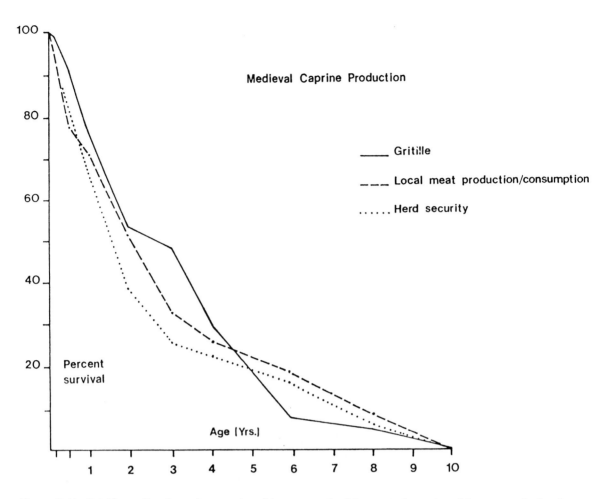

Figure 5:11. Gritille medieval caprine survivorship compared with expected survivorship pattern for local meat production/consumption and for maximization of herd security.

TABLE 5:16. EPIPHYSEAL FUSION DATA FROM GRITILLE MEDIEVAL CATTLE, PHASES 5–8 ($n = 159$)

Element	Fusion age (mos.)	Fused	Fusing	Unfused
1.5 Years				
Dist. scapula	7–8	9	0	1
Dist. humerus	12–18	11	0	1
Prox. radius	12–18	12	0	1
Prox. first phalanx	18	1	0	0
Prox. second phalanx	18	2	0	0
3.0 Years				
Dist. metacarpal 3–4	24–30	25	0	5
Dist. tibia	24–30	14	1	5
Dist. metatarsals 3–4	27–36	18	0	2
4.0 Years				
Calcaneum	36–42	3	0	2
Prox. femur	42	5	1	3
Dist. radius	42–48	9	1	3
Prox. humerus	42–48	2	0	1
Prox. ulna	42–48	1	0	0
Dist. femur	42–48	10	0	4
Prox. tibia	42–48	4	0	2

No. of cases

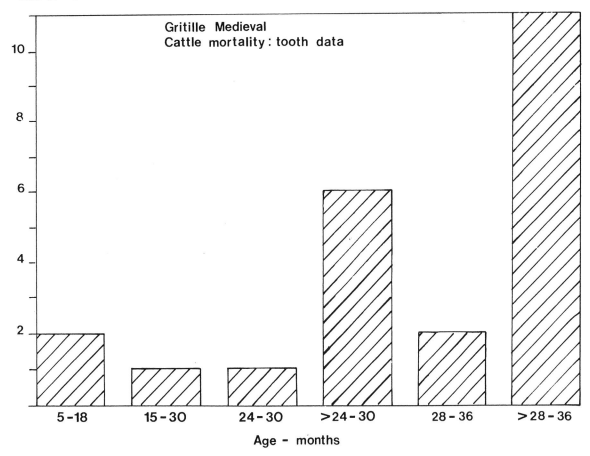

Figure 5:12. Gritille medieval cattle mortality: tooth data.

one would expect very little culling of juveniles (younger than three years) combined with a major culling of young adult males in the three and a half to four-year age range, when they approach 90 percent of their full adult weight and their growth rate levels off.[38] As shown above, the Gritille cattle show no evidence for a major culling of young adults. This strongly suggests that the medieval herders did not follow a meat production strategy.

In contrast with meat production, herders emphasizing dairy production would follow a management strategy that culled large numbers of juvenile males while having very low mortality among young adults. This model corresponds only in part with the medieval data. Although the Gritille cattle match the dairy production pattern in the treatment of young adults, there is no evidence for a major culling of juvenile males. In other words, late medieval herders at Gritille do not seem to have concentrated exclusively on dairy production.

Production strategies using cattle for traction castrate males and retain them as draft animals for plowing and/or transport. The resulting survivorship pattern would show low mortality among both juveniles and young adults, thereby leaving an adult population composed mostly of females along with significant numbers of oxen (castrates). The high proportion of

---

[38] Higham and Message, "Assessment of a Prehistoric Technique," 328; Legge, "Agricultural Economy," 86–89.

adults in the Gritille sample closely matches the survivorship pattern associated with the use of adult oxen for traction. Although we cannot determine sex ratios for the medieval cattle, the maintenance of a viable herd would have required a high proportion of females. Presumably these females would have served as both a breeding population and as a major source of dairy products. If this were, in fact, the case, then a compromise herding strategy of dairy and traction would also explain the partial match between the Gritille data and the dairy production model. In addition, a cattle production strategy combining dairy goods with the use of oxen for traction suggests an emphasis on agriculture which accords well with the relatively dense pattern of late medieval settlement in the fertile bottomlands of the Karababa basin.[39]

CONCLUSIONS: MEDIEVAL HERDING AND AGRICULTURE AT GRITILLE

The Gritille late medieval fauna are consistent with an overall economic pattern consisting of several generalized, multipurpose herding strategies. Mortality data and survivorship patterns for pigs, sheep, goats, and cattle show no evidence for large-scale specialized production of surplus animals or their products. Several aspects of late medieval herding strategies may make the most sense when considered as adjustments to the agricultural regime practiced in the Karababa basin.

Pigs, the most common animal in the faunal sample, seem to have been the main meat source of medieval Gritille. Swineherds apparently followed a nonintensive pannage system in which the pigs were permitted to range freely for most of the year. The mortality data indicate that most (80%) of the pigs were culled before the age of two and a half years. The combination of early culling and the very high natural fecundity of pigs means that these animals were consumed far more frequently than the other main domesticates. This high consumption rate would have made sense as part of a mixed farming system. Both wild and domesticated pigs are notorious for their depredations on agricultural crops.[40] Thus, periodic culling would have been necessary to limit crop damage arising from the rapid growth of a population of free-ranging pigs.

Caprines, mainly goats, form the second major component of the Gritille late medieval animal economy. Survivorship data suggest that sheep and goat herders pursued a generalized, subsistence-oriented strategy emphasizing either herd security or meat production for local consumption. The heavy emphasis on pigs in the meat diet may indicate that caprines were less important as a meat source than as a versatile and low-risk form of animal capital. This generalized strategy of risk reduction would have produced not only a steady supply of meat, but also reasonable amounts of dairy goods, hides, fiber, and wool for local consumption. The medieval emphasis on goats rather than sheep may have stemmed from the goats' greater natural rate of increase, and higher yield (in volume) of dairy products. Herders at Gritille may also have favored goats because of the latter's greater adaptability to the deforested environment of the Karababa basin and the generally degraded range conditions that frequently develop in the pastures closest to settlements practicing non-transhumant stock raising on fallow or harvested fields as part of an integrated agropastoral system.[41]

Cattle form the third major component of the pastoral economy. Culling patterns suggest that cattle herding followed a combined strategy that emphasized both dairy production and the use of oxen as draft animals for transport and/or plowing. Such an emphasis seems especially reasonable given the fact that cattle far surpass sheep and goats as dairy producers, while providing additional benefits to agriculture as a source of traction power and possibly dung fertilizer. Although probably not a primary production goal, cattle dung may well have served as an important fuel source along with

---

[39] For the agricultural outliers in the immediate vicinity of Gritille, see Chapter 7, this volume; for medieval settlement patterns in the Karababa basin as a whole, see Özdoğan, *Lower Euphrates Basin*, Pl. 17.

[40] Lay, "Study of the Mammals of Iran," 223; see also Mackin, "Dynamics of Damage," 447–458.

[41] Martin, "Conservation," 160.

brushwood from the banks and islands of the adjacent Euphrates River.[42]

Late medieval herders at Gritille seem to have followed generalized or composite production goals aimed at meeting local subsistence needs. In addition to providing important animal products, management strategies for all the major domesticates seem to have operated in ways that minimized conflict with the agricultural system practiced at Gritille.

ACKNOWLEDGMENTS

This chapter is a substantially revised and abridged version of Chapters 7 and 8 in my 1988 doctoral dissertation, "Pastoral Production in Complex Societies: Mid-Late Third Millennium B.C. and Medieval Faunal Remains From Gritille Höyük in the Karababa Basin, Southeast Turkey" (Anthropology Department, University of Pennsylvania). I wish to thank the director of the Gritille excavations, Richard Ellis (Bryn Mawr College), for permission to study the Gritille material. The first stage of this analysis was funded by a Fulbright-IIE travel grant. I am grateful to Dr. Nurettin Yardımcı of the Turkish General Directorate of Monuments and Museums for his cooperation and assistance. I was able to use the comparative faunal collections at the British Institute of Archaeology in Ankara through the courtesy of its director, Dr. David French, and co-director, Ms. Ann Murray. Dr. Toni Cross, director of the American Research Institute in Turkey (ARIT), Ankara Branch, was of invaluable assistance in conducting this research. The second stage of the analysis was conducted in the U.S., funded by a research fellowship from the University of Pennsylvania University Museum, Museum Applied Science Center for Archaeology (MASCA). I am grateful to Stuart Fleming, scientific director of MASCA, and Pamela Crabtree for their support of this part of the project. I also wish to thank Kent Flannery for permitting me to use the Zooarchaeology Laboratory at the University of Michigan Museum of Anthropology for the final stages of analyzing the medieval material. Discussions of the Gritille medieval stratigraphy with Mary Voigt (College of William and Mary) and Scott Redford (Georgetown University) were of great assistance in clarifying the chronological framework of this study. I thank John Hudson (Northwestern University) and the William and Marion Haas Fund for their assistance in preparation of illustrations for this paper. Finally, I would like to acknowledge Scott Redford for his constructive suggestions on the organization of this chapter.

---

[42] Ellis and Voigt, "Excavations at Gritille, Turkey," 321; Miller and Smart, "Intentional Burning of Dung," 15–28; and Miller, Chapter 6, this volume.

VI

PATTERNS OF AGRICULTURE AND LAND USE AT MEDIEVAL GRITILLE

Naomi F. Miller

Gritille was a small mound in Adıyaman province, southeastern Turkey. Even before it was flooded by the lake behind the Atatürk Dam, part of it had been cut away by the Euphrates River. The site yielded a wealth of plant remains from Neolithic, Early Bronze Age, and medieval levels. This report deals only with the medieval deposits, when the site was occupied by Christians, at first under Christian rule and later under Muslim. Gritille was situated about 10 kilometers upstream from Samsat, its regional center.[1] A previous report that dealt with the Crusader period fortress appeared in *Anatolica* and is incorporated in the present chapter.[2]

Gritille lies well within the rainfall agriculture zone; annual precipitation in the nearest city, Adıyaman, is 835 millimeters,[3] though Gritille is probably between the 500 and 600 millimeter isohyets.[4] The site is located in the steppe-oak forest zone of southeastern Turkey near its border with two other major phytogeographical zones: to the west lies the Mediterranean woodland climax, also an oak dominated steppe-forest, and to the south lies the northern extension of the Syrian steppe.[5] A remnant of open oak forest on steep slopes lies only about 20 kilometers

from the site.[6] Riparian forest (poplar, willow, and tamarisk) probably grew adjacent to the site. Based on historical references[7] as well as the archaeobotanical data, one can imagine fields, both irrigated and unirrigated, and pasture surrounding the site.

ARCHAEOLOGICAL BACKGROUND

A number of medieval occupation phases have been delineated. Following S. Redford's advice,[8] the archaeological contexts have been combined for purposes of analysis as follows:

Phase 2: Small eleventh-century A.D. Byzantine garrison, excavated in a small area. Only two samples from this phase were available for study.

Phase 3: Crusader-period fortress and farming village occupied during the middle of the twelfth century A.D. under the sovereignty of the County of Edessa (Urfa), until it was sacked and burned. Most of the samples come from the domestic area of the burnt fortress and consist of in situ seed deposits and fallen construction debris. Samples from Phase 3 non-destruction lev-

---

[1] Redford, "Excavations at Gritille (1982–1984)."

[2] Miller, "Crusader Period Fortress."

[3] Meteoroloji Bülteni, *Ortalama ve Ekstrem Kıymetler Meteoroloji Bülteni.*

[4] Atalay, *Türkiye Vejetasyon Coğrafyasına Giriş,* 17, Fig. 7.

[5] Zohary, *Geobotanical Foundations.*

[6] Gil Stein, personal communication.

[7] Redford, this volume.

[8] Information provided by Redford, letter of April 15, 1995.

el occupation debris have been combined for analysis with those from Phase 4.

Phase 4: Brief reoccupation of the site, with botanical samples consisting of occupation debris.

Phases 5 and 6: First occupation of the site under Muslim rule. Most of the excavated samples appear to be the result of intermittent industrial activity, though these deposits also include mudbrick collapse. It is not clear whether people actually lived on the site.

Phases 7 and 8: During the first 40 years of the thirteenth century A.D., Gritille once again appears to have been a small farming community, still under Muslim rule. It was probably abandoned in the third decade of the thirteenth century.

ARCHAEOBOTANICAL RESEARCH QUESTIONS

The medieval plant assemblage from Gritille represents the first such assemblage reported from this period in Anatolia, and one of the only ones in the entire Near East.[9] Fortunately there is at least some documentary evidence for agricultural and land use practices.[10] But as is true of historic sites in general, textual evidence pertaining to any particular site is rarely available, and historical records are no substitute for evidence out of the ground.

The first task of the archaeobotanist is simply to record the presence of agricultural products and other evidence of land use practices. Archaeobotanical studies of Bronze Age sites are helpful in developing interpretations of the plant remains, even though they bear little direct relationship to medieval remains.

The second task is to attempt to see if and how known historical events or processes affected plant use and whether they are reflected in the assemblage. Redford proposes that Gritille's circumstances were tied to those of Samsat. When Samsat was a reasonably secure local center (Phases 3/4, 7/8), Gritille would have been important for its agricultural hinterland in a relatively well-populated valley, and when Samsat and its region declined in importance (Phases 5/6), lower intensity land use strategies would have prevailed.[11]

SAMPLING AND LABORATORY PROCEDURES

The samples come from a variety of deposit types, including hearths and ovens, pits, ashy fill, and wall collapse (Table 6:1). Out of the 138 flotation and unfloated seed samples taken, about half could be assigned to one of the architectural phases (2 through 8), and analysis concentrated on these samples (Table 6:2).

The archaeobotanist did not participate in the excavation. Gil Stein had a SMAP-type flotation device constructed locally[12] and organized the sampling. Staff members who volunteered carried out flotation in the shade of the Euphrates riparian vegetation. Excavators were instructed to take 8-liter soil samples from a variety of deposits and to record the volume. In some cases, volume information was not recorded or is not available, so density of charred material is not always calculated. For very large samples that were subsampled before laboratory analysis, soil volume is calculated in proportion to the quantity analyzed.

In the laboratory, archaeobotanical samples were poured through nested geological sieves. Plant material caught in the 2 millimeter mesh was sorted totally into three categories and weighed: wood charcoal, seeds and seed fragments, and other (rachis and straw fragments, grape peduncles, pod fragments). Charred dung was also separated out and weighed. In the size fraction between 1 and 2 millimeters, whole seeds and identifiable seed and other plant part fragments were separated out and identified. In the size fraction smaller than 1 millimeter, only whole seeds and identifiable rachis fragments were separated out and identified.

---

[9] E.g., Samuel, "Plant Remains"; see Miller, "The Near East."

[10] See A. Watson, "Agricultural Innovation."

[11] Chapter 2, this volume.

[12] Named for the Shell Mound Archaeological Project (Kentucky), this flotation device uses an oil drum modified so that pumped water flows in at the bottom and is directed upward and over a spout. Soil is poured into a screened insert set into the tank. Heavy material is caught in the screen ("heavy fraction") and examined for sinking plant materials, bone, chipped stone, etc. Floating material ("light fraction") is caught in a small-mesh screen after it flows past the spout. See P. J. Watson, "In Pursuit of Prehistoric Subsistence."

TABLE 6:1. CATALOG OF ANALYZED ARCHAEOBOTANICAL SAMPLES
FROM GRITILLE MEDIEVAL LEVELS

GT #	Yr	Op	Locus	Lot	Phase	Description
105	82	9	5	8	8	Oven
113	82	9	11	10	8	Ash
365	82	9	16	18	7	Oven
627	82	9	15	34	7	Oven
631	82	9	23	35	Upper	Oven
1422	82	10	38	40	-	Pit
1754	82	10	52	47	-	Hearth
1763	82	10	49	49	-	Pit
1959	82	10	61	60	-	Oven
2341	82	11	26	41	6	Pit
3135	82	8	53	99	Upper	Exterior surface
3314	82	8	54	109	Upper	Oven
4558	83	25	28	32	8	Floor deposit
4587	83	25	31	41	7	Pit
4593	83	25	32	42	7	Pit
4908	83	27	2	16	8	Oven
4923	83	27	3	19	8	Oven
5515	83	26	20	29	7	Pit
5543	83	26	20	34	7	Pit
5566	83	25	35	61	5	Ash lenses
5580	83	25	5	64	7	Oven
5831	83	26	21	44	7	Pit
5845	83	26	21	44	7	Pit
6307	83	25	47	77	3	Ash, above burnt phase
6710	83	11	11	48	5	Pyrotechnic installation
6731	83	11	25	47	3B	Fill over floor
6982	83	26	11	70	7	Trash
7318	83	31	4	12	Upper	Oven
7327	83	31	2	13	7	Oven and pit
7660	83	26	32	78	5	Oven
7868	83	25/10	58	95	8	Pit w/ ashy lenses
7884	83	25/10	61	98	5	Ash
8075	83	11	41	75	4	Pit
8113	83	25/10	57	103	3B	Animal pen roof
8151	83	31	9	22	Upper	Ashy fill & wall collapse
8165	83	31	15	24	Upper	Pit
8567	83	11	46	88	3	Pit
8721	83	25/10	68	115	5	Floor deposit
8748	83	25/10	70	119	5	Between floors
9002	83	11	49	92	3	Oven
9187	83	25/10	75	128	3B	Burnt debris assoc w/ burnt level
13725	83	31	26	48	Upper	Brick collapse
13803	83	25/10	75	133	3B	Animal pen, surface
13806	83	25/10	75	133	3B	Animal pen, surface
13809	83	25/10	75	130	3B	Animal pen, not floated
13815	83	25/10	75	133	3B	Animal pen, not floated
13828	83	25/10	75	140	3B	Animal pen, surface, not floated
13832	83	25/10	75	140	3B	Animal pen, surface, not floated
15572	84	9	6	7	5	Pit
15746	84	42	12	13	5	Bricky wash on surface
16271	84	43	17	17	-	Pyrotechnic installation
16662	84	43	22	21	-	Oven
16915	84	42	19	28	3B	Surface
17048	84	26/27	22	23	4	Oven or exterior surface
17137	84	26/27	24	31	4	Above road
17748	84	47	10	13	4	Wall
17830	84	26/27	31	47	4	Oven, on exterior surface
18164	84	26/27	35	55	4	Oven, on exterior surface

TABLE 6:1 (CONT.). CATALOG OF ANALYZED ARCHAEOBOTANICAL SAMPLES FROM GRITILLE MEDIEVAL LEVELS

GT #	Yr	Op	Locus	Lot	Phase	Description
18210	84	26/27	40	62	Upper	Pit
18245	84	26/27	43	69	3B	Hearth
18249	84	26/27	44	70	3B	Oven
18377	84	45	15	21	3B	Bricky collapse on floor
18380	84	45	16	22	Upper	Bricky collapse on surface
18824	84	26/27	56	85	3B	Oven
18875	84	10	58	124	3B	Floor, in stable
19119	84	26/27	43	95	3B	Hearth
19579	84	26/27	72	111	2	Oven
19591	84	26/27	76	115	4	Pit
19598	84	26/27	77	116	2	Pit
20959	84	55	19	26	-	Oven
22091	84	55	38	44	-	Oven
22467	84	10	88	185	3B	Pit
22469	84	55	43	51	-	Oven
22492	84	55	41	48	Upper	Oven
22495	84	55	40	49	-	Oven
22606	84	47	25	34	-	Oven
22663	84	9	90	190	3B	Oven

TABLE 6:2. DISTRIBUTION OF GRITILLE MEDIEVAL ARCHAEOBOTANICAL SAMPLES BY PHASE

Phase	2	3*	4	5	6	7	8	Upper	Med.
No. taken	2	33	8	11	4	11	7	22	40
No. different loci	2	17	7	11	4	7	7	11	37
No. loci analyzed	2	14	7	11	3	7	7	10	6
No. analyzed	2	21	8	11	3	8	7	10	6

*Phase 3 includes several samples from the same burnt room, Locus 75, but from different deposits recognized as seed concentrations on the floor.

The data charts (Tables 6:3–6:8) are organized by phase, and within phase by operation, locus, and lot. Basic descriptive data head the charts. The plant taxa are listed as follows: cereals, pulses and other economic/food plants, and then wild and weedy plants listed in alphabetical order by family. Charred plant parts and mineralized seeds complete the tables. Weight of cereals and pulses is reported because these types occur mostly as fragments. To estimate whole-seed equivalents, conversion factors can be applied to the cereals. Seed identifications were made with the help of modern comparative material housed at the Ethnobotanical Laboratory of the University of Pennsylvania Museum, seed atlases, and published seed illustrations.[13]

The provenience of the samples is designated by excavation square (operation) and stratigraphic unit (locus). The lot number defines the actual unit of excavation. Sample numbers are prefixed "GT."

The Taxa

Most of the samples contain mixtures of various amounts of charcoal, cultigens, and wild and weedy plant seeds. Just a few taxa account for the bulk of the cultivated plants: durum/bread wheat, barley, lentil, and grape. It is only the samples from the burnt Crusader period settlement which had in situ concentrations of crop plants: fava beans, vetchling, and wheat. Other cultigens occur in such low quantities that they may have been incidental admixtures from animal fodder or dung fuel, or crops whose seeds accidentally fell into a fire: einkorn, foxtail millet, rice, vetchling, bitter vetch (probably a fodder crop), chickpea, pea, cotton, and flax. Fig and tentatively identified fenugreek, pistachio,

---

[13] E.g., van Zeist and Bakker-Heeres, "Archaeobotanical Studies in the Levant."

TABLE 6:3. GRITILLE ARCHAEOBOTANICAL SAMPLES, PHASES 2, 3, AND 4

GT no.	19579	19598	22663	8567	9002	6307	18249	18824	17748	8075	17048	17137	17830	18164	19591
Year	84	84	84	83	83	83	84	84	84	83	84	84	84	84	84
Operation	26/27	26/27	9	11	11	25	26/27	26/27	47	11	26/27	26/27	26/27	26/27	26/27
Locus	72	77	90	46	49	47	44	56	10	41	22	24	31	35	76
Lot	111	116	190	88	92	77	70	85	13	75	23	31	47	55	115
Phase	2	2	3	3	3	3	3	3	4	4	4	4	4	4	4
Volume (l)	8	4	8	8	8	?	8	8	8	8	?	8	8	8	3.84
Density (g/l)	0.55	0.91	0.50	0.24	0.15	n/c	0.30	0.23	0.29	1.64	n/c	0.08	0.10	0.52	2.02
Charcoal >2mm (g)	3.75	3.60	2.29	1.69	1.06	0.67	2.24	1.50	2.14	12.14	4.56	0.65	0.70	4.06	7.45
Seed >2mm (g)	0.61	0.01	1.59	0.19	0.17	0.10	0.19	0.30	0.20	0.98	0.14	0.01	0.09	0.13	0.32
Misc. >2mm (g)	+	0.01	0.11	.	+	+	.	0.03	+	0.02	+	.	.	.	+
Seed/charcoal (g/g)	0.16	+	0.69	0.11	0.16	0.15	0.08	0.20	0.09	0.08	0.03	0.02	0.13	0.03	0.04
Wild seed (#)	145	.	859	67	63	11	29	40	19	466	20	6	61	10	148
Wild seed/charcoal (#/g)	39	.	375	40	59	16	13	27	9	38	4	9	87	2	20
Wild/cereal (#/g)	279	.	573	419	394	157	161	138	633	590	167	n/c	871	100	1480
Cereal (g)															
Hordeum distichum	0.17	0.01	0.90	0.05	0.04	0.03	0.03	0.07	.	0.06	0.09	+	.	0.01	0.01
Triticum durum/aestivum	0.18	.	0.36	0.08	0.08	.	0.03	0.06	.	0.51	.	.	0.06	0.08	0.01
T. monococcum	+	.	.	.	.	.	.	.	.	.	.	.	.	.	.
Triticum sp.	+	.	.	.	.	0.01	.	.	0.02	.	+	.	.	.	0.03
Cereal indet.	0.17	+	0.24	0.03	0.04	0.03	0.12	0.16	0.01	0.22	0.03	.	0.01	0.01	0.05
Pulse (g)															
Cicer	.	.	.	.	.	.	.	.	.	.	.	.	.	.	.
Lathyrus	.	.	.	.	.	.	.	.	.	0.10	.	.	.	.	.
Lens	0.04	.	0.13	.	0.01	0.03	0.03	0.01	0.11	0.06	0.01	.	.	0.01	0.06
Pisum	.	.	.	.	+	.	.	.	.	.	.	.	.	.	.
Vicia ervilia	.	.	.	0.01	.	.	.	.	.	.	.	.	.	.	.
Pulse indet.	.	.	0.02	0.01	.	.	0.01	0.01	0.01	0.16	.	.	.	.	0.04
Other food/economic items															
cf. Pistacia (g)	0.01	.	.	.	.	0.02	.	.	.	.	.	.	.	.	.
Gossypium	.	.	.	.	.	.	.	.	.	.	1	.	.	.	.
Ficus	1	7	1	3	3	.	.	.	.	5	.	.	3	.	.
Secale	.	.	2	1	1	.	.	1	.	.	.	.	.	.	.
Setaria	.	.	1	1	.	.	.	.	.	.	.	.	.	.	.
Vitis	.	.	1	1	.	.	.	.	.	.	1	.	2	.	.

TABLE 6.3 (CONT.). GRITILLE ARCHAEOBOTANICAL SAMPLES, PHASES 2, 3, AND 4

GT no.	19579	19598	22663	8567	9002	6307	18249	18824	17748	8075	17048	17137	17830	18164	19591
Wild and weedy															
GT-Apiaceae 2	4														
Apiaceae			14					1	1				1	1	86
Centaurea			2		1		1	4		1	1				
GT-Asteraceae 1	2		28					1							
Asteraceae				1						3	1				
Heliotropium			1	1	4					2	1		1		
cf. Alyssum			3				2								
Brassicaceae	2		12						2	6					
Capparis			10							12			2		
Gypsophila	1								1						
Silene			2												
Chenopodium			2		1		1			5					
GT-Chenopodiaceae 1	2		7							1					
cf. Salsola			1												
Chenopodiaceae	14									2					
Carex			4				1			3					
cf. Scirpus	1		5		2	2		1	1	6					
Cyperaceae (GT-7)										1			1		2
Cyperaceae			2	2				1		1					
Cephalaria	2		5					2		2					
Euphorbia										1					
Astragalus			5				2			2					1
Coronilla	4		12	3	3				1	7			2		
Glycyrrhiza				1											
Medicago	1									1					
Prosopis	2						1								
Trifolium/Melilotus	1		23	1	1	1		2	2	14	1		8	1	
Trigonella astroites-type			43		2					1					
Trigonella	6		40	2	25	2		2		29	3		2	3	4
GT-Fabaceae 4	8		29	2	1		1			64					
GT-Fabaceae 5				7	2				2	9			10		
Fabaceae	7		47		8		1	2			3		2		2
Ajuga	1							1							
Ziziphora			7												
Lamiaceae			1	1											
Malva								4	2	46					
Fumaria										12					

TABLE 6:3 (CONT.). GRITILLE ARCHAEOBOTANICAL SAMPLES, PHASES 2, 3, AND 4

GT no.	19579	19598	22663	8567	9002	6307	18249	18824	17748	8075	17048	17137	17830	18164	19591
Papaver			5							1					
cf. *Plantago*			2												
Bromus			6									1			
Hordeum murinum-type			3												
Hordeum			3												
Lolium remotum-type				2											
Lolium										1					
Phleum-type	15		145	24		2	4	2		46	1	4	1		25
GT-Poaceae 1			1	1											
GT-Poaceae 3										2			1		
GT-Poaceae 5										8					
GT-Poaceae 7	1														
GT-Poaceae 8	15		174	2	1										
GT-Poaceae 12			4												
Poaceae	10		41	2		1	1	6	3	13	4	1	5	3	3
Rumex			4	1					1						
Portulaca	3		6	1											
Androsace			2							2					
Adonis			1			1	1			2					
Reseda			6	2						1			2		
Galium			1					2		2					
GT-Rubiaceae 1			3						1	6					1
Hyoscyamus											1				
Solanum										1					
Thymelaea								1							
Valerianella coronata	1		3						1						
Valerianella dentata	1														
Verbena			3	2			1						1		
Peganum					1		1				1				
Unknown, GT-5	1				1										
Unknown, GT-11															
Unknown, GT-15													2		
Unknown, GT-23										1					
Unknown, GT-25										1					
Unknown, GT-28										1					
Unknown, misc.	40		142	9	10	2	11	7	3	145	3		17	1	24

TABLE 6:3 (CONT.). GRITILLE ARCHAEOBOTANICAL SAMPLES, PHASES 2, 3, AND 4

GT no.	19579	19598	22663	8567	9002	6307	18249	18824	17748	8075	17048	17137	17830	18164	19591
Other charred plant parts															
Hordeum int.	21	.	100	2	.	1	.	8	.	9	1	.	2	.	1
Triticum durum/aestivum int.	17	.	50	1	.	.	.	8	.	3	1	.	.	.	.
Triticum gb	19	.	.	4	1	2	.	23	1	47	.	.	.	.	.
Trit mono/dicoccum sf	.	.	1	1	.	.	.	1	1	.	.	.	.	.	.
grass culm node	6	.	20	.	.	.	1	13	1	1	1	.	.	.	2
Vitis peduncle	.	2	.	.	.	.	.	.	.	.	.	.	.	.	.
Vitis fruit	.	.	1	.	.	.	.	.	.	.	.	.	.	.	.
Mineralized seeds															
Asteraceae	3	.	.	.	.	.	.	.	.	.	.	.	.	.	.
Alkanna	.	.	.	.	.	.	.	1	.	.	.	.	.	.	.
Lithospermum tenuifolium	.	.	.	4	.	.	.	1	.	.	.	.	1	.	.
cf. Capparis	1	.	.	.	.	.	.	.	.	.	.	.	.	.	1
Chenopodiaceae	1	.	.	.	.	.	.	.	.	.	.	.	.	.	.
Fimbristylis	17	.	2	1	3	.	.	.	.	1	.	.	1	.	1
Cyperaceae	1	.	1	1	3	.	.	.	.	1	.	.	.	.	.
Ficus	.	.	.	2	.	.	.	.	.	.	.	4	.	.	.
Papaver	.	.	.	2	.	.	.	.	.	.	.	.	.	.	1
Unknown, misc.	1	.	.	.	.	.	.	1	.	.	.	.	.	.	.

Abbreviations for Tables 6:3–6:8

nf = not floated; n/c = not calculable; int. = internode; gb = glume base; sf = spikelet fork; frg = fragment

TABLE 6:4. GRITILLE ARCHAEOBOTANICAL SAMPLES, PHASES 5 AND 6

GT no.	2341	1763	1422	8748	7884	8721	16662	15746	7660	5566	6710	1959	1754	15572
Year	82	82	82	83	83	83	84	84	83	83	83	82	82	84
Operation	11	10	10	25/10	25/10	25/10	43	42	26	25	11	10	10	9
Locus	26	49	38	70	61	68	22	12	32	35	11	61	52	6
Lot	41	49	40	119	98	115	21	13	78	61	48	60	47	7
Phase	6	6	6	5	5	5	5	5	5	5	5	5	5	5
Volume (l)	8	3.8	8	?	?	1.8	8	4	8	8	?	6	6	4.3
Density (g/l)	0.03	2.10	0.17	n/c	n/c	0.86	0.16	2.56	0.13	0.02	n/c	0.19	0.05	0.07
Charcoal >2mm (g)	0.07	7.71	0.18	10.42	0.58	1.26	0.84	9.62	0.96	0.08	0.02	1.05	0.26	0.11
Seed >2mm (g)	0.15	0.24	1.15	0.21	0.05	0.27	0.45	0.56	0.06	0.04	0.22	0.06	0.02	0.17
Misc. >2mm (g)	+	0.02	+	.	0.02	0.01	.	0.04	.	.	0.01	0.02	.	0.04
Seed/charcoal (g/g)	2.14	0.03	6.39	0.02	0.09	0.21	0.54	0.06	0.06	0.50	11.00	0.06	0.08	1.55
Wild seed (#)	17	64	123	17	250	1815	37	68	35	62	252	181	99	15
Wild seed/charcoal (#/g)	243	8	683	2	431	1440	44	7	36	775	12600	172	381	136
Wild/cereal (#/g)	850	221	96	89	8333	15125	142	105	583	2067	813	3017	3300	125
Cereal (g)														
Hordeum	.	0.05	0.37	0.04	0.02	0.08	0.02	.	0.01	0.01	0.03	+	.	0.08
Triticum durum/aestivum	.	0.10	0.44	0.10	.	0.04	0.07	0.55	0.05	.	0.20	.	.	0.02
Triticum sp.	+	.	.	.	+	.	0.01	.	.	0.01	.	+	.	.
Cereal indet.	0.02	0.14	0.47	0.05	0.01	+	0.16	0.10	.	0.01	0.08	0.06	0.03	0.02
Pulse (g)														
Cicer	.	.	.	.	.	.	0.10	.	.	.	.	.	.	.
Lens	+	0.01	+	0.03	.	.	0.02	0.01	+	.	.	0.01	.	.
Vicia ervilia	+	.	.	.	.	.	.	.	.	.	0.01	.	.	.
Pulse indet.	0.13	.	.	0.01	.	0.01	0.07	.	.	.	0.03	.	.	0.04
Other food/economic items														
Linum	.	.	.	.	.	.	.	.	.	.	.	.	.	.
Gossypium	.	.	.	.	.	2	1	.	.	.	.	.	.	.
Ficus	.	.	.	.	2	3	2	4	.	.	.	.	.	.
Setaria	.	.	.	.	.	20	.	.	.	.	.	.	.	.
Prunus (almond; g)	.	.	.	.	.	.	.	.	.	.	.	.	0.01	.
Vitis	1	.	.	.	.	1	4	1	.	.	.	.	.	.

TABLE 6:4 (CONT.). GRITILLE ARCHAEOBOTANICAL SAMPLES, PHASES 5 AND 6

GT no.	15572	1754	1959	6710	5566	7660	15746	16662	8721	7884	8748	1422	1763	2341
Wild and weedy														
GT-Apiaceae 2	.	.	2	.	.	.	.	.	7	.	.	.	1	.
Centaurea	.	.	1	2	.	.	1	.	5	2	.	.	.	.
GT-Asteraceae 1	.	2	.	.	.	.	.	.	6	.	.	.	.	.
Asteraceae	.	.	.	.	.	.	.	.	2	.	.	.	1	.
Heliotropium	.	.	1	.	.	1	.	.	.	.	.	.	.	.
cf. Alyssum	.	.	.	1	.	.	.	.	.	.	.	.	.	.
Brassicaceae	.	2	.	63	1	1	3	.	14	.	.	.	.	2
Capparis	.	.	.	.	.	.	2	.	1	.	.	.	.	.
Gypsophila	.	.	.	1	.	.	.	.	.	.	.	.	.	.
Silene	.	2	.	.	.	.	.	.	.	.	.	.	.	.
Vaccaria	.	.	.	.	.	.	.	.	5	.	1	.	.	.
Caryophyllaceae	.	.	1	.	.	.	.	.	.	.	.	.	.	.
Atriplex	.	.	.	.	.	.	.	1	.	.	.	.	.	.
Chenopodium	.	.	2	.	.	13	2	.	4	5	.	.	4	1
GT-Chenopodiaceae 1	.	1	.	.	1	1	3	.	8	.	.	1	.	.
Suaeda	.	.	.	.	.	1	.	.	.	.	.	.	.	.
Chenopodiaceae	.	.	.	.	.	.	.	.	1	1	1	.	.	.
cf. Scirpus	.	1	.	.	.	.	.	.	9	.	.	.	3	.
Cyperaceae (GT-7)	.	1	4	.	.	.	.	.	15	3	.	.	.	.
Cyperaceae	.	.	.	.	2	.	2	.	.	.	.	.	.	.
Cephalaria	.	.	.	.	.	.	.	1	11	.	3	1	.	.
Astragalus	.	.	2	2	6	.	2	.	12	2	.	1	.	.
Coronilla	.	.	.	.	1	.	.	.	17	1	.	.	2	.
Glycyrrhiza	4	.	.	.	.	.	.	.	.	.	.	.	.	.
Medicago radiata	.	.	.	.	.	.	.	.	.	.	.	.	.	.
Medicago	.	.	1	.	.	.	1	.	1	.	.	.	.	1
Trifolium/Melilotus	.	6	1	4	6	.	1	.	10	.	.	.	3	.
Trigonella astroites-type	.	4	.	.	1	1	.	.	3	12	.	1	.	.
Trigonella	.	39	7	.	12	3	.	4	30	21	4	1	3	2
GT-Fabaceae 4	.	11	.	.	.	.	.	.	.	.	1	.	.	.
GT-Fabaceae 5	.	.	1	3	1	.	5	.	90	.	.	.	1	1
Fabaceae	.	3	5	1	7	.	3	6	8	5	2	.	3	.
Hypericum	.	.	.	.	.	.	.	.	.	.	.	.	.	.
Ajuga chamaepitys-type	.	.	.	.	.	.	.	.	.	.	.	1	.	.
cf. Nepeta	.	.	.	.	.	.	.	.	2	.	.	.	.	.

TABLE 6:4 (CONT.). GRITILLE ARCHAEOBOTANICAL SAMPLES, PHASES 5 AND 6

GT no.	15572	1754	1959	6710	5566	7660	15746	16662	8721	7884	8748	1422	1763	2341
Teucrium	.	.	2	.	.	.	.	.	2	2	.	.	.	.
Ziziphora	.	.	.	.	.	.	.	.	.	1	.	.	1	.
Lamiaceae	.	.	.	.	.	.	.	.	.	.	.	.	1	.
Malva	.	.	.	.	.	.	.	.	2	6	1	.	.	.
Fumaria	.	.	.	.	.	.	.	.	1	.	.	.	.	.
Papaver	.	.	1	47	.	.	.	.	.	.	.	.	.	.
Bromus	.	.	.	.	.	.	.	.	1	.	.	.	.	.
Hordeum murinum-type	.	.	1	.	.	.	.	.	.	1	.	1	1	.
Hordeum	.	.	1	.	.	.	.	.	.	.	.	.	.	.
Lolium remotum-type	.	.	.	.	1	.	.	.	.	.	.	.	.	.
Lolium	.	.	.	.	.	.	.	.	3	.	.	.	.	.
Phalaris	.	.	.	.	.	.	.	.	1	.	.	.	.	.
Phleum-type	.	6	97	55	10	.	10	4	1138	96	.	2	6	1
GT-Poaceae 3	.	.	.	.	.	.	.	.	23	.	.	.	.	.
GT-Poaceae 5	.	.	.	.	.	.	.	.	1	.	.	.	.	.
GT-Poaceae 7	.	.	.	1	.	.	.	.	.	.	.	.	.	.
GT-Poaceae 8	2	2	3	.	.	.	2	2	77	4	.	.	.	.
GT-Poaceae 12	.	1	2	.	.	1	.	.	4	.	.	.	.	.
Poaceae	9	3	15	4	5	1	5	1	125	12	.	14	6	1
Polygonum persicaria-type	.	.	.	.	.	.	.	.	.	1	.	.	.	.
cf. *Polygonum*	.	.	1	.	.	1	.	.	.	.	.	.	.	.
Portulaca	.	.	.	1	.	.	.	.	8	2	.	.	.	.
Reseda	.	.	4	2	.	3	.	.	15	.	.	85	1	.
cf. *Potentilla*	.	.	.	.	.	.	.	.	.	.	.	1	.	.
Galium	.	2	.	.	.	.	.	2	.	.	.	1	1	2
GT-Rubiaceae 1	.	.	.	2	.	.	.	.	4	1	.	.	.	.
Solanum	.	.	.	.	.	.	.	.	.	2	.	.	.	.
Solanaceae	.	.	.	.	.	.	2	.	.	.	.	.	.	.
Valerianella	.	.	1	.	.	.	.	.	1	.	.	.	.	.
Verbena	.	.	1	.	3	1	1	.	3	.	.	.	.	.
Peganum	.	.	.	.	.	.	.	.	.	.	1	.	.	.
Unknown, GT-5	.	.	.	.	.	.	.	.	1	.	.	.	.	.
Unknown, GT-23	.	1	.	.	.	.	.	.	.	.	.	.	.	.
Unknown, misc.	.	11	27	63	7	7	23	16	145	70	3	13	27	6

TABLE 6:4 (CONT.). GRITILLE ARCHAEOBOTANICAL SAMPLES, PHASES 5 AND 6

GT no.	15572	1754	1959	6710	5566	7660	15746	16662	8721	7884	8748	1422	1763	2341
Other charred plant parts														
Hordeum int.	2	.	17	.	1	.	.	.	74	28	.	1	.	2
Triticum durum/aestivum int.	5	8	7	2	.	.	.	.	.	17	1	1	13	.
Triticum glume base	25	.	24	54	1	3	.	.	31	.	.	.	.	21
T. mono/dicoccum sf	.	.	.	.	.	.	.	.	.	.	.	2	.	.
Grass culm node	3	1	10	2	.	.	1	.	11	1	.	1	5	3
Oryza glume frg	.	.	1	.	.	.	.	.	1	.	.	.	.	.
Vitis peduncle	2	.	1	.	.	.	.	.	1	.	.	.	.	1
Vitis fruit	+	.	.	.	.	.	.	.	.	.	.	.	.	.
Glycyrrhiza pod frg	1	.	.	.	.	.	.	.	.	.	.	.	.	.
Mineralized seeds														
Arnebia decumbens	.	.	.	.	.	.	.	2	.	.	.	.	.	.
Heliotropium	.	.	.	.	.	1	.	.	.	.	.	.	.	.
Fimbristylis	.	1	.	3	.	12	.	.	.	4	.	3	.	.
Cyperaceae	.	.	.	.	.	.	.	2	.	.	.	2	.	.
Ficus	.	.	.	.	.	.	.	.	.	.	.	.	11	.
Papaver	.	.	.	123	.	.	.	.	.	.	.	.	2	.
Unknown, misc.	.	1	.	.	.	.	.	.	.	.	.	.	1	.

TABLE 6:5. GRITILLE ARCHAEOBOTANICAL SAMPLES, PHASES 7 AND 8

GT no.	365	5580	4587	4593	6982	5515	5543	5831	5845	7327	105	113	627	4558	7868	4908	4923
Year	82	83	83	83	83	83	83	83	83	83	82	82	82	83	83	83	83
Operation	9	25	25	25	26	26	26	26	26	31	9	9	9	25	25/10	27	27
Locus	16	5	31	32	11	20	20	21	21	2	5	11	15	28	58	2	3
Lot	18	64	41	42	70	29	34	44	44	13	8	10	34	32	95	16	19
Phase	7	7	7	7	7	7	7	7	7	7	8	8	8	8	8	8	8
Volume (l)	8	8	8	8	8	8	?	?	8	?	8	8	8	8	?	8	?
Density (g/l)	0.19	0.21	0.02	0.04	0.12	0.08	n/c	n/c	0.07	n/c	+	0.11	0.02	0.12	n/c	+	n/c
Charcoal >2mm (g)	.	0.84	0.11	0.30	0.92	0.22	0.90	0.22	0.51	+	0.02	0.12	0.07	0.93	0.04	0.01	+
Seed >2mm (g)	1.37	0.40	0.01	0.05	0.03	0.40	0.03	0.34	0.04	+	.	0.78	0.01	0.05	0.41	+	0.02
Misc. >2mm (g)	0.15	0.41	.	.	.	0.01	.	0.03	.	.	.	0.09	0.09	.	0.03	.	.
Seed/charcoal (g/g)	n/c	0.48	0.09	0.17	0.03	1.82	0.03	1.55	0.08	n/c	.	6.50	0.14	0.05	10.25	n/c	n/c
Wild seed (#)	120	124	28	45	8	24	.	12	32	1	.	216	5	8	22	8	.
Wild seed/charcoal (#/g)	n/c	148	255	150	9	109	.	55	63	n/c	n/c	1800	71	9	550	800	n/c
Wild/cereal (#/g)	74	653	2800	1125	800	92	.	32	1600	n/c	n/c	225	500	800	138	n/c	n/c
Cereal (g)																	
Hordeum distichum	0.93	0.03	.	0.02	.	0.10	.	0.04	.	.	.	0.18	.	.	0.01	.	.
Triticum durum/aestivum	0.28	0.13	0.01	.	.	0.09	0.01	0.22	.	.	.	0.26	.	+	0.07	.	.
Triticum sp.	.	.	.	0.01	0.01	.	.	.	0.01	.	.	0.05	.	.	.	.	.
Cereal indet.	0.41	0.03	+	0.01	.	0.07	0.02	0.11	0.01	.	.	0.47	0.01	0.01	0.08	+	.
Pulse (g)																	
Lens	.	.	.	.	.	.	0.01	+	0.02	.	.	.	.	.	.	.	0.01
Pisum	.	.	.	.	.	0.02	.	.	.	.	.	.	.	.	0.01	.	.
Vicia ervilia	.	.	.	.	.	.	.	.	.	.	+	.	.	.	.	.	.
Pulse indet.	.	.	.	.	.	0.10	.	+	.	.	.	.	.	.	0.12	.	.
Other food/economic items																	
Setaria	.	4	.	.	.	.	.	.	.	.	.	.	.	.	.	.	.
Vitis	.	6	.	.	.	1	.	.	.	.	.	.	.	.	5	1	1
Wild and weedy																	
Centaurea	5	.	.	.	.	.	.	.	.	1	.	2	.	.	.	.	.
GT-Asteraceae 1	48	.	.	.	1	.	.	.	.	.	.	.	.	.	.	.	.
Asteraceae	2	.	.	.	.	.	.	.	.	.	.	2	.	.	.	.	.
Brassicaceae	.	5	.	.	1	.	.	1	.	.	.	3	.	.	.	.	.
Capparis	1	.	.	1	.	.	.	1	.	.	.	1	.	.	.	.	.

TABLE 6:5 (CONT.). GRITILLE ARCHAEOBOTANICAL SAMPLES, PHASES 7 AND 8

GT no.	365	5580	4587	4593	6982	5515	5543	5831	5845	7327	105	113	627	4558	7868	4908	4923
Silene	·	5	·	·	·	·	·	·	·	·	·	·	·	·	·	·	·
Chenopodium	3	1	1	·	·	·	·	·	·	·	·	·	·	·	·	·	·
GT-Chenopodiaceae 1	·	1	1	1	·	·	·	·	·	·	·	1	·	·	·	·	·
Convolvulus	·	1	·	·	·	·	·	·	·	·	·	·	·	·	·	·	·
cf. *Bryonia*	·	·	·	·	1	·	·	·	·	·	·	·	·	·	·	·	·
Cyperaceae (GT-7)	·	·	1	1	1	·	·	·	·	·	·	·	·	·	·	·	·
Cyperaceae	·	·	·	·	·	·	·	·	2	·	·	·	·	·	·	·	·
Cephalaria	·	·	·	·	·	1	·	·	·	·	·	1	·	·	·	·	·
Astragalus	1	1	2	·	·	·	·	1	·	·	·	1	·	·	·	·	·
Coronilla	·	1	1	1	·	·	·	1	·	·	·	·	·	·	·	·	·
Medicago	·	1	1	1	·	·	·	·	·	·	·	2	·	·	·	·	·
Prosopis	·	2	·	1	·	·	·	·	·	·	·	·	·	·	·	·	·
Trifolium/Melilotus	3	6	4	2	·	·	·	·	2	·	·	33	·	·	·	·	·
Trigonella astroites-type	·	·	·	·	·	·	·	·	2	·	·	·	·	·	·	·	·
Trigonella	·	3	1	9	·	7	·	3	8	·	·	1	·	·	·	1	·
GT-Fabaceae 4	·	·	·	2	·	·	·	1	·	·	·	·	·	·	·	·	·
GT-Fabaceae 5	·	2	·	·	·	·	·	1	·	·	·	·	·	·	·	·	·
Fabaceae	5	1	1	2	4	2	·	1	5	·	·	34	2	2	6	·	·
Hypericum	·	1	·	·	·	·	·	·	·	·	·	·	·	·	·	·	·
Lamiaceae	·	·	1	·	·	·	·	·	·	·	·	·	·	·	·	·	·
Malva	3	2	2	·	·	·	·	·	2	·	·	2	·	·	·	·	·
Avena	·	·	·	·	·	1	·	·	·	·	·	·	·	·	·	·	·
Hordeum murinum-type	2	·	·	·	·	·	·	·	·	·	·	·	·	·	·	·	·
Lolium remotum-type	·	9	·	·	·	·	·	·	·	·	·	·	·	1	·	·	·
Lolium	·	·	·	·	·	·	·	·	·	·	·	1	2	·	·	·	·
Phleum-type	14	13	8	3	·	·	·	·	·	·	·	20	1	·	3	5	·
Triticoid	·	9	·	·	·	·	·	·	·	·	·	1	·	·	·	·	·
GT-Poaceae 8	·	·	·	·	·	1	·	·	·	·	·	2	·	·	1	·	·
GT-Poaceae 11	11	·	·	·	·	·	·	·	3	·	·	2	·	·	1	·	·
GT-Poaceae 12	·	6	·	1	·	·	·	·	·	·	·	·	·	·	·	·	·
Poaceae	1	16	2	4	·	7	·	·	·	·	·	4	·	·	10	1	·
Polygonum lapathifolium-type	·	·	1	·	·	·	·	·	·	·	·	·	·	·	·	·	·
Rumex	·	3	·	·	·	·	·	·	·	·	·	·	·	·	·	·	·
Reseda	·	1	·	2	·	·	·	·	·	·	·	·	·	·	1	·	·

TABLE 6:5 (CONT.). GRITILLE ARCHAEOBOTANICAL SAMPLES, PHASES 7 AND 8

GT no.	365	5580	4587	4593	6982	5515	5543	5831	5845	7327	105	113	627	4558	7868	4908	4923
Galium	.	.	.	.	.	.	.	.	.	.	.	.	.	.	1	.	.
GT-Rubiaceae 1	.	.	.	.	.	.	.	.	.	.	.	2	.	.	.	.	.
Solanum	.	.	.	1	.	.	.	.	.	.	.	.	.	.	.	.	.
Solanaceae	.	.	1	.	.	.	.	.	.	.	.	.	.	.	.	.	.
Valerianella coronata	.	1	.	.	.	1	.	.	.	.	.	.	.	.	.	.	.
V. dentata	.	.	.	.	.	.	.	.	1	.	.	1	.	.	.	.	.
Verbena	.	.	.	.	.	.	.	.	.	.	.	1	.	.	.	.	.
Peganum	.	8	.	.	.	.	.	.	.	.	.	.	.	.	.	.	.
Unknown, misc.	21	23	4	13	1	4	.	2	7	.	.	101	.	5	1	1	.
Other charred plant parts																	
Hordeum int.	.	.	.	.	.	1	.	.	.	.	.	.	.	.	.	.	.
Triticum durum/aestivum int.	1	.	.	.	.	19	.	5	.	.	.	2	.	.	19	.	.
Triticum glume base	.	.	.	4	.	.	.	9	.	.	.	.	.	1	40	.	.
T. mono/dicoccum sf	.	1	.	.	.	.	.	.	.	.	.	.	.	.	3	.	.
Grass culm node	1	6	.	.	.	.	.	2	.	.	.	.	.	.	11	.	.
Fabaceae (pod fragment)	.	.	.	.	.	.	.	.	.	.	.	.	.	.	1	.	.
Vitis peduncle	.	2	.	.	.	.	.	.	.	.	.	.	.	.	1	.	.
Vitis fruit	.	3	.	.	.	.	.	.	.	.	.	.	1	.	.	.	.
Mineralized seeds																	
Centaurea	1	.	.	.	.	.	.	.	.	.	.	1	.	.	.	.	.
Onopordum	.	.	.	.	.	.	.	.	.	4	.	.	.	.	.	.	.
Alkanna	.	.	.	.	.	1	.	.	.	.	.	.	.	.	.	.	.
Heliotropium	.	.	.	.	.	.	1	.	.	.	.	.	.	1	.	.	.
cf. *Capparis*	.	.	.	.	.	.	.	.	.	1	.	28	.	.	.	.	.
Suaeda	.	.	.	.	.	.	.	.	.	1	.	.	.	.	.	.	.
Fimbristylis	.	46	.	.	.	.	.	.	.	.	.	.	.	.	.	.	.
Ficus	5	1	.	.	.	.	5	1	.	.	.	.	.	.	.	.	.
Fumaria	.	.	.	.	.	.	.	1	.	.	.	7	.	3	.	.	.
Papaver	.	.	.	.	.	.	.	.	.	.	.	1	.	.	.	1	.
Hyoscyamus	.	.	.	.	.	.	.	1	.	.	.	3	.	.	.	.	.
Solanaceae	.	.	.	.	.	.	.	1	.	.	.	.	.	1	.	.	.
Unknown, misc.	1	.	.	.	.	.	.	.	.	.	.	.	.	.	1	.	1

TABLE 6:6. GRITILLE ARCHAEOBOTANICAL SAMPLES, UPPER PHASES (5–8, ISLAMIC PERIOD)

GT no.	3135	3314	631	18210	7318	8151	8165	13725	18380	22492
Year	82	82	82	84	83	83	83	83	84	84
Operation	8	8	9	26/27	31	31	31	31	45	55
Locus	53	54	23	40	4	9	15	26	16	41
Lot	99	109	35	62	12	22	24	48	22	48
Volume (l)	8	8	8	8	?	8	8	6.9	8	8
Density (g/l)	0.02	0.06	0.07	0.29	n/c	0.29	0.15	1.76	0.33	0.21
Charcoal >2mm (g)	0.14	0.46	0.03	2.19	0.16	2.25	1.17	12.21	2.47	1.44
Seed >2mm (g)	+	+	0.55	0.13	0.36	0.10	0.06	0.02	0.15	0.20
Misc. >2mm (g)	.	.	.	+	.	.	.	.	+	.
Seed/charcoal (g/g)	+	+	18.33	0.06	2.25	0.04	0.05	.	0.06	0.14
Wild seed (#)	4	.	88	10	5	30	14	17	10	6
Wild seed/charcoal (#/g)	29	.	2933	5	31	13	12	1	4	4
Wild/cereal (#/g)	400	.	463	77	50	750	200	850	100	120
Cereal (g)										
Hordeum distichum	.	.	+	0.06	0.01	+	.	0.01	+	0.03
Triticum durum/aestivum	.	.	0.07	0.02	0.04	0.02	0.02	0.01	.	0.02
Triticum sp.	.	.	.	.	.	.	.	.	0.02	.
Cereal indet.	0.01	0.01	0.12	0.05	0.05	0.02	0.05	.	0.08	.
Pulse (g)										
Cicer	.	.	.	.	.	.	.	.	.	0.04
Lens	+	.	0.03	.	0.08	0.02	0.01	.	.	0.17
Pisum	.	.	.	.	0.09	.	.	.	.	.
Vicia ervilia	.	.	0.13	.	0.02	.	.	.	.	.
Pulse indet.	.	.	0.07	.	0.12	.	.	.	0.01	.
Other food/economic items										
Linum	.	.	.	.	.	2	.	.	.	.
Gossypium	.	.	5	.	.	.	.	.	2	.
Ficus	.	.	.	.	.	.	.	7	1	.
Setaria	.	.	.	.	1	.	.	.	.	.
Vitis	.	.	2	.	1	.	.	.	.	.
Wild and weedy										
Centaurea	.	.	.	.	.	1	1	1	.	.
Brassicaceae	.	.	2	2	1	.	1	.	.	.
Gypsophila	.	.	.	.	.	.	.	1	.	.
Chenopodium	.	.	.	.	.	.	.	1	.	.
Convolvulus	.	.	.	.	.	1	.	.	.	.
cf. *Scirpus*	.	.	.	.	.	.	.	.	1	.
Cyperaceae	.	.	1	.	.	.	.	.	1	.
Astragalus	.	.	.	.	.	1	1	.	.	.
Coronilla	1	.	.	2	.	.	.	1	.	.
Medicago	.	.	.	.	.	2	.	.	.	.
Trifolium/Melilotus	.	.	.	.	.	2	.	2	.	.
Trigonella astroites-type	.	.	.	.	.	6	.	.	.	.
Trigonella	.	.	12	1	.	2	3	.	.	.
GT-Fabaceae 4	.	.	.	1	.	.	.	.	.	.
GT-Fabaceae 5	.	.	1	.	.	1	.	1	.	.
Fabaceae	.	.	1	.	.	4	1	1	.	.
Lamiaceae	.	.	.	.	.	.	.	1	.	.
Malva	.	.	1	.	.	1	.	.	.	.
Papaver	.	.	1	.	.	.	.	.	.	.

TABLE 6:6 (CONT.). GRITILLE ARCHAEOBOTANICAL SAMPLES, UPPER PHASES (5–8, ISLAMIC PERIOD)

GT no.	3135	3314	631	18210	7318	8151	8165	13725	18380	22492
Phleum-type	.	.	3	.	.	.	2	.	1	.
GT-Poaceae 8	3	.	10	.	.	.	.	.	.	.
Poaceae	.	.	.	.	1	1	3	.	2	4
Adonis	.	.	.	.	.	.	.	2	.	.
Reseda	.	.	.	.	.	.	2	.	.	.
Galium	.	.	.	.	.	1	.	.	1	.
GT-Rubiaceae 1	.	.	3	.	.	.	.	.	1	.
Verbascum	.	.	.	.	1	.	.	.	.	.
Hyoscyamus	.	.	.	.	1	.	.	.	.	.
Solanum	.	.	1	.	.	.	.	.	.	.
Unknown, misc.	.	.	51	4	1	7	.	.	1	2
Other charred plant parts										
Hordeum int.	.	.	1	.	.	.	.	.	.	.
Triticum durum/aestivum int.	.	.	.	.	.	.	.	.	1	.
Triticum glume base	.	.	.	3	.	.	.	.	.	5
Grass culm node	.	.	.	3	.	.	.	1	1	.
Vitis fruit	.	.	+	.	.	.	.	.	.	.
Mineralized seeds										
Onopordum	.	.	.	.	1	.	.	.	.	.
Lithospermum tenuifolium	1	.	.	.	.	.	.	.	.	.
Boraginaceae	.	.	.	.	1	.	.	.	.	.
Fimbristylis	.	.	1	.	.	.	.	.	.	.
cf. *Reseda*	.	.	.	.	.	.	.	.	1	.

TABLE 6:7. GRITILLE ARCHAEOBOTANICAL SAMPLES, MEDIEVAL DEPOSITS
OF INDETERMINATE PHASE

GT no.	16271	22606	20959	22091	22495	22469
Year	84	84	84	84	84	84
Operation	43	47	55	55	55	55
Locus	17	25	19	38	40	43
Lot	17	34	26	44	49	51
Volume (l)	?	8	8	8	8	8
Density (g/l)	n/c	0.95	0.16	0.48	0.02	0.15
Charcoal >2mm (g)	1.02	6.75	0.49	2.90	0.11	0.97
Seed >2mm (g)	0.50	0.72	0.75	0.86	0.09	0.24
Misc. >2mm (g)	.	0.12	0.02	0.06	+	0.02
Seed/charcoal (g/g)	0.49	0.11	1.53	0.30	0.82	0.25
Wild seed (#)	152	521	76	340	12	46
Wild seed/charcoal (#/g)	149	77	155	117	109	47
Wild/cereal (#/g)	390	734	113	791	63	256
Cereal (g)						
Hordeum distichum	0.07	0.37	0.06	0.07	0.03	0.06
Triticum durum/aestivum	0.28	0.13	0.49	0.26	0.11	0.05
Cereal indet.	0.04	0.21	0.12	0.10	0.05	0.07
Pulse (g)						
Lathyrus	.	.	.	0.14	.	.
Lens	0.04	0.10	0.03	.	.	0.02
Vicia ervilia	.	.	.	.	0.01	.
Pulse indet.	.	0.01	.	0.20	0.01	.
Other food/economic items						
Trigonella foenum-graecum	.	.	.	3	.	.
cf. *Juglans*	.	.	.	.	.	+
Gossypium	1	.	.	5	.	1
Ficus	1	.	.	.	.	.
Vitis	1	.	2	1	.	.
Wild and weedy						
GT-Apiaceae 2	.	5	2	.	.	.
Centaurea	.	1	1	4	1	3
GT-Asteraceae 1	.	2	1	.	.	.
GT-Asteraceae 3	.	2	.	.	.	.
Asteraceae	.	1	1	7	.	1
Heliotropium	.	3	.	2	.	.
Brassicaceae	.	5	3	18	2	.
Capparis	1	.	.	.	.	.
Gypsophila	.	.	1	.	.	.
Silene	1	.	.	.	.	.
Vaccaria	.	.	1	.	.	.
Chenopodium	2	6	1	.	.	.
Chenopodiaceae	.	.	3	.	.	.
Carex	2	2	.	.	.	.
cf. *Scirpus*	1	.	.	.	.	.
Cyperaceae	.	4	.	.	.	.
Cephalaria	.	.	2	5	.	.
Astragalus	1	2	.	2	.	.
Coronilla	2	22	2	2	.	1
cf. *Hippocrepis*	.	.	.	.	.	1
Medicago	.	.	.	2	.	.
Trifolium/Melilotus	.	.	1	9	.	1

TABLE 6:7 (CONT.). GRITILLE ARCHAEOBOTANICAL SAMPLES, MEDIEVAL DEPOSITS OF INDETERMINATE PHASE

GT no.	16271	22606	20959	22091	22495	22469
Trigonella astroites-type	.	.	3	.	.	1
Trigonella	20	7	.	67	.	1
GT-Fabaceae 4	.	.	.	2	.	.
GT-Fabaceae 5	10	24	1	.	.	.
Fabaceae	4	21	3	7	.	8
cf. *Nepeta*	2	.	.	.	.	.
Teucrium	1	2	.	.	.	.
Ziziphora	2	.	.	.	.	.
Malva	1	.	.	1	.	.
Fumaria	.	.	.	.	.	1
Papaver	.	.	.	.	.	1
Aegilops	.	1	.	.	.	.
Avena	.	2	1	.	.	.
Bromus sterilis-type	.	6	.	.	.	.
Hordeum murinum-type	.	3	.	.	.	3
Lolium remotum-type	.	.	3	.	.	.
Lolium	.	.	.	1	.	.
Phalaris	.	.	5	1	.	.
Phleum-type	7	86	5	1	1	11
GT-Poaceae 1	1	.	.	.	.	.
GT-Poaceae 3	.	.	.	.	.	1
GT-Poaceae 5	2	.	.	.	.	.
GT-Poaceae 7	1	.	13	.	.	.
GT-Poaceae 8	19	180	.	2	.	1
GT-Poaceae 12	6	.	.	.	.	.
Poaceae	49	60	14	10	3	2
cf. *Polygonum*	.	.	1	.	.	.
Rumex	1	.	.	.	.	1
Androsace	1	.	.	.	.	.
Adonis	.	1	1	.	.	.
Reseda	3	1	.	3	.	.
GT-Rubiaceae 1	.	2	.	3	.	.
Valerianella coronata	.	2	.	.	.	.
Verbena	.	.	.	1	.	.
Peganum harmala	.	.	.	116	.	.
Unknown, GT-19	.	2	.	.	.	.
Unknown, misc.	10	66	7	73	5	8
Other charred plant parts						
Hordeum int.	4	95	.	11	.	1
Triticum durum/aestivum int.	1	38	4	29	.	6
Triticum glume base	.	95	2	124	5	9
Aegilops glume base	.	3	.	.	.	.
Grass culm node	.	40	1	22	1	2
Vitis peduncle	.	.	.	3	.	1
Asteraceae (capitulum)	.	1	.	1	.	.
Glycyrrhiza pod segment	.	1	.	.	.	.
Mineralized seeds						
Arnebia decumbens	.	.	.	.	1	.
Lithospermum arvense	.	1	.	1	.	.
L. tenuifolium	1	.	.	1	.	.
Fimbristylis	.	7	.	.	.	1
Cyperaceae	.	1	.	.	.	.
Ficus	.	3	.	.	.	.

TABLE 6:8. GRITILLE ARCHAEOBOTANICAL SAMPLES, BURNT DEPOSITS OF CRUSADER-PERIOD SETTLEMENT (PHASE 3)

GT no.	18875	22467	6731	8113	9187	13809	13803	13806	13815	13828	13832	18245	19119	16915	18377
Year	84	84	83	83	83	83	83	83	83	83	83	84	84	84	84
Operation	10	10	11	25/10	25/10	25/10	25/10	25/10	25/10	25/10	25/10	26/27	26/27	42	45
Locus	58	88	25	57	75	75	75	75	75	75	75	43	43	19	15
Lot	124	185	47	103	128	130	133	133	133	140	140	69	95	28	21
Volume (l)	8	?	?	8	?	nf	1	0.6	nf	nf	nf	?	1	?	3
Density (g/l)	9.99	n/c	n/c	0.47	n/c	n/c	27.70	21.60	n/c	n/c	n/c	n/c	31.04	n/c	2.03
Charcoal >2mm (g)	79.91	21.04	8.12	3.45	14.02	·	3.07	0.82	·	0.04	0.05	1.35	0.24	4.98	5.61
Seed >2mm (g)	0.03	0.11	0.19	0.28	0.19	31.39	23.61	11.73	0.01	81.63	8.14	2.55	29.86	1.84	0.63
Misc. >2mm	+	0.27	0.02	+	0.01	·	0.04	+	+	·	·	+	+	·	·
Seed/charcoal (g/g)	·	0.01	0.02	0.08	0.01	n/c	7.69	14.30	n/c	2040.80	162.80	1.89	124.42	0.37	0.11
Wild seed (#)	2	37	46	78	100	1	482	271	1	·	·	275	79	102	4
Wild seed/charcoal (#/g)	·	2	6	23	7	n/c	157	330	n/c	·	·	204	329	20	1
Wild/cereal (#/g)	67	925	242	709	1457	n/c	17	19	100	n/c	·	75	2	84	5
Cereal (g)															
Hordeum	·	·	0.05	0.02	0.01	+	0.49	0.17	+	·	·	0.21	0.24	0.08	+
Triticum durum/aestivum	·	0.04	0.10	0.02	0.06	·	28.45	9.47	0.01	·	·	3.10	31.74	0.96	0.62
T. mono/dicoccum	·	·	·	·	·	·	0.14	0.22	·	·	·	·	·	·	·
T. monococcum	·	·	·	·	·	·	0.05	·	·	·	·	+	·	·	·
Triticum sp.	0.02	·	·	·	·	·	·	3.64	·	·	0.09	0.04	·	·	·
Cereal indet.	0.01	+	0.04	0.07	+	·	·	0.66	·	·	·	0.33	0.06	0.17	0.12
Pulse (g)															
Lathyrus	·	·	·	·	0.07	0.01	0.11	0.09	·	·	7.98	·	·	·	·
Lens	·	0.04	0.04	·	0.05	·	0.15	0.05	·	0.05	0.05	0.18	0.04	0.04	·
Pisum	·	·	·	·	·	1.06	·	·	·	1.40	·	·	·	·	·
Vicia faba	·	·	·	·	·	31.32	·	·	·	80.17	·	·	·	0.67	·
Pulse indet.	·	·	0.01	·	·	0.11	0.16	·	·	0.01	·	·	·	·	·
Other food/economic items															
Linum	·	·	·	·	·	·	·	·	·	·	·	2	4	·	·
Gossypium	·	·	·	·	·	·	·	·	·	·	·	7	31	·	·
Ficus	·	1	2	·	·	·	·	·	·	·	·	7	·	7	·
Secale	·	·	·	·	2	·	1	·	·	·	·	·	·	·	·
Vitis	·	·	1	·	·	·	·	·	·	·	·	1	1	2	·
Nutshell/pit frg (g)	·	·	·	·	·	·	·	·	·	·	·	0.04	·	·	·

TABLE 6:8 (CONT.). GRITILLE ARCHAEOBOTANICAL SAMPLES, BURNT DEPOSITS OF CRUSADER-PERIOD SETTLEMENT (PHASE 3)

GT no.	18875	22467	6731	8113	9187	13809	13803	13806	13815	13828	13832	18245	19119	16915	18377
Wild and weedy															
GT-Apiaceae 2	.	.	1	.	2	.	.	.	.	.	.	1	2	3	.
Apiaceae	.	.	.	.	1	1	.	.	.	.	.	.	.	2	.
Centaurea	.	.	.	.	.	.	.	.	1	.	.	.	.	.	.
GT-Asteraceae 1	.	.	.	1	2	.	.	.	.	.	.	3	.	.	.
GT-Asteraceae 3	.	.	.	.	1	.	.	.	.	.	.	.	.	.	.
Asteraceae	.	.	.	.	.	.	.	.	.	.	.	4	.	2	.
Heliotropium	.	.	.	1	2	.	.	.	.	.	.	1	.	1	.
cf. Alyssum	.	.	.	.	1	.	.	.	.	.	.	.	.	.	.
Brassicaceae	.	.	1	.	.	.	.	.	.	.	.	2	1	1	1
Capparis	.	.	.	1	.	.	.	.	.	.	.	1	.	2	.
Vaccaria	.	.	.	.	.	.	4	1	.	.	.	.	.	.	.
Chenopodium	.	.	.	.	2	.	.	.	.	.	.	15	1	.	.
GT-Chenopodiaceae 1	.	.	.	.	3	.	.	.	.	.	.	6	.	2	.
Chenopodiaceae	.	.	.	5	.	.	2	.	.	.	.	.	.	.	.
cf. Scirpus	.	.	.	2	3	.	.	.	.	.	.	1	.	.	.
Cyperaceae (GT-7)	.	.	.	9	.	.	.	.	.	.	.	.	.	.	.
Cyperaceae	.	.	.	.	.	.	.	.	.	.	.	.	.	.	.
Cephalaria	.	.	3	.	4	.	68	63	.	.	.	4	29	2	.
Astragalus	.	2	2	1	.	.	.	.	.	.	.	11	.	4	.
Coronilla	.	.	2	4	2	.	3	.	.	.	.	8	.	2	.
Prosopis	.	.	.	2	.	.	.	.	.	.	.	.	.	.	.
Trifolium/Melilotus	.	.	2	2	.	.	.	.	.	.	.	16	.	1	.
Trigonella astroites-type	.	.	.	.	.	.	.	.	.	.	.	1	.	.	.
Trigonella	.	1	3	10	4	.	13	.	.	.	.	26	2	17	.
GT-Fabaceae 5	.	.	1	1	1	.	6	.	.	.	.	.	2	.	.
Fabaceae	.	2	1	1	1	.	7	3	.	.	.	29	2	13	.
Ajuga	.	.	.	.	.	.	.	.	.	.	.	.	.	.	.
Teucrium	.	.	.	.	1	.	.	.	.	.	.	.	.	.	.
Malva	.	.	.	.	2	.	.	.	.	.	.	.	1	.	.
Fumaria	.	.	.	.	1	.	.	.	.	.	.	.	.	.	.
Lolium remotum-type	.	.	.	.	3	.	315	186	.	.	.	6	10	.	.
Phleum-type	.	4	2	.	1	.	2	.	.	.	.	70	4	1	.
Triticum cf. boeoticum	.	.	.	.	.	.	14	.	.	.	.	.	.	.	.

TABLE 6:8 (CONT.). GRITILLE ARCHAEOBOTANICAL SAMPLES, BURNT DEPOSITS OF CRUSADER-PERIOD SETTLEMENT (PHASE 3)

GT no.	18875	22467	6731	8113	9187	13809	13803	13806	13815	13828	13832	18245	19119	16915	18377
GT-Poaceae 3	·	·	·	·	7	·	·	·	·	·	·	2	·	·	·
GT-Poaceae 5	·	·	·	·	·	·	·	·	·	·	·	·	1	·	·
GT-Poaceae 8	·	1	1	1	·	·	·	·	·	·	·	4	·	4	·
GT-Poaceae 7	·	1	·	·	·	·	·	·	·	·	·	2	·	·	·
GT-Poaceae 12	·	·	1	·	·	·	·	·	·	·	·	1	·	·	·
Poaceae	·	13	6	12	3	·	21	10	·	·	·	5	4	10	2
Polygonum cf. lapathifolium	·	·	·	1	1	·	·	·	·	·	·	·	·	·	·
cf. Polygonum	·	·	·	·	·	·	·	·	·	·	·	·	·	1	·
Adonis	·	·	·	·	·	·	2	·	·	·	·	·	·	·	·
Ranunculus repens-type	·	·	·	·	1	·	·	·	·	·	·	·	·	·	·
Reseda	1	·	5	2	2	·	·	·	·	·	·	1	7	2	·
Galium	·	·	·	·	1	·	12	2	·	·	·	1	·	1	1
GT-Rubiaceae 1	·	·	·	4	·	·	·	·	·	·	·	·	·	·	·
Solanum	·	·	2	·	·	·	·	·	·	·	·	·	·	·	·
Thymelaea	·	·	·	·	·	·	·	·	·	·	·	·	·	·	·
Verbena	·	·	1	·	1	·	·	·	·	·	·	1	·	1	·
Unknown, GT-15	·	·	·	·	·	·	·	·	·	·	·	·	·	·	·
Unknown, GT-23	·	·	1	2	·	·	·	·	·	·	·	·	·	·	·
Unknown, misc.	1	13	11	17	49	·	13	6	·	·	·	53	13	30	·
Other charred plant parts															
Hordeum int.	·	1	1	4	3	·	·	·	·	·	·	·	5	·	·
Triticum durum/aestivum int.	·	·	·	2	6	·	14	10	·	·	·	·	1	·	·
Triticum gb	1	·	3	·	·	·	·	·	·	·	1	·	·	1	·
T. mono/dicoccum sf	·	4	2	·	·	·	2	·	·	·	·	·	·	·	·
Grass culm node	·	·	·	·	·	·	1	·	·	·	·	·	5	·	·
Vitis peduncle	·	·	·	·	·	·	·	·	·	·	·	1	·	·	·
Mineralized seeds															
cf. Capparis	·	3	·	·	·	·	·	·	·	·	·	·	·	·	·
Ficus	·	·	·	·	2	·	·	·	·	·	·	·	·	·	1

TABLE 6:9. MISCELLANEOUS ITEMS FOUND IN FLOTATION SAMPLES

GT No.	Dung, >2 mm (g)	Silicified cereal awns, straw	Other items
1422	+	Many	Silicified Asteraceae capitulum
1959	21.84		Silicified *Oryza* glume fragment
2341	+	Many	
5845	+		
6710	0.20*	Many	Many square stem fragments (mint?)
			*Includes 2 sheep/goat pellets
6731			Silique (Brassicaceae)
7868	11.76*	Many	*Sheep/goat pellet fragments
7884	0.08	Many	
8721	0.43		
8748	0.01		
9002		Many	
9187			Many twiglets
13803			Pod (Fabaceae)
13806			Pod (Fabaceae)
13809			9 larvae (in fava bean sample)
13815	9.39	Many	Dung sample, not floated
13828			33 larvae (in fava bean sample)
15572	7.68	Many	
17048	0.20		
18249		Many	
18824		Many	
19579	0.79	Many	
19591		Many	1 larva
22467			*Phragmites* (reed) culm fragment
22492	0.44*	Many	*Includes 3 sheep/goat pellets
22606	0.15*	Many	*Sheep/goat pellet fragments
22663	0.13	Many	

TABLE 6:10. GRITILLE ARCHAEOBOTANICAL SUMMARY*

Phase	2	3/4	5/6	7/8
No. samples	2	12	13	5 (6‡)
Mean				
Seed/charcoal (g/g)	0.08	0.15	1.74	4.12
Wild/charcoal (#/g)	20	58	1302	532
Wild/cereal (#/g)	140	475	2639	202 ‡
% wheat (relative to barley)	33	51	68	46 ‡
Total amount wheat & barley (g)	0.36	2.62	2.24	2.39 ‡

* Includes only samples with at least ≥1.0 g charcoal, ≥0.1 g seed, or ≥ 50 wild/weedy seed.
‡ Includes GT 365.

and walnut constitute the remainder of the likely food plants.

Before Gritille was flooded by the waters behind the Atatürk Dam, land use around the village emphasized "cereal farming with viticulture and a minor component of lentil cultivation. Cash crops include[d] rice along some perennial streams as well as tobacco [a post-1492 introduction] and cotton."[14]

CEREALS

WHEAT

The most numerous cereal grain in these samples is a naked wheat, either durum wheat or bread wheat (*Triticum durum* or *T. aestivum*; Pl. 6:1). Many of the grains have a compact form. The rachis internodes do not have a shield shape, but they are so short that a compact hexaploid wheat cannot be ruled out. Two deposits from an animal pen in the Crusader period settlement (GT 13803 and GT 13806) consisted of the harvested crop plus a few weed contaminants. The grains in that sample are fairly small (about 0.96 to 0.98 g/100 grains). In contrast, the grains of wheat samples from a contemporary hearth weigh approximately 1.55 grams/100 grains (GT 19119) and 1.10 grams/100 grains (GT 18245). A few grains of einkorn (*T. monococcum*), and possibly emmer (*T. dicoccum*) occur as minor components of some samples.

BARLEY

The barley is from the two-row type (*Hordeum vulgare* var. *distichum*).[15] Compared with what is found in many other sites in the Near East, the amount of barley is quite low relative to wheat, although it is more ubiquitous. None of the barley occurs in high densities; in the seed concentrations of the burnt Crusader settlement, it occurs either as a crop contaminant or mixed in with fuel remains. For example, in the sample containing the most barley, only two-thirds of the identified cereal grain is barley; the rest is wheat (GT 22663, see below). Barley grains weigh about 0.01 gram, but because the Gritille barley is scattered, weight per 100 grains cannot be calculated. Note, however, that in GT

22663, 77 grains weigh 0.64 gram, or approximately 0.79 gram/100 grains.

FOXTAIL MILLET

A few samples contain a few grains of foxtail millet. The puffed grains cannot be measured accurately, but based on size and shape at least some are likely to be the cultivated type, *Setaria italica* (Fig. 6:1F).[16] Given the small number, it is not certain that millet was grown at Gritille. If it were, it would have been an irrigated, summer-sown crop.

RICE

Rice (*Oryza sativa*) glumes can be recognized by their characteristic wafflelike texture. At Gritille, a single sample contained one charred and one silicified glume fragment, not quite enough on which to base any conclusions about trade or agriculture! If grown locally, rice would have been irrigated.

OTHER CEREALS

Many fragments of cereal grains could not be further distinguished, though they are almost certainly wheat or barley. Similarly, charred culm nodes of grasses are probably from wheat or barley straw. A number of samples contained a substantial amount of silicified culm and awn fragments of grasses, but quantification was not possible (many fragments fall through even a 0.5 mm mesh sieve) (Table 6:9).

PULSES

Fava bean (*Vicia faba*; Pl. 6:2) and vetchling (*Lathyrus*; Pl. 6:3) are the only two pulses found in concentrations in the Crusader period settlement.

FAVA BEAN

The two samples of nearly pure fava beans are probably part of the same seed stock, for they come from the same area in the Burnt Phase building complex (GT 13809 and GT 13828). Field beans (*V. faba* var. *equina*), which are usually used as a high quality fodder, are about 10 to 17 millimeters (uncharred), and broad beans (*V. faba* var. *minor*), which are eaten

---

[14] Wilkinson, *Town and Country*, 49–50.

[15] Miller, in "Crusader Period Fortress," mistakenly identified the barley as the six-row type.

[16] Cf. Nesbitt and Summers, "Some Recent Discoveries of Millet."

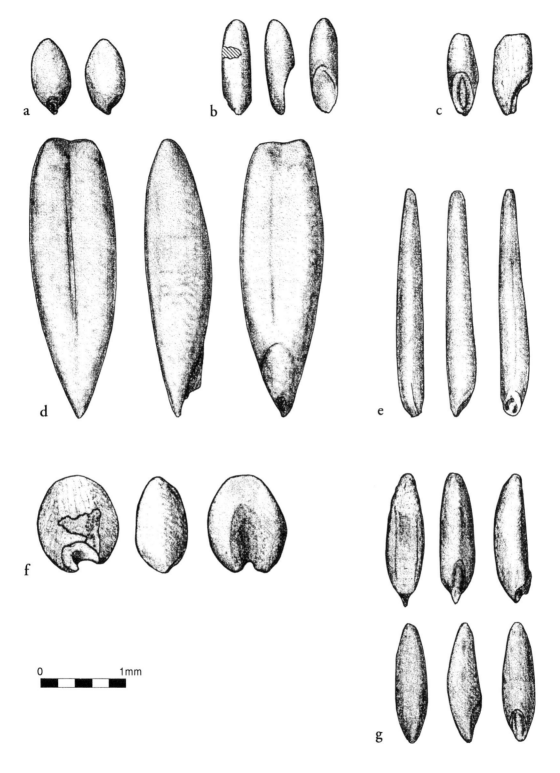

Figure 6:1. Grasses. (A) Phleum-*type [GT 22663]; (B) GT-Poaceae 7 [GT 6710]; (C) GT-Poaceae 12 [GT 22663]; (D)* Hordeum murinum-*type [GT 22663]; (E) GT-Poaceae 5 [GT 16271]; (F)* Setaria *[GT 22663]; (G) GT-Poaceae 8 [GT 22663].*

by people, are about 15 to 25 millimeters (uncharred).[17] Since the Gritille fava beans are quite small, less than 11 millimeters long, it seems likely that the material represents stored fodder. The store was infested with bruchid larvae;[18] about 10 percent of the whole beans had bruchid holes, and many of the individual cotyledons did as well. Some of these holes contained the charred remains of their creators.

Vetchling

One nearly pure sample of vetchling (*Lathyrus* sp.) was recovered from the same area of the Burnt Phase as the fava beans (GT 13832). Like the fava beans, these seeds probably came from a store of fodder. Although vetchling can be eaten by humans, it requires special processing to remove the toxins that bring on lathyrism and is usually grown as a fodder crop.[19]

Other Pulses

Lentil (*Lens culinaris*), the most common pulse in the ordinary occupation debris, was probably also grown locally. Chickpea (*Cicer arietinum*), pea (cf. *Pisum*), and bitter vetch (*Vicia ervilia*) occur in such small numbers that their importance in the agricultural and subsistence systems appears to be minor.

Fiber Plants

Cotton

Cotton seeds (*Gossypium* sp.) occur in consistently low numbers in Phases 3 through 5 and possibly later (Fig. 6:2F, G). These large seeds are very variable in shape. The seed coat can show a distinctive crackled texture, and a beak is sometimes preserved at one end.[20] Sometimes the seed coat is not preserved on these specimens. Cotton is thought to have spread to the Near East in the first millennium B.C. from the Indian subcontinent, where it had been established since the second millennium B.C.[21] Cotton provides both oil and fiber. Being an irrigated summer crop, its presence is an indicator of fairly intensive agriculture. If, as Andrew Watson stipulates, "Crusader villages tended to concentrate on subsistence, not cash crops" like cotton,[22] the Gritille finds would represent a minor contribution to the local economy. It is not possible to argue that the absence of cotton from levels clearly postdating Phase 5 reflects a significant agricultural shift in the region or at the site, because chance factors of recovery cannot be ruled out.

Trade in cotton cloth was widespread, but Watson puts the northern limit of cotton-growing before A.D. 1100 in the Near East to just north of Urfa.[23] Cotton seeds are more direct evidence of agricultural production than cloth, so cotton-growing by the mid-twelfth century is now documented as far north as Gritille. Finds from medieval deposits at Gordion (Phase 1 in the Yassıhöyük Stratigraphic Sequence)[24] extend the range into central Anatolia, but precise dating is not yet available.[25] Elsewhere in Anatolia, cotton seeds have been recovered from deposits dated to the twelfth to fourteenth centuries A.D. at Aşvan and to the sixteenth to eighteenth centuries A.D. at Kaman-Kalehöyük.[26]

Flax

A few flax (*Linum usitatissimum*) seeds were seen. Some are small, and may be wild, but others are large enough (more than 4 mm long) to be considered the domesticated type. Like cotton, flax could have provided oil or fiber.

Other Economic Plants

A single seed tentatively identified as the culinary herb fenugreek (*Trigonella foenum-graecum*) was seen.

---

[17] Townsend and Guest, *Leguminales*; Gill and Vear, *Dicotyledonous Crops*.

[18] So-called poppy seeds in GT 13809 (Miller, "Crusader Period Fortress") are actually charred bruchid larvae (Eva Panagiotakapulu, personal communication, June 11, 1996).

[19] Townsend and Guest, *Leguminales*.

[20] Delwin Samuel, personal communication, April 16, 1996.

[21] Zohary and Hopf, *The Domestication of Plants*, 127.

[22] A. Watson, *Agricultural Innovation*, 183 fn. 18.

[23] Ibid., 33.

[24] Author's unpublished laboratory notes.

[25] Mary Voigt, personal communication.

[26] Mark Nesbitt, personal communication, April 24, 1996.

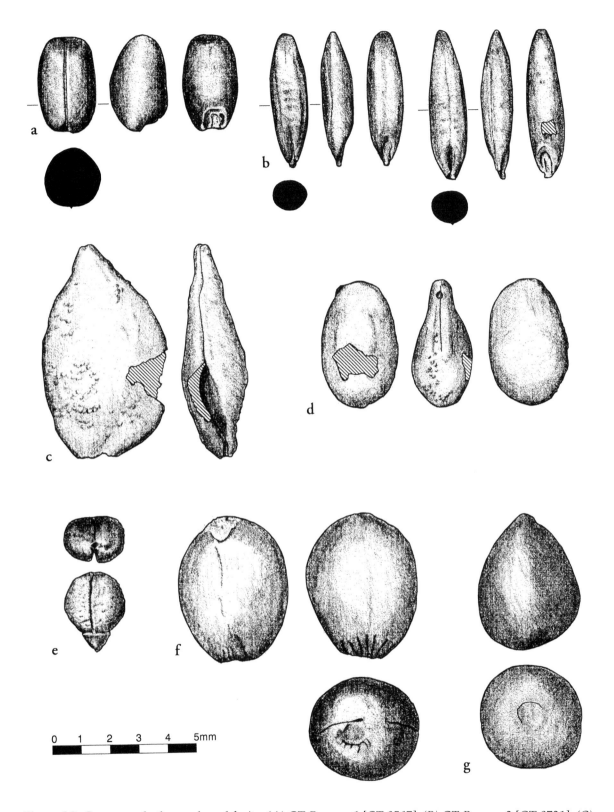

Figure 6:2. Grasses and other seeds and fruits. (A) GT-Poaceae 1 [GT 8567]; (B) GT-Poaceae 3 [GT 8721]; (C) Glycyrrhiza glabra *pod segment [GT 15572]; (D) cf.* Bryonia *[GT 6982]; (E) GT-19 [GT 22606]; (F)* Gossypium *[GT 8721]; (G)* Gossypium *[GT 8721].*

FRUIT

Remains of grape (*Vitis vinifera*) appear in small numbers throughout the sequence, primarily as seeds, but also as peduncles (fruit stems) and charred bits of the fruit itself still attached to seeds. Although grape is a natural part of the riparian vegetation, it is more likely that grape at Gritille was cultivated. Fig seeds (*Ficus carica*), sometimes burned, sometimes mineralized, also occur throughout the sequence but are a little more numerous in the earlier phases (3/4).

NUTSHELL

A small amount of almond (*Prunus* sp.), pistachio (cf. *Pistacia*), and a fragment of walnut (cf. *Juglans*) were encountered.

WILD AND WEEDY PLANT TAXA

Most of the wild seed types found at Gritille are known from other archaeological sites in the Near East. The most common ones in this assemblage are members of the pea (Fabaceae) and grass (Poaceae) families, especially *Trigonella* and cf. *Phleum*. Most are herbaceous and are palatable to livestock.

Many of the seeds have been determined only to family or genus. At that taxonomic level, it is usually not possible to infer growth habit (e.g., herb or shrub) or environmental requirements (e.g., disturbed ground, moisture). Where possible, however, I have tried to indicate the type of plant(s) under consideration, based on descriptions in the *Flora of Turkey*.[27]

Small seeds were recovered primarily from the flotation samples, but unfloated crop samples were not totally devoid of wild seeds. For example, two large seed types, vetchling and fava bean, occurred in such high concentrations they were just sampled en masse, without processing by flotation. Only a few wild seeds remained, probably because simple sieving by the medieval inhabitants had removed seed impurities before storage.

Archaeobotanical reconstructions presume the material is earlier than or contemporary with the artifacts associated in the same deposit. By Near Eastern archaeological standards, the Gritille medieval material is not very old, so one can imagine that degradation in the soil matrix might be incomplete. For that reason, some taxa that are occasionally encountered in partially charred form (e.g., *Reseda*, some Chenopodiaceae) are counted along with the charred seeds. It should further be noted that some small uncharred black seeds are not readily distinguished from their charred counterparts. This is particularly true for *Chenopodium*, *Portulaca*, and *Reseda*. If these small seeds are modern, the only plausible source would be as contamination in the river water used in flotation. I think this unlikely, however, as there are too many of them scattered throughout the samples. In this analysis, these probably charred seeds have been counted as archaeological rather than recent. In contrast, seeds that have become mineralized, frequently silicified, are treated separately, as they do not appear to have been preserved through burning.

APIACEAE

A few members of the carrot family were seen.

ASTERACEAE

Members of the daisy family occur sporadically. Only the very diverse genus *Centaurea* has been distinguished. One unknown, GT-Asteraceae 1 (Fig. 6:3G), is reminiscent of *Anthemis* or *Matricaria*. Two charred specimens of an Asteraceae capitulum (flower head) were also seen.

BORAGINACEAE

A few silicified achenes of boraginaceous plants are found (*Alkanna*, *Arnebia*, *Heliotropium*, *Lithospermum arvense*, *L. tenuifolium*). They are not included in calculations concerning the charred seeds, however, because of differences in preservation processes. One type, *Heliotropium*, does occur in charred form.

BRASSICACEAE

Several members of the mustard family have been seen but not further classified. A few are reminiscent of *Alyssum*, and a few look somewhat like *Hirschfeldia*.

---

[27] Davis, *Flora of Turkey*.

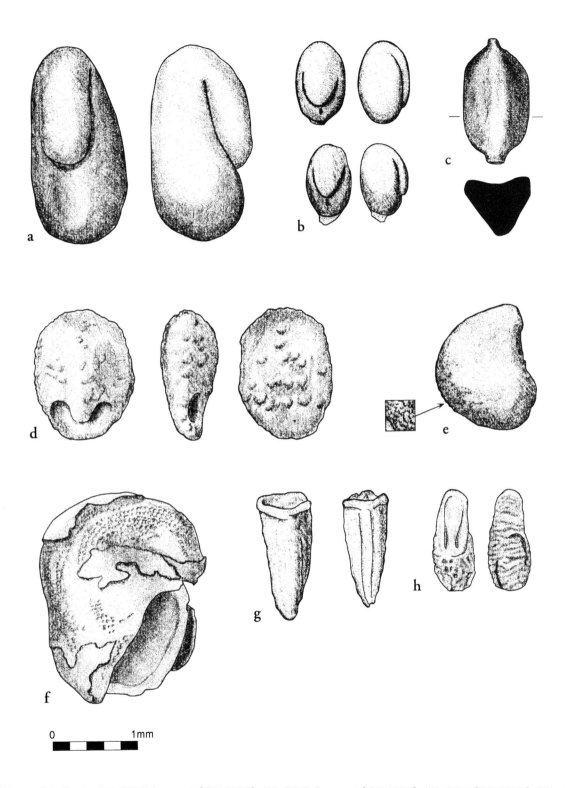

Figure 6:3. Seeds. (A) GT-Fabaceae 5 [GT 8075]; (B) GT-Fabaceae 4 [GT 1754]; (C) GT-7 [GT 8075]; (D) cf. Nepeta congesta-*type [GT 8721]; (E) cf.* Potentilla *[GT 1422]; (F)* Capparis *[GT 4593]; (G) GT-Asteraceae 1 [GT 22663]; (H)* Ajuga chamaepitys-*type [GT 1422].*

CAPPARIS

Caper seeds occur in small numbers throughout the sequence, usually charred but occasionally mineralized. Caper is a thorny shrub, but buds, fruits, leaves, and shoots have culinary uses, and animals can feed on the plants as well.[28] In some examples, the seed coat has fallen off, revealing the distinctive texture of the inner seed (Fig. 6:3F).

CARYOPHYLLACEAE

Several genera of the pink family were recognized. *Gypsophila* and *Silene* are quite diverse genera. Only one species of *Vaccaria* occurs in Turkey, *V. pyramidata*; it is a field weed.

CHENOPODIACEAE

Chenopodium is the most common genus of the goosefoot family represented. Small numbers of *Atriplex*, *Salsola*, *Suaeda*, and unidentified Chenopodiaceae are also seen.

CONVOLVULUS

Morning glory is represented by a couple of seeds.

CF. BRYONIA

The sole example of this seed makes it difficult to be certain of its identity (Fig. 6:2D). It is most probably from a trailing plant of the cucumber family.

CYPERACEAE

Sedges are typically plants of moist ground and might be expected to be found growing near the Euphrates, along canals, and in natural seeps. *Carex* and cf. *Scirpus* have been distinguished, but several other types occur as well. Silicified examples of small sedges also occur, primarily *Fimbristylis*; they are presumed modern as no charred examples were seen.

CEPHALARIA

Cephalaria is a noxious weed whose seeds are about the same size as the cereals and therefore cannot be removed from seed corn by simple sieving. Van Zeist and Bakker-Heeres note that though quite common today, it is rare up to the early historic period.[29] We can now demonstrate its increasing numbers by the twelfth century A.D.

EUPHORBIA

The sticky latex of spurge renders it unpalatable to herbivores when fresh.

FABACEAE

Small-seeded legumes, mainly *Trigonella* and *Trifolium* (clover) or *Melilotus*, constitute a substantial portion of the wild seed remains. Most had probably been eaten by herbivores. *Trigonella*, the most numerous type, is commonly a plant of the steppe. *Glycyrrhiza* (licorice) might be an indicator of degraded pasture, as it tends to be avoided by animals. *Prosopis* is shrubby, and like *Glycyrrhiza*, has a deep taproot that allows it to become established in cultivated fields. *Coronilla* is most likely a field weed. *Trifolium/Melilotus* would have grown on relatively moist ground. *Astragalus* is such a complex genus that not much can be deduced from its presence.

Glycyrrhiza (Fig. 6:2C) is today widespread in the Middle East, thanks to its deep taproot (harvested for licorice) and unpalatable leaves. It is rarely found in archaeobotanical assemblages.

GT-Fabaceae 4 may be a very small-seeded clover type (Fig. 6:3B). GT-Fabaceae 5 remains unidentified (Fig. 6:3A).

HYPERICUM

Like *Euphorbia*, St. John's wort is avoided by herbivores. It is a varied and widespread genus.

LAMIACEAE

It has been possible to identify four mints to genus: *Ajuga*, *Teucrium*, *Ziziphora*, and *Nepeta* (Fig. 6:3D). One example of a long *Ajuga* resembles *A. chamaepitys* (Fig. 6:3H), a plant that grows on stony slopes and in vineyards. Several unidentified members of the mint family also occur.

MALVA

Mallow occurs sporadically in the samples and is recognized by its wedge-shaped seed. (In sample GT 113, a bit of pericarp remains attached.)

---

[28] Townsend and Guest, *Cornaceae to Rubiaceae*, 140.
[29] "Archaeobotanical Studies in the Levant," 289.

PAPAVERACEAE

Three members of the poppy family have been recognized: *Fumaria*, *Glaucium*, and *Papaver*. Of these, *Papaver* (poppy) occurs in both charred and mineralized form (sometimes it is white, and probably silicified).

CF. *PLANTAGO*

Plantain is only tentatively identified.

POACEAE

Along with legumes, the grass family contributes a substantial number to the wild seed remains. Grasses are notoriously difficult to classify when fresh. This is even more the case with the seeds. Even so, several determinations are proposed:
Aegilops. Goat-face grass is rare.
Hordeum. A small-seeded barley whose size and shape is similar to that of the widespread species *Hordeum murinum* (Fig. 6:1D) is a minor constituent of the assemblage.
cf. *Phleum* (Fig. 6:1A) is tentatively assigned to a small rounded seed less than 1 millimeter in length. It is the most numerous wild grass in the assemblage.
Several as yet unidentified grasses are illustrated (Figs. 6:1B, C, E, G; 6:2A, B).

POLYGONACEAE

Both cf. *Polygonum* and *Rumex* were seen in very small numbers. One of the *Polygonum* seeds compares well with *P. lapathifolium*, and another with *P. persicaria*.

PORTULACA

Purslane seeds, rarely reported on Near Eastern archaeological sites, occur here in low numbers. Unfortunately, this tiny seed is black, and it is possible that some or all are recent.

ANDROSACE

This is another little herbaceous plant. It occurs only early in the sequence.

RANUNCULACEAE

Adonis and *Ranunculus repens*-type are the two members of the buttercup family recognized in these samples.

RESEDA

Reseda, which is a relatively common plant today, has not been reported in ancient times. Its habitat in Turkey is mainly rocky ground, but the most common species, *R. lutea*, is ubiquitous also as a weed. The seeds are small and black.

CF. *POTENTILLA*

A few examples of this seed are reminiscent of *Potentilla*, a herbaceous member of the Roseaceae (Fig. 6:3E).

GALIUM

Galium occurs in moderate amounts and is one of the larger wild seed types. It is easily recognized by its spherical shape with a hole on one side. GT-Rubiaceae 1 may simply be an undeveloped *Galium*.

SCROPHULARIACEAE

Verbascum (mullein), with its large, candelabra-like inflorescence, is a prominent part of late spring/early summer vegetation in Turkey but appears only sporadically in the archaeological samples.

SOLANACEAE

Hyoscyamus and *Solanum* occur in the samples, recognized by a reticulate surface. *Hyoscyamus* tends to be more oblong, and *Solanum* flatter and rounder in outline.

THYMELAEA

A few examples of this seed occur.

VALERIANELLA

On morphological grounds, two types as described by van Zeist and Bakker-Heeres have been distinguished: *Valerianella coronata* and *V. dentata*.[30]

VERBENA OFFICINALIS

Designation to species is plausible because *V. officinalis* is the more common type of those growing in Turkey.

PEGANUM HARMALA

This monospecific genus is widespread today, and in large quantity might be evidence

---

[30] Van Zeist and Bakker-Heeres, "Archaeobotanical Studies in the Levant."

of degraded pasture. It is not palatable to live-stock when fresh and tends to expand with overgrazing, as tastier plants are eaten. In the traditional ethnobotanical system, the seeds of *Peganum* are tossed onto fires against the evil eye.

ILLUSTRATED UNKNOWN TYPES

A number of types were encountered that are distinctive but not identifiable to genus, or even to family. They include GT-5 (Fig. 6:4A), GT-7 (Fig. 6:3C), GT-11 (Fig. 6:4D), GT-15 (Fig. 6:4E), GT-19 (Fig. 6:2E), GT-23 (Fig. 6:4C), GT-25 (Fig. 6:4F), GT-28 (Fig. 6:4B).

WOOD CHARCOAL

Poplar (*Populus*), tamarisk (*Tamarix*), and ash (*Fraxinus*) have been identified from one of the flotation samples. In addition to poplar and tamarisk, pine (*Pinus*), oak (*Quercus*), and possibly buckthorn (*Rhamnus*) have been noted from some of the medieval hand-picked charcoal samples.[31] As Willcox found in the Keban region,[32] pine charcoal occurs first in medieval deposits; it has not been seen in Chalcolithic through Hellenistic samples.[33]

DEPOSITS FROM THE CRUSADER PERIOD SETTLEMENT

Material dating to the destruction by fire of the Crusader period settlement is analyzed separately because it consists primarily of construction debris and stored crops (Table 6:8). The rest of the assemblage is probably the remnants of spent fuel mixed in with incidentally burned trash from the daily activities of the inhabitants (e.g., crop-processing debris) (Table 6:3).

Charred botanical materials are abundant in several of the burned rooms in the Crusader period fortress. Charred seed concentrations found in place identify crop storage areas within a room thought to be an animal pen.

ANIMAL PEN? (OP. 25/10, LOCUS 75)

Room just inside the fortification wall, with internal subdivisions.

LOT 133. MATERIAL IN NORTH SIDE OF ROOM

The nearly pure dung ash (unfloated; GT 13815) could be stable litter. Two flotation samples from Lot 133 are essentially pure wheat deposits, and their contents are virtually identical (GT 13803, GT 13806). The floated deposit was described in the field notes as "dark brown earth with seeds and very little else on top of straw deposit."

LOT 140. MATERIAL IN SOUTH HALF OF ROOM

Two unfloated samples were analyzed, one a collection of vetchling seeds (GT 13832), the other a collection of fava beans (GT 13828). Lot 140 "contains burnt planks, twigs, clay, and seeds," and is therefore presumed to include roofing material.[34] The virtually pure seed samples analyzed here presumably come from material that had been stored in the room before the roof fell.

LOT 130

Directly above Lot 140 (material in south side of room; GT 13809); virtually identical to the lower fava bean sample.

Op. 25/10, Locus 75 was thought to be an animal pen.[35] The independent archaeobotanical evidence supports this interpretation, as fodder seems to have been stored in the structure; the floor, at least in the north side of the room, was covered with dung.

ROOF OF "ANIMAL PEN"? (OP. 25/10, LOCUS 57)

Directly above Locus 75 "animal pen."

LOT 103

Described in the field notes as consisting of mudbrick chunks with "large lumps of charcoal

---

[31] Miller, "Gritille Charcoal."

[32] Willcox, "History of Deforestation."

[33] See also Miller, "Vegetation and Land Use."

[34] S. Redford, personal communication.

[35] S. Redford, personal communication.

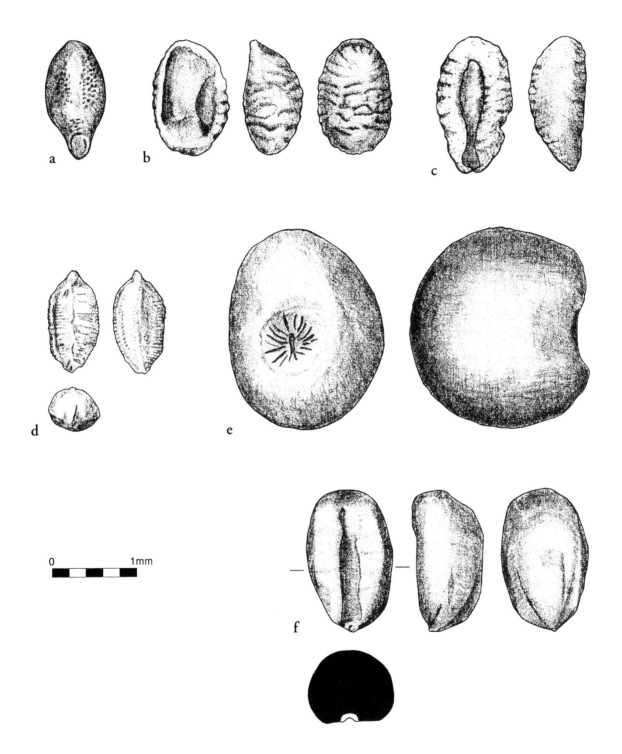

Figure 6:4. Unknown seeds. (A) GT-5 [GT 8721]; (B) GT-28 [GT 8075]; (C) GT-23 [GT 1754]; (D) GT-11 [GT 17748]; (E) GT-15 [GT 8075]; (F) GT-25 [GT 8075].

and lime and a lot of burnt pottery and unburnt bone" (GT 8113).

Its composition is quite different from the other Locus 75 samples in that it is primarily charcoal. The charcoal seems to be poplar/willow, which is consistent with the interpretation that the deposit consists of fallen roofing material. The roof would have protected the fodder stored in the Locus 75 "animal pen." The only cultigens are cereals, but one cannot tell from the plans or notes whether the sample was taken from the north or south side of the room, or from somewhere else. Many of the seeds are glossy and distorted by popping, probably from having been burned in an intense blaze.

FLOOR DEPOSIT IN ROOM NORTH OF "ANIMAL PEN" (OP. 10, LOCUS 58)

LOT 124

The sample consists almost entirely of wood charcoal. Three types in approximately equal quantities were noted: poplar, tamarisk, and ash wood (GT 18875).[36] Since a large proportion of the pieces in the flotation sample are twiglets and small branches, with diameters under 20 millimeters, this sample could be from a store of firewood. Roofing material is a less likely identification, because of the small diameters; furthermore, the excavator does not mention other construction debris (mud or plaster).

PIT (GT 22467, OP. 10, LOCUS 88)

Like the previous deposit, this sample is nearly all wood charcoal and probably is just burnt building debris that incidentally fell into the pit.

FILLS OVER FLOOR

Two samples consisting primarily of charcoal are most readily explained as fallen and burnt building debris: GT 6731 (Op. 11, Locus 25) and GT 18377 (Op. 45, Locus 15). Surface deposit GT 16915 has a greater seed admixture, but because of its relatively high amount of charcoal, it may be explained as mixed fallen debris.

OVEN IN ROOM NORTH OF "ANIMAL PEN," FIRST OCCUPATION PHASE OF THE MEDIEVAL PERIOD (OP. 9, LOCUS 90)

LOT 190

For a Phase 3 sample, GT 22663 contains a high proportion of seeds relative to charcoal, both wild and cultivated. The cultigens consist primarily of barley, but also include wheat and lentil. The density of wild seeds and barley rachis segments is extremely high. Since the sample comes from an oven, it is reasonable to suppose that the wood is the residue of fuel. The seeds may be plausibly explained in at least two ways, either as the discarded and burnt residue of grain cleaning,[37] or as burnt dung.[38]

Several points can be made in support of the first interpretation, that the seeds come from grain cleaning debris, which was then tossed in a fire: (1) The ratio of wild and weedy seeds to cereal (#/g) is 573. In contrast, the ratio of wild and weedy seeds to cereal in a nearly pure wheat sample (GT 13806) is only 19. (2) Most of the seeds are much smaller than cereals, and simple sieving (rather than hand-picking) would have separated grain from small impurities. Rodent(?) droppings, too, are a plausible impurity in grain, easily removed by sieving. (3) There is a close correspondence between the sample composition and that described for "fine sievings (smaller than prime grain)" in Hillman's chart describing glume wheat crop products.[39] The grain in this sample consists of barley and durum/bread wheat, so there is not an exact analogy. Nevertheless, most of the assemblage consists of seeds smaller than prime grain, and there are many barley rachis internodes. This stage of processing frequently occurs just prior to use; in the present day, the debris is commonly fed to animals, especially fowl, or tossed into a fire.[40] Even if the defenders of the Crusader fortress did not engage in agricultural production,[41] the residents had to eat. This type of residue is what might be expected in a food preparation context, since fine-sieving, as a

---

[36] Number of pieces, type, and weight: 6 poplar (4.77 g); 8 tamarisk (5.47 g), and 6 ash wood (6.52 g).

[37] Hillman, "Interpretation of Archaeological Plant Remains."

[38] Miller and Smart, "Intentional Burning of Dung."

[39] Hillman, "Interpretation of Archaeological Plant Remains," 10.

[40] Ibid., 4.

[41] S. Redford, personal communication.

household task, occurs toward the end of the grain processing sequence.

Some evidence supports the view that the seeds represent dung fuel residue: (1) The bulk of the flotate consists of charcoal, as expected for the material greater than 2 millimeters. The flotate less than 2 millimeters has many charred and some silicified straw fragments; this would be expected of dung fuel, which is frequently mixed with straw. The very high density of barley rachis internodes might also have come from straw and poorly cleaned grain in an animal's diet. (2) The wild seeds come from common fodder plants, some of which are not common in grain fields (e.g., *Carex*, *Scirpus*); many of the types in GT 22663 are those reported in sheep dung by Bottema.[42] Unfortunately, one cannot directly compare the densities of seeds in modern dung with those from a flotation sample, which, after all, has been mixed with dirt and other debris. (3) Barley, which is more likely than wheat to be grown as a fodder crop, predominates in this sample.[43]

It is possible that fine sievings were tossed into a fire fueled by wood and dung; this would account for ambiguities in the interpretation.

OVEN (OP. 26/27, LOCUS 43)

The two samples taken from this oven demonstrate the complexity of the archaeobotanical record. One, GT 19119, is a nearly pure wheat sample. It could have come from the accidental burning of food that occurred in the conflagration that destroyed the fortress. The other (GT 18245), probably lying above, shares many taxa and general characteristics (e.g., wheat predominates), but a closer examination reveals that it is more of a mixed deposit, like that described just above (GT 22663). It contains much more charcoal, and many more wild seed impurities; perhaps it is mixed with building debris fallen from above.

Comparison with two samples from the animal pen (Op. 25, Locus 75, Lot 133) is also instructive. Of the four samples, the two from the animal pen had the lightest (smallest) grains, the mixed oven sample had intermediate weight grain, and the pure wheat deposit in the oven had the heaviest, prime grain. In this instance,

one might surmise that the poorest grain was fed to animals and prime grain was saved for human consumption. This leaves the intermediate weight grain (GT 18245) unexplained, except perhaps as a mixed sample.

CRUSADER-PERIOD SETTLEMENT SUMMARY

The samples reported here are of three general types: stored crops, accidentally burned in the conflagration that destroyed the Crusader-period fortress; material deposited on the floors of the intramural settlement before or during the conflagration (dung in the "animal pen," roof collapse, and/or the remains of stored fuel or furnishings); and concentrated fuel remains found in or near ovens.

The deposits from the Burnt Phase reflect a moment in time over a restricted area. There is no way to tell how representative of crop choice and agricultural practices these remains are for Gritille, let alone for the medieval period of southern Turkey and northern Mesopotamia generally. The stored crops that have been preserved, especially the fava beans and vetchling, are probably fodder supplies; the wheat is likely to be a store of food. The cultigen admixtures of pea, lentil, cotton, barley, emmer, and einkorn found in these samples as well as in the trashy debris samples of the entire medieval occupation indicate that the medieval inhabitants of Gritille also grew these crops to feed people or animals.

INTERPRETATIONS OF THE REST OF THE ASSEMBLAGE

In interpreting archaeobotanical assemblages, it is usually helpful to compare results with nearby sites. Contemporary assemblages are not available, but plant remains from several sites along the Euphrates have been examined. The most relevant are from Kurban Höyük, a few kilometers downstream and across the river from Gritille.

Results are tentative owing to an inadequate data base; there are many unknowns, and the number of samples analyzed per phase is too low to encompass the full variability of the assemblage. Nonetheless, previous research has

---

[42] Bottema, "Composition of Modern Charred Seed Assemblages."

[43] Cf. Miller, "Interpretation of Carbonized Cereal Remains."

suggested some useful ratios to evaluate characteristics of the economy and vegetation. These ratios should not be taken as absolute numbers that directly reflect vegetation or economic variables, but rather as relative measures that allow some degree of comparison between samples, sites, or time periods. Because between-sample variability is so high, the numerical mean of the ratios discussed here is not meaningful and is reported in Table 6:10 merely as a summary of the bar graphs in Figures 6:5 through 6:7.

DISTRIBUTION OF TAXA THROUGH TIME

There are no major changes discernible in the distribution of the plant taxa through time. Most common taxa are spread throughout the sequence. Three possible exceptions are cotton, fig, and sedges, all of which seem to be a bit more common earlier. Given the relatively small number of samples, chance is a more plausible explanation for the distribution.

The stability in the assemblage over time probably reflects what actually happened in the past. That is, the medieval settlement period is less than 200 years, and land use practices did not change to an extraordinary degree. The limits of interpreting small amounts of data may also be a factor. As most taxa occur in only one or two of the seven phases, inferences concerning the disappearance or arrival of a rare taxon are not valid.

RATIOS AS INDICATORS OF THE AGROPASTORAL ECONOMY AND LANDSCAPE

In the ancient Near East, the proportion of seeds relative to charcoal is a rough indication of the state of the woody vegetation.[44] Based on the idea that the seeds originated in dung used as fuel and that wood is a preferred fuel, these ratios reflect the availability of wood in fairly close proximity to the site. Although one cannot use the information predictively, high levels of population and industry, ordinarily associated with prosperity, are also frequently associated with deforestation. Subsequent population declines may sometimes allow a degree of forest recovery as indicated by a reduction in the average value of seed/charcoal.

SEED/CHARCOAL (G/G), WILD AND WEEDY/CHARCOAL (#/G)

Although relative proportions of seeds and wood charcoal could be calculated in a variety of ways, I have found two to be most useful.[45] First, the weight in grams of seed and charcoal material that is caught in a 2 millimeter mesh generally compares material from cultivated grain fodder with wood fuel. Second, the number of seeds of wild and weedy plants (all sizes) compared with the weight of the wood charcoal larger than 2 millimeters is useful for skeptics who consider most charred cultigens to represent food.

Ideally, one would calculate the various ratios in order to determine mean values and standard deviations for each period. For the current set of samples, this is not statistically appropriate because for each ratio there are outlier values that strongly affect the mean. The distribution of the values for the various ratios by time period illustrates the point. That said, however, there are two subjective generalizations that can be made (Figs. 6:5–6:7). (1) The seed-to-charcoal ratio is higher in later periods than in earlier ones; and (2) the wild seed-to-charcoal ratio is somewhat higher later than earlier. Both these ratios are indicators of dung fuel use relative to wood. There does appear to be a general increase over time, which suggests an overall decline in woody vegetation, presumably due to fuel cutting.

WILD AND WEEDY/CEREAL (#/G)

If one accepts the notion that the charred seeds originated in dung fuel, then the proportion of wild seeds (count) to cereal greater than 2 millimeters (weight) can be a way to evaluate pasture and foddering practices. That is, a relatively large amount of cereal in the assemblage would suggest people devoted substantial effort to growing fodder for the herds, whereas a large number of wild seeds would suggest animals were being sent out to pasture. At Gritille, the wild and weedy-to-cereal ratios are highest in Phase 5.

To interpret this pattern, it is instructive to consider other sites along the Euphrates. In the arid steppe of north Syria, where sheep/goat

---

[44] Miller, "Clearing Land"; idem, "The Near East," 154.
[45] Miller, "Ratios in Paleoethnobotanical Analysis."

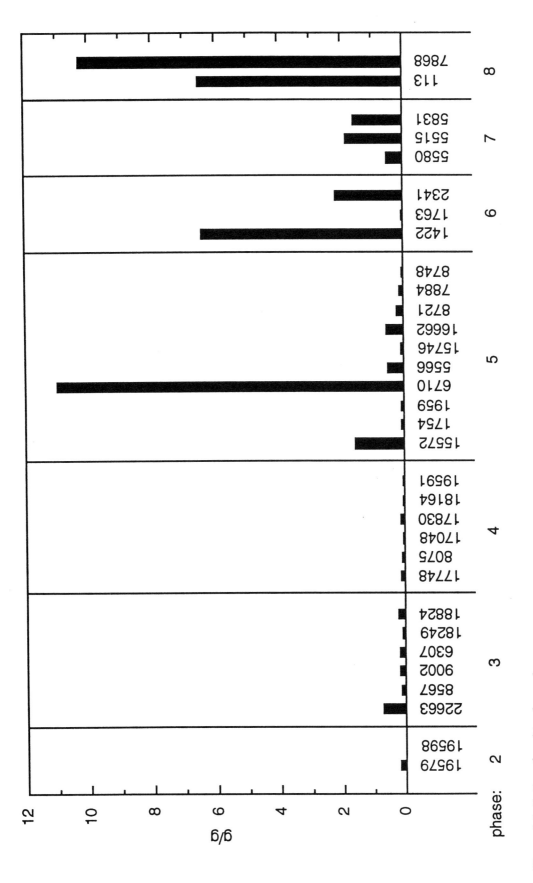

Figure 6:5. Ratios of seed to charcoal.

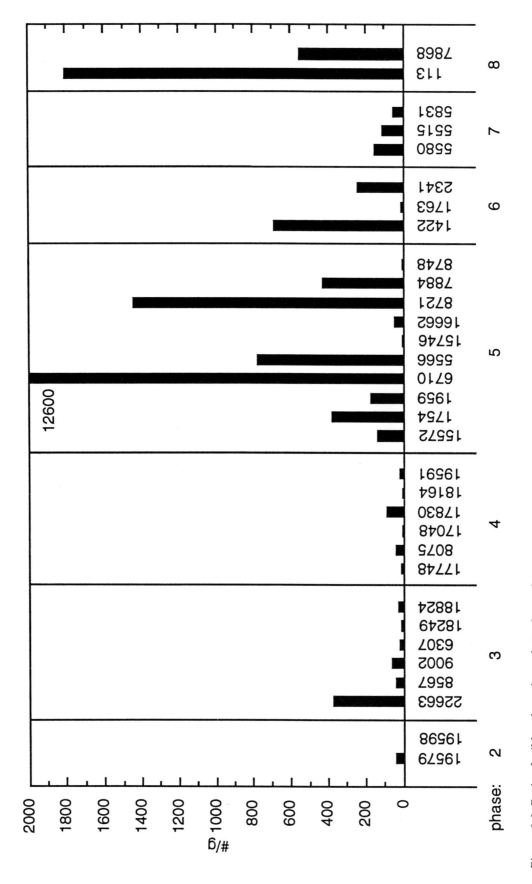

Figure 6:6. Ratio of wild and weedy seeds to charcoal.

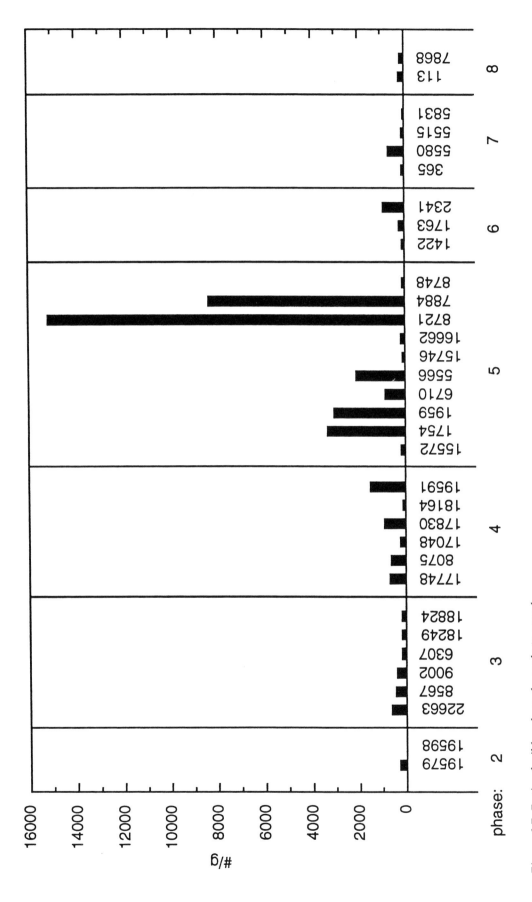

Figure 6:7. Ratio of wild and weedy seeds to cereal.

pastoralism would have prevailed, this ratio is particularly high.[46] At Kurban Höyük, I have noted a general correspondence between high proportions of wild seeds and high sheep/goat relative to pig and cattle.[47] Periods in which cultigens constitute relatively high proportions of fodder seem associated with high pig and/or cattle proportions.

It is therefore of some interest that exactly in the phase characterized by impermanent settlement on the Gritille mound, and relatively unsettled conditions in the region, this evidence for nonintensive land use is highest. As at Bronze Age Kurban, the faunal remains show a corresponding maximum of sheep/goat relative to cattle and pig in Phases 5/6 (Table 6:11).[48] (The modern Samsat district figure suggests that sheep/goat have simply replaced pig for the local Muslims.)

PERCENT WHEAT

In archaeobotanical assemblages from Chalcolithic and Bronze Age sites along the Euphrates, the importance of wheat relative to barley tends to follow rainfall: wheat is preferred for food, but it has a higher moisture requirement.[49] Where precipitation is limited, wheat is a riskier crop. Gritille is relatively well watered compared with the sites downstream, so one would expect wheat to be relatively more popular there than it is at sites to the south. For comparison, at Kurban, wheat generally comprises one-quarter to one-half of the identified cereal. At Gritille, similar calculations give figures that run between 33 and 68 percent.

It is likely that the livestock were primarily fed straw rather than grain, and that most of the wheat and some of the barley is from grain heads incidentally left with the straw. If the wheat and barley were ingested by animals, it would seem that high proportions of wheat represent a relatively intense land use pattern, with an emphasis on wheat cultivation. One might expect this situation to be more current in times of prosperous security because: (1) the labor situation would be stable; and (2) perhaps greater integration into a market economy permits the high risk/high gain strategy represented by wheat farming (i.e., you can sell your wheat in town if you have a good harvest, but if the crops fail, the regional distribution system will let you buy wheat in town if you need to).

It is therefore somewhat unexpected that the phase with the evidence for an extensive pastoral strategy (high wild-to-cereal ratio, Phase 5) also shows the highest wheat proportions. Possible explanations include (1) small sample size; (2) the wheat mixed in the ordinary trash samples did not come from dung fuel; and (3) intensive cropping around the site concentrated on the highly valued wheat, and very little land was devoted to fodder[50]—wheat would constitute a relatively large proportion of what little grain the animals ate.

Although the first two explanations cannot be ruled out at this point, the third is preferred by the author.

ASSESSING THE ARCHAEOBOTANICAL EVIDENCE FROM GRITILLE AGAINST THE HISTORICAL RECORD FOR THE REGION

One might expect, based on the modern vegetation distribution and comments by the Arab geographers, that the region between Malatya and Samsat was a producer of fruits, nuts, and other forest products.[51] Considering how close Gritille was to the uplands, the paucity of wild fruits and nuts and orchard products is a little surprising. This suggests that Gritille itself did not have direct access to forest products.

Some questions shall remain unanswered, as they depend on a knowledge of pre-Muslim medieval conditions for comparison. For example, since the new rulers treated non-Muslims

[46] Miller, "Farming and Herding."

[47] Ibid. Faunal data from Wattenmaker, *Social Context of Household Production.*

[48] Stein, *Pastoral Production in Complex Societies*; idem, Chapter 5, this volume.

[49] Miller, "Farming and Herding."

[50] Phase 5 has the only evidence for rice in the form of two tiny glume fragments; like wheat and cotton, rice would be an indicator of a more intensive agriculture or of trade.

[51] al-Idrīsī, *Géographie d'Édrisi*, 138. Travel time between Samsat and Malatya was about two and a half days (ibid.).

TABLE 6:11. COMPARISON OF MEDIEVAL ANIMAL BONE REMAINS WITH RECENT CENSUS DATA.

	Phase 5/6* % Bone count (N = 2866)	Phase 7/8* % Bone count (N = 2407)	Samsat district‡ % Livestock (N = 9533)
Sheep/goat	35	23	75
Cattle	20	25	25
Pig	45	52	-
	100	100	100

*Stein, *Pastoral Production in Complex Societies*, Table 8.2.
‡ Ibid., Table 2.1; from recent census data.

differently from Muslims for tax purposes, did this affect peasant villager strategies?[52] If land rather than animals were taxed, would Christians have been more likely to emphasize pastoral production at the expense of field crop production? The meager evidence from Phases 3 and 4 is not really enough to establish a baseline.

Redford has asked whether the influx of Turkish-speaking nomads generated change in the settled Christian community. For example, by filling the pastoral niche, did local nomads change the optimal combinations of food and fodder crops of the villagers? This question, too, cannot be answered at the present time.

There is one aspect of the data that does fit reasonably well the sociopolitical conditions posited by Redford. The Crusader-period settlement seems to have been a participant in a fairly intensive land use system, as evidenced by the presence of fava bean, apparently grown as a fodder crop, and cotton, an irrigated one. The Phase 5 settlement exhibits the most pastoral economy based on the wild and weedy-to-cereal ratio, although the presence of cotton and rice and a high proportion of wheat point to a system that requires irrigation. In Phases 6, 7, and 8, the emphasis on agriculture over pastoralism as indicated by a low wild and weedy-to-cereal ratio points to a subsequent return to pre-Islamic land use practices. This might be explained if the imposition of Islamic rule initially caused some disruption to agriculture and

commerce during Phase 5, when the site may not even have been occupied, but later on political stability permitted the traditional mode of agricultural production to return. One cannot, however, exclude the possibility that the evidence reflects site-specific rather than regional history.

THE MEDIEVAL LANDSCAPE AS INFERRED FROM THE ARCHAEOBOTANICAL ASSEMBLAGE

During the medieval period the village of Gritille participated in an agricultural system whose staple crops were wheat and barley supplemented by pulses (lentil and pea for food, bitter vetch, vetchling and fava bean for fodder). Evidence of other useful plants occurs in small quantities. Grape, fig, cotton, and flax were cultivated; pistachio, almond, and walnut may have provided the occasional treat. The presence of cotton and a tiny amount of millet and rice hints at some summer irrigation; the emphasis on wheat may have encouraged irrigation of at least some of that crop.

Around the village there was probably a patchwork of cultivated and fallow fields and vineyards. Near the village, trees would have grown along the Euphrates, in natural or cultivated groves. Pasture land would have extended farther away and, as is the case today, open oak woodland would have covered some of the

---

[52] In the absence of actual tax records for Gritille, it might be noted that in lands under Muslim rule, non-Muslims were subject to the *kharaj*, or land tax on productive real property, "whether or not the owner cultivated the land" (Aghnides, *Mohammedan Theories of Finance*, 385); animals belonging to non-Muslims do not seem to have been taxed (see also Ismail, *Das islamische Steuersystem*).

slopes nearby. Over time, however, the woodland would have thinned out or receded from the village.

ACKNOWLEDGMENTS

Between 1981 and 1984 the Gritille excavations were sponsored by Bryn Mawr College with the cooperation of the University of North Carolina, Chapel Hill, and the participation of the University of Pennsylvania Museum under the direction of Dr. Richard Ellis and under the auspices of the Directorate General of Ancient Monuments and Museums. Archaeobotanical work was funded by the National Endowment for the Humanities. Scott Redford provided the provenience information.

Seed illustrations were prepared for publication by Denise Hoffman from original pencil drawings by the author. I am grateful to Delwen Samuel for identifying two formerly "unknown" types as cotton.

VII

Medieval Regional Settlement Organization in the Gritille Hinterlands

Gil J. Stein

The 1982–1984 Gritille regional survey collected information on modern land use and archaeological settlement patterns in a 43 square kilometer area around the mound. Data on small-scale rural settlement helps place the medieval occupation of Gritille within its broader context by documenting the organization of economic activities in the hinterlands between this site and its larger neighbor Samsat. This chapter has two parts. The first provides an overview of the physical environment of the Karababa basin. The second part summarizes the survey data on medieval settlement systems in the Samsat-Gritille area. Comparison of the medieval pattern with earlier Byzantine rural organization shows the effects of increasing warfare in the twelfth to thirteenth centuries on site size, site location, and the intensity of agricultural production in this frontier zone.

The Physical Environment of the Karababa Basin

Topography, Climate, and Water Resources

In southeastern Turkey, the three parallel ranges of the eastern Taurus mountains form the southern edge of the Anatolian plateau. From the outer ranges of these highlands, a series of broad, moderately dissected limestone plateaus slope down gently southward to below 400 meters at the edge of the North Syrian steppe.[1] The primary drainages for this part of southeastern Turkey are the Tigris and Euphrates rivers. The Euphrates cuts through the southern margins of the Taurus by a series of gorges in the Şakşak and Gerger regions. In the foothills south of Gerger, the Euphrates valley widens enough to permit settlement and cereal cultivation. At Karababa Dağ (mountain), the limestone cliffs converge on the Euphrates, defining a sinuous, northeast–southeast oriented basin. About 35 kilometers long and 2 to 10 kilometers wide, before being flooded by the construction of the Atatürk Dam, the Karababa basin lay in the center of the transition zone between the Eastern Taurus mountains and the North Syrian plain.

The Karababa basin consisted of several distinct geomorphological strips or zones parallel to the Euphrates River. On the west (right) bank, the rolling terrain of the Adıyaman plain overlooked the basin, while the somewhat lower hills on the east bank formed the division between the Euphrates and Balīkh river drainages. Below this plateau/hill zone, a strip of highly dissected marl and limestone "badlands" marked the drop-off into the Euphrates valley proper. Pleistocene river terraces, defined by a calcium carbonate and cobble conglomerate, de-

---

[1] Pamir, *Explanatory Text*, 69–74.

scended in steps toward the river.[2] Brown and reddish brown calcareous soils overlay the terrace conglomerates and formed the basis for agriculture in the valley. These soils characterize much of southeast Turkey[3] and probably eroded down onto the Euphrates terraces from the plateau/hill and badland zones. Crosscutting the terraces, a series of irregularly spaced seasonal watercourses fed into the Euphrates. The lowest terrace, at 400 meters elevation, formed a bluff 20 meters high overlooking the river.

Where the Euphrates had first cut into the cliffs and then shifted course, recently deposited alluvial silts formed patches of flat irrigable bottomland. Although the bluffs marked the outer limits of shifts in the Euphrates channel, the dating and periodicity of these movements remain unclear. Severe erosion of the medieval levels on the eastern (river) side of Gritille indicates that at least some minor channel shifts have taken place within the last thousand years. Comparison of 1976 LANDSAT images with older maps of the area also indicate small shifts in the river channel. In several parts of the Karababa basin, the braided Euphrates channel formed low, impermanent islands whose brush and grasses provided grazing for herd animals and winter fuel for the inhabitants of the area.[4]

The Karababa had three main water sources: the Euphrates, rainfall, and a series of springs associated with the margins of the main Pleistocene river terraces; all were seasonally variable. The Euphrates River flow shows a marked intra- (and inter-) annual fluctuation, with 42 percent of the river discharge taking place in April and May. April discharges of 650 million cubic meters have been recorded at Birecik, just south of the Karababa basin.[5] Before the completion of the Keban Dam in the mid-1970s, flooding was common in the spring, usually from March through June, caused by the melting of the Eastern Taurus snows.[6] The lowest flow rates of the Euphrates generally occur in August and September, although fluctuations occur from year to year.

Mean annual precipitation in the Euphrates headwaters ranges from 800 to 1500 millimeters (much of it falling as snow), declining from north to south. The Karababa basin in the foothill zone received 400 to 600 millimeters annual precipitation, a figure comparable with rainfall levels in the dry farming belt of north Syria.[7]

Groundwater formed the third main water resource of the Karababa basin. Drawing on the absorption of runoff from the outer slopes of the Taurus, the west (right) bank of the Euphrates had much greater accessible groundwater resources than the east bank. Groundwater percolated from the Adıyaman plateau down into the Karababa basin and emerged as a series of springs along the edge of the 450 meter Pleistocene terrace on the west side of the river valley. These springs were extremely important resources for human settlement, as can be seen below in the close correlation between springs and archaeological site locations in the Gritille area. By contrast, the east side of the Karababa basin (in Urfa/Şanlıurfa province) drew on a much smaller, lower watershed, and for that reason had far fewer springs than the west. Many of the smaller springs dried up almost completely during the hot and dry summer months.

FLORA AND FAUNA

Topography and climate both placed the Karababa basin on the boundary between the Anatolian highlands and the North Syrian plain. This stretch of the Euphrates River valley also lay at the juncture of three different vegetation zones. Mediterranean woodland climax, Irano-Turanian steppe and desert vegetation, and Kurdo-Zagrosian steppe-forest were all found within a few kilometers of the Karababa basin.[8]

The Mediterranean vegetation zone, dominated by pine and oak, extended from the coast over the Amanus mountains, as far east as the open country between the Euphrates River and the city of Şanlıurfa. However, in the semi-arid

---

[2] Ibid., 74–75.
[3] Zohary, *Geobotanical Foundations*, 41.
[4] Ellis and Voigt, "Excavations at Gritille, Turkey," 321.
[5] Beaumont et al., *The Middle East*, 334–335.
[6] Great Britain, *Turkey*, 171.
[7] Tanoğlu et al., *Atlas of Turkey*, Map 25; Weiss, "Origins of Tell Leilan," Fig. 6.
[8] Zohary, *Geobotanical Foundations*, Map 7.

eastern zone adjacent to the Karababa basin, the Mediterranean vegetation declined from its arboreal climax into a more impoverished semi-steppe belt of increasingly sparse dwarf shrubs.[9]

To the east and south of the Mediterranean zone, the Irano-Turanian steppe and desert vegetation extended from the Şanlıurfa area across the North Syrian plain. Sage (*Artemesia herba alba*), spurge (*Euphorbia*), *Phlomis* (a member of the mint family), caper (*Capparis ovata*), and milk vetch (*Astragalus platyraphis*) predominated in this lowland region.[10] In winter and early spring, the grasslands of this area received enough rainfall to provide local pastoralists with a major grazing resource for their herds.[11]

Until the early twentieth century, wild fauna of the Irano-Turanian plains included gazelle, jackal, hyena, fox, wolf, and onager (*Equus hemionus*) among the medium and large mammals. With the exception of gazelle, who survive in a preserve at Ceylanpınar in Şanlıurfa province, most of these species are now either extinct or extremely rare in the area.[12]

Immediately to the north of the Irano-Turanian zone, the Kurdo-Zagrosian steppe-forest stretched across the foothills and slopes of the eastern Taurus. Oak (mainly *Quercus branii*) and pistachio (*Pistacia khinjuk* and *P. atlantica*) predominated in the open forest, while wild cereals such as einkorn wheat (*Triticum boeoticum*), emmer wheat (*T. dicoccoides*), and barley (*Hordeum spontaneum*) flourished in the hillsides and clearings of this zone.[13] The wild varieties of the grape vine (*Vitis vinifera silvestris*), pea (*Pisum*), and lentil (*Lens*) also occurred naturally in this part of southeast Anatolia.[14] The sloping plateaus of this foothill zone also formed an important resource for summer grazing. Millennia of agriculture, pastoralism and wood cutting for fuel removed almost all of the original arboreal vegetation from the lower slopes and valleys of this area.

In the river valleys of the Kurdo-Zagrosian zone, willow (*Salix*), plane tree (*Platanus*), licorice (*Glycyrrhiza*), tamarisk (*Tamarix*), and poplar (*Populus*) flourished, the last often planted in groves along the riverbanks. Marshy areas along the rivers supported stands of reeds and brush. However, aside from riparian vegetation and orchards (mainly apricot and pistachio), by the mid-twentieth century, prime agricultural areas such as the Karababa basin were almost totally devoid of natural tree cover.

The naturally occurring fauna in the once-forested hilly areas bordering the Euphrates valley formerly included black and brown bear, hyena, fox, roe deer, fallow deer, red deer, big horned ibex, and wild goat. The forests and particularly the marshy parts of the river valleys and the Euphrates islands provided an ideal habitat for wild pig. In the Van and Hakkari mountains to the east, wild sheep inhabited the open upland areas until early in this century.[15]

TRADITIONAL LAND USE: SETTLEMENT, AGRICULTURE, PASTORALISM, AND COMMUNICATIONS

The relatively flat topography, fertile soils, adequate water, and rich native flora and fauna have made the Karababa an attractive area for human settlement for at least the last 9,000 years. Population in the area was relatively high—especially in sites such as Samsat, Lidar, and Gritille—up through the thirteenth century, when the Mongol invasions led to widespread abandonment of settlements in the region. In trying to reconstruct medieval patterns of settlement and rural economy, present-day traditional patterns of land use can serve as a useful baseline for comparison. In the twentieth century, the Karababa basin has had a relatively low

[9] Ibid., 500, Map 7.
[10] van Zeist et al., "Studies of Modern and Holocene Pollen," 23; Zohary, *Geobotanical Foundations*, 473.
[11] Great Britain, *Turkey*, 248.
[12] Ibid., 251.
[13] Zohary, "Progenitors of Wheat and Barley," 43–55; idem, *Geobotanical Foundations*, 583.
[14] Zohary and Spiegel-Roy, "Beginnings of Fruit Growing," 319–327; Zohary and Hopf, "Domestication of Pulses," 887–894.
[15] Great Britain, *Turkey*, 251; Harrison, *Mammals of Arabia*, 11:330–376.

population density of 20 to 23 people per square kilometer. Settlement in this area has consisted almost entirely of small villages with average populations (in 1964) of 320 to 400 inhabitants.[16] The traditional land use system in the Karababa basin has combined rain-fed cereal agriculture with extensive herding of sheep, goats, and (to a lesser degree) cattle. Wheat sown on the river terraces has formed the major crop; barley has been of secondary importance. Vineyards and apricot orchards have utilized the chalky slopes at the boundary between the upper river terraces and the dissected badlands which enclosed the Karababa basin.

The embayment around Samsat and Gritille has been one of the most productive agricultural areas in the Karababa basin. Almost all (98.5%) of the Samsat administrative district lands have been classified as arable. Of these 27,871 hectares, 80.7 percent have been cultivated fields, the highest percentage of farmland in Adıyaman province. The Bozova district on the east side of the river in Şanlıurfa province has shown a comparable intensity of agricultural land use.[17]

Village inventory studies conducted in 1964 by the Turkish government provide a good picture of dry farming in the Karababa before tractors came into widespread use in the area. Farmers used an alternate year fallow system, supplemented by crop rotation (with lentils and chickpeas) and in some villages the application of dung fertilizer to the fields. In the Samsat district, sowing took place in September, with a July harvest. Villagers reported seeding rates of 130 to 200 kilograms/hectare and yields of 600 to 1200 kilograms/hectare of cereals on slightly rolling terrain. On more productive flat land, seeding ratios of 150 to 300 kilograms/hectare produced yields of 900 to 2400 kilograms/hectare.[18] Based on these figures, seed-to-yield ratios in the Karababa ranged from 1:5 to 1:7, indicating a relatively high productivity for a traditional dry-farming system.

Livestock raising also has played an important role in the rural economy of the Karababa basin and southeast Turkey. Sheep—most com-monly the fat-tailed variety—have predominated numerically, with goats second, and cattle a distant third. Sheep and goats are particularly well suited to grazing the slopes and badlands at the margins of the Karababa. Sheep herding in this part of southeast Turkey has been "multi-purpose," with animals kept for a combination of meat, milk, and wool. Sheep also have been raised for interregional exchange. In the traditional land use system before tractors became common in the area, the primary economic role of cattle seems to have been as draft animals, to judge from the 2.35 to 1 ratio of draft animals to milk cows in the 1964 village inventories.[19]

The herding system was organized so as to minimize spatial and temporal conflicts with the cropping cycle. Studies of modern land use conducted from 1982 to 1984 in conjunction with the Gritille regional survey determined that local herders used the badlands area on the edges of cultivation as the main source of winter grazing for sheep and goats, while cattle were given fodder, mainly chaff. By late spring, these resources were generally almost entirely exhausted. Consequently, as soon as the cereal fields had been harvested, sheep, goats, and cattle would be brought in to graze on the stubble. During the summer, the islands in the Euphrates also served as an important grazing resource. At the time of the land use study, herds did not range beyond the Karababa basin for forage, although they may well have done so in the past.

Most herds in the Karababa basin belonged to the sedentary villagers rather than to nomadic pastoralists. Average holdings ranged from 5.4 to 8.3 sheep and goats per family,[20] although the 1982–84 land use survey noted that some wealthier families had herds of more than 400 head. Smaller holdings would often be grouped together for herding by hired shepherds, usually old men from the villages. In addition, nomadic Yörük pastoralists passed through the Karababa as part of their seasonal round.[21]

Historical references suggest that for at least three millennia, agricultural and pastoral goods were the most abundant and best-known prod-

[16] Republic of Turkey, *Köy Envanter Etudlerine Göre Adıyaman*; idem, *Köy Envanter Etudlerine Göre Urfa*.
[17] Republic of Turkey, *Adıyaman*, 39, 1 17; idem, *Urfa*, Tables 14–15.
[18] Republic of Turkey, *Adıyaman*, Tables 5, 20, converted from donum to hectares.
[19] Dewdney, *Turkey*, 109; Republic of Turkey, *Adıyaman*, Table 25.
[20] Republic of Turkey, *Adıyaman*; idem, *Urfa*, Table 25.
[21] Scott Redford, personal observation, 1986.

ucts of the Karababa area. The Assyrian kings Asurnasirpal I and Shalmaneser III took grain, wine, cattle, sheep, and goats as tribute from the communities of Kummuh, as the Karababa area was known in the ninth century B.C.[22] In the first century B.C., Strabo emphasized the fertility of the Karababa area, noting especially its fruit trees, olives, and grapes.[23] The medieval Arab geographer al-Idrīsī also commented on the abundance of vines and other fruit trees in the hills surrounding Samsat.[24]

In addition to its role as a prime area of agricultural and pastoral production, the importance of the Karababa basin also derived from its strategic position astride several major routes of communication and trade. South of the Taurus mountains, the widening of the Euphrates valley creates three main river crossing points in the transitional area between the Anatolian highlands and the North Syrian plain: Carchemish (modern Jerablus) in the south, Zeugma and Birecik in the middle, and the Karababa basin in the north. In the Karababa, the main river crossing was at Samsat, with a subsidiary crossing point at Gritille. Exact itineraries varied depending on the season of travel and security conditions; however, the Karababa area river crossings often formed an important part of the east–west route from northern Mesopotamia to the Mediterranean and Anatolia.

The Karababa basin also lay on the Euphrates River north–south transportation route connecting Anatolia with Syria and Mesopotamia. The Euphrates first became consistently navigable at Samsat, although materials were rafted down from farther north.[25] Lumber and iron may have passed from east-central Anatolia down the Euphrates to Syria and Mesopotamia.[26] Herodotus reports a heavy traffic of leather boats along the Euphrates from Anatolia to Babylon.[27] Huge rafts made of wood and hundreds of inflated goat skins traveled south from the Karababa area as recently as the early part of the twentieth century.[28] This combination of agropastoral productivity and strategic location along key communications routes accounts for the long-term occupation of the Karababa basin from the Aceramic Neolithic up through the present.

THE GRITILLE REGIONAL SURVEY

The first systematic archaeological survey of the Karababa basin was conducted in the mid-1970s by Mehmet Özdoğan and a team from Istanbul University to record the sites threatened with inundation by the construction of the Atatürk Dam.[29] This survey identified Gritille as a major site for rescue excavations. As part of the Bryn Mawr College–University of North Carolina joint salvage program at Gritille, surveys of archaeological site location and agropastoral land use were conducted from 1982 to 1984. The Gritille survey sought to extend and amplify the coverage of Özdoğan's initial site inventory by focusing intensively on the history of smaller-scale rural settlement and specialized agropastoral land use in the hinterlands surrounding Samsat and Gritille. The survey was also intended to complement T. J. Wilkinson's detailed regional study of the catchment area around Kurban Höyük, a short distance downstream from Gritille on the Urfa side of the Euphrates.[30] The Gritille program included intensive walking transects, recording of modern cropping and herding practices, mapping and systematic surface collections of artifacts at sites ranging from the early Ceramic Neolithic through Ottoman periods in a 5 kilometer radius around the site of Gritille. The survey covered an area of approximately 43 square kilometers, bounded to the south by the site of Samsat, to the east by the Euphrates River, and to the north and west by the dissected badland terrain

---

[22] Jankowska, "Some Problems of the Economy," 256, 258, 270; Luckenbill, *Ancient Records of Assyria and Babylonia*, 599, 769, 772.

[23] Strabo 16.2.3; 12.2.1.

[24] al-Idrīsī, *Géographie d'Édrisi*, 138.

[25] Chesney, *Expedition*, 45.

[26] Maxwell-Hyslop, "Assyrian Sources of Iron," 139–154; Rowton, "Woodlands of Ancient Asia," 261–277; Voigt and Ellis, "Excavations at Gritille, Turkey: 1981," 89.

[27] Herodotus 1.194.

[28] Great Britain, *Turkey*, 177–178.

[29] Özdoğan, *Lower Euphrates Basin*.

[30] Wilkinson, *Town and Country in Southeastern Anatolia*, Vol. 1.

which enclosed the Samsat-Gritille embayment below the 500 meter contour line. This area consisted of two topographic zones: an upper terrace which ran northeast–southwest at an elevation of 450 meters, parallel to the Euphrates, and a lower terrace at 400 meters, in a 2 kilometer wide strip along the river.[31]

SURVEY METHODOLOGY

The 5 kilometer radius around Gritille was divided into zones of greater and lesser transect coverage for an intensive walking survey, based on those topographical and environmental criteria that appeared to be most important for modern land use and ancient settlement location, according to an initial reconnaissance and Özdoğan's survey. Given the land and water resources of the Karababa basin (as described above), these features were defined as the Euphrates River, seasonal watercourses, seasonal or perennial springs, and more or less level agricultural land. Those locations where seasonal watercourses cut across the eastern edge of the 450 meter upper terrace, exposing perennial springs, were targeted as prime areas for investigation.

Fourteen 200 meter wide transects were defined for investigation, including the area along the Euphrates from Hardiyan in the north to the outskirts of Samsat in the south; the east edge of the 450 meter upper terrace; all major seasonal watercourses; and several control transects to investigate the areas lying between the seasonal watercourses. The following watercourses were investigated: Hamışkan, Bolunca, Memişan, Değirmen, Gevrik, Alikan, Aşma, Karadut, Hederm, and Dina Deresi (Fig. 7.1a).[32] Members of the five-person survey crew, spaced 20 meters apart, walked each transect in two 100 meter

wide segments. All sites and artifact scatters were recorded and collected. Site locations were triangulated using a Brunton pocket transit and recorded on enlarged versions of the published Özdoğan survey maps. Sites were mapped using compass and tape. Multicomponent sites such as Sürük Mevkii were gridded and systematically surface collected in 10 by 10 meter units in order to determine the extent of occupation in different periods.[33] At small single-component sites, nonsystematic judgment samples of diagnostics were collected. For each site, the following information was recorded: nearest drainage, nearest available water, topography, vegetation, soils, site dimensions, disturbances (if present), artifact densities, and occupation periods. Diagnostic ceramics were drawn and photographed from each site. The sites were dated mainly by comparing the surface collected survey ceramics with stratigraphically excavated assemblages from Gritille, Lidar, Samsat, and Kurban Höyük.[34]

As part of the studies of prehistoric land use, the survey also investigated the intensity of ancient agriculture in the Gritille area by making a series of transect collections of the low density sherd scatters lying between settlements, and especially around Gritille itself. Field scatters apparently reflect the fairly common field fertilization practice in which farmers would have dug up ash from their settlements and spread it, along with manure, on their fields.[35] By mapping the distributions of these field scatters and dating the collected sherds, it was possible to identify periods of high intensity agricultural land use in a given region. These periods generally correlate well with periods of urbanization and/or high density rural settlement in the dry farming zone of southeast Anatolia, north Syria, and north Mesopotamia.

---

[31] The Gritille survey in the Atatürk Dam reservoir zone was later complemented by the British Institute of Archaeology's much larger scale survey of the adjacent upland areas, notably the Adıyaman plain and several key tributary watercourses feeding into the Euphrates in the vicinity of Samsat. See Blaylock, French, and Summers, "The Adıyaman Survey," 81–135.

[32] Özdoğan, *Lower Euphrates Basin*, Maps 41–43.

[33] For full discussions of the controlled surface collection methodologies employed, see Whallon, *Archaeological Survey of the Keban Reservoir Area*.

[34] Algaze, *Town and Country in Southeastern Anatolia*, Vol. 2; Wilkinson, *Town and Country in Southeastern Anatolia*, Vol. 1. These materials were made available for study in the field by the excavators of these sites: Professors Richard Ellis, Harald Hauptmann, Nimet Özgüç, and Leon Marfoe. The assistance of Scott Redford in identification of the medieval ceramics is gratefully acknowledged.

[35] Wilkinson, "Definition of Ancient Manured Zones," 323–333; idem, "Extensive Sherd Scatters," 31–46; idem, *Town and Country in Southeastern Anatolia*, Vol. 1.

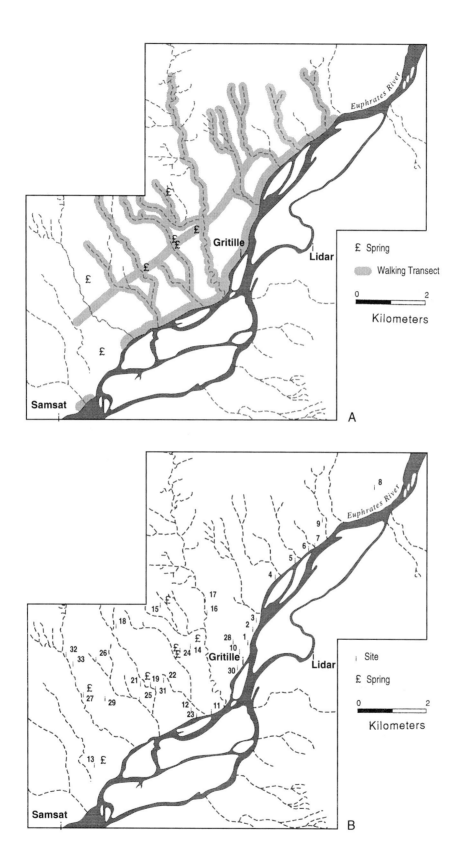

Figure 7:1. (A). Gritille regional survey walking transects; (B) survey sites and field scatters, all periods.

SURVEY RESULTS

In examining the results of the 1982–84 survey, it is important to recall that the 43 square kilometer survey area represents a very small portion of a larger-scale regional system, dominated by urban settlements such as Samsat, and fortified villages/river crossings such as Gritille and Lidar. The extent to which small-scale specialized outlying settlements were found in the Samsat-Gritille embayment was determined by the political and economic fortunes of those three larger settlements. This is analogous to the way the occupation of Gritille itself was very much dependent on events at Lidar and Samsat. Thus it should come as no surprise that the sites in the Gritille survey area were small and either single-component or sporadically occupied in a pattern that reflects broader regional-level processes.

The survey recorded 25 sites (along with a number of field scatters associated with agricultural practices such as manuring) within a 5 kilometer radius of Gritille (Fig. 7.1B). The sites ranged in time from the early Ceramic Neolithic through the Late Ottoman period (Tables 7:1, 7:2).[36] The sites were generally quite small—21 of the 25 sites were less than 0.5 hectare in area—a size range consistent with the identification of most as hamlets or individual farmsteads. The 4.5 hectare size of the largest site (number 31) cannot be considered reliable since it completely underlies the modern village of Biriman/Kovanoluk. Most periods were represented in the survey area, although Halaf, Middle Bronze Age, and early Iron Age sites were absent. Since Halaf ceramics are easily recognizable, it is probable that their absence accurately reflects the lack of Halaf sites in the intensive survey zone. The absence of second and early first millennia B.C. sites in the Gritille survey area is consistent with the major settlement shifts that took place in the Kurban Höyük hinterlands just across the river.[37] However, since the ceramics of the Middle Bronze Age and early Iron Age of southeast Turkey remain poorly known, it is quite possible that the lack of

sites dating to these periods reflects the problems of recognition or "archaeological visibility," rather than an absence of small settlements dating to these periods.

Settlement density was generally quite low—with only two to three small sites in the 43 square kilometer survey area during most periods up through the late Iron Age. The number of sites then increased to seven during the Late Hellenistic/Early Roman period (roughly from the second century B.C. to the early third century A.D.). The peak period for settlement in the Samsat-Gritille hinterlands appears to have been the Late Roman/Byzantine period, corresponding to the late third through seventh centuries A.D. (Fig. 7:2A). Seventeen sites were noted; these were almost all farmstead-sized localities smaller than 0.5 hectare. This matches the regional patterns noted on the Kurban Höyük side of the Euphrates, where settlement reached its peak both in the number of sites and in aggregate site area in the Late Roman/Byzantine period as well.[38]

The distribution of Byzantine sites in the Samsat-Gritille hinterlands reveals some interesting patterns which differ noticeably from the later secondary peak in settlement during the medieval period. First of all, the high concentration of Byzantine settlement took place at a time when the mound of Gritille was not occupied. Second, all field scatters noted in collection transects dated to the Late Roman/Byzantine period; this suggests the practice of manuring on the 400 meter lower terrace as part of an intensive farming system in this period (no evidence for manuring was noted on the 450 meter upper terrace). Finally, sites were widely and evenly distributed on prime agricultural land throughout the survey area. Eight sites were located on the lower terrace, strung out along a 10 kilometer stretch of the Euphrates from Samsat in the south to Hardiyan in the north. Nine sites were located on the upper terrace. The large number of small sites, their wide dispersal, their location in exposed positions along the river, the field scatter evidence for manuring, and the lack of a fortified occupation at Gritille in the Late Ro-

---

[36] For neolithic sites, see Stein, "Archaeological Survey at Siirtik Mevkii," 19–32.

[37] Wilkinson, *Town and Country in Southeastern Anatolia*, 1:109–111.

[38] Scott Redford, personal communication.

TABLE 7:1. GRITILLE REGIONAL SURVEY SITES

Site	Site size (ha)	Neo-lithic	L. Chalco-lithic	Early EBA	Mid EBA	Late Iron	Hellenistic/ Roman	Byzantine	Abbas.	Medieval	Post-medieval	Comments
Gritille	1.50	X			X	X				X		
2	0.20						X	X				
3	0.05										X	
4	0.48			X			X	X				
5	2.00		X									Karatut Mekvii
6	0.20		X									
7	0.15							X				
8	0.13							X		?		
9	0.01											Plundered cemetery
10	0.18						X					
11	0.29							X	?	X		
12	0.38							X				
13	0.21							X				
14	0.60							X	X			Alikan Mevkii (Özdoğan site no. T51/10)
15	1.17	X				X	X	X		X	X	Sürük Mevkii (Özdoğan site no. T51/13)
16	1.28			?		?	?	?		X		Haraba Çukan (Özdoğan site no. T51/12)
17	0.14						X	X	X			
18	0.15										X	
21	0.43							X		X		
24	0.20					?		X		X		
25	0.31							X	?			
26	1.02							X		X		Salahan Mevkii (Özdoğan site no. T51/20)
27	0.33						X	X	X	X		Hamiskan Mevkii (Özdoğan site no. T51/21)
30	0.05				X							
31	4.50			X		X	X	X	?	X	X	Biriman
32	0.18			X								

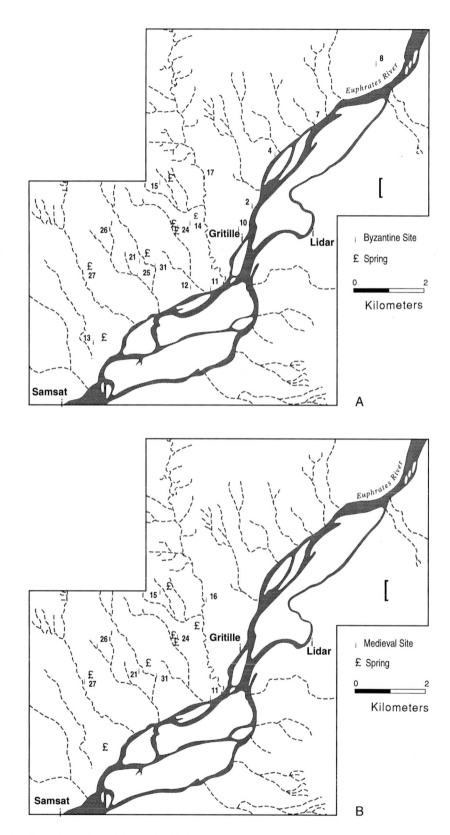

Figure 7:2. (A) Byzantine sites; (B) medieval sites.

TABLE 7.2. GRITILLE REGIONAL SURVEY, BREAKDOWN OF SITE OCCUPATIONS BY PERIOD

Period	Number of sites
Postmedieval	3
Medieval	7
Abbasid	2
Byzantine	17
Hellenistic/Roman	7
Late Iron Age	3
Mid-Late 3rd millennium BC	2
Early 3rd millennium BC	3
Late Chalcolithic	2
Ceramic Neolithic	2
Aceramic Neolithic	1

Counts include documented occupations at Gritille Höyük.

man/Byzantine all suggest a period of intensive agricultural production under relatively secure conditions in the countryside north of Samsat.

The medieval settlement system contrasts markedly with the Late Roman/Byzantine pattern. During the Byzantine period, seventeen sites were occupied. However, in the medieval period, only eight sites were occupied in the Samsat-Gritille hinterlands: Sites 11, 15, 16, 21, 24, 26, 27, and 31 (Fig. 7:2b). These settlements were generally quite small; controlled surface collections at Sites 15, 21, and 27 yielded distributions of medieval ceramics (Fig. 7:3) and ground stone agricultural processing tools which suggest that these were small hamlets or farmsteads.

Shifts in settlement locations appear to reflect a need for protection under significantly less secure political conditions. In the Late Roman/Byzantine period, sites were located all along the river, and Gritille itself was unoccupied until the eleventh century. In the medieval period, Gritille was well fortified, and all but one (Site 11) of the smaller settlements along the river and the lower terrace were abandoned. The embayment to the north of Gritille no longer had any small agricultural outliers. Instead, the medieval sites clustered away from the river, on the upper terrace next to perennial springs, in the area lying between the major fortified sites of Samsat and Gritille. Overwhelmingly, it

was the small sites that were abandoned. Those medieval outliers that remained in place were on the average larger (mean size 1.19 ha) than the Late/Roman Byzantine settlements (mean size .63 ha). Since the total area of all sites occupied in each period was virtually identical (10.73 ha for Byzantine; 10.72 ha for medieval), this probably does not reflect any kind of change in rural population levels. Instead, the difference in mean site area suggests an aggregation of the farming population for increased security; this was consistent with the abandonment of exposed settlements on the lower terrace and in areas distant from the fortified outpost at Gritille. Concurrent with the abandonment of exposed settlements and aggregation in more protected locales, the lack of medieval field scatters suggests that the earlier intensive agricultural practices such as manuring were also given up in the twelfth to thirteenth centuries. These small agricultural outliers could only survive under the protection of the fortified river crossings at Gritille and Samsat. Once Gritille was destroyed, all were abandoned, with the exception of Site 21 (Okul Mevkii), whose occupation continued for perhaps less than a century, before its inhabitants left as well.

Overall, the survey data suggest that significant shifts took place in land use between the Late Roman/Byzantine and medieval periods. The Byzantine system of widely dispersed, small unprotected agricultural outliers was only tenable under stable political conditions and military security. During the period of increased warfare in the twelfth to thirteenth centuries, agricultural outliers could only survive in protected locations. Thus the medieval settlement history of the Samsat-Gritille hinterlands shows strong evidence for a decline in the scope and intensity of rural production owing to the more difficult conditions of life on a dangerous, militarized frontier.

MEDIEVAL SITE INVENTORY

SITE 11

Location: Lower terrace.
Nearest water: Euphrates River, 200 meters to the east.

---

[39] Scott Redford, personal communication.

FIGURE 7:3. SELECTED GRITILLE MEDIEVAL SURVEY CERAMICS

A. Site 15. Orange ware rim. Diameter 52 cm. Unevenly fired. Core is gray (5 YR 5/1), trending to light reddish brown (5 YR 6/4) at surface. Red paint/slip on rim. Medium-sized grit temper.

B. Site 15. Rim. Diameter 24 cm. Unevenly fired. Core is dark reddish gray (5 YR 4/2), trending to red (2.5 YR 5/6) toward surface. Horizontal register of impressed ovals 0.5 cm below lip. Medium-sized grit temper.

C. Site 21. Orange ware bowl. Diameter 20 cm. Evenly fired brown paste. Slightly thickened rim. Diagonally impressed lines on exterior surface 4 cm below the rim. Interior and exterior are covered with matte red slip. Medium-sized grit temper.

D. Site 27. Handle. Unevenly fired. Core is gray (2.5 YR N5) trending to reddish brown (2.5 YR 5/4) at surface. Crudely smoothed handle with roughly rectangular cross-section. Coarse grit temper with frequent limestone inclusions.

E. Site 21. Orange ware rim. Diameter 11 cm. Unevenly fired. Core is reddish gray (5 YR 5/2) trending to yellowish red (5 YR 5/6) toward the exterior surface. Surface is plain, matte, undecorated reddish yellow. Medium-sized grit temper. Wheelmade.

F. Site 27. Orange ware rim. Diameter 11 cm. Evenly fired red (2.5 YR 5/6) paste. Exterior is covered with red paint/slip extending over the lip. Medium-sized grit temper.

G. Site 21. Orange ware rim. Diameter 13 cm. Evenly fired 5 YR 6/6 reddish yellow paste. Surface is plain, matte, undecorated reddish yellow (7.5 YR 7/6). Medium-sized grit temper. Wheelmade.

H. Site 11. Molded buff ware. Evenly fired light gray (10 YR 7/2). Molded design of circles and diamonds. Fine to medium-sized grit temper.

I. Site 11. Green and yellow glazed bowl-body sherd. Evenly fired red (2.5 YR 5/6) paste. Bowl exterior is plain, matte, undecorated. Interior is decorated with a green glaze diagonal band on a yellow glaze background. Fine-to-medium grit temper.

J. Site 21. Lid. Unevenly fired. Core is yellowish brown (10 YR 5/4) trending to reddish yellow (5 YR 6/6) toward the top of the lid. Top of lid is decorated with at least eight incised concentric circles, with impressed oval intersecting one circle. Two wide red splash-painted lines cover portions of the incised/impressed design.

K. Site 15. Lid. Unevenly fired. Core is gray (5 YR 5/1) trending to light reddish brown (5 YR 6/4) at surface. Top has low rounded knob at center of concentric circular ridges. Medium-sized grit temper. Wheelmade.

L. Site 21. Handle. Unevenly fired. Core is dark reddish gray (5 YR 4/2) trending to dark reddish brown (5 YR 3/2) and yellowish red (5 YR 4/6) toward the surface of the handle. Exterior surface has three vertical ribs or ridges, with red painted lines running parallel. Medium-to-coarse grit temper.

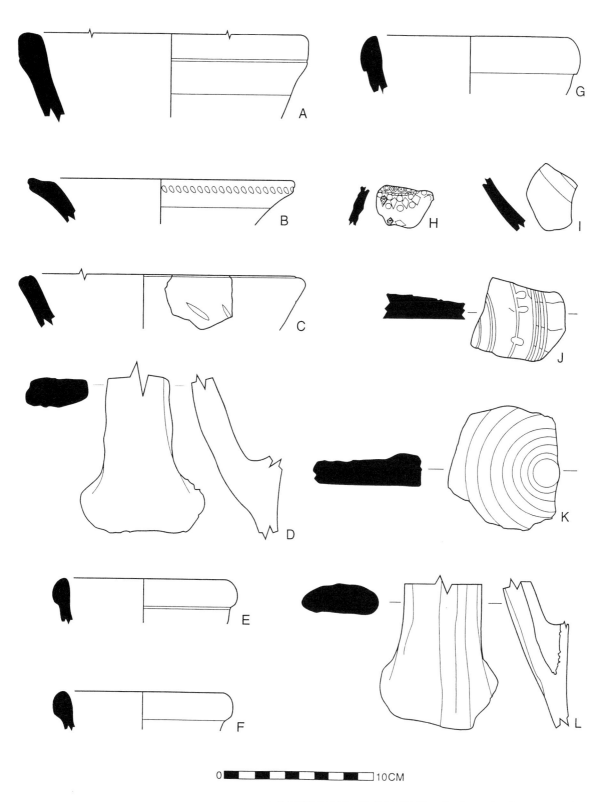

FIGURE 7.3. SELECTED SURVEY CERAMICS

Dimensions: 57 x 51 meters.

Collection procedures: Site limits flagged. Compass and tape mapping. Nonsystematic collection of surface ceramics.

Dating: Late Roman/Byzantine; early/late medieval?

Medieval ceramics: Molded buff ware (probably a Syrian import dating to the 11th–14th century),[39] three yellow and green-glazed fine-to-medium grit-tempered red wares. These do not match either Abbasid glazes or the glazes from the Gritille medieval. Based on the molded buff ware and the glazes, the site would probably date to either the post-Abbasid early medieval (ca. 11th–12th centuries), or the post-Gritille fourteenth century.

Other artifacts: Roof tiles, limestone door socket, limestone tesserae, basalt grinding stone fragment.

Site 15 (Sürük Mevkii: Özdoğan 1977 survey site number T5 1/13)

Location: 2 kilometers northwest of Gritille, by a spring on the upper terrace, at the outer edge of the embayment next to dissected badlands and along the tributary of Gevrik Deresi.

Nearest water: Three perennial springs at the northeast corner of the site.

Dimensions: 90 x 130 meters.

Collection procedures: Controlled surface collections (Fig. 7:4). Three transects consisting of 28 10 x 10 meter collection units. All diagnostics were collected.

Dating: Ceramic Neolithic, Late Iron Age, Late Hellenistic/Roman, Late Roman/Byzantine, late medieval, postmedieval occupations

Medieval ceramics: Grit-tempered red-slipped and burnished orange wares, grit-tempered red splash/drip-painted orange wares, friable brown ware with limestone temper, brown splash/drip-painted ware, and everted rim cooking pot ware.

Site 16 (Haraba Çukan: Özdoğan 1977 survey site number T5 1/12)

Location: Upper terrace, 1.2 kilometers northwest of Gritille on low spur along the east bank of the Gevrik Deresi.

Nearest water: Small perennial spring in Gevrik Deresi, 150 meters west of the site.

Dimensions: 116 x 110 meters.

Collection procedures: Site limits flagged.

Compass and tape mapping. Divided into two collection units for nonsystematic collection of diagnostic ceramics.

Dating: Possible early third millennium? Possible Late Iron Age, Late Roman/Byzantine, or late medieval.

Medieval ceramics: One turquoise glazed bowl rim and orange wares.

Other artifacts: Late Roman/Byzantine roof tiles and limestone tesserae, late medieval glass bangle fragments, and basalt millstone fragments. Architectural remains were visible on the surface at the south end of the site.

Site 21 (Okul Mevkii/Duzbaşı Mevkii)

Location: Eastern edge of the upper terrace, 200 meters southwest of Biriman/Kovanoluk village.

Nearest water: Perennial spring 10 meters northwest of the site.

Dimensions: 74 x 58 meters.

Collection procedures: Controlled surface collections. Three transects consisting of 24 10 x 10 meter collection units. All diagnostics were collected.

Dating: Late Roman/Byzantine, late medieval to thirteenth century. Overlaps with the final medieval occupation of Gritille.

Medieval Ceramics: Green, blue, yellow, and dark purple glazes, splash/drip painted wares, decorated lids.

Other artifacts: Medieval glass bangle fragments, iron, vitrified clay.

Site 24

Location: Eastern edge of the upper terrace, about 1 kilometer west of Gritille on the Şikeft/Değirmen Deresi.

Nearest water: Two perennial springs in the Değirmen Deresi, 37 meters south of the site.

Dimensions: 56 x 36 meters.

Collection procedures: Site limits flagged. Compass and tape mapping. Nonsystematic collection of surface ceramics.

Dating: Late Iron Age?, Late Roman/Byzantine, medieval.

Medieval ceramics: Green glazes, red and orange wares, painted wares. No red-slipped and burnished ware was recovered.

Other artifacts: Late Roman/Byzantine roof tiles, limestone tesserae.

SITE 26 (SALAHAN MEVKII: ÖZDOĞAN 1977 SURVEY SITE NUMBER T5 1/20)

Location: Western edge of the upper terrace, on the upper reaches of the Bolunca Deresi, at the base of badlands enclosing the Samsat-Gritille embayment, 3 kilometers west of Gritille.

Nearest water: Perennial spring 100 meters south-southeast of the site on Bolunca Deresi.

Dimensions: 136 x 75 meters.

Collection procedures: Site limits flagged. Compass and tape mapping. Nonsystematic collection of surface ceramics.

Dating: Late Roman/Byzantine, medieval.

Medieval ceramics: Glazes and red-slipped burnished ware.

Other artifacts: Late Roman/Byzantine roof tiles and limestone tesserae, and basalt grinding stone fragment.

SITE 27 (HAMIŞKAN MEVKII: ÖZDOĞAN 1977 SURVEY SITE NUMBER T5 1/21)

Location: On the upper terrace, on the Hamışkan Deresi, about 3.25 kilometers west-southwest of Gritille.

Nearest water: Perennial spring at the site.

Dimensions: 75 x 44 meters.

Collection procedures: Controlled surface collections. Two transects consisting of 20 10 x 10 m collection units. All diagnostics were collected.

Dating: Late Hellenistic/Roman, Late Roman/Byzantine, medieval.

Medieval ceramics: Late medieval twelfth- to thirteenth-century ceramics: jar handle with large grit and limestone temper. Other pieces from the same period include a flattened oval cross-section, comb-incised ware; red-slipped tan/orange ware; brittle "cooking pot" ware; red splash-painted wares; red-slipped and burnished jar rim; tan/orange grit-tempered green-glazed bowl fragment; and blue glazes.

Other artifacts: Marble fragments (GT 2765), stone bead, (GT 2764), and vitrified clay (GT 2766).

SITE 31 (BIRIMAN)

Location: At the east edge of the upper terrace, on Memisan Deresi. The site underlies the modern village of Biriman/Kovanoluk.

Nearest water: Perennial spring on site.

Dimensions: 300 x 150 meters (est.)

Collection procedures: Site limits flagged. Compass and tape mapping. Nonsystematic collection of surface ceramics.

Dating: Early to mid-third millennium, Late Iron Age, Late Hellenistic/Roman, Late Roman/Byzantine, Abbasid?, medieval, postmedieval.

Medieval ceramics: Grit-tempered red splash/drip-painted orange wares.

ACKNOWLEDGMENTS

I wish to thank Prof. Richard Ellis of Bryn Mawr College, director of the Gritille project, for allowing me to conduct archaeological surveys and land use studies in the Gritille site catchment from 1982 to 1984. In developing the site sampling methodology, I benefited greatly from discussions with Tony Wilkinson (now at the University of Chicago, Oriental Institute). I would also like to thank Mr. Andrew Weiss (now at Stanford University) for his assistance in the Gritille land use study. Guillermo Algaze, Richard Ellis, Charles and Marie-Henriette Gates, Mehmet Özdoğan, Scott Redford, Glenn Schwartz, Geoff Summers, Mary Voigt, and Tony Wilkinson all gave comments and suggestions that were extremely helpful in dating the ceramic collections made as part of the Gritille survey. Julie Perlmutter's work in preparing computer graphic versions of the maps and ceramic illustrations for publication greatly improved the quality of the original field drawings. I also wish to thank John Hudson (Northwestern University) and the William and Marion Haas Fund for their assistance in preparation of PMT illustrations for this paper. Final responsibility for any errors of fact or interpretation remains my own.

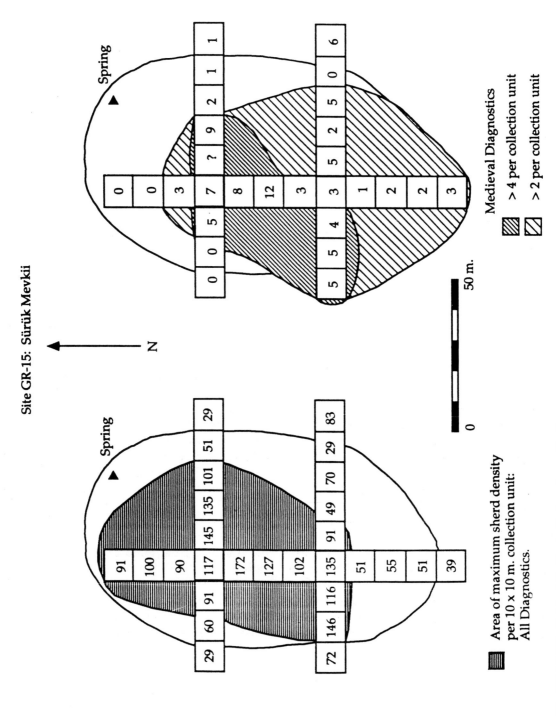

Figure 7:4. Site GR 15 (Sürük Mevkii). Controlled surface collections.

VIII

INTERPRETING MEDIEVAL GRITILLE

"Such wider issues as the inter-relationship between towns and the nomadic groups present in the area of the Diyār Bakr, as well as the treatment of the Christians, who probably outnumbered the Muslims . . . must remain almost entirely undiscussed through lack of information."[1]

In this concluding chapter, I would like to join topics raised severally in this study. The first two concern the characteristics of the region, specifically, the regional identity of the Karababa basin in the eleventh to the thirteenth centuries; and the delineation of a regional man-made environment, and architectural and artifactual koine of medieval settlements in this part of the Near East. Other topics joined here, too, are regional, but deal with larger historical trends: the Crusades, the nomadification and depopulation upon the Turkish influx, and the practical effect of the iqṭa', or medieval Islamic appanage system.

Two factors contributed to the importance of the Karababa basin in the medieval period. The first was the position of Samsat at the river crossing of a major route leading to and from the eastern Anatolian plateau. Islamic states of the region depended on this route in the early

Islamic centuries for the institutionalized warfare along the thughūr as well as for commerce. The recovery of eighth- to tenth-century ceramics and other remains from Samsat, Tille, and Eski Kâhta reinforce the importance of the area near the Anti-Taurus for border warfare. The recovery of a contemporaneous caravansaray at Kurban Höyük and possibly another at Lidar emphasizes the trade and travel routes mentioned by early medieval geographers.[2]

Gritille was not inhabited in this earlier Islamic period, and the Karababa basin in general saw little of the settlement activity that it did in the eleventh to thirteenth centuries. The importance of Samsat and the Karababa basin were enhanced by the rise of the Kingdom of Armenian Cilicia, which blocked off the direct route between central Anatolia and northern Syria, just as the massive buildup of the Cilician area of the thughūr had contributed to the comparative underdevelopment of the Samsat-Malatya area of the frontier in the ninth and early tenth centuries.

The second major reason for the importance of the Karababa basin in the medieval period was its function as the breadbasket of Urfa, the major settlement of the region. According to

---

[1] Hillenbrand, "Establishment of Artuqid Power," 149.

[2] Algaze, *Town and Country in Southeastern Anatolia*, 2:199 (for a plan of the caravansaray), 391–395, 431–432 (for other aspects of this occupation). Harald Hauptmann ("Lidar Höyük 1981," 94) reports the recovery of a large courtyard-centered building of about 20 by 18 meters below medieval strata at Lidar. This building is dated to the 4th to 7th centuries. In later conversations with Prof. Hauptmann, he expressed the opinion that the building may have been contemporaneous with the caravansaray at Kurban. For Abbasid-period finds at Tille, see Moore, *Tille Höyük 1*, 181 ff.; for Abbasid pottery from Kâhta, see Goell and Otto-Dorn, "Keramikfunde aus dem Mittelalter," 249 ff.

twelfth-century chroniclers, the valley around Samsat, small but fertile, sent its herds and harvests to Urfa.

Because Gritille lay in the hinterland of Samsat, in this study its settlement has been related to periods of intensive exploitation of the valley. Because there also existed a military component to several periods of Gritille's settlement, the issue of the defense of Samsat must be considered as an additional factor.

There are objections to be raised to both of these rationales. A major portion of the stratigraphic sequence at Gritille (Phases 6–8) occurred when the fortification wall around the mound had fallen into disrepair. (The square structure erected in Phase 7 cannot have been more than a watchtower.) Moreover, with the sack of Urfa in 1144, Samsat, and with it Gritille, lost the major market for its produce, yet settlement at Gritille persisted for about another century. Gil Stein's analysis of medieval faunal material from Gritille in Chapter 5 concludes that pastoral production at Gritille during the latter part of the sequence (Phases 5–8) followed generalized herding practices with no specialized production, concomitant with subsistence and minimal disruption of agriculture. Still, Gritille would have benefited the rulers of Samsat in terms other than those of pastoral surplus. Examples of such benefits not readily recoverable from the archaeological record include corvée labor and the tithing of crops. Naomi Miller's analysis of plant remains from medieval strata at Gritille in Chapter 6 posits that wheat was likely the principal crop. Wheat would have had a higher value to town dwellers at either Samsat or Urfa than barley or other grain crops.

The disappearance of settlement from Gritille can be attributed to the end of a slow and long decline in the region. With the defeat of the Seljuks at the hands of the Mongols in 1243, the principal Anatolian power in the region was neutralized. The Seljuks had used the Malatya-Samsat corridor as their principal route for the invasion of northern Syria, again because of the presence of the Kingdom of Armenian Cilicia hindering ready passage through the Cilician Gates. The Mongols, who entertained strong interest in the region, had access to northern Syria both from the east and north, and their alliance

with the Armenians allowed them to use Birecik to the west as their major crossing point of the Euphrates. The Samsat region declined in strategic importance, and also lost population, no doubt as a result of renewed warfare in Syria, this time between Mongol and Mamluk armies. Gil Stein's survey data in Chapter 7 show that settlement around Gritille after the middle of the thirteenth century dwindled to a handful of smaller sites near springs, none of them as large as Gritille.

Within the rather broad sweep of medieval Near Eastern history, it is possible to propose a more restricted "microclimatic" explanation for the cycle of fortification and occupation at Gritille. Samsat was the center of this microclimate, whose boundaries were those of the Karababa basin. Modifications to Gritille and other sites in the Karababa basin related directly only to Samsat. Larger economic and political trends were always filtered through Samsat.

To summarize the settlement sequence: Gritille was fortified during the Byzantine occupation in the early eleventh century, abandoned, reoccupied and refortified during the Crusader period of the first half of the twelfth century, sacked, reoccupied, partially abandoned with neglect of fortification, and then rebuilt and reinhabited. It was definitively abandoned in the middle of the thirteenth century, not to be reoccupied until the Ottoman period.

At Lidar, the medieval settlement was larger and its occupation more complicated. Within the two main phases of the medieval there, Lidar saw three layings of pebbled streets (as opposed to two at Gritille) and three major destructive fires (as opposed to one at Gritille).[3] In addition, despite parallels with Gritille in terms of architectural layout, with spoke walls radiating in from the fortification wall, Lidar also had a street paralleling the edge of the mound, and this street seemed to serve as a divider between houses of greater and lesser size, a marker of social differentiation.[4]

Still, at times in their medieval sequences, the architectural layout at both sites betokened planned settlement associated with a centralized military authority. This is different from the petty feudal lords' residences that dominated the fortified settlements at medieval Horis and

---

[3] Hauptmann, "Lidar Höyük 1981," 251; Akkermans, "Lidar Excavation Notebook F/G/H 42 (1980–81)," 164.
[4] Ibid.

Tille. The difference in site organization between Lidar and Gritille and the other two sites outside the Karababa basin can be attributed to distance from or proximity to a major center of state authority at Samsat.

According to the model proposed above, the settlement sequence at Gritille is linked directly with periods when Samsat was the primary seat of governance for the Karababa basin. Accordingly, it was the location of the seat of government at Samsat proper that caused investment in the settling and/or fortification of Gritille.

This explanation is strongest for the Crusader period (Phase 3) and the middle Ayyubid period (Phase 7). We have seen that the refortification of the site in Phase 3 was extensive, even though the actual accumulation of occupational debris was not. This phase ended in a conflagration whose debris included a hoard of Crusader coins and most of the human skeletal remains analyzed by Denise Hodges in the appendix. If we accept that Gritille was the site identified in the Anonymous Syriac Chronicle as being sacked in 1148, then the reoccupation and refortification of Gritille in Phase 3 must have occurred after the fall of Urfa in 1144, when Crusader sovereignty at Samsat became precarious, Samsat constituting the end of a string of Crusader-held forts widely spaced along the Euphrates and to its west.

Similarly, by numismatic means it is possible to associate the laying of the upper street, the erection of the tower, and other features typifying Phase 7 with the reign of al-Afḍal, Saladin's renegade eldest son, who received Samsat as part of a larger northern Syrian appanage and, shorn of his other dependencies, ended up ruling the Samsat region alone as a quasi-independent polity from 1202 to 1225. During both of these periods, the two rationales outlined above—the defense of Samsat and the exploitation of its agricultural hinterland—would have been paramount.

The reoccupation of the West End in Phase 4 is of such brief duration that it can be viewed as an immediate reaction to the sack of Gritille. It must have occurred between 1148 and the fall of

Samsat to the Artuqids in 1150. The presence of distinctive decorated ovens in this phase alone but also at Lidar could mean that Gritille was resettled from Lidar in Phase 4.

Phases 5 and 6, during which settlement at Gritille moved almost entirely off the mound, coincide with the period during which the Artuqid emirs of Mardin occupied the area. Coins bearing the countermarks of previously unknown or misidentified origin were retrieved from these levels. Because of their findspot, and because of the presence of Artuqid governors at Samsat for thirty-odd years from the early 1150s to the early 1180s, the strong probability exists that these are the countermarks of one or more of the Artuqid governors of Samsat.

The decentralization of power in the medieval Jazīra beginning in the late eleventh century, particularly under the Artuqids, is well known.[5] A separate countermarked coinage of the governors of Samsat confirms this practice of decentralization. It has been noted for the twelfth century that

> [t]he whole Syrian and eastern area was in turmoil as rivals marched and plundered: what villagers and nomads thought and did about currency may well have been quite different from what remote centres of government intended.[6]

To this list of creative misusers of coinage one might also add individuals higher up the social scale than villagers and nomads, namely, governors.

Samsat lay on the western frontier of the Artuqid principality of Mardin. It is known that the emirs of Mardin often replaced, in rapid succession, the Artuqid governors they had earlier installed. While this practice may bring into question the decentralization of power implicit in a separate countermarked coinage, it is possible, too, that governors were replaced so often for the very reason that their independence on this post at the edge of Artuqid territories was threatening to the central power to which they owed allegiance. Nevertheless, the Artuqid rebuilding in stone of the citadel perimeter wall at

---

[5] See Väth, *Die Geschichte der artuqidischen Fürstentumer*, 186–187, for the rights and responsibilities of the Artuqid governors; also Cahen, "L'évolution de l'iqta'," 44–45, for the hereditary nature of Zangid and Ayyubid appanages in Syria and the Jazīra. His conclusions do not apply to Samsat, given its peculiar history.

[6] Lowick, Bendick, and Whitting, *The "Mardin" Hoard*, 15.

Samsat and construction of a palace there imply a degree of interest and control commensurate with an emir rather than a governor.

During this period, the fortification wall at Gritille fell out of use, the top of the mound ceased to be used for domestic constructions, and extant settlement at Gritille was located on the northern and western flanks of the mound. It is likely that little attention was paid to the defense or rehabilitation of Gritille at this time precisely because the territories of the Artuqid governors of Samsat extended beyond the Karababa basin—that is to say, it had ceased to be part of a frontier region.

Little is known of the Byzantine level at Gritille (Level 2) aside from the brevity of its occupation, and the close resemblance its layout bears to that of the garrison fort at Taşkun Kale, and also to Lidar. However, we need not extend our regional explanation to this initial period of occupation for the simple reason that, as in Roman times, this area constituted the frontier of the Byzantine state, and as such must have participated directly in a greater system of defense, a *limes* of intervisible watchtowers and garrison forts principally located along the Euphrates River.[7]

On a more limited scale, of course, intervisible sites and fortified strongholds serving as refuge and garrison points must have constituted the defense of the Samsat region throughout the medieval period. Gritille and Lidar, on opposite banks of the Euphrates, together would have surveyed the northern end of the Karababa basin. Samsat is clearly visible from both sites. During the Artuqid period and the Ayyubid period before the reign of al-Afdal, however, the *iqta'* of Samsat stretched beyond the valley down to the Shabakhtān, where the garrisons in numerous forts would have alerted the governor in Samsat to any intrusion from the south or west.

I have proposed a regional raison d'être for medieval habitation at Gritille that in many ways does not extend beyond the limits of the Karababa basin. Be that as it may, many indications point to participation by the inhabitants of medieval Gritille in the economy of the region at large. The alignment of the Karababa basin with a greater power—Anatolian, Jazīran, or north

Syrian—determined patterns of long-distance trade. Under the Byzantines in the early eleventh century and intermittently by the Rum Seljuks in the early thirteenth century, this area was held by an Anatolian power. Yet the distance of Samsat from Anatolian centers of power necessitated the presence of strong local vassals: Armenians such as Philaretos for the Byzantines, and disaffected Ayyubids such as al-Afdal for the Seljuks. Control was indirect and of short duration.

The Jazīran Artuqids and the Syrian Ayyubids were closer to Samsat geographically, but they, too, experienced difficulty in securing this area. As for the County of Edessa, it lasted as long as it did largely because of the participation of the local Christian populace, and its fall can be seen as resulting from a failure to secure the protection of either a strong Jazīran or a strong north Syrian state. The direct effect of the First Crusade on this region can be seen as providing a catalyst toward greater political unity than the region had known for several centuries. Zangī's success lay in his ability to unite both regions and to reduce the Artuqids to vassal status. As a consequence, the Crusader counts had no allies to counterbalance the Zangid armies.

The Crusaders failed in this, their first major attempt, to expand inland from coastal strongholds. Their failure condemned them to an existence on the Levantine littoral. It was not until the early thirteenth century that one can identify material culture of a Crusader state in the Outremer: sgraffiato pottery bearing distinct Crusader motifs and images. The County of Edessa lasted too short a time to have evolved more than the beginnings of a material expression of its sovereignty. As was the case with the Artuqids, the coins of the County of Edessa consisted of overstrikes of eleventh-century Byzantine copper coins or minting of coppers of the same general size and weight. And, as the Gritille hoard attests, European silver was also still the coin of the realm, used because of the paucity of silver coinage circulating in the Levant in the eleventh and twelfth centuries. These coins partially filled the void created by the collapse of Byzantine political and economic hegemony in Anatolia. The use of Byzantine imagery on Artuqid coins until the latter half of the twelfth

---

[7] Edwards, *Armenian Fortifications of Cilicia*, 41–42, details such a system in medieval Armenian Cilicia.

century (in this region the change occurs with the coins of Najm al-Dīn Alpī)[8] and the recovery of late eleventh-century Byzantine gold coins from late twelfth- or early thirteenth-century levels at Gritille point to a continued dependence on the tangible and intangible aspects of Byzantine economy and authority.

POTTERY AND REGIONAL ORIENTATION

The cessation of hostilities in the mid-twelfth century allied Gritille with the material culture of greater Syria. This can be seen nowhere more clearly than in its glazed ceramics. Glazed fritwares, calcareous clay glazed wares, and lusterwares, especially those with a manganese glaze, are found throughout the sequence, and in shape and glaze they pertain to the group traditionally (but, in this writer's opinion, incorrectly) known as Raqqa ware. Green lustered wares imitate the designs of Syrian glazed ceramics, albeit in a more cursive, slap-dash manner. This integration strengthened under the Artuqid hegemony (Phase 5) with the introduction of underglaze painted fritwares, green luster on a clear glaze, and molded cream ware "pilgrim flasks," all pottery types typical of medieval Syria. Enameled and gilded glass is also introduced into this region, although not until the Ayyubid period.

In this way, the Karababa basin formed its closest ties with northern Syria despite changing political fortunes. The hold of Anatolian powers was brief and superficial, and the Jazīra, at least its westernmost components the Diyār Muḍar and the Diyār Bakr, was always culturally subordinate to north Syria in the medieval period.

Furthermore, Samsat must be posited as the source of much of the glazed (as well as unglazed) pottery found at Gritille. Until the evidence of pottery production found by the excavators of Samsat is published, the kind and extent of pottery production there can only be wagered, but the quantity and standardization of much of the Gritille ceramic corpus is commensurate with a regional ceramic center of some size. Small-scale metallurgy at a variety of small medieval sites in the region has been un-

covered, along with metal vessels and implements of varying quality. Ceramic production may not have been as decentralized and small-scale as metalworking.

At Gritille, the sequence of wares and their association can be determined fairly precisely. Similarities of shape, glaze, fabric, and temporal distribution have been noted for both lustered and unlustered manganese-glazed frit or calcareous clay bowls. At the very least, these must constitute members of the same family of wares, produced locally. Other glazed wares may have been added to the repertoire when peace returned to Samsat in the 1150s.

Reintegration of this area into the Islamic world after the defeat of the Crusaders can be seen in the ceramics of Phases 5 and 6, when Iranian and Syrian imports were found at Gritille despite its half-ruined state. If prosperity can be measured by variety of imports, then Gritille can be said to have fared better under *pax islamica* than under Crusader rule.

The hypothesis of regional domination advanced above can be expanded to include the unglazed pottery. In considering ceramics of all kinds, we can raise the second topic, that of defining a regional koine. Cooking pot ware and orange ware at Gritille exhibited a remarkable consistency of decoration, shape, fabric color, and temper throughout the sequence. New handle types, kinds of decoration, and shapes were introduced in every type category over the sequence, but all bespeak an evolutionary trend without major breaks. With the exception of Phase 2, which produced little of the sample, the stratigraphic sequence at Gritille in the medieval period spanned a period of less than a century. As a result, despite major upheavals in the lives of Gritilleans, the variation of body, rim, and handle shape, and decoration of the pottery they used was minor, and basic ware types remained constant. Likewise, the size of the various vessel types did not vary much from phase to phase. The major alteration in the decorative vocabulary of the unglazed wares occurred with the introduction of rows of stamped motifs on pithos shoulders, but major decorative techniques such as splash/drip and red-slip painting remained at relatively constant levels. Instead, the political and military volatility of the region in this period shows itself in the import-

---

[8] See Spengler and Sayles, *Turkoman Figural Bronze Coins*, e.g., 83.

ed wares. Such production consistency requires a local production center like Samsat, which could have supplied the region throughout the period of Gritille's existence.

By no means were these unglazed wares unique to the inhabitants of Gritille. They were found close at hand at Lidar and Samsat and other sites in the Karababa basin, upstream at Tille, and even farther north at the sites of the Keban region. Habitation at all of these major sites continued past the end of the Gritille medieval sequence.

Because all of these sites were inhabited by Christians (Gritille, Lidar, Tille, Aşvan, and Taşkun) or had a significant Christian population (Samsat), we can isolate a regional ceramic style to be associated with the indigenous Christian agriculturalist stock of the eleventh through fourteenth centuries. It is the regional aspect of this equation that is to be emphasized here: there seems to be no explicit or implicit religious component to it. Moreover, as we have seen, sectarian rivalries were at times as least as fierce between Jacobites and Armenians as they were between Muslims and Christians.

Nevertheless, the probability that the majority of the population in this region remained non-Muslim over five centuries after the spread of Islam gives rise to interesting speculation about the degree of "Islamicity" found here, despite its cultural and political domination by Islamic power centers in Syria and the Jazīra. Bulliet has suggested that Islamic society cannot properly be called such until the majority of its populace belongs to that faith.[9] This is in direct conflict with Hodgson's ecumenical term *Islamicate* used earlier in the Introduction.

On one hand, a non-elite, annalistic approach accords with the archaeological delimitation of a region of ceramic homogeneity described above. On the other hand, institutions of Islamic society were by and large urban in character, and rural settlements such as those listed above, whether Christian or Muslim, would have had only indirect contact with them. Moreover, no Christian institutions were uncovered either. To the regional nature of this ceramic distribution, then, one can add a component of class identification. Tillers and herders, regardless of their religion, would not have participat-

ed in much of the political, juridical, and cultural systems in larger, more densely settled and central areas.

Monasticism helped disseminate and perpetuate culture and identity outside of large urban areas in this period. Chronicles such as those of Michael the Syrian, Matthew of Edessa, and Bar Hebraeus contain more information about events occurring outside of the major cities, and especially in this region, precisely because of an acquaintance with the countryside born of the monastic experience. But, while the Anti-Taurus mountains south of Malatya and the gorges of the upper Euphrates were home to many monasteries, the relative accessibility of the Karababa basin and surrounding terrain seems to have militated against that particular institutionalization of rural life for the Christian villagers of the region. Religious affiliation is attested by the recovery of small pectoral crosses and decorated ovens; if there was a church in the medieval settlement it was not recovered at Tille, Lidar, or Gritille.

Nevertheless, the decentralization characterizing this period did bear some curious fruit. Glazed wares produced in small rural settlements can be related to the dominance of an urban Islamic culture rather than any force of tradition. This is to be observed most conspicuously at Aşvan Kale, where local Christians produced sgraffiato pottery imitating Islamic calligraphy and even an Islamic figural style, but also at Gritille, and Samsat, where we have proposed a regional center of fritware production.[10]

Unglazed ceramics in this peripheral region reflect a local tradition carried on by an indigenous rural, provincial population. Luxury ceramics, by contrast, derived from the taste of urban Muslim cultural elites. *Derived* is a key word in this context, for, whatever their origins, these luxury wares were found at sites as small as Gritille in constant and significant enough quantities to suggest their use at every level of the medieval social order. Exactly how these glazed vessels were used remains to be determined. We have seen that glazed pottery occurred almost entirely in the form of bowls. It is noteworthy that unglazed bowls formed an inconsequential percentage of the Gritille ceramic assemblage at every level, pointing to the conclusion that

---

[9] Bulliet, *Conversion to Islam*, 2.
[10] For Aşvan Kale, see Mitchell, *Aşvan Kale*, 55, Fig. 26, No. 5.

bowls were not used in daily eating or food preparation. Consequently, we can infer that glazed bowls were status items, even if status value was not limited to a non-elite, rural settlement. Their value may have derived more from their decorative merits than from any special ceremonial use—perhaps as a kind of "Sunday china." The small chips of glazed fritware embedded in the decorated ovens of Phase 4 seem to demonstrate the value placed on this decorative aspect. The retrieval of glazed fritwares from Gritille, however poor in quality, may in addition simply be a marker of increased trade and prosperity.

Thus, the delineation of separate systems of local, unglazed wares, and imported, urban, elite-influenced "luxury" wares sets up a false dichotomy. In many ways, the production of glazed and unglazed wares paralleled each other. We have proposed Samsat as the regional production center for commonly found types of both glazed and unglazed pottery found at Gritille: cooking pot ware and orange ware, glazed earthenwares including sgraffiato and fritware including luster. These "luxury" wares, however, imitated forms and styles found in larger centers of pottery production in Syria.[11]

In a similar way, almost all unglazed ceramics came from the same source, although the presence of a few extraordinarily decorated unglazed vessels may indicate that they were imported.[12] Imported nonglazed status items were the molded tan/buff "pilgrim flasks," which imitate closely the less elaborate examples of this type of vessel known from central Syria. Similar to glazed wares, these molded vessel fragments were found only in the later phases at Gritille, when the Karababa basin was in direct and continuous contact with northern Syria.

We have also seen certain examples of glazed bowl forms imitating unglazed bowl forms, and fritware bowl forms imitating those of glazed earthenwares. Lusterware, too, shared glaze, fabric, and shape criteria with plain frit-

wares. Cross-fertilization of this sort must have also taken place at the local production level.

Although medieval Levantine and Anatolian plainwares have not been much studied,[13] we can assume that the jugs, basins, and cooking pots of Syria and central Anatolia were different from those of the area of comparison available for this study, namely, the Euphrates valley from the edge of northern Syria to the rim of the Anatolian plateau. For example, the sites of this area have little of the thin-walled buff-colored unglazed pottery common in Iraq and Syria. Within this area, too, production of unglazed earthenwares was quite homogeneous.

Glazed earthenwares, including sgraffiato, were found in substantial numbers at Gritille only after Phase 4, that is, after 1150, and are most widely found in Phase 7, corresponding to the early to mid-thirteenth century. Sgraffiato wares were found throughout the medieval Near East and eastern Mediterranean for many centuries, although the date of their introduction into Syria has never been proposed. At Takht-i Sulaymān in Azerbaijan, Schnyder has dated the introduction of a particular kind of sgraffiato to the second half of the twelfth century and has associated it with the wide-scale immigration of Turkish tribes.[14]

The introduction of sgraffiato at Gritille was coincident with the establishment of Artuqid Turkish control over the region, but because slip-incised glazed earthenwares predated the arrival of the Turks in the Levant, it is hard to assign an ethnic identity to their appearance in this border region.[15] At Aşvan Kale, Mitchell did note the increased incidence of sgraffiato pottery in twelfth- and thirteenth-century levels there, and it is the predominant glazed ware at late thirteenth- and early fourteenth-century levels at Taşkun, Aşvan, and Korucutepe: the latter two sites were also known to have produced this ware. Owing to its high incidence in Level 7 at Gritille, certainly we can posit the production of glazed earthenwares, including

---

[11] For examples of this production, see Öney, "Pottery from the Samosata Excavations, 1978–81," 293–294.

[12] Fig. 3:9F represents one such piece: its handle was elaborately scored and punctated, and it had a skillfully fashioned "snake" thumbstop.

[13] Day, "Islamic Finds at Tarsus," 145: " . . . the coarse, common unglazed pottery (which, like the poor, we have always with us). . . ."

[14] Schnyder, "Political Centres and Artistic Powers in Saljuq Iran," 207.

[15] See Allan, "Incised Wares of Iran and Anatolia," 17–18, for a résumé of Byzantine sgraffiato.

sgraffiato, at neighboring Samsat during the Ayyubid period.

On one hand, it is difficult to apportion ethnic affiliation to ceramic styles and techniques such as sgraffiato. On the other hand, it is equally difficult to explain the popularity of glazed earthenwares at a time when fritwares were already widely distributed. One cannot speak of technological advance, for fritware was, even at the low end of the production scale, a lighter ware capable of finer potting and more elaborate decorative techniques such as molding and luster.

It is possible, however, that the regional distribution of glazed earthenwares and fritwares in the last half of the twelfth and the first half of the thirteenth centuries was caused by technological simplicity. Fritware never became established in Anatolia, where we have noted many kiln sites for the manufacture of glazed earthenwares, including sgraffiato. No kilns producing sgraffiato wares in eastern Anatolia during the Byzantine period have been found. There is abundant evidence that sgraffiato was used and traded by Byzantines and Crusaders throughout the Aegean, western Anatolian littoral, and eastern Mediterranean.[16] It seems evident that sgraffiato was found primarily in coastal regions such as these, and also in Iran and Iraq. The sgraffiato wares were found in securely dated levels at Gritille, levels that predate all sgraffiato production sites on the Anatolian plateau, suggesting that sgraffiato, although not unknown, was not produced in inner Anatolia, the Jazīra, or Syria before the mid-twelfth century. This ware was introduced into the Samsat region with the establishment of links with the Jazīra, Iraq, and Azerbaijan via the Artuqids, although by the time of Ayyubid control (Phase 7), it was stylistically indistinguishable from sgraffiato of the northern Syrian type.

ARCHITECTURE AND REGIONAL IDENTIFICATION

Gritille partook of a regional koine in its built environment, too. This vernacular can be defined both horizontally and vertically. Farther south, in Harran and Bālis, baked brick was used for domestic structures in sites of more than average size and importance.[17] However, at Samsat, Lidar, Tille, Eski Kâhta, Taşkun Kale, Aşvan Kale, Korucutepe, Pirot, and other sites along the Euphrates, mudbrick on stone footings was used for domestic architecture. This suggests that, at this level of the social order, mudbrick construction was used exclusively in the region under study, while brick was more widely used farther south and in Syria proper. The deep roots of this building tradition in this region are emphasized by late Antique/early Byzantine levels at Eski Malatya, whose excavator stressed shared characteristics of construction and organization with late Roman settlements elsewhere in Anatolia and later.

> I villaggi dell'Anatolia, per tutto il periodo romano fino alla conquista turca, rimasero quello che sono, in parte, ancora oggi, mere agglomerazioni di capanne contadinesche con una piazza centrale e locali per le autorità del paese e i funzionari governativi. La populazione dei villaggi non dovette mai sollevarsi da un'organizzazione tribale.[18]

The striking similarity between the unglazed ceramics recovered in Eski Malatya and those of medieval sites a millennium later also speaks eloquently for the conservatism of the region.

At Tille and other sites mapped by the Adıyaman survey, a typically feudal settlement pattern is observable. However, at Gritille and Lidar, we have seen that the military component of the site has lent even subsequent occupational periods an organization that counters the idea of a settlement as a mere agglomeration of houses around a central square.

Military architecture, too, was constructed using the same materials: mudbrick and rubble socle fortifications were found at Lidar, Tille, Gritille, Taşkun, and Pirot. Vertical separation is evident, however, in the military architecture of larger, more important sites which were furnished with stone fortifications; witness the

---

[16] See Pringle, "Medieval Pottery from Caesarea," passim.

[17] Yardımcı, "1985 Harran Kazı ve Restorasyon Çalışmaları," 1:280–281; Golvin, "A la recherche de la cité médiévale de Bâlis," 391.

[18] Equini Schneider, *Malatya-II,* 10 (for shared characteristics), 8 (for the quote).

hasty construction of rubble and lime mortar defensive walls by the Crusaders at Keysun, the ashlar and rubble Artuqid citadel walls and the (Crusader?) keep at Samsat, and the castles at Eski Kâhta and Gerger. It is also to be found in the main residence building at Tille, which was constructed of limestone and river cobble.

MACROHISTORY AND THE MARGINS

The archaeological record presents no clear evidence relating the sequence of occupation at Gritille to two wider trends noted for Anatolia proper in the late eleventh and twelfth centuries: the interrelated phenomena of depopulation and nomadification coincident with the Türkmen migrations into Syria and Anatolia.[19]

At first blush, Gritille would seem to have been an ideal site for the testing of these macrohistorical trends in an archaeological context. It was a small settlement whose Christian inhabitants were engaged in agriculture and animal husbandry—the type of settlement one would expect to have been affected most directly by the influx of large numbers of Türkmen nomads into the region. However, upon reflection, certain geographical and historical factors appear, placing Gritille outside the mainstream.

First of all, the history of the Karababa basin was not that of Byzantium: Byzantine rule was relatively short-lived in this region and, as we have seen, effected largely through the agency of local Armenian officials who enjoyed considerable autonomy. It is to be assumed that their policies were not those of Byzantine Anatolia, where absentee landlords, large estates, and tax farming were legion. In addition, extended Crusader rule in this region is also a localized phenomenon. That the Crusader period wreaked havoc on the economy of this area is clear from the numerous reports of crop and orchard burnings and massacres of peasants and livestock alike during the first half of the twelfth century. Whatever the changed circumstances of the Artuqid governors of Samsat, they must have ushered in a welcome surcease to the constant war footing of the County of Edessa.

Nevertheless, from Balduk, the ruler of Samsat in the late eleventh century, through the Artuqid governors of Samsat in the late twelfth century, to Baba Resūl, the millenarian heretic who arose near the Samsat region in the early thirteenth century, we are assured of the presence of Türkmen nomads in the region during most of the lifespan of medieval Gritille. Presumably, nomadic and other groups were excluded from the economic order (such as it was), or at least kept in check, under Crusader rule. At Gritille, the period to examine is that after Phase 4.

Here again, one may tie the viability of Gritille as a community to direct rule over the Karababa basin from Samsat. Although settlement continued under Artuqid rule, Gritille witnessed renovation only during the reign of al-Afḍal. If from historical sources one knows of conflict between peasant and nomad, it is during the period of Phases 5 and 6 that one might suppose it to have happened.

On this score, the archaeological record is mute. Increased prosperity brought on by a cessation of hostilities in this region can be inferred from the presence of new types of glazed wares. Real renovation of the settlement of Gritille, however, had to wait until the mid-Ayyubid period.

The eventual abandonment of Gritille can be tied to a neglect of central authority at Samsat. This is itself due to strategic reasons: the expansion of the Mamluk frontier north past Samsat and the Mamluk subjugation of Armenian Cilicia. But also, the nomadic influx continued and became incorporated during the fourteenth century as part of the regional economy, a trend that continued into the modern period. Buckingham, crossing the area between Birecik and Urfa in the early nineteenth century, called it "the Plains of the Turcomans" owing to the numbers of Türkmen nomads he found there.[20] Stein's survey data show that settlement around Gritille survived the abandonment of the site, but only in the form of small sites near springs. These settlements, if involved with agriculture, could not have competed with large-scale nomadic activity, but it is possible they could have been part of a largely nomadic exploitation of this area of the Karababa basin.

So far, the presence of local rule at Samsat has been advanced several times to explain the history of settlement and fortification at Gritille.

---

[19] The standard source for these issues in Anatolia is Vryonis, *Decline of Medieval Hellenism.*
[20] Buckingham, *Travels in Mesopotamia*, 41–42.

During the period of Islamic rule, Artuqid governors ruled Samsat as an *iqta'* from the emir in Mardin. Two sets of contradictions arise from an examination of the history of Artuqid rule in relation to the archaeological remains from Phases 5 and 6 at Gritille. The first is historical and concerns the degree of freedom enjoyed at Samsat. Countermarks on coins at Gritille imply a great deal of freedom in running economic affairs there. Be that as it may, frequent replacement of the governors at Samsat implies that that freedom was a precarious one.

The second contradiction concerns the prosperity of Gritille under the Artuqid *iqta'* system. On one hand, the decay of the fortification wall, abandonment of settlement within the walled area, and the wall's use in the West End as a demarcation of an industrial area do not signal economic expansion; instead the picture is one of ruin and decline. On the other hand, defensive neglect could be interpreted as indicative of peace. From Operations 30 and 8 we know that settlement continued around the base of the mound even when the top itself had fallen into desuetude. In addition, these phases contained a much wider variety of glazed wares, including sherds of imported wares from Syria and Iran.

During the reign of al-Afḍal the top of the mound at Gritille was once again repopulated and furnished with a paved street and a tower. Glazed earthenwares and sgraffiato were found in abundance alongside fritwares. Unfortunately, these signs of relative prosperity cannot be related to the *iqta'* system, since al-Afḍal's domain at Samsat must be considered as a quasi-independent state possessed of much more freedom than a governor's concession.

In summary, we may address ourselves to the quotation that heads this chapter. While it is impossible to delineate exact relationships between ruler and ruled, nomad and peasant in this period, the remains of medieval Gritille do allow the examination of the economic bases at a settlement during the time within which such contacts were taking place. The material culture of the settlement did not change drastically at this time. There is no sign of impoverishment or interrupted local trade networks such as an increase in the number of handmade vessels. Indeed, more and different kinds of glazed wares came into use. However, faunal analysis shows that animals raised at Gritille were for local consumption and not part of a larger regional system such as historical sources document for the previous century. The growing of wheat at Gritille as a major crop may be the firmest archaeological indicator of its participation in a larger regional economic system.

In architecture, a paved street was still used as the central organizing factor, and structures on both sides of it shared common long walls and courtyards. The materials of construction remained the same. All these factors, plus the sheer continuation of settlement at Gritille, point to a degree of control over the nomadic influx and some governmental interest in the upkeep of rural agricultural settlements. In this study this interest has been tied to the nearby presence of a seat of power in Samsat.

The data from Gritille provide views of a stratum of the medieval Near East not often seen in chronicles, and suggest a range of activity, adaptation, and contact therein, parts of which are known for other places and times, but not hitherto in one spot over the course of one century.

In this one spot, archaeological and textual information can be blended to form a picture. It is of a landscape of hills dotted with wild fruit and nut trees and a valley rich in irrigated gardens and dry-farmed fields. By the edge of the river running through this valley lay a mound; on it stood a small settlement rising behind and around a mudbrick parapet. There, a farming and herding people lived in flat-roofed mudbrick dwellings with courtyards and stables where they cooked, processed, and stored the produce of the land. These surroundings were enlivened occasionally by vessels of bright turquoise, purple, or green. The walls of the settlement provided scant shelter from the conflict surrounding it, but long stretches of time passed when the inhabitants did not look for protection to the ruined walls. They looked instead to a high mound clearly visible downstream, to the citadel of the ruler of Samsat, who governed this valley and their lives. For long stretches of time their safety and servitude centered on that fortified town, and for it they labored.

THE FRONTIER

In earlier centuries, the Karababa basin had constituted a part of the *arrière-pays* of the *thughūr*, when there was an actively contested and recognized frontier zone between Byzantium and the Abbasid Empire and its successors. The terminology developed in this period continued during the medieval era, but the twelfth and early thirteenth centuries saw a much more dynamic and rapidly changing frontier develop. Franks, Armenians, Syriac Christians, Türkmen nomads, Bedouins, and Islamic armies and dynasties composed of Arabs, Turks, and Kurds all contested this region. Lines of contestation stretched east–west as well as north–south.

This situation stands in contrast to medieval Spain. With the collapse of the northern border zone centering on the Ebro, the Christian expansion into the heavily populated lands of Andalusia brought populations of Christians and Muslims into close contact with each other for the first time, and there were extensive efforts to colonize newly won lands. In the region between Anatolia and Syria, the frontier between Byzantium and the Turks shifted to central and western Anatolia, it is true, but the old region of the *thughūr* remained a contested zone first between Crusaders and Zangids, then Artuqids and Ayyubids, Ayyubids and Seljuks, and finally, lying outside the limits of this study, Mamluks and Mongols.

During the last years of the County of Edessa and the period of Artuqid hegemony, the Karababa basin was an actual frontier. But even when it was not near or at the border between states, it participated in the flux and decentralization (or localization) of authority characteristic of a frontier region. The power vacuum set up by the collapse of Byzantine rule in Anatolia and by the Turkish and Crusader influx raised two marginal characters to brief prominence in the historical record, individuals who perhaps personify the struggle of and for authority and ideology. The first is Kogh Vasil, lord of Keysun. He exemplifies the lawlessness of the period between Manzikert and the Second Crusade, when robber barons profited from the breakdown of central authority to carve out their own territories. Even when they were nominally subservient to a larger entity such as the County of Edessa, such feudal barons enjoyed great degrees of autonomy.

The second is Baba Resūl, the Türkmen religious leader whose syncretistic beliefs caught fire in the 1230s, spreading from his base near Keysun among a largely nomadic, recently Is-

lamicized constituency to almost topple the Seljuk state. Baba Resūl is an extremely important figure in the development of Islam in Anatolia. Despite the defeat of his movement, several later dervish orders important in the formation of the Ottoman state traced their origins to him. The lack of state systems of religious instruction and worship in this region created a vacuum that allowed such charismatic preaching to spread.

These two men exemplify different aspects of a frontier society, in which cultures and religions, while confronted, also mingled; where distance from central authority permitted the emergence of centers of local authority based on factors as different as personal charisma or force; a zone in which military authority is paramount.

In terms of material culture, this frontier culture was marked in three different ways. First was an innate conservatism born of the uncertainty and poverty operative in a frontier zone lacking in major institutions and centers of population and production. In this border region, unglazed ceramic and building traditions continued largely unaltered from the previous millennium. This koine of ceramic production and mudbrick domestic architecture stretched to military architecture. It is only occasionally that centralized state authority devoted resources to the building of fine stone constructions such as the keep at Samsat and the Mamluk fortifications at Besni, Gerger, and Eski Kâhta.

The second characteristic of this frontier zone was the small settlement of Christian agriculturalists, either under the control of a local power center such as Samsat or living around the skirts of a fortified residence of a petty feudal lord as at Tille, which had enough open space within its walls to shelter them and their flocks. Militarization of the social order extended to its lowest rural rung in this period.

Third, the economic chaos of the twelfth and early thirteenth centuries is best embodied by its coinage. The practice of countermarking was widespread, marking both the localization of authority and its impoverishment. At Gritille this was evident in several ways. In the Crusader era, coins imported from Europe seem to have remained important and widely accepted. And Byzantine coinage continued to be used, whether as countermarked copper coinage or gold coinage, until the thirteenth century, or imitated by Artuqid dynasties in their own copper coinage until the mid-to-late twelfth century.

In these ways, the inhabitants of medieval Gritille and their coevals participated, survived, and at times prospered in this border land marked by a great river flowing between mountain and plain.

Appendix

THE HUMAN SKELETAL REMAINS FROM THE MEDIEVAL OCCUPATION OF GRITILLE

Denise C. Hodges

Numerous human bones were encountered during the excavation of the medieval occupation of Gritille. Most of the bones were found in ashy layers with mudbrick collapse rather than in formal burials or graves. The remains of individuals are thus very fragmentary, with only a few bones present from most of the individuals. The remains were examined to determine the age and sex of the individuals. A complete study of the bones was made, including a series of measurements, scoring of nonmetric traits, and recording of pathologies. The results of the analysis are reported below with brief descriptions of the excavation context, the human remains, and a summary section.

METHODOLOGY

The age and sex of the individuals were determined using standard dimorphic features of the skeleton.[1] These determinations are presented in Table A:1. A series of measurements were made on the bones and teeth following the measurement definitions of Bass, Moore-Jansen and Jantz, Howells, Olivier, and Goose.[2] The cranial and mandibular measurements are reported in Table A:2. The postcranial measurements are reported in Table A:3. The dental measurements appear in Table A:4. Nonmetric traits were

TABLE A:1. AGE AND SEX INVENTORY OF THE GRITILLE HUMAN REMAINS

Lot Number	Sex	Age
GT 13717	?	Adult
GT 13721		3-5 years
GT 15197	Female	15-20 years
GT 17704		1.5-2 years
GT 17113	?	Adult
GT 18965	Male	35-40 years
GT 19745A	Male	25-35 years
GT 19745B	Male ?	Adult
GT 19745C		Subadult, < 10 years
GT 19747A	Male	20-25 years
GT 19747B	Female ?	Adult, young
GT 19747C	Male ?	Adult
GT 19747D		Subadult, < 10 years
GT 19747E		Subadult, adolescent
GT 22741A	Male	25-30 years
GT 22741B	Male	Adult

recorded following the scoring definitions of Finnegan, El-Najjar and McWilliams, and Bass.[3] The cranial and postcranial nonmetric traits are reported in Table A:5. The dental inventory and occurrences of dental pathologies are reported in Table A: 6. The frequency of dental nonmetric traits are reported in Table A:7.

---

[1] Bass, *Human Osteology*; Moore-Jansen and Jantz, "Data Collection Procedures."

[2] Bass, *Human Osteology*; Moore-Jansen and Jantz, "Data Collection Procedures"; Howells, *Cranial Variation*; Olivier, *Practical Anthropology*; Goose, "Dental Measurement."

[3] Finnegan, "Non-metric Variation"; El-Najjar and McWilliams, *Forensic Anthropology*; Bass, *Human Osteology*.

Bone Descriptions by Lot Number

GT 13717

Excavation context: Operation 31, Locus 26, Lot 47. Excavated 29 July 1983. Remains found in locus containing ash lenses and mudbrick collapse.

Human remains: A single bone was recovered: a left radius with both the proximal and distal epiphyses missing. The length and width of the bone shaft indicated the bone was from an adult individual. The individual's sex could not be determined.

No pathologies or abnormalities were noted.

GT 13721

Excavation context: Operation 31, Locus 26, Lot 47. Excavated 30 July 1983. Remains found in locus containing ash lenses and mudbrick collapse.

Human remains: The human remains consisted of a fragmentary mandible, a fragment of the frontal bone, the sphenoid bone, a right clavicle, a right humerus with the proximal epiphysis missing, nine rib fragments, and two cervical vertebrae fragments.

The individual was a subadult aged 3 to 5 years old at the time of death, based on the stage of crown and root formation of the permanent central incisors.[4]

No pathologies or abnormalities were noted on the bones.

There were twelve teeth present: the deciduous maxillary lateral incisors, the deciduous maxillary and mandibular canines, the deciduous maxillary right first molar, the deciduous mandibular left first molar, and all four permanent central incisors. Tooth measurements are reported in Table A:4, the dental status and pathology inventory are reported in Table A:6, and the nonmetric traits for the permanent teeth are reported in Table A:7.

No abnormalities or pathologies were observed on the teeth.

GT 15197

Excavation context: Operation 44, Locus 12, Lot 11. Excavated 30 June 1984. Remains were found in a dark, ashy layer next to a wall. The skull was resting face down in the dark, ashy, pit fill, with its face approximately 6 cm above the hard surface at the bottom of the dark, ashy layer. The hand was lying next to the skull; the remainder of the skeleton was underneath the balk.

Human remains: The human remains from this lot included a nearly complete cranium, mandible, and eight hand bones. The age of the individual was estimated at 15 to 20 years based on the incomplete fusion of the hand phalanges and metacarpals, the incomplete fusion of the basilar suture, and the partial eruption of the third molars.[5] The individual was a female based on the appearance of standard dimorphic cranial features.[6]

The skull displayed a slight warping owing to postdepositional forces. The cranial and mandibular measurements that could be taken are reported in Table A:2. The scores for nonmetric cranial and mandibular features are reported in Table A:5.

No pathologies or abnormalities were observed on the cranium, mandible, or hand bones.

Thirty teeth were present in the alveolar bone. The maxillary third molars were congenitally absent. Tooth size measurements are reported in Table A:4. Tooth status and pathology are reported in Table A:6, and nonmetric dental trait scores are reported in Table A:7.

All eight of the central and lateral incisors and the two mandibular canines displayed slight calculus deposits. Linear enamel hypoplasia, a defective groove in the enamel, was present on each of the four canines. Two hypoplastic defects were present on the mandibular left canine; the other three canines each had a single hypoplastic defect. Linear enamel hypoplasias

---

[4] Moorrees, Fanning, and Hunt, "Age Variation of Formation Stages."
[5] Bass, *Human Osteology.*
[6] Ibid.

TABLE A:2. CRANIAL METRICS (MM)

Measurement	15197	19745A
Maximum cranial length	167	173
Maximum cranial breadth		
Basion-bregma height	135	
Porion-bregma height		
Basion-porion height		
Auricular height		
Minimum frontal breadth	98	92*
Total facial height	112	
Upper facial height	65	
Bizygomatic breadth		
Upper facial breadth		
Nasal height	51	
Nasal breadth	27	
Orbital height	32(L)	
Orbital breadth	39(L) 41(R)	
Bimaxillary-frontal diameter		
Maxilloalveolar length	55	
Maxilloalveolar breadth	66	
Palatal length	42	
Palatal breadth	39	
Basion-nasion length	102	
Basion-prosthion length	99	
Bicondylar breadth		
Bigonial breadth	97	
Ramus length	53(R)	59(R)
Minimum breadth of ramus	34(L) 32(R)	36(L)
Maximum breadth of ramus		
Mandibular body height	26(L&R)	28(L)
Mandibular body length	90(R)	
Symphysis height	32	32
Breadth mandibular body		
Gonial angle	124o	
Condyle medial-lateral length	21(R)	
Condyle anterior-posterior length	7(R)	
Nasio-occipital length		
Foramen magnum length		

L = left
R = right
* = estimate

are produced when an individual suffers a stress episode that temporarily halts the formation of enamel.[7] Stress episodes capable of disrupting enamel formation can be caused by nutritional deficiencies, serious illness, or a combination of dietary and health problems.[8] Once the stress episode passes enamel formation resumes, but a small depression or groove is left on the tooth surface.

The etiology of an enamel hypoplasia cannot be determined by its appearance, but the presence of hypoplasias on archaeological spec-

---

[7] Goodman, Armelagos, and Rose, "Enamel Hypoplasias as Indicators of Stress."
[8] Ibid.

TABLE A:3 (1). POSTCRANIAL METRICS (MM)

Measurement	17113 L	18965 L	18965 R	19745A L	19745A R	19745B R
HUMERUS						
Maximum length	318					
Maximum diameter at midshaft	22					
Minimum diameter at midshaft	19					
Maximum diameter of head	45					
Vertical diameter of head	44					
Transverse diameter of head	34					
Least circumference of shaft	65					
Epicondylar width						
Articular width						
FEMUR						
Maximum length					439*	
Bicondylar length					438*	
AP diameter at mid-shaft		30	31		27	
ML diameter at mid-shaft		30	30		27	
Maximum diameter of head					47	
Vertical diameter of head						
Circumference of midshaft		94	93		86	
Subtrochanteric AP diameter					24	
Subtrochanteric ML diameter					32	
Bicondylar breadth		85			80	
TIBIA						
Maximum length				364		
Physiological length				353		
AP diameter at N.F.						
ML diameter at N.F.						
Circumference at N.F.						
Proximal breadth				80		
Distal breadth						
FIBULA						
Maximum length				346		
TALUS						
Maximum length				57	57	53
CALCANEUS						
Maximum length						
Middle breadth						
INNOMINATE						
Maximum height		141*				
Maximum breadth						
Pubis length						
Ischium length						
SACRUM						
Maximum anterior height		90		114		
Maximum anterior breadth		106		116		
Max. transverse. diameter of base						
SCAPULA						
Scapula length						
Glenoid cavity length						
Maximum breadth						

TABLE A:3 (2). POSTCRANIAL METRICS (MM)

Measurement	19747A R	19747B R	22741A L	22741A R
HUMERUS				
Maximum length			331	
Maximum diameter at midshaft			23	
Minimum diameter at midshaft			21	
Maximum diameter of head			47	
Vertical diameter of head				
Transverse diameter of head				
Least circumference of shaft			67	
Epicondylar width			63	
Articular width			46	
FEMUR				
Maximum length				457
Bicondylar length				453
AP diameter at midshaft				28
ML diameter at midshaft				28
Maximum diameter of head			46	48
Vertical diameter of head			45	46
Circumference of midshaft			89	
Subtrochanteric AP diameter			25	26
Subtrochanteric ML diameter			33	34
Bicondylar breadth				86
TIBIA				
Maximum length		349		
Physiological length		337		
AP diameter at N.F.	31	26		
ML diameter at N.F.	34	27		
Circumference at N.F.	105	81		
Proximal breadth	80	74		
Distal breadth		43*		
TALUS				
Maximum length		52		
SACRUM				
Maximum anterior height			99*	
Maximum anterior breadth			103	
Max. transverse. diameter of base				
SCAPULA				
Scapula length				
Glenoid cavity length			40	
Maximum breadth				

KEY
L = Left
R = Right
AP = Anterior-Posterior
ML = Medial-Lateral
N.F. = Nutrient foramen
* = estimate

TABLE A:4. DENTAL METRICS (MM)

Tooth	13721 Max.	13721 Mand.	15197 Max.	15197 Mand.	17704 Max.	19745A Mand.
Incisor 1, Left						
M-D	8.8	5.7	9.1	5.8		
B-L	7.2	6.1	8.2			
Crown height	11.9	10.3				
Incisor 1, Right						
M-D	9.0	5.9	9.1	5.8		
B-L	7.3	6.2	8.2	6.9		
Crown height	12.3	10.4				
Incisor 2, Left						
M-D	5.1^d		6.5	6.3		
B-L	4.5		7.7	7.3		
Incisor 2, Right						
M-D			7.2	6.4		
B-L			7.5	7.1		
Canine, Left						
M-D	7.3^d	6.1^d	8.5	7.1		
B-L	6.9	6.0	9.7	9.0		
Canine, Right						
M-D	7.2^d	6.5^d	8.7	7.2		
B-L	6.8	6.0	10.0	8.9		
Premolar 1, Left						
M-D			7.2*	7.3		
B-L			10.2	8.4		
Premolar 1, Right						
M-D			7.4	7.4		6.6
B-L			10.0	8.7		7.9
Premolar 2, Left						
M-D				7.9		
B-L			10.4	9.0		
Premolar 2, Right						
M-D			7.6	7.6		
B-L			10.3	9.0		
Molar 1, Left						
M-D			10.7*	11.6*	7.6^d	
B-L			11.9	11.0	9.4	
Molar 1, Right						
M-D	7.5^d		11.3*	11.5*	7.6^d	11.3
B-L	8.7		11.8	11.2	9.5	
Molar 2, Left						
M-D			10.4*	11.4*		
B-L			12.4*	10.6		
Molar 2, Right						
M-D			10.2*	11.3*	9.7^d	
B-L			11.5*	10.5	10.5	
Molar 3, Left						
M-D						
B-L						
Molar 3, Right						
M-D						
B-L						

M-D = Mesial-distal breadth   B-L = Buccal-lingual breadth
Max. = Maxilla   Mand. = Mandible
^{d} = Deciduous   * = Estimate

TABLE A:5 (1). CRANIAL AND POSTCRANIAL NONMETRIC TRAIT SCORES

Cranial traits	15197 L	15197 R	19745A L	19745A R
Epipteric bone	A	A	A	
Asterionic bone	A	P	A	
Parietal notch bone	A	A	A	
Os lambdoidal suture	A		P	
Os coronal suture	P		A	
Os sagittal suture	A		A	
Os japonicum	A	A		
Inca bone	A		A	
Bregma bone				
Metopic suture	A		A	
Supra-orbital foramen	N	N	N	N
Pterion shape	A	A		
Parietal foramen	P	P	P	A
Sup. sagittal sulcus dir.	R		R	
Mastoid foramen exsutural	PI	PI	PI	
Postcondylar foramen	P	A		
Hypoglossal canal bipartite	A	A	A	PC
Foramen ovale incomplete		PC		
Pterygospinous bridge/spur	A	A		
Auditory exostosis	A	A	A	
Tympanic dehiscence	A	A	A	
Multiple infraorbital foramen	A	A		
Infraorbital suture	A	A		
Multiple zygomatic foramen	A	A		
Palatine torus	A	A		
Mandibular torus	A	A	A	
Mylohyoid bridge	A	A	A	A
Multiple mental foramen	A	P	A	A

KEY
A = Absent
P = Present
R = Right
N = Notch
PI = Present, incomplete
PC = Present, complete
S = Single
D = Double

imens does indicate the occurrence of early childhood stressors. The location of the defect on the tooth surface can be used to determine at approximately what age the hypoplasia producing stress had occurred based on standards of tooth development.[9] The defects on this individual were located in the cervical half of the tooth crown and indicate that a stress episode had occurred between 4 to 4.5 years of age.

No other dental pathologies or abnormalities were noted.

---

[9] Ibid.

TABLE A:5 (2). CRANIAL AND POSTCRANIAL NONMETRIC TRAIT SCORES

Postcranial traits	17113	18965		19745A		19745B	19747A	
	L	L	R	L	R	R	L	R
Allen's fossa					A			
Poirier's facet					A			
Plaque					A			
Hypotrochanteric fossa					P			
Trochanteric fossa exostosis					P			
Third trochanter					P			
Medial tibial squatting facet				A	A			
Lateral tibial squatting facet				P	P			
Supracondyloid process	A							
Septal aperture	A							
Acetabular crease								A
Accessory sacral facet-Inn.			A					
Accessory sacral facet		A		A	A			
Sacralization of L-5		A		A				
Vastus notch		P						
Vastus fossa		P						
Emarginate patella		A						
Os trigonum				A	A	A		
Medial talar facet				A	A	A		
Lateral talar extension				P	P	P		
Inferior talar articular surface				S	S	A		
Anterior calcaneal facet				A	A			
Peroneal tubercle					P			
Atlas facet form								
Transverse foramen bipartite (C3-7)							A	
Atlas posterior bridge								
Atlas lateral bridge								
Acromial articular facet								
Suprascapular foramen								
Circumflex sulcus								
Sternal foramen								

GT 17704

Excavation context: Operation 47, Locus 4, Lot 1. Excavated 11 August 1984. Remains were found in bricky decay from the upper phase domestic structures.

Human remains: The human remains from this lot included a cranium missing the right temporal and facial bones, a fragmentary left scapula, the distal two-thirds of the left tibia, the proximal third of the right femur shaft, the proximal two-thirds of the right tibia, and three rib fragments.

The individual was a subadult estimated at 1.5 to 2 years of age at death, based on the stage of crown formation of the permanent first molars.[10]

Cribra orbitalia, a pitting of the roof of the eye orbit, was observed in both the left and right orbits. The porosity was slight with small, diffuse pits. Cribra orbitalia is a condition associated with hemolytic anemias, including thalassemia, sickle-cell anemia, and iron deficiency anemia.[11] Thalassemia is a hereditary anemia that is found in eastern Mediterranean populations. Iron deficiency anemia can be caused by

---

[10] Moorrees, Fanning, and Hunt, "Age Variation of Formation Stages."
[11] Ortner and Putschar, *Identification of Pathological Conditions*.

TABLE A:5 (3). CRANIAL AND POSTCRANIAL NONMETRIC TRAIT SCORES

Postcranial traits	19747B R	22741A L	22741A R	22741B L
Allen's fossa		A	P	
Poirier's facet		A	A	
Plaque		A	A	
Hypotrochanteric fossa		A	A	
Trochanteric fossa exostosis			A	
Third trochanter		P	P	
Medial tibial squatting facet	A			
Lateral tibial squatting facet	P			
Supracondyloid process		A		
Septal aperture		A		
Acetabular crease				
Accessory sacral facet-Inn.				
Accessory sacral facet				A
Sacralization of L-5		P		A
Vastus notch				
Vastus fossa				
Emarginate patella				
Os trigonum	A			
Medial talar facet	A			
Lateral talar extension	P			
Inferior talar articular surface	D			
Anterior calcaneal facet	A			
Peroneal tubercle	P			
Atlas facet form				
Transverse foramen bipartite (C3-7)				
Atlas posterior bridge				
Atlas lateral bridge				
Acromial articular facet				
Suprascapular foramen		A		
Circumflex sulcus		A		
Sternal foramen				

an insufficient intake of iron, a parasitic infection which interferes with the absorption of iron in the body, or a combination of dietary and poor health factors.[12] Sickle-cell anemia is caused by a genetic defect in the structure of hemoglobin. Sickle-cell anemia is found primarily in African populations[13] and can be ruled out as the cause of this case of cribra orbitalia.

Thalassemia affects individuals in early childhood, with the most severe changes occurring in the skull.[14] The diploe of the cranial vault expands, and later the outer table is progres-

sively eroded. The maxilla and zygomatic bones may also display expanded dimensions. In prehistoric samples from the eastern Mediterranean, Angel has diagnosed cases of cribra orbitalia as due to thalassemia.[15] In this individual from Gritille, though, no expansion or erosion was observed on the cranial vault bones. The facial bones were missing. It seems unlikely that the individual had thalassemia since no other lesions were observed on the skull. The cribra orbitalia was most likely due to an iron deficiency anemia. The anemia may have been due to a

[12] Ibid.

[13] Steinbock, *Paleopathological Diagnosis.*

[14] Ortner and Putschar, *Identification of Pathological Conditions.*

[15] Angel, "Porotic Hyperostosis."

TABLE A:6 (1). DENTAL INVENTORY AND PATHOLOGY SCORES

Tooth	Status L/R	Caries L/R	Pulp Exposure L/R	Alveolar Abscess L/R	Hyper-cementosis L/R	Calculus L/R
13721						
UI1	$1^P/1^P$					
UI1	$9^d/9^d$					
UI2	$1^d/1^d$	0/0	0/0	0/0	0/9	0/0
UC	$1^d/1^d$	0/0	0/0	0/0	0/9	0/0
UP1						
UP2						
UM1	$9^d/1^d$	/0	/0	/0	/9	/0
UM2	$9^d/9^d$					
UM3						
LI1	$1^P/1^P$					
LI1	$9^d/9^d$					
LI2	$9^d/9^d$					
LC	$1^d/1^d$	0/0	0/0	0/0	0/0	0/0
LP1						
LP2						
LM1	$1/9^d$	0/	0/	0/	0/	0/
LM2	$9/9^d$					
LM3						
15197						
UI1	2/2	0/0	0/0	0/0	0/0	1/1
UI2	2/2	0/0	0/0	0/0	0/0	1/1
UC	2/2	0/0	0/0	0/0	0/0	0/0
UP1	2/2	0/0	0/0	0/0	0/9	0/0
UP2	2/2	0/0	0/0	0/0	9/0	0/0
UM1	2/2	0/0	0/0	0/0	9/9	0/0
UM2	2/2	0/0	0/0	0/0	9/9	0/0
UM3	8/8					
LI1	2/2	0/0	0/0	0/0	9/0	1/1
LI2	2/2	0/0	0/0	0/0	0/0	1/1
LC	2/2	0/0	0/0	0/0	0/0	1/1
LP1	2/2	0/0	0/0	0/0	0/0	0/0
LP2	2/2	0/0	0/0	0/0	0/0	0/0
LM1	2/2	0/0	0/0	0/0	9 /9	0/0
LM2	2/2	0/0	0/0	0/0	9/9	0/0
LM3	6/6					
17704						
UI1	$5^d/5^d$					
UI2	$5^d/5^d$					
UC	$5^d/5^d$					
UM1	$2^d/2^d$	0/0	0/0	0/0	9/9	0/0
UM2	$6^d/6^d$					
UM1	$7^P/7^P$					
19745A						
LI1	5/5					
LI2	5/5					
LC	5/5					
LP1	5/2	/0	/0	/0	/0	/0
LP2	5/5					
LM1	2/9	$2^1/$	0/	0/	9/	0/
LM2	4/9					
LM3	9/9					

TABLE A:6 (2). DENTAL INVENTORY AND PATHOLOGY SCORES

Tooth	Attrition Degree/Form Left	Attrition Degree/Form Right	Enamel Defects Type/No. Left	Enamel Defects Type/No. Right	Alveolar Resorption (mm) L/R
13721					
UI2d	2/1	2/2	0	0	
UCd	2/1	2/1	0	0	
UM1d		2/1		0	
LCd	2/1	2/1	0	0	
LM1d	2/1		0		
15197					
UI1	3/1	3/1	0	0	
UI2	1/1	1/1	0	0	
UC	2/1	2/1	$4/1^2$	$4/1^2$	
UP1	1/1	1/1	0	0	
UP2	1/1	1/1	0	0	
UM1	2/1	2/1	0	0	
UM2	1/1	1/1	0	0	
LI1	2/1	2/1	0	0	
LI2	2/1	2/1	0	0	
LC	1/1	1/1	$4/2^2$	$4/1^2$	
LP1	1/1	1/1	0	0	
LP2	1/1	1/1	0	0	
LM1	2/1	2/1	0	0	
LM2	1/1	1/1	0	0	
17704					
UM1	1/1	1/1	0	0	
19745A					
LP1		3/1		0	
LM1	3/5		0		2.3/

KEY

Status
1 = Present, tooth only
2 = Present, tooth in socket
3 = Antemortem loss (socket resorbing)
4 = Antemortem loss (socket resorbed)
5 = Postmortem loss
6 = Partial eruption
7 = Unerupted
d = Deciduous
P = Permanent
8 = Congenital absence
9 = Unknown

Caries
0 = Absent
2 = Pit to 1/2 of surface destroyed
1 = Interproximal surface

Pulp exposure
0 = Absent
1 = Due to attrition

Calculus
0 = Absent
1 = Slight or flex
2 = Moderate, up to 1/2 crown covered

Attrition degree (Hinton, "Form and Patterning of Anterior Tooth Wear")
Incisors and canines
1 = Unworn to polish or small facets (no dentin exposure)

2 = Hairline of dentin exposure
3 = Dentin line of distinct thickness
Premolars
1 = Unworn to polish or small facets (no dentin exposure)
2 = Moderate cusp removal
3 = Full cusp removal and/or moderate dentin patches
Molars
1 = Unworn to polish or small facets
2 = Moderate cusp removal
3 = Full cusp removal and/or some dentin exposure

Attrition form (Hinton, "Form and Patterning of Anterior Tooth Wear")
1 = Natural face or slightly blunt
2 = Flat
5 = Rounded

Alveolar abscess
0 = Absent
9 = Unknown

Hypercementosis
0 = Absent
9 = Unknown

Enamel defect type
0 = Absent
4 = Hypoplasia (horizontal groove)

Enamel hypoplasia distances:
UC, left = 2.8 mm
UC, right = 2.6 mm
LC, left = 5.9 mm, 2.9 mm
LC, right = 3.1 mm

TABLE A:7. NONMETRIC DENTAL TRAIT SCORES

| Dental nonmetric traits | 13721[a] | | 15197 | | 19745A |
	Max.	Mand.	Max.	Mand.	Mand.
Enamel pearl	0/2	0/2	0/14	0/14	0/2
Enamel extension	0/2	0/2	0/14	0/14	0/2
Peg tooth	0/2	0/2	0/14	0/14	0/2
Carabelli cusp[b]			2/4		
Shoveling[c]	0/2	0/2	0/4	0/4	
Supernumerary tooth	0/2	0/2	0/14	0/14	0/2
Taurodontic			0/14	0/14	
Rotation			0/14	0/14	0/2
Crowding			0/14	0/14	0/2

a = Permanent teeth
b = Observed on maxillary molars only
c = Observed on incisors only

dietary deficiency, a parasitic infection, an interference in the absorption of iron, or a combination of these health and nutritional problems. The proximate cause of the iron deficiency cannot be determined from the appearance of the lesions on the skeleton.

No other pathologies or abnormalities were noted on the remains.

Only two of the deciduous teeth were present: both maxillary first molars. The deciduous canines and incisors had been lost postmortem. The deciduous second molars were unerupted. The permanent first molars were visible in the tooth sockets. The tooth measurements are reported in Table A:4. The tooth status and pathology inventory are reported in Table A:6.

No pathologies or abnormalities were noted on the teeth.

GT 17113

Excavation context: Operation 26/27, Locus 17, Lot 27. Excavated 7 July 1984. Remains were found in a soft, ashy outdoor surface associated with the lower street and an oven.

Human remains: The human remains from this lot consisted of a single left humerus. The epiphyses had fused, indicating the bone was from an adult individual; a specific age range could not be assigned. The sex of the individual could not be estimated; the bone was not particularly robust or gracile in its muscle markings.

The measurements of the bone are reported in Table A:3. The stature of the individual was estimated at 162 ± 4.2 cm using Trotter's formula for white females.[16] The female formula was chosen because the bone was not particularly robust and thus may have been from a female.

No pathologies or abnormalities were noted on the bone.

GT 18965

Excavation context: Operation 45, Locus 13, Lot 39. Excavated 28 July 1984. The remains were found in bricky collapse on a burned floor (Locus 19). The remains comprised a burial/skeleton consisting of the upper leg, the pelvis, and the lumbar region. It was found lying face down with legs spread apart and extended. The upper parts of the skeleton were encased with hard bricky collapse, with soft ashy soil packed around the bones close to the flooring.

Human remains: The human remains from this lot consisted of a fragment of the sternum, fragmentary left and right innominates, a complete sacrum, a left patella, the shaft of the right femur, the distal two-thirds of the left femur, two rib fragments, and all five lumbar vertebrae.

The individual was a male based on the appearance of standard dimorphic features of the pelvis and sacrum.[17] The age of the individual was estimated at 35 to 40 years based on the av-

---

[16] Trotter, "Estimation of Stature."
[17] Bass, *Human Osteology*.

erage ages determined from the morphology of the pubic symphysis (stage IV-2, average = 35.2 years, range 23 to 57 years)[18] and the sacro-iliac surface (stage I, 35 to 39 years).[19]

The measurements of the bones are reported in Table A:3. The nonmetric trait scores are reported in Table A:5.

Slight osteophyte formations were present on the superior and inferior body margins of the second through fifth lumbar vertebrae.

No other pathologies or abnormalities were noted on the bones. The excavation notes on this lot report "slash mark on right knee (outside of bottom of femur), perhaps from sword or ax." Unfortunately the right distal femur was badly fragmented and could not be reconstructed. No cutmarks were observed on the bone fragments, but this does not preclude the possibility that this individual had suffered a traumatic injury.

GT 19745

Excavation context: Operation 47, Locus 18, Lot 26. Excavated 4 August 1984. Remains were found in a locus consisting of bricky collapse, thick ash, and charcoal deposits. The remains were scattered on a burned floor.

Human remains: The human remains from this lot represent a minimum of three individuals: two adults and one subadult. Individual A was an adult male, Individual B was an adult male, and Individual C was a subadult. The presence of two adults was indicated by the presence of two left radii, two right tali, and two right calcanea. The bones were matched, and those remaining were assigned to one of the two individuals based on size differences. It is possible that some of the bones may have been from additional adult individuals.

INDIVIDUAL A

The human remains from this individual consisted of a cranium missing the right temporal and facial bones, an incomplete mandible, a sacrum, twelve tarsals, ten metatarsals, two foot phalanx, a left tibia, a left fibula, a left radius and ulna, both missing the distal two-thirds of the shafts, a right femur, a right tibia and fibula, both missing the proximal two-thirds of the shafts, five rib fragments, and three thoracic vertebrae fragments.

The individual was a male based on the appearance of sexual dimorphic features of the sacrum and cranium.[20] The individual was aged between 25 to 35 years based on the stage of closure of the ectocranial sutures.[21]

The cranium was warped; the measurements that could be taken are reported in Table A:2. The postcranial measurements are reported in Table A:3. The cranial and postcranial nonmetric trait scores are reported in Table A:5.

The stature of the individual is estimated at 168 ± 3.4 cm using Trotter's tibia formula for white males.[22] The tibia was used to estimate stature because the femur maximum length could not be measured.

The maxilla was missing from the cranium but a mandible, missing the right ramus, was present. Only the left first molar and the right first premolar were present. The left second molar had been lost antemortem; the remaining teeth were lost postmortem or were missing. Dental measurements are reported in Table A:4, tooth status and pathology are reported in Table A:6, and the nonmetric dental trait frequencies appear in Table A:7. The first molar had a carious pit on the interproximal surface. The caries had destroyed over a quarter of the enamel surface and had also affected the root.

No other pathologies or abnormalities were noted on the teeth.

Several pathologies and traumatic injuries were present on the cranium and the postcranial remains.

Trauma: (1) The left second metatarsal had a healed fracture on the distal quarter of the shaft. Extra bone formation from the healing process was still present, but bone formation was not active at or near the time of death.

(2) The left third metatarsal also had a healed fracture on the distal quarter of the shaft. The fracture most likely occurred in the same

[18] Suchey, Brooks, and Katz, *Use of the Suchey-Brooks System.*

[19] Lovejoy et al., "Chronological Metamorphosis."

[20] Bass, *Human Osteology.*

[21] Meindl and Lovejoy, "Ectocranial Suture Closure."

[22] Trotter, "Estimation of Stature."

incident that fractured the second metatarsal. Extra bone formation was still present at the fracture site, but bone formation was not active.

(3) The fourth right metatarsal had a healed fracture on the proximal end of the shaft. Bone formation and remodeling was evident, but the fracture appeared to be nearly healed.

(4) A single cutmark was present on the right frontal bone of the cranium at the location of the minimum postorbital constriction (Pls. A:1, A:2). The cutmark appears to have been made by a sharp ax or sword that was delivered by a blow from the right side of the individual. The attacker struck the victim from behind with the blade piercing the outer table at about a 45 degree angle. A small section of bone was sliced off posteriorly to the cutmark and another anteriorly to the cutmark, including a portion of the supraorbital torus. It appears that the individual received a single blow to the skull, and that the removal of bone flakes and slicing around the cutmark occurred when the attacker was attempting to remove the blade from the skull. No evidence of healing was found near the cutmark. The cutmark did not pierce the inner table nor the brain; thus the blow may not have led to the death of the individual, but the lack of healing and the increased susceptibility to further attacks in the battle probably contributed to his death.

Pathology: (1) The right femur has a slight periosteal reaction on the anterior and medial surfaces of the proximal shaft. The lesion consisted of slight new bone formation that was active at the time of death. The lesion indicates an infectious condition was affecting the bone.

(2) The left tibia had a slight periosteal reaction on the medial surface at the mid-shaft. The lesion consisted of a slight amount of new bone formation that was active and localized at the time of death.

(3) The left fibula had a medium to large bony exostosis on the posterior surface of the head (Pl. A:3). The possible diagnoses for this exostosis are myositis ossificans, osteochondro-ma, and an occupational stress marker. Myositis ossificans is a condition in which muscle or tendon fibers at a site of insertion are ossified.[23] Myositis ossificans is usually associated with trauma. The formation of bone in the muscle can become part of the existing bone tissue. There is no evidence of trauma at the proximal end of the fibula. The exostosis also appears as an extension of the fibular head, not the attachment of ossified muscle tissue. These two features of the Gritille specimen argue against a diagnosis of myositis ossificans.

An osteochondroma is a benign bone tumor. Osteochondromas occur on bones that develop by endochondral ossification and occur at or near the epiphyseal line.[24] The bone formed in an osteochondroma is normal in structure. Osteochondromas are usually solitary lesions; rarely are multiple osteochondromas observed in a skeleton.[25] Steinbock has suggested that these tumors may be a congenital anomaly rather than a true neoplasm.[26] The exostosis on this individual does occur at the epiphyseal line, is normal in its structure, and is a continuation of the bone of the fibular head. Osteochondroma appears to be a possible diagnosis for the exostosis.

Another possibility is that the exostosis may represent a rare occupational stress marker. Although no description of an exostosis of the fibular head could be found in the literature on occupational stress markers,[27] it is possible that the exostosis is due to occupational use. The soleus muscle has its origin on the posterior surface of the fibular head at the location of the exostosis. The soleus inserts on the heel of the calcaneus and acts to extend the foot. The muscle is active, along with other foot extensor muscles, when an individual is standing, walking, dancing, or leaping. Prolonged extension of the foot could have led to overuse of the muscle. The stress of overuse would have resulted in external forces pulling on the bone and led to the bony formation. The interosseous crest was very prominent on the shaft of the fibula which sug-

[23] Ortner and Putschar, *Identification of Pathological Conditions.*
[24] Steinbock, *Paleopathological Diagnosis.*
[25] Ibid.
[26] Ibid., 321.
[27] Kennedy, "Skeletal Markers of Occupational Stress."

gests that the muscles of the individual were well developed and tends to support a diagnosis of an occupational stress marker.

This fibular exostosis was observed in a second individual in the Gritille sample (GT 19747C). The fact that the exostosis was observed in two individuals in the sample would tend to argue in favor of an occupational stress marker. However, osteochondroma cannot be ruled out, as a single osteochondroma lesion may be the result of a congenital anomaly, and thus its genetic basis could explain the presence of two cases.

INDIVIDUAL B

The remains of this individual consisted of a right talus, a right calcaneus, three metatarsals, three metacarpals, the proximal third of the left radius, and the distal one-third of the left ulna. The metacarpals, ulna, and radius all had partially charred surfaces present.

The individual was probably a male, based on the maximum length of the talus.[28] The age at death could not be determined, but the individual was an adult.

The postcranial metrics are reported in Table A:3. The nonmetric trait scores are reported in Table A:5.

A lesion of porosity or bone loss was present on both the calcaneus and talus. The talus displayed bone loss and pitting on the posterior surface of the calcaneus articular surface. The area affected was oblong in shape, measuring 12 mm by 8 mm. The lesion was confined to the articular surface. On the calcaneus a small area of pitting was observed surrounding the posterior and lateral sides of the posterior talar articular surface. The pits ranged from small to moderately large in size. The articular surface was not affected on the calcaneus. The lesions probably represent a localized infection on the talus that had affected the adjacent surface of the calcaneus.

No other pathologies or abnormalities were noted on the bones.

INDIVIDUAL C

A partial left clavicle with unfused epiphyses was the only remains of the subadult indi-

vidual. The small size of the clavicle suggested that the individual was probably less than 10 years of age at the time of death.

No abnormalities or pathologies were noted on the bone.

GT 19747

Excavation context: Operation 47, Locus 18, Lot 27. Excavated 7 August 1984. Remains were found in a locus consisting of bricky collapse, thick ash, and charcoal deposits. The remains were scattered on a burned floor.

Human remains: The human remains from this lot represent a minimum of five individuals: three adults and two subadults. The identification of three adults is based on the presence of two right tibia and two right fibula, of which one tibia and fibula belonged to the same individual (A) while the other fibula and tibia clearly did not match, thus determining a minimum of three adults. The subadults were both represented by a single bone. The adult bones were matched to the identified individuals based on size and robusticity differences.

INDIVIDUAL A

This individual consisted of a right tibia missing the distal third, a left fibula missing the distal third, a scapula fragment, a partial right innominate, and four cervical and thoracic vertebrae.

The individual was a male, based on the appearance of dimorphic features of the innominate.[29] The age at death is estimated at 20 to 25 years based on the average ages determined from the morphology of the pubic symphysis (stage I, average = 18.5 years, range 15 to 23 years),[30] and the sacro-iliac surface (phase C, 25 to 29 years).[31]

The measurements of the bones are reported in Table A:3. The nonmetric trait scores are reported in Table A:5.

A traumatic injury was observed on the scapula fragment (Pl. A:4). The fragment consisted of only the acromion process which had been sliced off with a sharp instrument approximately where the scapula spine meets the acromion process. A hinge break was present on

---

[28] Bass, *Human Osteology.*

[29] Ibid.

[30] Suchey, Brooks, and Katz, *Use of the Suchey-Brooks System.*

[31] Lovejoy et al., "Chronological Metamorphosis."

the inferior surface of the bone. It is quite likely that the injury contributed to the death of this individual.

No other pathologies or abnormalities were observed.

INDIVIDUAL B

This individual consisted of a complete right tibia, a right talus, a right calcaneus, seven metatarsals, and three foot phalanges. The individual was probably a female, based on measurements of the tibia's circumference at the nutrient foramen, the proximal breadth, and the distal breadth.[32] The individual was probably a young adult, as the articular surfaces displayed no evidence of aging; a precise age range could not be determined.

The measurements of the bones are reported in Table A:3. The nonmetric trait scores are reported in Table A:5.

A healed fracture was present on the right second metatarsal. The fracture had healed with a slight misalignment. Bone formed during the healing process was still present, although no active bone formation was indicated.

No other pathologies or abnormalities were observed.

INDIVIDUAL C

This individual consisted of a right fibula missing the lateral malleolus. The length and robusticity of the bone suggested it may have been from an adult male.

The fibula displayed a bony exostosis on the posterior and inferior surface of the head. The exostosis is nearly identical to that found in GT 19745 Individual A. As discussed above, the exostosis is probably an osteochondroma or an occupational stress marker.

INDIVIDUAL D

This individual consisted of a femur distal epiphysis from a subadult. Based on the size of the epiphysis, the individual was probably less than 10 years of age at the time of death.

No pathologies or abnormalities were observed on the bone.

INDIVIDUAL E

This individual consisted of a metatarsal with an unfused head epiphysis. The head of the metatarsals typically fuses between 12 to 22 years of age.[33] The age of the individual at the time of death was 12 to 22 years old. The sex of the individual could not be determined.

No pathologies or abnormalities were noted on the bone.

GT 22741

Excavation context: Operation 55, Locus 45, Lot 61. Excavated 24 August 1984. The remains were found in a layer with charcoal and below a layer of mudbrick.

Human remains: The human remains from this lot consisted of two adult individuals based on the presence of two sacra and two left innominates. The remains were assigned to one or the other of the individuals based on size and robusticity differences.

INDIVIDUAL A

This individual consisted of a partial left scapula, a left innominate, a partial right innominate, a sacrum, a left humerus, the proximal half of the left femur, a right femur, nineteen ribs and rib fragments, three cervical and one lumbar vertebrae.

The individual was a male, based on the dimorphic features of the innominate and sacrum.[34] The age of the individual was estimated at 25 to 30 years based on the average ages determined from the morphology of the pubic symphysis (stage II-1, average age = 23.4, range 19 to 34 years)[35] and the sacro-iliac surface (phase E, 30 to 35 years).[36]

The measurements of the postcranial remains are reported in Table A:3. The nonmetric trait scores are reported in Table A:5.

The stature of the individual is estimated at 170 ± 3.3 cm using Trotter's femur formula for white males.[37]

The individual displayed a sacrilization of the fifth lumbar with a nearly complete fusion

---

[32] Bass, *Human Osteology.*

[33] Brothwell, *Digging up Bones.*

[34] Bass, *Human Osteology.*

[35] Suchey, Brooks, and Katz, *Use of the Suchey-Brooks System.*

[36] Lovejoy et al., "Chronological Metamorphosis."

[37] Trotter, "Estimation of Stature."

of the vertebra to the sacrum. Sacrilization is a nonmetric trait; its expression is determined in part by the genetic makeup of the individual.[38]

The left femur had been fractured at the mid-shaft (Pl. A:5). There is no evidence of cutmarks or carnivore activity on the bone, nor any signs of attempted union and healing. The fracture was a perimortem fracture occurring at or near the time of death. There is a dark rim surrounding the breakage with some evidence of burning around the fractured end. This pattern of a proximal femur displaying a clearly defined rim with burning at the fracture site has been observed in a forensic science case where the lower leg had been burned using an accelerant.[39] It would appear, then, that the lower part of the leg had been burned while the flesh was intact, leaving only the proximal end of the femur present.

No other pathologies or abnormalities were noted on the bones.

INDIVIDUAL B

This individual consisted of a complete sacrum, a fragment of the left innominate, and the third and fourth lumbar vertebrae. The individual was a male, based on the shape of the sacrum.[40] The age of this adult individual could not be determined.

Measurements of the sacrum are reported in Table A:3. Nonmetric trait scores of the sacrum are reported in Table A:5.

No pathologies or abnormalities were noted on the bones.

INTERPRETATIONS AND CONCLUSIONS

A minimum of sixteen individuals were identified among the human remains recovered in the medieval strata. Five of the individuals were subadults: four were younger than 10 years old at the time of death, while the fifth subadult was an adolescent at the time of death. Of the eleven adults, two individuals were identified as females, six as males, and the sex of the other three adults could not be determined. Although the sample is rather small, the high frequency of adult males (75% of individuals with sex determined) may indicate that many of the women and children were absent from the village during the attack. Of the four adults whose age could be determined, all were aged under 40 years at the time of death.

The fragmentary nature of the remains precluded age and sex determination for many of the individuals. None of the sixteen individuals was represented by a complete skeleton. However, the bones that were present had good bone preservation. This combination of good bone preservation but poor skeletal representation reflects the lack of formal burial of these individuals. Nearly all of the individuals in this sample were found in association with ashy lenses or mudbrick collapse, with no evidence of grave construction. The individuals appear to have been killed in a battle or died during the destruction of the village, the bodies being left in the rubble.

The skeletal remains provide clear evidence of the warfare that led up to the destruction of the village. At least two individuals had severe traumatic injuries that most likely occurred during the fighting: GT 19745A had a cutmark from a sword or ax on the cranium; and GT 19747A had a cutmark on the scapula from a sword or ax. A third individual, GT 18965, probably also had a sword or ax wound to the knee based on the excavator's observations of the bones in situ. No evidence of healing was observed at the site of these injuries, which suggests the traumas may have led to the death of these individuals. All three of the individuals were young adult males.

Individual GT 22741A displayed a fracture of the femur that probably resulted when the lower leg had been burned while the flesh was intact. This condition may have occurred at the time of death or just after death. Either way it reflects the warfare activities that led up to the abandonment of the site.

In addition to the warfare related injuries, the remains displayed a few other pathologies. One individual, GT 18975, displayed osteophyte formation on the lumbar vertebrae. The presence of osteophytes on the articular margins of bone joints represents the early stages of osteoarthritis. Osteoarthritis develops as part of the

---

[38] Brothwell, *Digging up Bones.*
[39] Julie M. Saul, Lucas County Coroner's Office, Ohio, personal communication.
[40] Bass, *Human Osteology.*

normal aging process, but when present in young adults may be attributed to mechanical stress on the joint.[41] This individual was aged between 35 and 40 years; thus it is probable that the osteophytes observed on his spine were due to the normal aging process.

Infectious lesions were observed on two individuals: GT 19745A had slight periosteal reactions on the femur and tibia, and GT 19745B had an infection on the talus and calcaneus. In both cases the infections were localized and had been active at the time of death.

One case of cribra orbitalia was observed: GT 17704, a subadult aged 1.5 to 2 years of age. Two other individuals had intact frontal bones, but did not display the lesions of cribra orbitalia. No evidence of healing was observed on the affected individual. While thalassemia is a possible diagnosis for the lesion, the lack of additional cranial lesions suggests that iron deficiency anemia is a more like diagnosis.

Four fractured metatarsals were observed among the sample. Three of the fractures were found on GT 19745A and one fracture on GT 19747B. All four fractures had healed before the death of the individuals.

Two of the adult males displayed a bony exostosis on the posterior fibula head. The exostosis appears to be an osteochondroma or an occupational stress marker.

The dentition of the individuals displayed few pathologies. Only one dental caries was present out of the four individuals with teeth (1 of 40 teeth). No alveolar abscesses or pulp exposures were present on the two adult individuals with teeth. One of the two adults had slight calculus deposits on the teeth (10 of 28 teeth on the individual). Enamel defects were observed on one of the four individuals; an adult female had linear enamel hypoplasias on all four canines. No defects were observed on the deciduous teeth of the subadults. In general, few pathologies were observed among the dentition.

In conclusion, the Gritille skeletal sample described in this report represent a fragmentary collection of sixteen individuals, minimally. Most of the individuals probably died during a battle and/or destruction of the village. The sample was skewed toward young adult males (75% among the adults whose sex could be determined), although subadults and adult females were also represented. Several traumatic injuries were observed on the bones, including perimortem sword or ax wounds and fractures. Healed fractures of the foot bones were also common. Additional health problems observed included mild periosteal infections, cribra orbitalia, enamel hypoplasias, and dental caries. These conditions were found at relatively low frequencies, indicating the population had few sinificant health problems prior to the warfare that ended in the destruction of Gritille.

---

[41] Jurmain, "Stress and the Etiology of Osteoarthritis."

BIBLIOGRAPHY

Abu'l Fidā'. *Kitāb Taqwīm al-Buldān*. Paris: Imprimerie Royale, 1840.

Adams, Robert McC. *Heartland of Cities*. Chicago: University of Chicago Press, 1980.

—. "Tell Abū Sarīfa. A Sassanian-Islamic Ceramic Sequence from South Central Iraq." *Ars Orientalis* 8 (1970): 87–119.

Aghnides, Nicolas P. *Mohammedan Theories of Finance*. New York: AMS Press, 1969 [1916].

Ahrweiler, Hélène. "La frontière et les frontières de Byzance en Orient." *Actes du XIVe Congrès International des Études Byzantines*, 1:209–230. Bucharest: Editura Academiei Republicii Socialiste Romînia, 1974.

Ainsworth, William. *A Personal Narrative of the Euphrates Expedition*. London: Kegan, Paul, Trench, 1888.

Akkermans, Peter. "Lidar Excavation Notebook F/G/H 42, 1980–81." Manuscript. Heidelberg: Institute for Prehistoric Archeology of the University of Heidelberg.

Albert of Aachen (Albert d'Aix). *Histoire des croisades*. Edited by M. Guizot. Collection des mémoires relatifs à l'histoire de France, Vol. 20. Paris: J.-L.-J. Brière, 1824.

Algaze, Guillermo, ed. *Town and Country in Southeastern Anatolia*. Vol. 2, *The Stratigraphic Sequence at Kurban Höyük*. University of Chicago Oriental Institute Publications, Vol. 110. Chicago: Oriental Institute, 1991.

Allan, James W. "Incised Wares of Iran and Anatolia in the 11th and 12th Centuries." *Keramos* 64 (1974): 15–22.

Amouroux-Mourad, Monique. *Le comté d'Edesse*. Institut Français d'Archéologie du Proche-Orient. Bibliothèque Archéologique et Historique, Vol. 128. Paris: Librairie Orientaliste Paul Geuthner, 1988.

Anadolu Medeniyetleri (Anatolian Civilizations). Vol. 3. Ankara: Ministry of Tourism, 1983.

Angel, J. Lawrence. "Porotic Hyperostosis, Anemias, Malarias and Marshes in the Prehistoric Eastern Mediterranean." *Science* 153 (1966): 760–763.

Anonymous. "The First and Second Crusades from an Anonymous Syriac Chronicle." Translated by A. S. Tritton. *Journal of the Royal Asiatic Society* (1933): 69–101, 273–305.

Atalay, İbrahim. *Türkiye Vejetasyon Coğrafyasına Giriş*. Ege Üniversitesi Edebiyat Fakültesi Yayınları 19. İzmir: Ege University, 1983.

Azuar Ruiz, Rafael. "El Sur del Pais Valenciano. Una Posible Frontera en Epoca Almohade (Segunda Mitad del Siglo XII, Primera Mitad del Siglo XIII)." *Castrum* 4 (1992): 99–107.

Bakırer, Ö. "The Medieval Pottery and Baked Clay Objects." In *Korucutepe*, Vol. 3, edited by M. van Loon. Amsterdam: North Holland Publishing Company, 1980.

Balog, Paul. *Coinage of the Ayyubids*. Royal Numismatic Society Special Publication, No. 12. London: Royal Numismatic Society, 1980.

Banser, Ewald. *Die Türkei. Ein modern Geographie*. Berlin: Georg Westermann, 1919.

Bar Hebraeus. *The Chronography of Gregory Abu'l Faraj the Son of Aaron*. Edited and translated by E. A. W. Budge. London: Oxford University Press, 1932.

Bass, William M. *Human Osteology*. 3d ed. Columbia: Missouri Archaeological Society, 1987.

Bates, D. *Nomads and Farmers: A Study of the Yörük of Southeastern Turkey*. Anthropological Papers 52. Ann Arbor: University of Michigan, Museum of Anthropology, 1973.

Bates, Michael, and D. M. Metcalf. "Crusader Coinage with Arabic Inscriptions." In *A History of the Crusade*. Vol. 6, *The Impact of the Crusades on Europe*, edited by H. Hazard and N. Zacour, 421–473. Madison: University of Wisconsin Press, 1989.

Bazzana, André Pierre Guichard, and Philippe Sénac. "La frontière dans l'Espagne médiévale." *Castrum* 4 (1992): 35–59.

Beaumont, Peter, Gerald Blake, and J. Malcolm Wagstaff. *The Middle East: A Geographical Study*. London: John Wiley and Sons, 1976.

Bernus Taylor, Marthe. "The Islamic Glazed Pottery." In *The River Qoueiq, Northern Syria, and its Catchment*, edited by J. Matthers, 473–498. Oxford: British Archaeological Reports, 1981.

Bianquis, Thierry. "Les frontières de la Syrie au XIe siècle." *Castrum* 4 (1992): 135–150.

—. "L'ânier de village, le chevalier de la steppe, le cavalier de la citadelle, trois personnages de la transition en Syrie." In *Proceedings of the Fifth International Conference on the History of Bilad al-Sham. Bilad al-Sham During the Abbasid Period*, edited by Muhammad al-Bakhit and Robert Schick, 91–104. Amman: Ministry of Culture, 1991.

Biddick, K. "Pig Husbandry on the Peterborough Abbey Estate from the 12th to the 14th Century A.D." In *Animals and Archaeology* 4: *Husbandry in Europe*, edited by C. Grigson and J. Clutton-Brock. International Series No. 202. Oxford: British Archaeological Reports, 1984.

Blackman, M. James, and Scott Redford. "Calcareous Clay Glazed Ceramics from Gritille, Turkey." *Muqarnas* 11 (1994): 32–35.

Blaylock, Stuart, D. H. French, and G. D. Summers. " The Adıyaman Survey: An Interim Report." *Anatolian Studies* 40 (1990): 81–135.

Boessneck, J. "Osteological Differences Between Sheep (*Ovis aries Linne*) and Goat (*Capra hircus Linne*)." In *Science in Archaeology*, edited by D. Brothwell and E. S. Higgs. London: Thames and Hudson, 1969.

Boessneck, J., and A. von den Driesch. "Tierknochenfunde vom Korucutepe bei Elazığ in Ostanatolien." In *Korucutepe*, Vol. 1, edited by M. van Loon. Amsterdam: North Holland Publishing Company, 1975.

Bonner, Michael. "Some Observations Concerning the Early Development of Jihad on the Arab-Byzantine Frontier." *Studia Islamica* 75 (1992): 5–31.

Boone, J. "Defining and Measuring Midden Catchment." *American Anthropologist* 52 (1987): 336–345.

Bosworth, C. Edmund. "Byzantium and the Syrian Frontier in the Early Abbasid Period." In *Proceedings of the Fifth International Conference on the History of Bilad al-Sham. Bilad al-Sham During the Abbasid Period*, edited by Muhammad al-Bakhit and Robert Schick, 54–62. Amman: Ministry of Culture, 1991.

Bottema, S. "The Composition of Modern Charred Seed Assemblages." In *Plants and Ancient Man*, edited by W. van Zeist and W. A. Casparie, 207–212. Rotterdam: A. A. Balkema, 1984.

Brothwell, D. R. *Digging up Bones*. 3d ed. Ithaca: Cornell University Press, 1981.

Bryer, Anthony. "The Historian's *Digenes Akrites*." In *Digenes Akrites. New Approaches to Byzantine Heroic Poetry*, edited by Roderick Beaton and David Ricks, 93–102. London: Variorum, 1993.

Buckingham, J. S. *Travels in Mesopotamia*. London: Henry Colburn, 1827.

Budge, E. A. W. *Assyrian Sculptures in the British Museum*. Oxford: Oxford University Press, 1914.

Bulliet, Richard. *Conversion to Islam in the Medieval Period*. Cambridge, Mass.: Harvard University Press, 1979.

Bulut, Lale. "Samsat İslami Devir Sırsız ve Tek Renk Sırlı Seramikleri" (Unglazed and Monochrome Glazed Islamic Period Ceramics from Samsat). Ph.D. diss., Ege University, 1991.

Cahen, Claude. "Contribution à l'histoire du Diyār Bakr au quatorzième siècle." *Journal asiatique* 243 (1955): 65–100.

—. "L'évolution de l'iqtā' du IXe au XIIIe siècle." *Annales. Économies, sociétés, civilisations* 8 (1953): 25–52.

—. "Les tribus turques d'Asie Occidentale pendant la période seljukide." *Wiener Zeitschrift für die Kunde des Morgenlandes* 51 (1948–52): 178–187.

—. "Le régime rural syrien au temps de la domination franque." *Bulletin de la Faculté des Lettres de Strasbourg* 29 (1951): 286–310.

—. "Le service de l'irrigation en Iraq au début du XIe siècle." *Bulletin d'études orientales* 13 (1949–51): 117–143.

—. "La première pénétration turque en Asie Mineure." *Byzantion* 18 (1946–48): 5–67.

—. *La Syrie du nord.* Paris: Paul Geuthner, 1940.

—. "Le Diyār Bakr au temps des premiers Urtukides." *Journal asiatique* 237 (1935): 219–276.

—. "La Djazira au milieu du treizième siècle." *Revue des Études Islamiques* 8 (1934): 109–128.

Canard, Marius. "Al-ʿAwāṣim." *The Encyclopaedia of Islam.* Vol. 1. 2d ed. Leiden: E. J. Brill, 1960.

—. *Histoire de la dynastie des Hamdanides de Jazira et de Syrie.* Paris: Presses universitaires de France, 1951.

—. *Byzance et les arabes.* Brussels: Éditions de l'Institut de Philologie et d'Histoire Orientales, 1935.

Castagnoli, F. *Orthogonal Town Planning in Antiquity.* Cambridge, Mass.: MIT Press, 1971.

Chesney, F. R. *The Expedition for the Survey of the Rivers Euphrates and Tigris.* London: Longman, Brown, Green, and Longmans, 1850.

Crow, J. G., and D. H. French. "New Research on the Euphrates Frontier in Turkey." In *Roman Frontier Studies 1979,* edited by W. Hanson and L. Keppie, 903–912. Oxford: British Archaeological Reports, 1980.

Dagron, Gilbert. "Guérilla, places fortes et villages ouverts à la frontière orientale de Byzance vers 950." *Castrum* 3 (1988): 43–48.

Dahl, G., and A. Hjort. *Having Herds: Pastoral Herd Growth and Household Economy.* Stockholm: Department of Anthropology, University of Stockholm, 1976.

Dalliere-Benelhadj, Valérie. "Le 'chateau' en al-Andalus: un problème de terminologie." *Castrum* 1 (1983): 63–67.

Davis, Peter, ed. *Flora of Turkey.* 10 vols. Edinburgh: University Press, 1965–1988.

Day, Florence. "The Islamic Finds at Tarsus." *Asia* 41 (1941): 143–148.

Dédéyan, Gérard. "Razzias 'turcomanes' et contre-razzias arméniennes dans le Diyâr Bakr au début du XIIe siècle: les Banou Bôgousag de Sewawerak contre les Mamikonian de Karkar." *Res orientales* 6 (1994): 49–58.

Dennis, George. *Three Byzantine Military Treatises.* Washington, D.C.: Dumbarton Oaks, 1985.

Dewdney, J. C. *Turkey, An Introductory Geography.* New York: Chatto and Windus, 1971.

Dörner, F. K., and Theresa Goell. *Arsameia am Nymphaios.* Berlin: Gebr. Mann, 1963.

Dörner, F. K., and R. Naumann. *Forschungen in Kommagene.* Istanbuler Forschungen 10. Berlin: Deutsches Archäologisches Institut, 1939.

Doruk, Seyhan. "Horis Kale Kazıları" (Horis Kale Excavations). In *II. Kazı Sonuçları Toplantısı,* 167–169. Ankara: İşletme Müdürlüğü, 1981.

Dozy, R. *Supplément aux dictionnaires arabes.* 3d ed. Leiden: E. J. Brill, 1967.

Dussaud, René. *Topographie historique de la Syrie antique et médiévale.* Paris: Paul Geuthner, 1927.

Edwards, Robert. *Armenian Fortifications of Cilicia.* Washington, D.C.: Dumbarton Oaks, 1987.

El-Najjar, Mahmoud Y., and K. Richard McWilliams. *Forensic Anthropology.* Springfield, Ill.: Charles C. Thomas, 1978.

Ellis, Richard. "Gritille 1984." In *VII. Kazı Sonuçları Toplantısı,* 261–270. Ankara: Ministry of Tourism, 1985.

—. "The 1983 Season at Gritille." In *VI. Kazı Sonuçları Toplantısı,* 65–70. Ankara: Ministry of Tourism, 1984.

—. "The Gritille Project." In *V. Kazı Sonuçları Toplantısı,* 117–121. Ankara: Ministry of Tourism, 1983.

Ellis, Richard, and Mary Voigt. "1981 Excavations at Gritille, Turkey." *American Journal of Archaeology* 86 (1982): 319–332.

Equini Schneider, Eugenia. *Malatya*-II. *Rapporto Preliminare Delle Campagne 1963–1968. Il Livello Romano Bizantino e le Testimonianze Islamiche.* Orientis Antiqui Collectio 10. Rome: Centro per le Antichità e la Storia dell'Arte del Vicino Oriente, 1970.

Farmayan, Hafez, and Elton Daniel, eds. and trans. *A Shi'ite Pilgrimage to Mecca 1885–1886. The Safarnameh of Mirza Mohammad Hosayn Farahani.* Austin: University of Texas Press, 1990.

Felix, Wolfgang. *Byzanz und die islamische Welt im Frühern 11. Jahrhundert.* Vienna: Verlag der Österreichischen Akademie der Wissenschaften, 1981.

Fiey, Jean Maurice. "The Syriac Population of the Thughur al-Shamiya and the 'Awasim, and its Relation with the Byzantines and Muslims." In *Proceedings of the Fifth International Conference on the History of Bilad al-Sham. Bilad al-Sham During the Abbasid Period*, edited by Muhammad al-Bakhit and Robert Schick, 45–53. Amman: Ministry of Culture, 1991.

Finnegan, Michael. Non-metric Variation of the Infracranial Skeleton. *Journal of Anatomy* 125 (1978): 23–37.

Foss, Clive. "The Defenses of Asia Minor Against the Turks." *The Greek Orthodox Theological Review* 27 (1982): 145–205.

French, D. H. "New Research on the Euphrates Frontier: Supplementary Notes 1 and 2." In *Armies and Frontiers in Roman and Byzantine Anatolia*, edited by S. Mitchell, 71–101. Oxford: British Archaeological Reports, 1983.

French, D. H., J. Moore, and H. F. Russell. "Excavations at Tille 1979–1982. An Interim Report." *Anatolian Studies* 32 (1982): 161–187.

Georgiev, G. G. "Old Bulgarian Writing Implements from Pliska and Preslav." *Arkeologya* 22 (1980).

Gibb, H. A. R. "Notes on the Arabic Materials for the History of the Early Crusades." *Bulletin of the School of Oriental and African Studies* 7 (1933–35): 739–754.

—. *The Damascus Chronicle of the Crusades.* London: Luzac & Co., 1932.

Gill, N. T., and K. C. Vear. *Dicotyledonous Crops, Agricultural Botany*, Vol. 1. 3d ed. London: Duckworth, 1980.

Goell, Theresa. "Samosata Archeological Excavations, Turkey, 1967." In *National Geographic Society Research Reports 1967*, edited by P. Oehser. Washington, D.C.: National Geographic Society, 1974.

Goell, Theresa, and K. Otto-Dorn. "Keramikfunde aus dem Mittelalter und der frühosmanischen Zeit." In *Arsameia am Nymphaios*, by F. K. Dörner and T. Goell. Berlin: Gebr. Mann, 1963.

Golvin, Lucien. "A la recherche de la cité médiévale de Bâlis." In *Le moyen Euphrate*, edited by J.-Cl. Margueron, 389–396. Leiden: E. J. Brill, 1980.

Goodman, Alan H., George J. Armelagos, and Jerome C. Rose. "Enamel Hypoplasias as Indicators of Stress in Three Prehistoric Populations from Illinois." *Human Biology* 52 (1980): 515–528.

Goose, Denys H. "Dental Measurement: An Assessment of its Value in Anthropological Studies." In *Dental Anthropology*, edited by D. R. Brothwell, 125–148. New York: Macmillan, 1963.

Grant, A. "The Use of Tooth Wear as a Guide to the Age of Domestic Ungulates." In *Ageing and Sexing Animal Bones from Archaeological Sites*, edited by B. Wilson, C. Grigson, and S. Payne, 91–108. British series No. 109. Oxford: British Archaeological Reports, 1982.

Grayson, D. *Quantitative Zooarchaeology.* New York: Academic Press, 1984.

Great Britain. *Turkey. Naval Intelligence Division Handbook.* London, 1942.

Grigson, C. "Porridge and Pannage, Pig Husbandry in Neolithic England." In *Archaeological Aspects of Woodland Ecology*, edited by S. Limbrey and M. Bell, 297–304. Oxford, 1982.

Haase, Claus-Peter. "Madinat al-Far/Hisn Maslama: First Archaeological Soundings at the Site and the History of an Umayyad Domain in Abbasid Times." In *Proceedings of the Fifth International Conference on the History of Bilad al-Sham. Bilad al-Sham During the Abbasid Period*, edited by Muhammad al-Bakhit and Robert Schick, 206–225. Amman: Ministry of Culture, 1991.

Haldon, J. F., and Hugh Kennedy. "The Arab-Byzantine Frontier in the Eighth and Ninth Centuries: Military Organisation and Society in the Borderlands." *Zbornik Radova Vizantoloskog Instituta* 19 (1980): 79–116.

Harrison, D. *The Mammals of Arabia.* Vol. 11, *Carnivora, Artiodactyla, Hyracoidea.* London, 1968.

Hartmann, R. "al-Ḥadath al-Ḥamrā." *Istanbuler Forschungen* 17 (1950): 40–50.

Harvey, Alan. *Economic Expansion in the Byzantine Empire, 900–1200.* Cambridge: Cambridge University Press, 1989.

Hauptmann, Harald. "Die Grabungen auf dem Lidar Höyük, 1979." In *Lower Euphrates Project 1978–1979 Activities*, 257–263. Middle East Technical University Lower Euphrates Project Publications Series 1, No. 3. Ankara: Middle East Technical University, 1987.

—. "Lidar Höyük, 1981." *Türk Arkeoloji Dergisi* 26 (1983): 93–103.

Hellenkemper, Hansgerd. *Burgen der Kreuzritterzeit in der Grafschaft Edessa und im Königreich Kleinarmenien*. Bonn: Rudolf Habelt, 1976.

—. "Zur mittelalterlichen Landschaftsgeschichte zwischen Tauros und Euphrat." *Antike Welt* 6 (1975): 82–85.

Higham, C. F. W. "Stock Rearing as a Cultural Factor in Prehistoric Europe." *Proceedings of the Prehistoric Society* 33 (1967): 84–103.

Higham, C. F. W., and M. A. Message. "An Assessment of a Prehistoric Technique of Bovine Husbandry." In *Science in Archaeology*, edited by D. Brothwell and E. S. Higgs. London: Thames and Hudson, 1969.

Hild, Friedrich. *Das byzantinische Strassensystem in Kappadokien*. Tabula Imperii Byzantini 2. Vienna: Verlag der Österrechischen Akademie der Wissenschaften, 1977.

Hillenbrand, Carole. "The History of the Jazīra, 1100–1250: A Short Introduction." In *The Art of Syria and the Jazīra, 1100–1250*, edited by Julian Raby, 9–19. Oxford: Oxford University Press, 1985.

—. "The Establishment of Artuqid Power in the Diyār Bakr in the Twelfth Century." *Studia Islamica* 54 (1981): 129–153.

Hillman, Gordon C. "Interpretation of Archaeological Plant Remains: The Application of Ethnographic Models from Turkey." In *Plants and Ancient Man*, edited by W. van Zeist and W. A. Casparie, 1–41. Rotterdam: A. A. Balkema, 1984.

Hinton, Robert J. "Form and Patterning of Anterior Tooth Wear Among Aboriginal Human Groups." *American Journal of Physical Anthropology* 54 (1981): 555–564.

Hinz, W. "Farsakh." *Encyclopaedia of Islam*. 2d ed. Leiden: E. J. Brill, 1965.

Hodgson, Marshall. *The Venture of Islam*. Chicago: University of Chicago, 1974.

Hole, Frank, Kent V. Flannery, and James A. Neely. *Prehistory and Human Ecology of the Deh Luran Plain*. Memoir 1. Ann Arbor: University of Michigan, Museum of Anthropology, 1969.

Honigmann, Ernst. *Le couvent de Barṣaumā et le patriarcat jacobite d'Antioche et de Syrie*. Louvain: L. Durbecq, 1954.

—. *Die Ostgrenze des byzantinischen Reiches*. Brussels: Editions de l'Institut de Philologie et d'Histoire Orientales, 1935.

Hook, David. "*Digenes Akrites* and the Old Spanish Epics." In *Digenes Akrites. New Approaches to Byzantine Heroic Poetry* , edited by Roderick Beaton and David Ricks, 73–85. London: Variorum, 1993.

Howells, W. W. *Cranial Variation in Man*. Papers of the Peabody Museum of Archaeology and Ethnology, Vol. 67. Cambridge, Mass.: Harvard University, 1973.

Humann, Karl, and Otto Puchstein. *Reisen in Kleinasien und Nordsyrien*. Berlin: Dietrich Reimer, 1890.

Humphreys, R. Stephen. *From Saladin to the Mongols*. Albany, N.Y.: SUNY Press, 1973.

Huntington, Ellsworth. "The Valley of the Upper Euphrates River and its People." *Bulletin of the American Geographical Society* 34 (1902): 301–310, 384–393.

Ibn al-'Adīm. *Bughyat al-Ṭalab fī Tārīkh Ḥalab*. Edited and translated by Ali Sevim. *Biyografilerle Selçuklular Tarihi*. Ankara: Türk Tarih Kurumu, 1982.

—. *Zubdat al-Ḥalab min Tārīkh Ḥalab*. Damascus: Institut Français, 1954.

Ibn al-Athīr. *Al-Kāmil fī al-Tārīkh*. Beirut: Dar Sader, 1967.

—. *Al-Tārīkh al-Bāhir fī al-Dawlat al-Atābakiyya*. Cairo: Dār al-Kutub al-Ḥadītha, 1963.

Ibn al-Azraq al-Fāriqī. *Tārīkh Mayyāfāriqīn wa Āmid* (*A Muslim Principality in Crusader Times. The Early Artuqid State*). Edited and translated by Carole Hillenbrand. Leiden: Nederlands Historisch-Archaeologisch Instituut te Istanbul, 1990.

Ibn al-Faqīh al-Hamadānī. *Kitāb al-Buldān*. Leiden: E. J. Brill, 1889.

Ibn al-Furāt. *Tārīkh al-Duwal wa'l-Mulūk* (*Ayyubids, Mamelukes and Crusaders*). Edited and translated by U. and M. C. Lyons. Cambridge: Cambridge University Press, 1971.

Ibn al-Qalānisī. *Dhayl Tārīkh Dimashq*. Leiden: E. J. Brill, 1908.

Ibn Bībī. *Das Seltschukengeschichte des Ibn Bibi*. Edited and translated by Herbert Duda. Copenhagen: Munksgaard, 1959.

Ibn Ḥawqal. *Kitāb Ṣūrat al-Arḍ*. Beirut: Dār Maktabat al-Ḥayāt, 1979.

Ibn Jubayr. *Riḥla*. Beirut: Dar Sader, 1964.

Ibn Khallikān. *Wafayāt al-'Ayān*. Beirut: Dār al-Thiqāfa, 1968.

Ibn Khurdādhbih. *Kitāb al-Masālik wa'l-Mamālik*. Leiden: E. J. Brill, 1889.

Ibn Rusta. *Kitāb al-'Alāq al-Nafīsa*. Leiden: E. J. Brill, 1892.

Ibn Shaddād. *al-'Alāq al-Khaṭīra fī Dhikr Umarā*

al-Shām waʾl-Jazīra (*Description de la Syrie du nord*). Translated by A. M. Eddé-Terasse. Damascus: Institut Français, 1984.

Ibn Waṣil. *Mufarrij al-Kurūb fī Akhbār Banī Ayyūb*. Cairo: Government Press, 1957.

al-Idrīsī. *Géographie d'Édrisi*. Translated by P. Amédée Jaubert. Paris: L'Imprimérie Royale, 1840 [1154].

—. *Kitāb Rujār*. Rome: IsMEO, 1976.

Isaac, Benjamin. *The Limits of Empire. The Roman Army in the East*. Oxford: Clarendon Press, 1990.

Ismail, Karim-Elmahi. *Das islamische Steuersystem vom 7. bis 12. Jahrhundert n. Chr. unter besonderer Berücksichtigung seiner Umsetzung in den eroberten Gebieten*. Wirtschafts- und Rechtsgeschichte 17. Köln: Müller Botermann Verlag, 1989.

Işık, Cengiz. "Horis Kale Kazıları 1981" (Horis Kale Excavations 1981). In *IV. Kazı Sonuçları Toplantısı*, 315–319. Ankara: Hacıtepe Sosyal ve İdari Bilimler, 1983.

al-Iṣṭakhrī. *Kitāb al-Masālik waʾl-Mamālik*. Leiden: E. J. Brill, 1927.

Jankowska, N. B. "Some Problems of the Economy of the Assyrian Empire." In *Ancient Mesopotamia. Socio-Economic History*, edited by I. M. Diakonoff, pp. 253–276. Moscow: Nauka, 1969.

Jones, A. H. M. *The Cities of the Eastern Roman Provinces*. Reprint. Amsterdam: Adolf M. Hakkert, 1983.

Jurmain, Robert D. "Stress and the Etiology of Osteoarthritis." *American Journal of Physical Anthropology* 46 (1977): 353–366.

Karaca, Özgen. "Pirot Höyük 1983 Kazıları" (1983 Pirot Höyük Excavations). In *VI. Kazı Sonuçları Toplantısı*, 37–46. Ankara: Ministry of Tourism, 1984.

—. "Pirot Höyük 1980 Çalışmaları" (1980 Work at Pirot Höyük). In *III. Kazı Sonuçları Toplantısı*, 109–116. Ankara: n.p., 1981.

Keddie, Nikki. "Material Culture, Technology, and Geography: Toward a Holistic Comparative Study of the Middle East." In *Comparing Muslim Societies: Knowledge and the State in a World Civilization*, edited by J. Cole, 31–62. Ann Arbor: University of Michigan, 1992.

Kennedy, Hugh. "Nomads and Settled People in Bilad al-Sham in the Third/Ninth and Fourth/Tenth Centuries." In *Proceedings of the Fifth International Conference on the History of Bilad al-Sham. Bilad al-Sham During the Abbasid Period*, edited by Muhammad al-Bakhit and Robert Schick, 105–113. Amman: Ministry of Culture, 1991.

Kennedy, Kenneth A. R. "Skeletal Markers of Occupational Stress." In *Reconstruction of Life from the Skeleton*, edited by Mehmet Yasar Iscan and Kenneth A. R. Kennedy, 129–160. New York: Alan R. Liss, Inc., 1989.

Kervran, Monique. "Les niveaux islamiques du secteur oriental du tépé de l'Apadana." *Cahiers de la Délégation Archéologique Française en Iran* 7 (1977): 75–165.

Killen, J. T. "The Wool Industry of Crete in the Last Bronze Age." *Annual of the British School at Athens* (1964): 5.

Koster, H. "The Ecology of Pastoralism in Relation to Changing Patterns of Land Use in the Northeast Peloponnese." Ph.D diss., Univ. of Pennsylvania, 1977.

Lane, Arthur. "Mediaeval Finds from al Mina in North Syria." *Archaeologia* 87 (1938): 19–78.

Lane, E. W. *An Arabic-English Lexicon*. Reprint ed. Beirut: Librairie du Liban, 1980.

Laurent, J. "Byzance et Antioche sous le Curopalate Philarète." *Revue des études arméniennes* 9 (1929): 61–72, 148–159.

—. "Des grecs aux croisés. Étude sur l'histoire d'Édesse entre 1071 et 1098." *Byzantion* 1 (1924).

Lay, D. "A Study of the Mammals of Iran Resulting from the Street Expedition of 1962–63." *Fieldiana Zoology* 54 (1967): 223.

Legge, A. "The Agricultural Economy." In *Grimes Graves, Norfolk: Excavations 1971–1972*, edited by R. Mercer, 79–103. Archaeological Reports 11. London: Department of Environment, 1981.

Lightfoot, C. S. "Tilli, A Late Roman *Equites* Fort on the Tigris?" In *The Defence of the Roman and Byzantine East*, edited by Philip Freeman and David Kennedy, 509–529. Oxford: British Archaeological Reports, 1986.

Lilie, Ralph. *Byzanz und die Kreuzfahrerstaaten*. Munich: Wilhelm Fink, 1981.

Lovag, Zsuzsa. "Byzantine Type Reliquary Pectoral Crosses in the Hungarian National Museum." *Folia Archaeologica* 22 (1971).

Lovejoy, C. Owen, Richard S. Meindl, Thomas R. Pryzbeck, and Robert P. Mensforth. "Chronological Metamorphosis of the Auricular Surface of the Ilium: A New Method for the Determination of Adult Skeletal Age at Death." *American Journal of Physical Anthropology* 68 (1985): 15–28.

Lowick, Nicholas, S. Bendall, and P. D. Whitting. *The "Mardin" Hoard.* London: A. H. Baldwin, 1977.

Luckenbill, Daniel David. *Ancient Records of Assyria and Babylonia.* Chicago: University of Chicago Press, 1926.

Lyman, R. L. "On the Analysis of Vertebrate Mortality Profiles: Sample Size, Mortality Type, and Hunting Pressure." *American Anthropologist* 52 (1987): 125–142.

Mackin, R. "Dynamics of Damage Caused by Wild Boar to Different Agricultural Crops." *Acta Theriologica* 15 (1970): 447–458.

Markwart, Jos. *Südarmenien und die Tigrisquellen nach griechischen und arabischen Geographen.* Vienna: Mechitharisten Buchdruckerei, 1930.

Martin, M. "Conservation at the Local Level: Individual Perceptions and Group Mechanisms." In *Desertification and Development Dryland Ecology in Social Perspective*, edited by B. Spooner and H. S. Mann. London: Academic Press, 1982.

al-Masʿūdī. *Murūj al-Dhahab wa Maʿādin al-Jawhar.* Beirut: Dār al-Andalus, 1975.

—. *Kitāb al-Tanbīh waʾl-Ashraf.* Leiden: E. J. Brill, 1894.

Mason, Robert. "Defining Syrian Stonepaste Ceramics: Petrographic Analysis of Pottery from Maʿarrat al-Nuʿman." In *Islamic Art in the Ashmolean Museum*, Vol. 1, edited by J. Allan. Oxford: Oxford University Press, 1995.

Mason, Robert, and Edward Keall. "The Abbasid Glazed Wares of Siraf and the Basra Connection: Petrographic Analysis." *Iran* 29 (1991): 51–66.

—. "Petrography of Islamic Pottery from Fustat." *Journal of the American Research Institute in Egypt* 27 (1990): 165–184.

—. "Islamic Ceramics; Petrography and Provenance." In *Proceedings of the 26th International Archaeometry Symposium*, edited by R. M. Farquhar et al., 184–187. Toronto: University of Toronto, 1988.

Matthew of Edessa. *Armenia and the Crusades Tenth to Twelfth Centuries. The Chronicle of Matthew of Edessa.* Edited and translated by Ara Edmond Dostourian. Lanham, Md.: University Press of America, 1993.

Maxwell-Hyslop, K. R. "Assyrian Sources of Iron: A Preliminary Survey of the Historical and Geographical Evidence." *Iraq* 36 (1974):139–154.

McNicoll, Anthony. *Taşkun Kale. Keban Rescue Excavations Eastern Turkey.* Oxford: British Archaeological Reports, 1983.

Meadow, R. "Animal Bones: Problems for the Archaeologist Together with Some Possible Solutions." *Paléorient* 6 (1980): 65–77.

Meindl, Richard, and C. Owen Lovejoy. "Ectocranial Suture Closure: A Revised Method for the Determination of Skeletal Age at Death Based on the Lateral-Anterior Sutures." *American Journal of Physical Anthropology* 68 (1985): 57–66.

Metcalf, D. M. "The Gritille Hoard of Coins of Lucca and Valence." *Numismatic Chronicle* 147 (1987): 92–95.

—. *Coinage of the Crusades and the Latin East.* London: Royal Numismatic Society, 1983.

Meteoroloji Bülteni. *Ortalama ve Ekstrem Kiymetler Meteoroloji Bülteni.* Ankara: Devlet Meteoroloji İşleri Genel Müdürlüğü, 1974.

Michael the Syrian. *Chronique de Michel le Syrien patriarche jacobite d'Antioche.* Edited and translated by J.-B. Chabot. Paris: E. LeRoux, 1899–1914.

Miller, Naomi F. "Farming and Herding Along the Euphrates: Environmental Constraint and Cultural Choice (Fourth to Second Millennia B.C.)." In MASCA Research Papers in Science and Archaeology, Vol. 14. Philadelphia: University of Pennsylvania Museum, in press.

—. "The Crusader Period Fortress: Some Archaeobotanical Samples from Medieval Gritille." *Anatolica* 18 (1992): 87–99.

—. "The Near East." In *Progress in Old World Palaeoethnobotany*, edited by W. van Zeist, K. Wasylikowa, and K.-E. Behre, 133–160. Rotterdam: A. A. Balkema, 1991.

—. "Clearing Land for Farmland and Fuel: Archaeobotanical Studies of the Ancient Near East." In *Economy and Settlement in the Near East: Analyses of Ancient Sites and Materials*, edited by N. F. Miller, 71–78. MASCA Research Papers in Science and Archaeology, supp. to Vol. 7. Philadelphia: University of Pennsylvania Museum, 1990.

—. "The Crusader Period Fortress: Some Archaeobotanical Samples from Medieval Gritille." MASCA Ethnobotanical Report 3. On file at the Museum Applied Science Center for Archaeology. Philadelphia: University of Pennsylvania Museum, 1989.

—. "Ratios in Paleoethnobotanical Analysis." In *Current Paleoethnobotany*, edited by C. A. Hastorf and V. S. Popper, 72–85. Chicago: University of Chicago Press, 1988.

—. "Gritille Charcoal: Preliminary Analysis." MASCA Ethnobotanical Laboratory Report 1. On file at the Museum Applied Science Center for Archaeology. Philadelphia: University of Pennsylvania Museum, 1987.

—. "Vegetation and Land Use." *Anatolica* 13 (1986): 85–89, 119–120.

—. "The Interpretation of Some Carbonized Cereal Remains as Remnants of Dung Cake Fuel." *Bulletin on Sumerian Agriculture* 1 (1984): 45–47.

Miller, Naomi F., and Tristine L. Smart. "Intentional Burning of Dung as Fuel: A Mechanism for the Incorporation of Charred Seeds into the Archeological Record." *Journal of Ethnobiology* 4 (1984): 15–28.

Miquel, André. "La perception de la frontière chez les géographes arabes d'avant l'an mil." *Castrum* 4 (1992): 129–133.

—. *La géographie humaine du monde musulman.* Paris: Mouton, 1967.

Mitchell, Stephen. *Aşvan Kale. Keban Rescue Excavations, Eastern Anatolia.* Oxford: British Archaeological Reports, 1980.

von Moltke, Helmut. *Briefe über Zustände und Begebenheiten in der Türkei.* Berlin: E. S. Mittler, 1893.

Moore, John. *Tille Höyük 1. The Medieval Period.* Ankara: The British Institute of Archaeology at Ankara, 1993.

Moore-Jansen, Peer H., and Richard L. Jantz. *Data Collection Procedures for Forensic Skeletal Material.* Report of Investigations, No. 48. Knoxville: Department of Anthropology, University of Tennessee, 1989.

Moorrees, Coenraad F. A., Elizabeth A. Fanning, and Edward E. Hunt, Jr. "Age Variation of Formation Stages for Ten Permanent Teeth." *Journal of Dental Research* 12 (1963): 1490–1502.

Mudar, K. "Early Dynastic III Animal Utilization at Lagash: A Report on the Fauna of Tell al Hiba." *Journal of the Near Eastern Society* 41 (1982): 26.

al-Muqaddasī. *Aḥsan al-Taqāsim fī Maʿrifaʾl-Aqālīm.* Leiden: E. J. Brill, 1906.

Nesbitt, Mark, and Geoffrey D. Summers. "Some Recent Discoveries of Millet (*Panicum miliaceum* [L.] and *Setaria italica* [L.] P. Beauv.) at Excavations in Turkey and Iran." *Anatolian Studies* 38 (1988): 85–97.

Noddle, Barbara. "A Comparison of the Animal Bones from Eight Medieval Sites in Southern England." In *Archaeozoological Studies*, edited by A. T. Clason, pp. 248–260. Amsterdam: Elsevier, 1975.

Nöldeke, Arnold. "Der Euphrat von Gerger bis Djerebis (Djerablus)." *Petermanns Geographische Mitteilungen* (1920): 15–20, 53–56.

Ocak, A. Yaşar. *La révolte de Baba Resul ou la formation de l'hétérodoxie musulmane en Anatolie au XIIIe siècle.* Ankara: Türk Tarih Kurumu, 1989.

Öğün, Baki. "Horis Kale Kazıları, 1978–1979" (Horis Kale Excavations 1978–1979). In *Lower Euphrates Project 1978–1979 Activities*, 145–152. Middle East Technical University Lower Euphrates Project Publications Series 1, No. 3. Ankara: Middle East Technical University, 1987.

Oikonomidès, Nicolas. "L'organisation de la frontière orientale de Byzance aux Xe-XIe siècles et le Taktikon de l'Escorial." *Actes du XIVe Congrès International des Études Byzantines*, 1:285–302. Bucharest: Editura Academiei Republicii Socialiste România, 1974.

Olivier, Georges. *Practical Anthropology.* Springfield, Ill.: Charles C. Thomas, 1969.

Öney, Gönül. "Pottery from the Samosata Excavations, 1978–81." In *The Art of the Saljuqs in Iran and Anatolia*, edited by R. Hillenbrand, 286–294. Costa Mesa, Calif.: Mazda Publishers, 1994.

—. "1978–79 Yılı Samsat Kazılarında Bulunan İslam Devri Buluntularıyla İlk Haber" (Preliminary Report on the Islamic Period Finds from 1978–79 Excavations at Samsat). *Arkeoloji-Sanat Tarihi Dergisi* 1 (1982): 71–80.

Orhonlu, Cengiz, and Turgut Işıksal. "Dicle ve Fırat Nehirlerinde Nakliyat" (Transport on the Tigris and Euphrates Rivers). *Tarih Dergisi* 12 (1961): 77–102.

Ortega, A. "Basic Technology: Lime and its Production." *Mimar* 17 (1985): 77–81.

Ortner, Donald J., and Walter G. J. Putschar. *Identification of Pathological Conditions in Hu-*

man Skeletal Remains. Washington, D.C.: Smithsonian Institution Press, 1981.

Özdoğan, Mehmet. *Lower Euphrates Basin 1977 Survey*. Publications series 1, No. 2. Ankara: Middle East Technical University, 1977.

Özgüç, Nimet. "Sümeysat Definesi" (The Samsat Treasure). *Belleten* 49 (1985): 441–450.

Pamir, Hamit. *Explanatory Text of the Geological Map of Turkey: Hatay*. Ankara: Maden, Tetkik ve Arama Enstitüsü Yayinlari, 1975.

Parker, S. Thomas. *Romans and Saracens. A History of the Arabian Frontier*. Winona Lake, Ind.: Eisenbrauns, 1986.

Payne, S. "Kill-Off Patterns in Sheep and Goats: The Mandibles from Aşvan Kale." *Anatolian Studies* 23 (1973): 281–303.

Pertusi, A. "Tra Storia e Leggenda: Akrítai e Ghâzi sulla Frontiera Orientale di Bisanzio." *Actes du XIVe Congrès International des Études Byzantines*, 1: 237–283. Bucharest: Editura Academiei Republicii Socialiste România, 1974.

Pesez, Jean-Marie. "Archéologie et stratification culturelle en Italie méridionale." *Castrum* 4 (1992): 253–257.

Ploug, Gunhild, et al. *Hama. Fouilles et recherches 1931–38*. Vol. 4, pt. 3, *Les petits objets médiévaux sauf les verreries et poteries*. Copenhagen: National Museet, 1969.

Porteous, John. "Crusader Coinage with Greek or Latin Inscriptions." In *A History of the Crusades*. Vol. 6, *The Impact of the Crusades on Europe*, edited by H. Hazard and N. Zacour, 354–420. Madison: University of Wisconsin Press, 1989.

—. "The Early Coinage of the Counts of Edessa." *Numismatic Chronicle* 15 (1975): 169–182.

Porter, Venetia. *Medieval Syrian Pottery*. Oxford: Ashmolean Museum, 1981.

Porter, Venetia, and Oliver Watson. "Tell Minis' Wares." In *Syria and Iran. Three Studies in Medieval Ceramics*, edited by J. Allan and C. Roberts, 175–248. Oxford: Oxford University Press, 1987.

Poujoulat, Baptistin. *Voyage à Constantinople, dans l'Asie Mineure, en Mesopotamie*. Brussels: J. Gregoir, V. Wouters, & Co., 1841.

Pringle, Denys. "Medieval Pottery from Caesarea: The Crusader Period." *Levant* 17 (1985): 171–202.

Puchstein, Otto. "Bericht über eine Reise in Kurdistan." *Sitzungberichte der königliche preussichen Akademie der Wissenschaften zu Berlin* 1 (1883): 29–64.

Puglisi, S. M., and P. Meriggi. *Malatya*-I. Rome: Centro per le Antichità dell'Arte del Vicino Oriente, 1964.

Redding, R. "The Role of the Pig in the Subsistence System of Ancient Egypt: A Parable on the Potential of Faunal Data." In *Animal Use and Culture Change*, edited by P. Crabtree and K. Ryan, 20–30. MASCA Research Papers in Science and Archaeology, Vol. 8. Philadelphia: University of Pennsylvania Museum, 1991.

—. "Decision Making in Subsistence Herding of Sheep and Goats in the Middle East." Ph.D. diss., University of Michigan, 1981.

Redford, Scott. "Medieval Ceramics from Samsat, Turkey." *Archéologie islamique* 5 (1995): 55–70.

—. "Ayyubid Glass from Samsat, Turkey." *Journal of Glass Studies* 36 (1994): 81–91.

—. "The Ceramic Sequence from Medieval Gritille, Southeast Turkey." Ph.D. diss., Harvard University, 1989.

—. "Excavations at Gritille (1982–1984): The Medieval Period. A Preliminary Report." *Anatolian Studies* 36 (1986): 103–136 and plates.

Redford, Scott, and M. James Blackman. "Luster and Fritware Production and Distribution in Medieval Syria." *Journal of Field Archaeology* 24 (1997), in press.

Republic of Turkey. *Köy Envanter Etudlerine Göre Adıyaman* (Village Inventory Studies of Adıyaman Province). Konya, 1967.

—. *Köy Envanter Etudlerine Göre Urfa* (Village Inventory Studies of Urfa Province). Konya, 1967.

Rice, D. S. "Studies in Medieval Harran I." *Anatolian Studies* 2 (1952): 36–84.

Riis, P., and V. Poulsen. *Hama. Fouilles et recherches 1931–1938*. Vol. 4, pt. 2. Copenhagen: National Museet, 1957.

Rogers, J. Michael. "Mediaeval Pottery at Apamaea in the 1976 and 1977 Seasons." In *Apamée de Syrie*, edited by J. Balty, 261–278. Brussels: Centre belge de recherches archéologiques Apamée de Syrie, 1984.

—. " Apamaea. The Mediaeval Pottery. A Preliminary Report." In *Apamée de Syrie. Bilan des recherches archéologiques 1969–71*, edited by J. and J. Ch. Balty, 253–270. Brussels: Centre belge de recherches archéologiques Apamée de Syrie, 1972.

Rosser, John. "The Role of Fortifications in the

Defense of Asia Minor Against the Arabs from the Eighth to the Tenth Century." *Greek Orthodox Theological Review* 27 (1982): 135–143.

Rowton, M. "The Woodlands of Ancient Asia." *Journal of Near Eastern Studies* 26 (1967): 261–277.

Runciman, Steven. *A History of the Crusades*. Cambridge: Cambridge University Press, 1951.

Russell, James. *Zoroastrianism in Armenia*. Cambridge, Mass.: Harvard University Department of Near Eastern Languages and Civilizations, 1987.

Russell, James. "Transformations in Early Byzantine Urban Life: The Contribution and Limitations of Archaeological Evidence." In *The 17th International Byzantine Congress. Major Papers*, 137–154. New Rochelle, N.Y.: Aristide Caratzas, 1986.

Saatçi, Tahsin. "Sümeysat Definesi Sikkeleri" (The Coins of the Samsat Treasure). *Belleten* 49 (1985): 451–466.

Samuel, Delwen. "Plant Remains from the Northwest Tell at Buṣrā." *Berytus* 34 (1986): 83–96.

Sarre, Friedrich, and Ernst Herzfeld. *Archäologische Reise im Euphrat- und Tigris- Gebiet*. Berlin: Dietrich Reimer, 1911.

Schmid, Elisabeth. *Atlas of Animal Bones*. Amsterdam: Elsevier, 1972.

Schnyder, Rudolf. "Mediaeval Incised and Carved Wares from North West Iran." In *The Art of Iran and Anatolia from the 11th to the 13th Century A.D.*, edited by W. Watson, 85–94. London: Percival David Foundation, 1974.

—. "Political Centres and Artistic Powers in Saljuq Iran." In *Islamic Civilisation, 950–1150*, edited by D. S. Richards, 201–209. Oxford: Cassirer, 1973.

Segal, J. B. *Edessa. The Blessed City*. Oxford: Oxford University Press, 1970.

Sénac, Philippe. "Une fortification musulmane au nord de l'Ebre: le site de La Iglesieta." *Archéologie islamique* 1 (1990): 123–145.

Serdaroğlu, Ümit. 1975 *Surveys in the Lower Euphrates Basin*. Ankara: Middle East Technical University, 1977.

Silver, I. A. "The Ageing of Domestic Animals." In *Science in Archaeology*, edited by D. Brothwell and E. S. Higgs, 285–286. London: Thames and Hudson, 1969.

Simon de Saint-Quentin. *Histoire des Tartares*. Edited by Jean Richard. Paris: Librairie Orientaliste Paul Geuthner, 1965.

Spengler, William, and Wayne Sayles. *Turkoman Figural Bronze Coins and Their Iconography*. Vol. 1, *The Artuqids*. Lodi, Wisc.: Clio's Cabinet, 1992.

Speth, J. *Bison Kills and Bone Counts: Decision Making by Ancient Hunters*. Chicago: University of Chicago, 1983.

Stein, Gil. "Archaeological Survey at Siirtik Mevkii: A Ceramic Neolithic Site in the Euphrates Valley, Southeast Turkey." *Anatolica* 18 (1992): 19–32.

—. "Strategies of Risk Reduction in Herding and Hunting Systems of Neolithic South Anatolia." In *Early Animal Domestication and Its Cultural Context*, edited by P. Crabtree, D. Campana, and K. Ryan, 87–97. MASCA Research Papers in Science and Archaeology, supp. to Vol. 6. Philadelphia, University of Pennsylvania Museum, 1989.

—. "Pastoral Production in Complex Societies: Mid-Late Third Millennium B.C. and Medieval Faunal Remains from Gritille Höyük in the Karababa Basin, Southeast Turkey." Ph.D. diss., University of Pennsylvania, 1988.

—. "Regional Economic Integration in Early State Societies: Third Millennium BC Pastoral Production at Gritille, Southeast Turkey." *Paléorient* 13 (1987): 101–111.

—. "Herding Strategies at Neolithic Gritille." *Expedition* 28 (1986): 35–42.

—. "Village Level Pastoral Production: Faunal Remains from Gritille Höyük, Southeast Turkey." *MASCA Journal* 4 (1986): 2–11.

Steinbock, R. Ted. *Paleopathological Diagnosis and Interpretation*. Springfield, Ill.: Charles C. Thomas, 1976.

Strabo. *The Geography of Strabo*. Translated by H. L. Jones. New York: Putnam, 1930.

Stronach, D. "Metallfunde in Arsameia am Nymphaios." In *Arsameia am Nymphaios*, by F. K. Dörner and T. Goell, 275–281. Berlin: Gebr. Mann, 1963.

Stratos, A. "Les frontières de l'empire au cours du VIIe siècle." In *Studies in 7th Century Byzantine Political History*, by A. Stratos. London: Variorum, 1983.

Suchey, Judy M., Sheilagh T. Brooks, and Darryl Katz. "Instructions for Use of the Suchey-Brooks System for Age Determination of the

Male Os Pubis." Instructional material accompanying male pubic symphyseal models of the Suchey-Brooks system. Distributed by France Casting, Fort Collins, Co., 1988.

Sucu, Mustafa. *Adıyaman İli ve İlçeleri*. Adana: Önder Matbaası, 1985.

Tanoğlu, Ali, Sirri Erinç, and Erol Tümertekin. *Atlas of Turkey*. Publication 903. Istanbul: Faculty of Letters, University of Istanbul, 1961.

Tate, Georges. "Frontière et peuplement en Syrie du nord et en haute Mésopotamie entre le IVe et le IXe siècle." *Castrum* 4 (1988): 151–159.

Ter-Grigorian Iskenderian, G. *Die Kreuzfahrer und ihre Beziehungen zu den armenischen Nachbarfürsten bis zum Untergang der Grafschaft Edessa*. Weida: Thomas & Hubert, 1915.

Thomas, D. H. "Great Basin Hunting Patterns: A Quantitative Method for Treating Faunal Remains." *American Anthropologist* 34 (1969): 392–401.

Toubert, Pierre. "Frontière et frontières: un objet historique." *Castrum* 4 (1992): 9–17.

Townsend, C. C., and E. Guest. *Cornaceae to Rubiaceae. Flora of Iraq*. Vol. 4 (2 parts). Baghdad: Ministry of Agriculture and Agrarian Reform, 1980.

—. *Leguminales. Flora of Iraq*, Vol. 3. Baghdad: Ministry of Agricultural Reform, 1974.

Trotter, Mildred. "Estimation of Stature from Intact Long Limb Bones." In *Personal Identification in Mass Disasters*, edited by T. Dale Stewart, 71–83. Washington, D.C.: Smithsonian Institution, 1970.

Turan, Osman. *Doğu Anadolu Devletleri Tarihi* (The History of the States of Eastern Anatolia). Istanbul: Nakışlar Yayınevi, 1973.

Türkiye'de Vakıf Abideler ve Eski Eserler (Antiquities and *Vakıf* [Piously Endowed] Monuments in Turkey), Vol. 1. Ankara: Vakıflar Genel Müdürlüğü, 1972.

van Loon, Maurits, ed. Korucutepe. *Final Report on the Excavations of the Universities of Chicago, California (Los Angeles) and Amsterdam in the Keban Reservoir, Eastern Anatolia 1968–1970*. 3 vols. Amsterdam: North Holland Publishing Company, 1975–1980.

van Zeist, W., and J. A. H. Bakker-Heeres. "Archaeobotanical Studies in the Levant 4. Bronze Age Sites on the North Syrian Eu-

phrates." *Palaeohistoria* 27 (1985–88): 247–316.

van Zeist, W., et al. "Studies of Modern and Holocene Pollen Precipitation in Southeastern Turkey." *Palaeohistoria* 14 (1968): 19–39.

Väth, Gerhard. *Die Geschichte der artuqidischen Fürstentumer in Syrien und der Ğazīra'l-Furātīya*. Berlin: Klaus Schwarz, 1987.

Vikan, Gary. *Byzantine Pilgrimage Art*. Washington, D.C.: Dumbarton Oaks, 1982.

Voigt, M., and R. Ellis. "Excavations at Gritille, Turkey, 1981." *Paléorient* 7 (1981): 89.

von den Driesch, A. *A Guide to the Measurement of Animal Bones from Archaeological Sites*. Cambridge, Mass.: Harvard University Press, 1976.

Vryonis, S. *The Decline of Medieval Hellenism in Asia Minor and Process of Islamization from the Eleventh Through the Fifteenth Century*. Berkeley: University of California Press, 1971.

Waagé, F. O. *Antioch-on-the-Orontes*, Vol. 4, pt. 1. Princeton: Princeton University Press, 1948.

Warner, Jörg. "Die Römer am Euphrat." *Antike Welt* 6 (1975): 68–82.

Watson, Andrew M. *Agricultural Innovation in the Early Islamic World: The Diffusion of Crops and Farming Techniques*. New York: Cambridge University Press, 1983.

Watson, Oliver. *Persian Lusterware*. London: Faber, 1985.

Watson, Patty Jo. "In Pursuit of Prehistoric Subsistence: A Comparative Account of Some Contemporary Flotation Techniques." *Midcontinental Journal of Archaeology* 1 (1976): 77–100.

Wattenmaker, Patricia A. "The Social Context of Household Production: The Development of Specialized Craft and Food Economies in an Early Near Eastern State." Ph.D. diss., University of Michigan, 1990.

Weiss, H. "The Origins of Tell Leilan and the Conquest of Space in Third Millennium Mesopotamia." In *The Origins of Cities in Dry Farming Syria and Mesopotamia in the Third Millennium BC*, edited by H. Weiss. Connecticut: Guilford, 1986.

Whallon, R. *An Archaeological Survey of the Keban Reservoir Area of East Central Turkey*. Ann Arbor: University of Michigan, Museum of Anthropology, 1979.

Wheeler, Everett L. "Rethinking the Upper Euphrates Frontier: Where Was the Western Border of Armenia?" In *Roman Frontier Stud-

ies 1989, edited by V. A. Maxfield and M. J. Dobson, 505–511. Exeter: University of Exeter Press, 1991.

Wilkinson, T. J. *Town and Country in Southeastern Anatolia*. Vol. 1, *Settlement and Land Use at Kurban Höyük and Other Sites in the Lower Karababa Basin*. University of Chicago Oriental Institute Publications, Vol. 109. Chicago: Oriental Institute, 1990.

—. "Extensive Sherd Scatters and Land Use Intensity: Some Recent Results." *Journal of Field Archaeology* 16 (1989): 31–46.

—. "Environmental Change and Local Settlement History." *Anatolica* 13 (1986): 38–46.

—. "The Definition of Ancient Manured Zones by Means of Extensive Sherd Sampling Techniques." *Journal of Field Archeology* 9 (1982): 323–333.

Willcox, G. H. "A History of Deforestation as Indicated by Charcoal Analysis of Four Sites in Eastern Anatolia." *Anatolian Studies* 24 (1974): 117–133.

William of Tyre. *A History of Deeds Done Beyond the Sea*. Translated by E. A. Babcock and A. C. Krey. New York: Columbia University Press, 1943.

Williamson, Andrew. "Regional Distribution of Mediaeval Persian Pottery in the Light of Recent Investigations." In *Syria and Iran. Three Studies in Medieval Ceramics*, edited by J. Allan and C. Roberts, 11–22. Oxford: Oxford University Press, 1987.

Woods, John. *The Aqquyunlu. Clan, Confederation, Nomadism*. Minneapolis: Bibliotheca Islamica, 1976.

Wünsch, J. "Meine Reise in Armenien und Kurdistan." *Mitteilungen der K. K. geographischen Gesellschaft in Wien* 26 (1883): 487–496, 513–520.

Xenophon. *The Persian Expedition*. Aylesbury, U.K.: Penguin, 1986.

Yāqūt al-Rūmī. *Muʿjam al-Buldān*. Beirut: Dar Sader, 1955–57.

Yardımcı, Nurettin. "1988 Dönemi Harran Kazı Çalışmaları" (Harran Excavations During 1988). In *XI. Kazı Sonuçları Toplantısı*, 2: 347–361. Ankara: Ankara University, 1990.

—. "1987 Dönemi Harran Kazı ve Restorasyon Çalışmaları" (Harran Excavation and Restoration Activities During 1987). In *X. Kazı Sonuçları Toplantısı*, 2: 287–306. Ankara: Ministry of Tourism, 1988.

—. "1985 Harran Kazı ve Restorasyon Çalışmaları" (1985 Harran Excavations and Restoration Activities). In *VIII. Kazı Sonuçları Toplantısı*, 1: 273–295. Ankara: Ministry of Tourism, 1987.

—. "Harran–1983." In *VI. Kazı Sonuçları Toplantısı*, 79–91. Ankara: Ministry of Tourism, 1984.

Yınanç, Refet, and Mesut Elibüyük. *Kanunî Devri Malatya Tahrir Defteri* (A Malatya Tax Register from the Period of Sultan Süleyman the Magnificent). Ankara: Gazi University, 1983.

Yorke, Vincent W. "A Journey in the Valley of the Upper Euphrates." *Geographical Journal* 8 (1896): 317–335, 453–474.

Zeder, Melinda A. *Feeding Cities*. Washington, D.C.: Smithsonian Institution, 1991.

Zohary, Daniel. "The Progenitors of Wheat and Barley in Relation to Domestication and Agricultural Dispersal in the Old World." In *The Domestication and Exploitation of Plants and Animals*, edited by P. Ucko and G. W. Dimbleby, 47–66. Chicago: Aldine, 1969.

Zohary, D., and M. Hopf. *Domestication of Plants in the Old World*. Oxford: Clarendon Press, 1994.

—. "Domestication of Pulses in the Old World." *Science* 182 (1973): 887–894.

Zohary, D., and P. Spiegel-Roy. "Beginnings of Fruit Growing in the Old World." *Science* 187 (1975): 319–327.

Zohary, Michael. *Geobotanical Foundations of the Middle East*. Stuttgart: Fischer Verlag, 1973.

INDEX

1:1. Gritille from upstream, July 1982.

1:2. View across the Euphrates from Gritille to Lidar, August 1984.

2:1. Innertube *kelek* raft with Gritille in background.

2:2. Operation 12 from the north showing upper phase wall cut off at eastern edge of mound.

2:3. Operation 2 (1984). View of splayed Phase 1 spoke wall rebuilt in Phase 3.

2:4. Operation 2 (1984). View of ledge of Phase 2
fortification wall with later fortification wall built
atop and Phase 3 and 4 walls abutting it.

2:5. The West End. General view in August 1984 with balks removed. Most structures visible date from Phase 3. Remnant of 1982 deep sounding visible in center left.

2:6. Operation 9. Mudbrick bin and surrounding curb wall.

2:7. Operation 26/27. Main structure, empty except for Phase 4 oven at back wall opposite entrance. Sunken oven in foreground.

2:8. Houses at Biriman village, July 1982. A roof roller (loğ taşı) is visible on the left-hand side of the roof of the house at the top left.

2:9. Operation 11 (1983). View of heavily burnt area of courtyard after removal of most wooden planking.

2:10. Operation 10/25. View of animal pens with collapsed roofing at back.

2:11. Operation 10. Phase 4 decorated two-chambered oven.

2:12. Detail of left-hand panel of oven in Plate 2:11.

2:13. Detail of right-hand panel of oven in Plate 2:11.

2:14. Operation 26/27. Phase 4 decorated two-chambered oven.

2:15. Detail of left-hand panel of oven in Plate 2:14.

2:16. Detail of right-hand panel of oven in Plate 2:14.

2:17. Operation 11. Detail of pyrotechnic feature, half in balk and surrounded by stone packing.

2:18. Disassembly of pyrotechnic feature in Plate 2:17, showing levels of plaster inside feature.

2:19. Operation 10. Undulating surface of mudbrick collapse with oval pyrotechnic feature at center right. Surface is also cut by later pits.

2:20. Operation 10/25. Bin partially built on top of fortification wall (visible at right).

2:21. Operations 2, 3, 6, 7. General view of foundations of Phase 7 tower building.

2:22. Operation 11. Upper street.

2:23. Operation 9. General view of Phase 8 remains and grapevine roots just below the surface of the mound.

2:24. Operation 53. General view from below showing mound erosion.

2:25. Operation 53. General view of bastion from the top of the mound.

2:26. Operation 39. Upper fortification wall.

2:27. Operations 9 and 2 (1984). General view of fortification wall.

2:28. Operation 25/10. Fortification wall tower with articulated mudbrick.

2:29. Operations 25/10 and 9. Same tower and fortification as in Plate 2:28, with wall stripped of mudbrick.

2:30. North End. General view of courtyard with Phase 3 surface cut in center by sounding and Phase 3 blocked doorway cleared in wall at bottom right. Press element at top is not contemporary with this phase.

2:31. North End. General view of courtyard with Phase 3 surface and post bases.

2:32. Operation 45. Human remains from Phase 3.

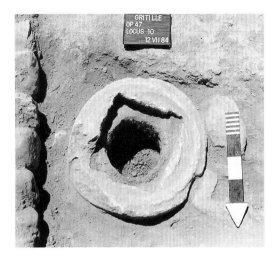

2:34. Detail of one element of the press.

2:33. Operation 47. Curb wall reemploying press elements.

2:35. Operation 43. General view showing tower.

2:36. Operation 42. General view showing street and domestic structure.

2:37. Operation 37. General view of Phase 7 structures.

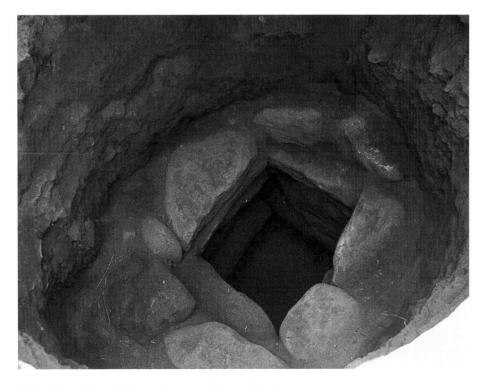

2:38. Operation 4. Stone storage pit opening.

4:1. Fishhook, copper/bronze. GR 82-346.

4:2. Spear point, iron. GR 81-88. See also Figure 4:2P.

4:3. Nail, iron. GR 81-77.

4:4. Nail, iron. 1981, Operation 2.

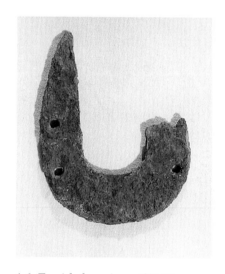

4:6. Equid shoe, iron. GR 84-244. See also Figure 4:3C.

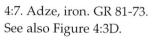

4:5. Nail, iron. GR 81-8.

4:7. Adze, iron. GR 81-73. See also Figure 4:3D.

4:8. Shackle, iron. GR 84-371. See also Figure 4:3E.

4:9. Tweezers, copper/bronze. GR 84-407.

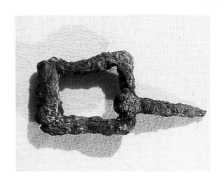

4:10. Buckle, iron. GR 84-219.

4:11. Sickle, iron. GR 82-335. See also Figure 4:4G.

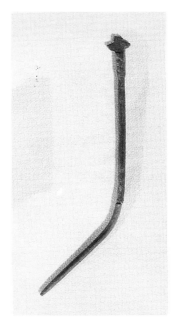

4:12. Pin, copper/bronze. GR 84-163. See also Figure 4:2M.

4:13. Pin (?), copper/bronze. GR 84-56. See also Figure 4:2G.

4:14. Bowl, copper/bronze. GR 84-243. See also Figure 4:5E.

4:15. Lamp, copper/bronze. GR 84-365. See also Figure 4:5F.

4:16. Lamp, copper/bronze. GR 84-52. See also Figure 4:5G.

4:17 and 18. Historiated phylactery, copper/bronze, obverse and reverse. GR 82-370. See also Figure 4:5A.

4:19. Cross, copper/bronze. GR82-311. See also Figure 4:5C.

4:20. Cross, copper/bronze. GR 82-369. See also Figure 4:5B.

4:21. Cross, copper/bronze. GR 83-167.

4:22. Grindstone, basalt. GR 84-364.

4:23. Grindstone, basalt. GR 82-95.

4:24. Bulgur maker, limestone. Op. 10, 1982.

4:25 and 26. Chancel screen (?), limestone (?), obverse and reverse. GT 22693.

6:1. *Triticum durum/aestivum* GT 13803.

6:2. *Vicia faba* GT 13809.

6:3. *Lathyrus* GT 13832.

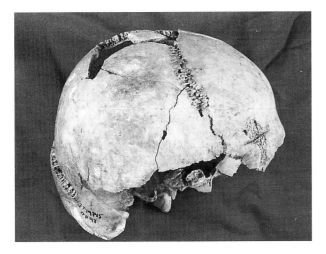

A:1. GT 19745A. Cranial cutmark from a sword or ax.

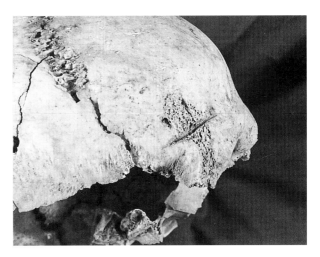

A:2. GT 19745A. Cranial cutmark.

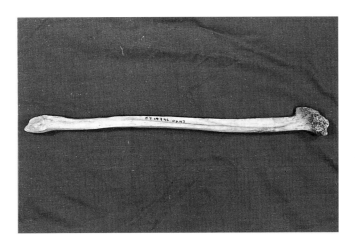

A:3. GT 19745A. Exostosis of fibula head.

A:4. GT 19747A. Cutmark on acromion process of scapula.

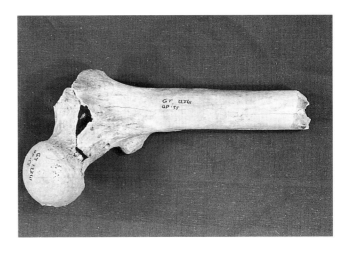

A:5. GT 22741A. Femur fracture.